W9-BXT-035

Foundations for Teaching English Language Learners

Research, Theory, Policy, and Practice

Wayne E. Wright
University of Texas, San Antonio

Caslon Publishing
Philadelphia

Copyright © Caslon, Inc. 2010

All rights reserved. Except for the quotation of short passages for the purposes of criticism and review, no part of this publication may be reproduced, stored in a retrieval system, or transmitted in any form or by any means, electronic, mechanical, photocopying, recording, or otherwise without prior written permission of the publisher.

Caslon, Inc.
P.O. Box 3248
Philadelphia, PA 19130
caslonpublishing.com

9 8 7 6 5 4 3

Library of Congress Cataloging-in-Publication Data

Wright, Wayne E.
Foundations for teaching English language learners : research, theory,
policy, and practice / Wayne E. Wright.
    p.   cm.
ISBN 978-1-934000-01-4 (soft cover)
1. English language—Study and teaching—Foreign speakers.   2. English language—
Study and teaching—Technological innovations.   3. English language—Study and
teaching—Technological innovations.   4. English language—Computer-assisted
instruction.   5. Web-based instruction.   I. Title.
PE1128.A2W75   2010
428.0071—dc22   2010006772

PREFACE

It is an exciting yet challenging time in education. English language learners (ELLs) are the fastest growing demographic in U.S. schools today, and most teachers and administrators around the country can expect to find ELLs in their classrooms and schools. Federal and state accountability policies include all students, and they require ELLs to take and pass the same standards-based tests as their English-proficient peers. Schools are also expected to test these learners' English language proficiency each year, and schools are held accountable for ensuring that ELLs make adequate yearly progress in learning English. Unfortunately, to date many teachers and administrators have not received adequate training in how to effectively address the academic, language, literacy, and learning needs of ELLs. Fortunately, this is changing.

An important premise of this book is that all educators—mainstream elementary and secondary teachers, special education and literacy specialists, administrators, ESL and bilingual educators—share responsibility for ELL education. These educators must work together to make important decisions about policies, programs, and practices for ELLs. These decisions must be grounded in a clear understanding of how ELLs learn a second language and how academic content can be taught to maximize learners' comprehension. Decisions must also be made with an understanding of the historical and sociocultural contexts in which schools, teachers, students, and their families are situated.

A Comprehensive Approach

Foundations for Teaching English Language Learners was written to provide current and future educators with a solid foundation from which to make informed decisions regarding ELLs. We take a comprehensive, learner-centered approach to research, theory, policy, and practice. The special features of the book and the companion Web site (indicated by the icon to the left and described later in detail) facilitate prospective teachers and administrators' learning about how to educate ELLs in their classes, schools, and communities.

Learner-Centered. *Foundations for Teaching English Language Learners* begins by looking closely at who ELLs are, emphasizing the diversity encompassed by the label *English language learner*. We discuss the challenges these learners face in school and outline what educators need to know and be able to do to address each learner's needs. Real-life examples of ELLs and teachers in classrooms and schools bring the book to life. Samples of ELL student work included for discussion and analysis give readers practical experience making the kinds of instructional decisions they will be called on as teachers to make.

Research. The practices, strategies, and techniques highlighted throughout this book are firmly grounded in the research. Each chapter provides a survey of what we know from scientific research related to the content of the chapter. These surveys include, for example, the findings of two national reviews of the literature on language and literacy instruction for ELLs. Readers look critically at the research, review current controversies in the field, and identify gaps in the research. Activities at the end of chapters and on the companion Web site provide students with opportunities to make research-based decisions about what constitutes effective policies, programs, and practices. Research activities also invite students to contribute to further research on practice in ELL education.

Theory. *Foundations for Teaching English Language Learners* synthesizes theories of second language acquisition, literacy development, and sociocultural perspectives. Academic language and literacy development are important concerns, and the spectrum of second language and literacy approaches and methods are critically reviewed. Students see how the sociocultural context shapes learning and teaching; they analyze how different theories of language and literacy development are reflected in policies, programs, and practice. Students are encouraged to develop their own approach to providing effective instruction for ELLs based on the theories and research reviewed and synthesized in the text.

Policy. *Foundations for Teaching English Language Learners* skillfully links macro language and education policy debates to the decision-making power that educators have within their local domains of authority. Chapters analyze the evolution of federal and state language and education policy for ELLs, review the range of program models that we find in schools, outline essential components of effective programs, and introduce students to the fundamentals of assessment and accountability. Special features of the book and companion Web site encourage students to critically review and respond to these policies, and to make decisions about effective programs and accountability systems for ELLs in schools.

Practice. *Foundations for Teaching English Language Learners* makes connections among theory, research, policy, and practice explicit. Chapters on oral language, reading, writing, content-area instruction, primary language support, and technology review the relevant research; theories of language; literacy, learning, and policy debates; and describe a range of research-based practices (i.e., approaches, methods, strategies, and techniques). This comprehensive, balanced approach to teaching equips prospective teachers with the knowledge and skills they need to provide equal educational opportunities for their ELLs.

Special Features

Foundations for Teaching English Language Learners introduces special features within the text to structure student learning, teaching, and research. These features also facilitate professors' course preparation and advance the field of ELL education.

Guiding Questions. Each chapter opens with a series of questions that preview the concepts and practical focus of the chapter. Guiding Questions encourage students to read with a concrete purpose in mind and to summarize and synthesize the major concepts. Guiding Questions also prepare students to apply what they learn in the chapter to ELL learning and teaching situations.

Key Terms. Key Terms are listed at the beginning of each chapter, and they offer a powerful way to approach the concepts discussed in the chapter. These terms are highlighted in the text and clearly defined when first used. For quick reference, every Key Term is defined in the Glossary.

Figures, Tables, and Boxes. Every chapter is supplemented with photographs, summaries, illustrations, demographic data, samples of student work, and resources for additional research and practice. This material is organized into figures, tables, and boxes that augment the discussions of issues and current controversies within the field, and prepare prospective teachers to address these issues in schools and classrooms.

Summaries.   Every chapter concludes with a brief Summary of the major concepts addressed in the chapter. Summaries are followed by Discussion Questions, Research Activities, and Recommended Readings that together ensure that students can respond to the Guiding Questions that open the chapter and apply what they have learned.

Discussion Questions.   When students respond to Discussion Questions, they reinforce their understanding of the material covered in the chapter. These questions also give students opportunities to reflect on and apply chapter content to their own ELL learning and teaching contexts. Discussion Questions can be responded to individually or used to guide group discussions.

Research Activities.   Research Activities offer students the opportunity to conduct classroom-based or school-based research on topics and issues raised in the chapter. Professors can ask students to extend these activities into larger culminating projects and incorporate them into their learning and teaching portfolios.

Recommended Readings.   Each chapter concludes with a list of books and articles recommended by the author. The author has annotated this list with suggestions for the further study of topics introduced in the chapter.

Glossary.   The Glossary provides a quick reference to the vocabulary used in the field and to the Key Terms highlighted in the book.

Companion Web Site

Foundations for Teaching English Language Learners takes full advantage of the power of the read-write Web with an extensive companion Web site that is included with the purchase of the book. This free Web site is an integral part of the course and is thus a real value for students and professors. The companion Web site icon appears in the left margin of the text to indicate the additional information, resources, and activities available on the Web site. The author and other professors across the country continually post new resources and information about recent developments in research, theory, policy, and practice on the Web site, ensuring that the text is always up-to-date in the rapidly changing field of ELL education.

Perhaps most important, the companion Web site provides a space where professors can structure interactions and collaborations that go beyond the traditional university class. Students can participate in discussions about course topics with their own classmates as well as with other students who use the text in classes around the country. Students are also encouraged to contribute to the *Foundations for Teaching English Language Learners* Wiki based on their own research in the field, thereby contributing to the development of a national database on teaching ELLs.

Features of the Companion Web Site

The companion Web site is organized into sections that align with chapters of the main text. Each section/chapter of the Web site includes the following features that enhance student learning and facilitate professors' class preparation.

Downloadable Files of Figures and Forms.   All figures, tables, boxes, and forms found in *Foundations for Teaching English Language Learners* can be downloaded for easy use.

Professors and students may incorporate figures from the text in PowerPoint or other multimedia presentations. Students can also complete and download forms used in assignments for class. Students will use many of these forms in their work as teachers of ELLs in the future.

On-line Extras.   Additional text, boxes, and information are provided for students and professors who are interested in pursuing a topic in greater detail, and these can be downloaded for easy use. Other on-line extras for students include links to additional resources, video-sharing sites, chapter review activities, an on-line discussion board, wiki-this research activities, and a bonus e-handbook on advocacy.

Links Cited in the Book.   Students and professors can simply click on the link and easily connect with on-line resources cited in the text.

Links to Additional Resources Relevant to Chapter Topics.   This feature takes students and professors beyond works cited in the book with links to full-text briefs, articles, and instructional resources.

Links to Videos on YouTube or Other Video-Sharing Sites.   Students and professors can view examples of instructional practices described in the book, and they can use the strategies and techniques described in the book to reflect on those practices.

Chapter Review Activities.   Students can use these activities to review concepts presented in the chapter and assess their learning.

On-Line Discussion Board.   The On-Line Discussion Board allows students to post their responses to selected discussion questions for each chapter. Most of these questions ask readers to share their thoughts, ideas, and experiences relevant to the chapter content. Readers can read and respond to answers provided by students within their class as well as to answers provided by students using this Web site in similar courses in other universities. In this way, students can participate in national conversations about ELL education and gain an appreciation for some of the variation we see across districts, communities, and states.

Wiki-This Research Activities.   One or more of the research activities for each chapter have been posted on a Wiki, ready for students to post their research findings and share them with the world. On the Wiki, readers can learn from each other about how ELL education issues play out in areas across the country. Students who add to the *Foundations for Teaching English Language Learners* Wiki are contributing to the development of a national database on ELL education.

Bonus e-Handbook

Providing Effective Instruction and Advocacy for ELLs.   Effective ELL educators often become advocates for ELL students and their families, and the companion Web site includes a downloadable bonus e-Handbook for Practitioners. The e-Handbook begins with a list of characteristics shared by effective ELL programs. The list is a synthesis of major ideas presented in the *Foundations for Teaching English Language Learners* text with additional attention paid to the key elements of advocacy and parental involvement. A detailed discussion of steps that educators can take to advocate on behalf of their ELLs and to involve ELL parents in their children's education follows. The e-Handbook concludes with a discussion of research needs relevant to ELL students and the role teachers can play as action-oriented researchers within their own classrooms.

Professors' Resource Room

This feature is for professors only. It provides a space for professors to download resources they can use in their classes and upload resources they can share with other professors using *Foundations for Teaching English Language Learners* in their courses. The Professors' Resource Room includes a sample course syllabus the author has developed that professors are free to use or modify for their courses, PowerPoint slides for use in lectures, examples of creative culminating projects for students, and resources to document student learning. The Professors' Resource Room also includes a discussion board where professors can connect and collaborate with other professors teaching similar courses across the country.

Access to the Companion Web site

Access to the companion Web site is included with the purchase of a new copy of *Foundations for Teaching English Language Learners*.[1] Professors and students can go to http://wright.caslonpublishing.com/register and use the access code found with this book to register as a user of the companion Web site.

1: Students who buy the book second-hand may buy access to the companion Web site. Go to www.caslonpublishing.com for more information.

ACKNOWLEDGMENTS

First and foremost I must acknowledge my former ELL students who taught me much about their strengths and unique language, academic, and cultural needs. Working in the Long Beach Unified School District for many years afforded me numerous opportunities to work with and learn from many outstanding administrators and teachers dedicated to providing high quality instruction for ELL students. There are too many to list here, but you know who you are. Thank you!

This book is a reflection of much of what I have learned from my graduate training from many excellent faculty. In particular I wish to thank my adviser, mentor, and friend Terrence G. Wiley, whom I had the good fortune of studying and working with in both California and Arizona. One could not ask for a better mentor. Other influential faculty members I've had the privilege of learning from include Alfredo Benavides, David Berliner, Eugene Garcia, Josué González, Sam Green, Gary Hanson, Kay Hunnicutt, Jeff MacSwan, Michelle Moses, Joseph Ryan, Mary Lee Smith, Marilyn Thomson, Caroline Turner, and L. Dean Webb. I also learned a great deal from my fellow doctoral student, officemate, and friend Gerda de Klerk.

This book was also made possible with the support of several graduate students at the University of Texas at San Antonio (UTSA). James Knaack and Mariana Kuhl helped track down resources, did extensive proofreading of early drafts, and provided many useful comments. Hsiao-Ping Wu, Pei-Yu Shih, and Sun-Yun Yang also provided much needed assistance. I am deeply grateful for my colleagues at UTSA, Juliet Langman, Peter Sayer, Bertha Perez, and Shannon Sauro, who read selected portions of early drafts and provided critical feedback. My colleagues Francis Hult, Howard Smith, and Patricia Sanchez were also very helpful in answering specific questions that came up as I wrote. I also wish to thank my graduate students at UTSA, who bring a wealth of language learning and teaching experience to my courses. Many also gave useful feedback on early drafts of these chapters. In addition, I wish to express my deep gratitude to my department chair, Robert Milk, and my dean, Betty Merchant, who have provided a great deal of support for my research, writing, and other academic endeavors.

I owe a great deal of gratitude to my editor, Rebecca Freeman Field. Having an editor who is a well-known scholar with intimate knowledge of the field has been a true blessing. Rebecca's enthusiasm for this book, her encouragement and patience, and her helpful feedback throughout the process were of tremendous help. Charles Field has also been a constant source of encouragement and guidance. Debby Smith, with her amazing copy editor's eye for detail, was instrumental in helping me prepare the final draft.

Finally, I wish to thank my dear wife, Phal Mao Wright, and our three energetic children, Jeffrey, Michael, and Catherine. Their experiences as students and learners and my interactions as a parent with their schools and teachers have given me new perspectives on education. Their love and patience, and their willingness to be neglected as I spent many long hours and late nights writing made this book possible.

CONTENTS

3   Language and Education Policy for ELLs   51

4   Program Models for ELLs   81

5 Assessment   111

6 Listening and Speaking   141

10 Primary Language Support   267

11 Technology   285

Foundations for Teaching English Language Learners

Who Are English Language Learners?

LEP Students are among the fastest-growing demographic group of students in the U.S.

—U.S. Department of Education (2008)

KEY TERMS

- English language learner (ELL)
- limited English proficient (LEP)
- fluent English proficient (FEP)
- redesignation
- emergent bilingual
- language minority students
- language majority students
- heritage language
- language-as-resource orientation
- subtractive bilingualism
- additive bilingualism

GUIDING QUESTIONS

1. What kinds of diversity do we find within the category "English language learners"?
2. What pros and cons do you see in the different labels for "English language learners"?
3. Where do we find English language learners in the United States, in the past and today?
4. Why do teachers need to know specific information about their English language learner students' home languages and literacies, English language proficiency, educational histories, and sociocultural experiences?
5. How can teachers learn about their English language learner students' backgrounds?

An English language learner (ELL) is a non-native speaker of English who is in the process of attaining proficiency in English. Despite the unifying label, however, ELLs are an extremely diverse group. Consider each of the following students, all of whom are officially classified by their schools as ELLs:

- Daniel, one of the "Lost Boys of Sudan," comes from a rural area where he had little access to public education. His parents were killed in the Sudanese Civil War, and he spent several years in a refugee camp in Kenya before coming to the United States. He entered school for the first time 2 years ago as a 10th grade high school student in the United States. While he is making good progress in speaking and listening, he struggles greatly with English reading and writing.
- Maria, a 4th grade student, immigrated to the United States from Mexico 3 months ago. She was a top student in her village school and has excellent literacy skills in Spanish, but she did not speak any English when she started school in the United States.
- Hiep, a 2nd grade student, was born in the United States. His parents, who immigrated to the United States from Vietnam 10 years ago, can speak only a little English. Hiep speaks Vietnamese with his parents, and he speaks mostly English with his older brothers and sisters. He cannot read or write

Vietnamese. He appears to be fluent in English yet struggles with the language demands of some academic tasks.

■ Chanyoung, a Korean student in 7th grade, arrived in the United States 1 year ago. Her parents, who speak only a little English, are well educated and own and operate a small market in an ethnically diverse neighborhood. Chanyoung lived in the capital city of Seoul and has attended school continuously since she was 4 years old. She is highly literate in Korean, and she excelled in all content areas in her Korean schools. She received instruction in English as a foreign language at school and in private English language classes after school, but she had no opportunities to speak English with native speakers. Although her reading and writing skills in English are good, Chanyoung struggles with speaking and listening.

As these few examples suggest, ELLs vary widely by race, ethnicity, native language, level of schooling, socioeconomic status, parents' level of education, parents' proficiency in English, proficiency and literacy in their native language, and proficiency in English. Many ELLs have had limited access to education, and some may have experienced disruptions in their education in their home countries or in refugee camps. Many have experienced war firsthand. Others come from stable countries with high quality educational systems to which they had access. Many ELLs have parents who have had limited or even no opportunities to attend school. Others have highly educated parents who may have some proficiency in English. Most ELL students are born in the United States, but the level of English spoken in their homes varies considerably. Nonetheless, all of these students are classified as English language learners by U.S. schools if it is determined that they are not yet "fluent" in English.

These students are entitled to equal access to educational opportunities in U.S. public schools. Equal access means ELLs are entitled to (1) high quality language instruction to develop proficiency in English, and (2) high quality academic instruction across the content areas. Both are needed for ELLs to be successful in school and in society.

Defining and Identifying ELLs

The federal No Child Left Behind Act of 2001 (NCLB) refers to ELL students as limited English proficient (LEP) students, defined as those

> whose difficulties in speaking, reading, writing, or understanding the English language may be sufficient to deny the individual—(i) the ability to meet the State's proficient level of achievement on State assessments . . . (ii) the ability to successfully achieve in classrooms where the language of instruction is English; or (iii) the opportunity to participate fully in society.[1]

The actual process of identifying ELL students, which is not laid out in the act, varies greatly from state to state and even from school district to school district within the same state.

In most states, parents must complete a home language survey when they enroll their children in school. The purpose of these surveys, which vary by state and school district, is to determine whether a language other than English is the primary language spoken at home and whether the student speaks that language. If the student does speak a language other than English at home, he or she is given a

---

1: Public Law 107-110, Section 9101(37).

test to assess English language proficiency. These tests, which, like the surveys, vary from state to state and from district to district, are far from perfect. Because language proficiency is a complex concept, no single test can give a true measure of a student's actual proficiency in English, and different tests may give different results for the same student.

Even more problematic is determining when an ELL student has attained enough proficiency in English to be redesignated as fluent English proficient (FEP). This redesignation means a student no longer requires English as a second language (ESL) or other special services and is considered ready to participate in mainstream classrooms. Redesignation procedures also vary widely from state to state and within the same state. Some rely on a single measure (the results of an English proficiency test), some also consider student scores on state standardized tests, and some consider subjective measures, such as teachers' recommendations.

Because of the limitations of English language proficiency testing, states and school districts have traditionally tried to err on the side of caution to ensure that ELL students receive the ESL instruction and other services to which they are entitled and that are necessary to ensure that they succeed academically. After 2001, however, many states created or adopted new statewide English proficiency tests and redesignation procedures in an effort to comply with the requirements and accountability provisions of NCLB for assessing English language proficiency and in response to the pressure to show improvements in learning English. There is growing concern in some states that these newer tests are underidentifying ELLs or redesignating them before they are ready. Thus, many students may be forced into mainstream classrooms even though they lack the English proficiency necessary to succeed in them.

Although official English language proficiency tests can be helpful, they provide only a snapshot of a student's performance at the date and time the test was given. A more reliable determination of an ELL student's proficiency in English is the teacher's informed observations. Teachers who have training in second language acquisition and who engage in effective instructional and authentic assessment practices speak to their students and listen to them talk every day. They read with their students and ask them questions about what they read. They read their students' writing and discuss their work with them throughout the school year.

Labeling ELLs

One major issue in the field is the lack of consistency and agreement about what to call students who are not yet proficient in English. In this book you will most often see *English language learner,* or *ELL.* First used by Mark LaCelle-Peterson and Charlene Rivera in 1994, *English language learner* has become the preferred term in the field. Sometimes shortened to *English learner,* or *EL,* this term is an improvement over the previous widely used label *limited English proficient* (*LEP*). Most scholars in the field object to the word *limited* because it suggests a deficit in the students themselves or that their lack of proficiency in English is a permanent condition. Nothing in the label *limited English proficient* indicates that students are actively learning and attaining proficiency in their new language.

The label *English language learner* has a more positive focus. It portrays students as actively learning English. According to the scholars who introduced the term, it

> underscores the fact that, in addition to meeting all the academic challenges that face their monolingual peers, these students are mastering another language—something

> too few monolingual English-speakers are currently asked to do in U.S. schools. The term follows conventional educational usage in that it focuses on what students are accomplishing, rather than on any temporary "limitation" they face prior to having done so, just as we refer to advanced teacher candidates as "student teachers" rather than "limited teaching proficient individuals," and to college students who concentrate their studies in physics as "physics majors" rather than as "students with limited physics proficiency." (LaCelle-Peterson & Rivera, 1994, p. 55)

Although *English language learner* is a much better label than *limited English proficient,* it has its own set of problems.

First, aren't native English speakers also English language learners? Oral language development is a focus of early childhood education for native English speakers, and native English-speaking students acquire new English vocabulary and learn new genres across content areas every year. Furthermore, the category *native English speaker* includes students who speak a nonstandard variety of English (e.g., Chicano English; Black vernacular English or Ebonics) and learn standard English at school.

Second, the term *English language learner* focuses attention only on English. Ofelia García (2009) introduced a less limiting term, emergent bilingual, which draws attention to the other language or languages in the linguistic repertoires of the students and situates them on a continuum of bilingual development. More important, the emergent bilingual label emphasizes that a fundamental goal of language education programs should be to help these students attain high levels of proficiency in both their first language and English.

Many other labels have been and continue to be used to describe this same population of students. One commonly used term is language minority students, which covers all students in the United States who speak languages other than standard English, including nonstandard varieties of English. In contrast, language majority students refers to students who speak the dominant societal language, standard English. Although ELLs clearly are language minority students, care should be taken not to use the term *language minority students* when referring exclusively to ELLs. Language minority students may be fluent in English and may even lack proficiency in their home language. Also, there is some concern about the use of the term *minority* because, in increasing numbers of schools and communities across the United States, the majority of students are speakers of "minority" languages. Some use the term *culturally and linguistically diverse students* to refer to the combination of ethnic and linguistic minority students. Although this term avoids the minority label and calls attention to culture and language, it excludes standard English speakers who are White. Are these students not also part of the cultural and linguistic diversity of our schools?

The label heritage language is used in the foreign/world language field. Students from homes where a language other than English is spoken and who speak or at least understand some of that language may be labeled as heritage language speakers, regardless of whether they are ELLs or fluent English speakers. As a group, heritage language speakers have a wide range of linguistic and cultural expertise on which educators can readily build; although some may be fully bilingual and biliterate, most have some degree of oral proficiency in the nonstandard variety of their home language but cannot read or write it. Although most people see the positive qualities in *heritage language speaker,* some have expressed concern that this label, with its emphasis on heritage, points more to the past than to the future (Wiley, 2001). A better alternative may be the terms *community languages* and *community language speakers,* which are used in Australia and some European countries, but these have not yet caught on in the United States.

Limited English proficient, unfortunately, is the legal term used in federal legislation (NCLB) and in some instances, in state legislation. This book therefore uses *LEP* when discussing these policies and *ELL* in all other contexts. Teachers are encouraged to look critically at the ways language learners are described and evaluated in their schools and communities, as well as in the media, and to consider the implications of these labeling practices.

Historical and Current Demographic Trends

The United States has always been a nation of immigrants and is currently experiencing high rates of immigration. Researchers from the Urban Institute, using data from the 2000 U.S. Census and the U.S. Current Population Survey, found that between 14 million and 16 million immigrants entered the United States during the 1990s, more than double the 7 million that entered during the 1970s and a further increase from the 10 million that entered during the 1980s (Capps et al., 2006). In 2000, 11 million out of the 58 million children enrolled in pre-kindergarten (pre-K) through 12th grade in the United States, or 1 in 5, were children of immigrants. In 2004 the total foreign-born population in the United States was over 34 million.

Although the absolute number of immigrants coming to the United States is at an all-time high, immigrants make up only about 12% of the total U.S. population—slightly lower than the percentage at the turn of the 20th century, when immigrants made up about 14% of the population. In the late 1800s and early 1900s, the vast majority of immigrants were from Europe and Canada, but now most immigrants are from Latin America or Asia (see Figure 1.1). In fact, the Urban Institute found that in 2000, over 50% of the elementary-school-aged immigrant students were from Mexico, other Latin American countries, and the Caribbean, whereas about 25% were from Asian countries.

A common misconception is that most children of immigrants are foreign born and that many are "illegal aliens." But according to the Urban Institute study, approximately 75% of children of immigrants were born in the United States and are therefore U.S. citizens. In 2000 undocumented immigrant children made up less than 2% of all students in elementary school (grades pre-K–5), and less than 3% of all students in secondary school (grades 6–12).

Another common misconception is that immigrants today are slow to learn

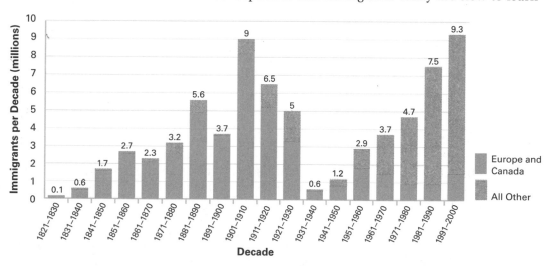

Figure 1.1   Immigration to the United States, 1820s to 2000   Jameson, 2003, p. 27.

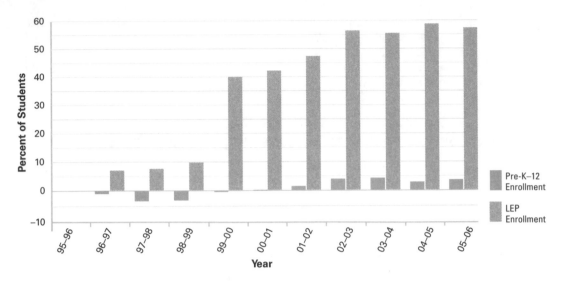

Figure 1.2   The growing numbers of limited English proficient students, 1995/96–2005/06   NCELA, 2009.

English and that most children of immigrants are LEP. According to the Urban Institute's analysis, however, while children of immigrants made up 19% of the school-age population, only about one third were classified as LEP. The Urban Institute also reported that the majority of LEP students are U.S.-born citizens, finding that 76% of elementary school LEP students and 56% of LEP students at the secondary level were born in the United States.

The National Clearinghouse for English Language Acquisition (NCELA) provides annual reports on ELL student enrollment in each state and the country as a whole. In 2006, the total ELL student enrollment was 5,074,572 out of a total student population of 49,324,849; thus, nationally, a little over 10% of students in that year were ELLs. However, the growth rate of ELL students far surpasses the growth rate of the total student population. Between 1995 and 2006, the total pre-K–12 student growth rate was less than 4%, whereas the ELL student growth rate exceeded 57% (see Figure 1.2).

Data from the NCELA (2009) reveal that in the 2005–2006 school year, most ELLs lived in just six states:

- California: 1,600,000 ELLs (25.1% of the total student population)
- Texas: 641,000 (14.2%)
- Florida: 253,000 (9.5%)
- New York: 235,000 (8.7%)
- Illinois: 205,000 (9.7%)
- Arizona: 153,000 (15.4%)

Although these states account for the majority, there are 27 other states or U.S. territories with over 20,000 ELLS, and 17 states or territories with over 5,000 (see Table 1.1).

A different picture emerges if we examine the density of the ELL student population. In 31 states or territories ELLs make up 5% or more of the total student population. Also revealing is the fact that in nearly half the states, the ELL growth rate from 1995 to 2006 was over 100%. This figure includes many states that are not typically known for their high levels of diversity, such as Alabama, Arkansas, Dela-

Table 1.1	Limited English Proficient (LEP) Students in U.S. K–12 Population, by State and Territory
Number of LEP students, 2005–2006 school year	
Over 100,000	Arizona, California, Florida, Illinois, New York, Puerto Rico, Texas
20,000–100,000	Alaska, Arkansas, Colorado, Connecticut, Federal States of Micronesia, Georgia, Indiana, Kansas, Maryland, Massachusetts, Michigan, Minnesota, Nevada, New Jersey, New Mexico, North Carolina, Ohio, Oklahoma, Oregon, Pennsylvania, South Carolina, Tennessee, Utah, Virginia, Washington, Wisconsin
5,000–20,000	Alabama, American Samoa, Delaware , Guam, Hawaii, Idaho, Iowa, Kentucky, Louisiana, Marshall Islands, Missouri, Montana, Nebraska, North Dakota, North Mariana Islands, Rhode Island
Less than 5,000	Maine, Mississippi, New Hampshire, Palau, South Dakota, Vermont, Virgin Islands, Washington DC, West Virginia, Wyoming
Density of LEP students, 2005–2006 school year	
Over 10%	Alaska, American Samoa, Arizona, California, Colorado, Federated States of Micronesia, , Guam, Marshall Islands, Nevada, New Mexico, North Mariana Islands, Oregon, Palau, Puerto Rico, Texas, Utah
5%–10%	Delaware, Florida, Hawaii, Idaho, Illinois, Kansas, Minnesota, Nebraska, New York, North Carolina, North Dakota, Rhode Island, , Virginia, Washington, Washington DC
Growth of LEP population, 1995 to 2006	
Over 200%	Alabama, Arkansas, Colorado, Delaware, Georgia, Indiana, Kentucky, Nebraska, New Hampshire, North Carolina, Puerto Rico, South Carolina, Tennessee, Virginia
100%–200%	Arizona, Iowa, Kansas, Minnesota, Missouri, Nevada, Pennsylvania

Source: NCELA, 2009.

Note: The population includes students in the 50 states, Washington, DC, and 8 territories or outlying areas (American Samoa, Federated States of Micronesia, Guam, Marshall Islands, North Mariana Islands, Palau, Puerto Rico, and U.S. Virgin Islands).

ware, Georgia, Idaho, Iowa, Kansas, Kentucky, Missouri, Nebraska, North Carolina, South Carolina, Tennessee, Utah, and West Virginia.

Because of this rapid growth in the ELL student population across the United States, it is imperative that future and current classroom teachers receive the necessary training and certification to provide effective language and content instruction. As these numbers indicate, teachers will likely find ELLs in their schools and classrooms regardless of where they teach.

Diversity of ELL Students

The descriptions of sample ELL students at the beginning of this chapter illustrate why using a singular label to encompass the immense diversity ELLs represent is problematic. This section explores the diversity of ELLs that teachers are likely to find in their schools. We begin with home languages, proficiency in English, socioeconomic status, and educational achievement. Next we explore special education considerations for ELLs, including the approach that should be followed to determine whether a student is in need of special education services. We conclude this section with a review of other important sociocultural factors that can influence the learning of ELLs, including first language literacy, prior schooling, cultural background, and issues of language, identity, and power.

Home Languages

About 80% of ELLs are Spanish speakers. The remaining 20% of ELLs represent over 400 different language groups. After Spanish, the languages most commonly spoken by ELLs are Vietnamese and Hmong, with between 70,000 and 89,000 speakers each, followed by Cantonese, Korean, Haitian Creole, Arabic, Russian, Tagalog, Navajo, Khmer (Cambodian), Mandarin, and Portuguese, with between 20,000 and 47,000 speakers each. Table 1.2 provides a partial list of the more than 400 languages spoken by ELL students in the United States.

Even within the large group of Spanish-speaking ELLs, there is great diversity. Although a large number of ELLs (or their parents) are from Mexico, many Spanish-speaking students come from other countries. Spanish, like English, is a major international language. Spanish is spoken by over 322 million people as a native language, and an additional 60 million people speak it as a second language (Gordon, 2005). Spanish is an official language in countries in Europe, the Caribbean, and North, Central, and South America, and it is widely spoken as a second language in many other countries throughout the world (see Box 1.1). Spanish, like

Table 1.2	Language Backgrounds of Limited English Proficient (LEP) Students in the United States and Outlying Areas, 2000–2001
Number of speakers	**Languages (sorted highest to lowest number of speakers in each category)**
Over 3,500,000	Spanish
70,000–89,000	Vietnamese, Hmong
20,000–47,000	Cantonese, Korean, Haitian Creole, Arabic, Russian, Tagalog (Pilipino, Filipino), Navajo (Dine), Khmer (Cambodian), Mandarin, Portuguese
10,000–19,000	Urdu, Serbo-Croatian (Serbian, Croatian, Bosnian, Montenegrin, Hrvatski), Lao (Laotian), Japanese, Chuukese (Truk, Trukese), Chamorro, Marshallese, Punjabi, Armenian, Polish, French, Hindi
5,000–10,000	Ukrainian, Pohnpeian (Ponapean), Farsi (Persian, Parsi, Dari), Somali, Cherokee (Tsalagi, Elati), Gujarati, Albanian, German, Yup'ik, Bengali (Bangla), Romanian (Moldovian), Ilocano

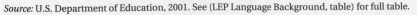

Source: U.S. Department of Education, 2001. See (LEP Language Background, table) for full table.

Note: Parentheses denote alternative spelling, names, or closely related variants or dialects of the language.

Data above exclude 14,817 students with unspecified Chinese dialects; 10,174 students with unspecified Native American languages; 4,874 students with unspecified African languages; 3,380 students with unspecified European languages; 3,219 students with unspecified Asian languages; 162 students with unspecified Pacific languages; 62 students with unspecified Creole or Patois; and 33,559 other students with unknown or unspecified languages.

Box 1.1

Spanish-Speaking Countries

Spanish-speaking ELLs may be from any of the countries on this list. In many of these countries Spanish is the national language; others have a different official or dominant language but large Spanish-speaking populations. The United States is the 5th largest Spanish-speaking country in the world.

Andorra	Colombia	Honduras	Philippines
Argentina	Costa Rica	Israel	Puerto Rico (U.S.)
Aruba	Cuba	Jamaica	Spain
Australia	Dominican Republic	Mexico	Sweden
Belgium	Ecuador	Morocco	Switzerland
Belize	El Salvador	Netherlands	Trinidad and
Bolivia	Equatorial Guinea	Antilles	Tobago
Canada	Finland	Nicaragua	United States
Canary Islands	France	Norway	Uruguay
(Spain)	Germany	Panama	Venezuela
Cayman Islands	Gibraltar	Paraguay	Virgin Islands
Chile	Guatemala	Peru	(U.S.)

Source: Gordon, 2005.

English, varies from country to country and region to region. Just as native English speakers from California, Texas, Boston, Australia, England, and New Zealand may speak a different variety of English, so too will Spanish-speaking ELLs speak different varieties of Spanish, according to their country and region of origin.

It is important to recognize that the fact that ELLs come from a Spanish-speaking country does not mean their native language is Spanish. A growing number of immigrant students come from indigenous groups within these countries and have their own, unique languages and cultures. Educators also need to be aware of the great linguistic diversity masked by the label *Asian*. Hundreds of different languages are spoken across 21 Asian countries (Asian Languages, box). Finally, it is important to understand that many students come from households that are bilingual or multilingual; thus children growing up in these homes may be acquiring two or more languages at once.

Proficiency in English

ELLs also differ substantially in their level of English proficiency. The ELL label covers students from those who speak little to no English to those who are highly advanced and ready to be redesignated as fluent English proficient. Stephen Krashen and Tracy Terrell identify five stages of English language proficiency in their widely used classification system. Juli Kendal and Outey Khuon (2006) describe these levels as follows:

1. *Preproduction.* Students are not ready to produce much language, so they communicate primarily with gestures and actions. They are absorbing the new language and developing receptive vocabulary.
2. *Early production.* Students speak using one or two words or short phrases. Their receptive vocabulary is developing; they understand approximately 1,000 words. Students can answer who, what, and where questions with limited expression.
3. *Speech emergence.* Students speak in longer phrases and complete sentences.

However, they may experience frustration at not being able to express completely what they know. Although the number of errors they make increases, the quantity of speech they produce also increases and they can communicate ideas.

4. *Intermediate.* Students may appear to be fluent; they engage in conversation and produce connected narrative. Errors are usually of style or usage. Lessons continue to expand receptive vocabulary, and activities develop higher levels of language use in content areas. Students at this stage are better able to communicate effectively.

5. *Advanced.* Students orally communicate very effectively in social and academic settings, but many may struggle with reading and writing.

An understanding of what ELL students can do with oral and written English at different stages of second language acquisition is crucial if teachers are to provide effective language and content area instruction.

Socioeconomic Status

David Berliner (2006) refers to poverty as the "unexamined 600 pound gorilla that most affects American schools today" (p. 4). High rates of poverty are associated with low levels of educational achievement. The Urban Institute, in its study of population trends, reports that in 1980, 41% of the children of immigrants enrolled in school came from low-income families and that between 1980 and 2000 that share rose substantially to reach just over half, or 51%. The institute found that most immigrant parents did not have high school diplomas and many had less than a 9th-grade education. The institute also found a strong correlation between LEP status and poverty. In 2000, 68% of LEP children in pre-K through 5th grade and 60% of LEP children in 6th through 12th grade were from low-income families. These rates were nearly twice as high as the rates for English proficient children in comparable grades. About 50% of LEP students have parents who have never completed high school, and 25% have parents with less than a 9th grade education. In contrast, only 11% of English proficient children have parents without a high school diploma, and only 2% have parents with less than a 9th grade education.

Educational Achievement

As these demographics reveal, the majority of ELLs are ethnic minorities from low-income families. Historically, the U.S. education system has done an inadequate job in providing equitable educational opportunities to poor and minority students. Today, despite tough talk about high standards and accountability, and policies that claim to leave no child behind, there continues to be a wide gap in academic achievement between poor, minority, and ELL students and middle- to upper-class White students.[2]

A 2008 report from the U.S. Department of Education reveals that in the 2005–2006 school year, for 3rd grade ELL students, only 21 states met their achievement targets for math, and only 9 met their targets for reading. The report notes further that the level of achievement decreased as grade level increased. Indeed, in grade 7, only 5 states met their target for math, and in grade 8 only 2 states met their target

---

2: For studies that examine this continuing gap in academic achievement, see AERA, 2004; Olson & Manzo, 2005; Poliakoff, 2006. For studies that examine the failure of the U.S. education system to provide equitable educational opportunities to ELLs, see Deschenes, Cuban, & Tyack, 2001; Tyack & Cuban, 1995; Weinberg, 1977; Wiley, 2002.

for reading for ELL students. Although these dismal results reflect major issues and flaws in the NCLB's accountability system for ELLs, they nonetheless reveal that states are failing to meet the achievement expectations for ELL students.

In addition, drop-out rates continue to be substantially higher for Latino students than for White students. In 1998 the graduation rate for Latinos was only 54%, compared with 78% for White students (Greene, 2002). But Latino students are not the only ones struggling. Despite the Asian model minority myth, which claims that Asian Americans students do well academically and Asian American families do well economically, a closer examination reveals that many Asian students are struggling in school, many of their families live in poverty, and many continue to face discrimination. In fact, the Asian model minority myth has been widely criticized for masking the educational and linguistic needs of Asian students, particularly Asian students who are ELLs.[3] In California, for example, the Legislative Analyst's Office found that two major Asian ELL student groups, Hmong and Khmer (Cambodian), made the least amount of progress in learning English in comparison with ELLs from other language minority groups (Hill, 2004).

Besides Latinos and Asians, other recent immigrant students face their own significant challenges. Schools today are seeing an increase in the number of students from war-torn Middle Eastern and African countries. Some of these students may be entering school for the first time, whereas others have experienced disruptions in their education. Many suffer from the trauma of war. Many students from African countries, such as the Somali Bantus, were subject to discrimination and were often denied access to education in their home countries.

In the past, some researchers placed the blame of underachievement on the students and their families with claims of lower IQs and cognitive inferiority. A number of scholars, however, have thoroughly refuted these out-dated claims.[4] Academic underachievement is better understood through the principle of opportunity to learn. Poor and minority students tend to be segregated in the most overcrowded and underfunded schools. An analysis in 2005 by researchers from the Education Trust found that nationally we spend approximately $900 less per year on each student in the school districts with the most poor students than we do in the school districts with the fewest poor students (Randolph-McCree & Pristoop, 2005). ELL students in particular tend to be very segregated. In California, for example, researchers from the Linguistic Minority Research Institute found that in 2005, at the elementary level, more than half of the state's ELLs attended 21% of the state's public schools, where they constituted more than 50% of the student body (Rumberger, Gándara, & Merino, 2006). The Urban Institute found that at the elementary level nationally, 70% of LEP students attended only 10% of the country's public elementary schools (de Cohen, Deterding, & Clewell, 2005).

Schools serving poor, minority, and ELL students usually have the least experienced teachers and the fewest resources. Researchers from the Education Trust found that poor and minority children are about two times more likely than all other students to be assigned to a novice teacher, and that at the secondary level, they are more likely to be taught by teachers who lack expertise in the subject they teach, that is, teachers without a major or minor in that subject. In discussing these findings, the researchers note the irony of assigning students with the greatest needs to the least qualified teachers. They conclude:

3: See Chun, 1995; Lee, 2005; Pang & Cheng, 1998; Park & Chi, 1999; Suzuki, 1995; Weinberg, 1997.

4: For examples of studies that place the blame for underachievement on students and their families, see Herrnstein & Murray, 1994; Jensen, 1995, 1998; Terman, 1916. For studies that refute these claims, see Fagan & Holland, 2002; Fish, 2002; Gould, 1981; Hakuta, 1986; Hout, 2002; Jencks & Phillips, 1998; Mensh & Mensh, 1991; Nisbett, 1998; Sacks, 1999.

Public education cannot fulfill its mission if students growing up in poverty, students of color and low-performing students continue to be disproportionately taught by inexperienced, under-qualified teachers. These manifestly unequal opportunities make a mockery of our commitment to equal opportunity and undermine genuine social mobility. What we have is a caste system of public education that metes out educational opportunity based on wealth and privilege, rather than on student or community needs. (Peske & Haycock, 2006, p. 15)

Additionally, poor and minority students, as noted earlier, tend to have parents with low levels of education who are unable to provide assistance with schoolwork. Those whose parents do not know English have a further obstacle to learning. Many also live in low-income neighborhoods, where living conditions are crowded, crime rates are high, and access to good school and community libraries is minimal. These conditions make finding quiet places to study, do homework, and obtain resources to complete school assignments a challenge. Krashen (1993, 1995) has found strong correlations between school and community libraries and student reading scores—the better the libraries, the better the test scores. Thus, poor and minority students, who have little access to interesting books and other reading materials from libraries and whose families are less able to purchase books for their children to read for pleasure at home, read less and have lower reading scores than students from wealthier neighborhoods. For many ELL students, all of these factors are compounded by the fact that they are still learning English at the same time they are receiving instruction through this new language.

Although limited resources and the challenges of learning English may impede opportunities to learn, ELL students can learn and reach the highest levels of academic achievement. Teachers, administrators, and political leaders must therefore take these challenges into consideration when creating policies, designing programs, and making instructional decisions. They also should build on the considerable strengths that ELLs bring with them to school, including their home languages and the funds of knowledge they have access to in their homes. *Funds of knowledge,* a concept developed by Luis C. Moll and his colleagues, refers to the body of knowledge, cultural artifacts, and cultural resources that are present in students' homes and communities and can be drawn on as a basis for learning (González, Moll, & Amanti, 2005).

Special Education Considerations

Many educators question how to distinguish between learning disabilities and language difficulties in ELLs. Else Hamayan, Barbara Marler, Cristina Sanchez-Lopez, and Jack Damico (2006) stress, however, that one must consider a wide range of factors to determine whether an ELL student is also learning disabled.

Hamayan and her colleagues have developed a framework within which to consider the needs of ELLs, and they offer a collaborative model of information gathering and service provision. They call for teams of special education and ESL/bilingual teachers who collectively have the expertise needed to explore factors that influence an ELL's response to intervention. These factors include the (1) learning environment created for ELLs, (2) personal and family issues, (3) physical and psychological development, (4) previous schooling, (5) social and academic language development in the first and the second language, (6) academic achievement in both languages, and (7) cultural differences. Team members work together to describe the learning difficulties they observe before diagnosing. Then they outline a continuum of interventions and measure the ELL's response to those interventions.

Sociocultural Factors

Research on ELL students' academic achievement, English language proficiency development, and cultural integration highlights a range of sociocultural factors that influence success at school (Genesee, Lindholm-Leary, Saunders, & Christian, 2006). Although current accountability requirements do not mandate collecting data on students' prior schooling, home language and literacy practices, or cultural background, teachers of ELL students should have this critical information in order to address the needs of this diverse population. Teachers also should consider how a school's ideological orientation toward linguistic and cultural diversity influences students' opportunities to learn.

Richard Ruiz (1984) made an important distinction between a language-as-resource orientation and a language-as-problem orientation. Effective schools take a language-as-resource orientation, recognizing that the first language and home culture of ELL students are not problems to be overcome but rich resources that can be used to help the students learn English and academic content. Schools where bilingual programs are not feasible can still value the native languages of their ELL students and draw on them as resources.

Educators who work with ELLs must be aware of the linguistic diversity in their schools and surrounding communities. The following questions can guide teachers' inquiry: What countries are the students or their families from? What languages are spoken in their homes? What are their ethnicities and to which cultural groups do they belong? How long have the students (or their families) been in the United States? What prior schooling have the students had, either in their home countries or in the United States? Can they read and write in their native languages? What are the parents' levels of education, and do they have literacy skills in their native languages? What are the students' neighborhoods like? What is each student's socioeconomic status? What birth position does each student hold among his or her siblings, or is he or she an only child?

Teachers must be able to answer these basic questions about the ELL students in their classroom if they are to provide effective instruction for them. Knowing a student's ethnicity and country of origin, for example, allows the teacher to incorporate appropriate multicultural education strategies and techniques into the curriculum. Knowing the student's home language or languages allows the teacher to provide primary language support that can accelerate the student's acquisition of English and comprehension of academic instruction. If the student has literacy skills in his or her native language, the teacher can use bilingual dictionaries and other written materials in that language to provide support and use strategies that facilitate literacy transfer from the first language to the second. Likewise, knowing what language and literacy skills the parents have helps the teacher determine in what language to send home notes and other school communications and whether to arrange for an interpreter at parent conferences or other school meetings.

Experience leads to expertise. Thus, the more the teacher knows about a student's experiences, the more he or she can assume about the expertise that student is likely to have. For example, if the student has attended school in his or her home country, the teacher may assume that the student has some literacy skills in his or her native language and also has learned academic content through that language. If the student has been educated mostly in the United States and has not participated in bilingual programs (or heritage language programs outside of school), the teacher may assume that the student cannot read or write in his or her native language because there have been no opportunities to develop these skills. If the parents have low levels of education, and if the family lives in a low-income neighborhood, the teacher should take into consideration the factors related to poverty discussed earlier and find ways to address these issues in the classroom. If the student is one of the younger children in the family, and the family has been in the United States for several years, it is likely that the older siblings speak English and use it often in the home. But if the student is the oldest or only child, such support is probably not present.

Teachers also need to know their students' cultural backgrounds and how culture influences learning at school. But what do we mean by culture? Culture involves much more than the food, dress, art, music, and holidays of an ethnic group. These outward manifestations of culture are what Else Hamayan (2006) refers to as the tip of the iceberg. Below the surface, the iceberg is massive, and this portion represents the norms and values that consist of the ways people interact with and makes sense of their surroundings. Some of these below-the-surface aspects of culture include eye contact, notions of modesty, ways of ordering of time, conversational patterns, approaches to problem solving, preferences for competition or cooperation, and conceptions of beauty and status and mobility. These below-the-surface aspects of the home culture may differ from or even be in conflict with aspects of the dominant culture that are privileged in the schools.

As teachers begin to understand their students' cultural backgrounds, they must be careful to avoid stereotypes and generalizations. For example, in many schools today there is a tendency to generalize the cultures of Mexico and China and assume they apply equally to all Latino and Asian students, respectively, and to focus on surface manifestations of culture. (For an indication of the cultural diversity teachers may find among Spanish-speaking ELLs, see Box 1.1, which lists all countries where Spanish is spoken.) In my former elementary school, the overwhelming majority of the Asian students (who made up about 45% of the school's population) were Cambodian Americans. Yet, the only Asian-related lesson some of the teachers in the school did all year was about Chinese New Year. The red envelopes, coloring sheets with dragons, and signs that read "Gung Hay Fat Choy" were just as foreign to the Cambodian American students as they were to other non-Chinese students in the school. Likewise, schoolwide celebrations for Cinco de Mayo—which is really more of a commercially contrived U.S. holiday than an authentic traditional Mexican holiday—hold little meaning for Spanish-speaking students whose families are not from Mexico. Although there may be similar cultural traits across students labeled as Latino, Asian, Native American, Middle Eastern, or African, it is important to be aware of the distinct history and culture of each ethnic group.

It is also important to recognize that ELL students may not necessarily come from a singular cultural or linguistic background. I have had Asian students who are fluent in Spanish because they came to the United States after living in South America. I recall one Korean student in particular whose family came to the United States from Peru. She worked in a small local Mexican market, and when customers wondered aloud in Spanish why a "Chinese" girl was working there, she shocked them by answering their question in fluent Spanish. While visiting a high school ESL class in San Antonio, Texas, I noticed many Middle Eastern students using bilingual Russian-English dictionaries. I learned that they had spent time and attended school in one or more Russian-speaking countries after escaping from war in their own countries. Educators must look beyond static notions of culture to consider the ways that students' specific histories and experiences influence their expertise.

Another common misconception is that all ELLs are immigrants (or "foreigners"), born outside of the United States. As noted earlier, most ELLs are U.S.-born citizens. Typically, U.S.-born ELLs represent the second generation, born to immigrant parents who may or may not speak English well. Very few ELLs are members of the third generation, meaning their parents were born in the United States but their grandparents were born in a different country. There are significant differ-

Box 1.2

Foreign-Born and U.S-Born ELLs

Teachers should consider some of the following differences between U.S.-born and foreign-born ELLs:

- U.S.-born ELLs receive extensive exposure to English before beginning school from radio, television, movies, video games, friends, older siblings, relatives, neighbors, and other community members.
- U.S.-born ELLs, unless they participate in bilingual education programs or heritage language programs outside of school, often do not have opportunities to fully develop their native language, particularly in the area of literacy.
- Foreign-born ELLs who attended school in their home country typically have strong native language skills, including literacy in their native language or languages.
- Foreign-born students with strong native language literacy skills may learn to read and write in English faster and better than U.S.-born ELLs.
- U.S.-born ELLs (unless they are in bilingual program) face the difficult task of learning to read and write first in their weaker language (English) and thus may learn more slowly.
- Some older foreign-born ELLs may have studied English as a foreign language in school. These programs typically place more emphasis on reading and writing than on listening and speaking.
- Some foreign-born ELLs have experienced disruptions in their education or never attended school in their home countries (or in refugee camps) because of poverty, oppression, or war.

ences between U.S.-born and foreign-born ELLs, even among students from the same ethnic group. ELLs in these two groups bring to school a different set of strengths and challenges (see Box 1.2).

While ELL students are learning at school, they are also developing their identities. Carolyn McKinney and Bonny Norton (2008) describe identity as "dynamic" and "multiple" and "a site of struggle," noting that a student's identity is shaped by the economic, historical, political, and cultural contexts in which he or she lives and learns. Language also plays a major role in the development of identity, because students' identities are socially constructed through their language-mediated interactions and relationships. ELL students often struggle as they learn and adjust to a new language and culture that may be vastly different from the language and culture of their home. ELLs formulate and reformulate their identities as they deal with and attempt to resolve the conflicts between what they encounter at home, in school, and in the dominant society culture. Their academic success depends in large part on how the school and the wider society treats them, their language, their culture, their families, and their communities.

Cultural Adjustment Issues

Classic and recent research studies have documented the effect that cultural differences can have on student success in the classroom.[5] Native English-speaking students from the dominant group generally find that the culture of the school

5: The classic studies are Heath, 1983; Philips, 1983. More recent studies include McCarty, 2005; McKinney & Norton, 2008.

closely matches that of their homes, and thus they have an advantage as they enter school. ELLs, however, may experience a cultural and linguistic mismatch between the culture and language of their home and the school's culture and language. They are disadvantaged when schools do not recognize, value, and incorporate these differences.

Helping ELLs succeed academically requires helping them adjust to the culture of the classroom and the school by giving them access to what McKinney and Norton (2008) call "dominant or privileged ways of knowing and doing" (p. 201). The goal of most education and language policies is assimilation, "the process by which a person or language group loses their own language and culture, which are replaced by a different language and culture" (Baker & Jones, 1999, p. 698). In the United States, education has and continues to function as a tool for assimilation to ensure that immigrant children abandon their home language and culture and become monolingual English-speaking Americans. Studies by Alejandro Portes and Rubén Rumbaut have shown, however, that students who assimilate quickly often have deep conflicts at home, and these conflicts can lead to academic and social difficulties (Portes & Rumbaut, 2006; Rumbaut & Portes, 2001).

Assimilation is the ideology behind the great melting pot, a metaphor for the notion that immigrants to the United States willingly abandon their language and cultural to become Americans. A serious flaw in the melting pot metaphor is that some immigrants, especially people of color, do not "melt" into the whole as easily as others. Regardless of how "Americanized" they become, many other Americans will nonetheless question their "American-ness." For example, when the U.S. ice-skating champion Michelle Kwan came in second place to fellow U.S. teammate Tara Lipinski in the 1998 Winter Olympics, Asian Americans were dismayed by an MSNBC.com headline announcing, "American beats out Kwan!" (The network removed the headline and apologized after receiving a flood of complaints.) Both skaters were born in the United States and both come from immigrant families—Kwan's from Hong Kong and Lipinski's from Poland. But why was Kwan's American identity questioned while Lipinski's was not? Simply put, Lipinski melts better because she is White. Many third-, fourth-, and fifth-generation Asian and Latino Americans who have never spoken any language other than English often have encounters with other Americans who assume they do not speak English, or who act with surprise when they hear them talk and ask, "How did you learn to speak English so well?" Worst yet, many have been told to "go back to your country" or have been the recipients of other comments or actions that send the subtle message, "You don't belong here."

Another problem with the assimilationist melting pot ideology is the assumption that immigrants must give up their native language and culture to become Americans. An alternative to assimilation, however, is acculturation—immigrants and their children can adapt to the new language and culture without having to sacrifice their own. Donna Gollnick and Philip Chin (2002), experts in multicultural education, point out that the melting pot metaphor is inaccurate for describing U.S. society, because, they say, "we are a nation of many cultural groups distinguished by our ethnicity, gender, class, language, and religion" (p. 15). As an alternative to the melting pot, the salad bowl metaphor has been suggested, wherein each ingredient maintains its unique characteristics but all ingredients together make up a single wonderful whole.

Students' efforts to maintain or develop their native culture while learning and adjusting to American culture is neither a simple nor a straightforward process. Culture is dynamic and multi-faceted. What is "American" culture anyway? And what exactly is the native "culture" of ELL students? Just as my "American" culture is not the same as my parents' "American" culture, the native culture of ELLs may be much different from the culture their parents attempt to bring with them from their home country. Parents often have idealized notions of what their culture is and should be, and they become dismayed when their children who are growing up in the United States do not fully adopt it. Rather than fully adopt "American" culture (whatever that may be), or adopt their parents' idealized notions of the native culture, many children of immigrants forge a style of cultural identity that is neither one nor the other but a hybrid of the two that is uniquely theirs. This hybridization is referred to by some scholars as a "third space."[6]

One example of hybridization is hip hop culture, which is highly influenced by young urban African Americans. Hip hop is the American culture many ELLs and other minority students experience growing up in inner cities. One example of a hip hop–influenced cultural identity is Asian pride (sometimes called AZN Pride or Pryde). Try typing "Asian pride" into Google. At the time of this writing, this phrase returned over 1.4 million hits. While not all Asian Americans have embraced it (particularly those from the older generations), it nonetheless illustrates the way many children of immigrants forge new ethnic identities for themselves in the United States that are constantly being negotiated.

Some Asian Americans and others mock newly arrived Asian immigrants by calling them FOBs—fresh off the boat. Although calling someone FOB is usually an insult, a new term has emerged, *fobulous*. The on-line Urban Dictionary (www .urbandictionary.com) contains this definition of *fobulous* (posted by a user):

> You speak perfect English and you are fluent in your native language.
> You have Asian friends as well as non-Asian friends.
> You listen to Asian pop as well as American music.
> You are equally aware of both popular American culture and Asian pop culture.
> For you, FOB stands for Fabulous Oriental Being.
> You have lots of Asian pride.

For many Asian American students, being "fobulous" is the ideal goal. It essentially represents a new ethnic identity, a third space, where one takes pride in being bilingual and bicultural in an American context.

School programs for ELLs should reach for similar goals, that is, they should help ELLs create new, positive sociocultural identities that can help them negotiate the dynamic new world in which they are living, rather than encourage students to assimilate to mainstream norms. Multicultural education can help prepare all students to live in our multicultural society, with attention to the complex social challenges—including racism, discrimination, and other issues of inequality—that continue to plague our society. In short, educators have a responsibility to help prepare the next generation to continue working on solving important social problems related to diversity that past generations have failed to fully address.

Most educators agree that multicultural education is important, but there are vast differences in how schools address it. James Banks (1994), one of the pioneers of multicultural education, looked at how schools provide multicultural education and identified four levels: (1) contributions, (2) additive, (3) transformative, and (4) social action. The first level entails briefly mentioning the contributions individual minorities or ethnic groups have made to the United States, for example, by celebrating Martin Luther King Jr. Day or reading a side-bar paragraph in the textbook about the Chinese workers who built the railroads. The second level entails making up for gaps in the mainstream curriculum by adding new material, such as a unit about the internment of Japanese Americans during World War II, which typically gets brief mention in core textbooks. At the third level, teachers move be-

---

6: See, e.g., Bhabha, 1994; Gee, 1996; Lipka, Sharp, Adams, & Sharp, 2007.

yond simply informing students of historical or current events and help them develop critical perspectives on issues of justice, equality, and democracy in society. For example, students might discuss continuing problems of school segregation and why schools with large numbers of immigrant and ELL students receive less funding than schools that serve majority students. At the final level, students go beyond discussing these issues and take on action research projects aimed at making positive changes in the name of social equity. For example, students might collect data on per-pupil spending and resources in minority and majority schools and present their findings to the school board and local press. Most teachers and schools appear to be more comfortable with levels 1 and 2. These provide a good start but are not sufficient to prepare students to understand and begin to address the unequal power relationships in our society that may limit the life opportunities of the students, their families, and their communities.

Rebecca Freeman Field (2008) emphasizes the importance for educators to have an understanding of power relationships between social identity groups in the communities in which they teach in order to develop policies, programs, and practices that can (1) help elevate the status of minority languages and their speakers, (2) provide more access to opportunities for language minority students, and (3) challenge the dominant identity and power relations that exist on the local level. McKinney and Norton (2008) argue:

> One of the greatest challenges in responding to cultural and linguistic diversity in language classrooms is to move beyond stereotyping differences or merely celebrating diversity as if it had no links to social inequality and no structural or material effects. Differences and power relations must always be considered together in pedagogy that responds meaningfully to diversity. (pp. 192–193)

Promoting Bilingualism on the Individual and Societal Levels

Subtractive bilingualism occurs when a new language replaces a student's home language. In contrast, additive bilingualism occurs when a student develops proficiency in a new language without losing his or her home language. This form of bilingualism should be the goal of all school language programs. Thus, as ELLs work diligently to learn their new language, English should be viewed as an additional language rather than as a replacement for their native language. Additive bilingualism is encouraged when schools value linguistic diversity, adopt a language-as-resource orientation, and provide opportunities for ELL students to use and develop their first language skills, alongside English, for academic purposes.

The concept of additive bilingualism, however, may be somewhat misleading. It suggests simply adding something to something that already exists. But most ELLs are born in the United States and grow up in homes where English may not be the dominant language. They are probably acquiring English at the same time they are learning their native language. Furthermore, for students (younger ones in particular) to become highly bilingual and biliterate, they must have opportunities to further develop their native language at school. Thus, rather than additive bilingualism, it may be more accurate to describe this phenomenon as emergent bilingualism (García, Kleifgen, & Falchi, 2008).

When ESL and content instruction in English pressure students to replace or demote the first language, subtractive bilingualism may occur. More accurately, such programs fail to provide ELLs the opportunity to develop and maintain the use of their first language for academic purposes. Schools that take this approach

Box 1.3

Consequences of Primary Language Loss

- Children are unable to communicate effectively with parents.
- Parents have difficulty passing on their values, beliefs, understandings, and wisdom.
- Breakdown in communication can lead to conflicts between children and their parents.
- Children may lose respect for their parents.
- Children experience difficulty, embarrassment, and shame when trying to communicate with older relatives and community members.
- Children may face humiliation and shame if they return to their (or their parents') home country and cannot effectively communicate.
- Children may become ashamed of their home language and culture and struggle with identity issues.
- Losing proficiency in the home language before attaining proficiency in standard English often leads to academic difficulties.
- Learning to read in English is more difficult if students cannot read in their home language.
- Students may have fewer job opportunities than they would have otherwise had they maintained their home language.
- The society as a whole loses needed linguistic resources to fulfill the language demands of national and international institutions, organizations, and agencies.

Sources: Fillmore, 1991; Wright, 2004a.

fail to take into consideration the needs of the student as a whole, and the needs of the student's family and community, as well as the wider society. Lily Wong Fillmore, in an article titled "When Learning a Second Language Means Losing the First," details the harsh consequences that can befall ELL students when English replaces their native language. My own research with Cambodian American students who received English-only instruction found similar consequences. These consequences are outlined in Box 1.3.

Encouraging ELLs to maintain and develop their home languages while they develop proficiency in English benefits the individual ELL and his or her family and community, as well as the nation overall. The United States needs bilingual citizens who can fulfill the myriad jobs in the government, service, business, and education sectors that require bilingual skills to interact with immigrants who have not yet learned English, to communicate with international tourists and other visitors, and to help ensure the country's success in international relations, global business, and national security (see Box 1.4).

Learning More About Your ELL Students

As outlined in the earlier discussion of the language-as-resource orientation, teachers need to know the following about each student: (1) the language and literacies used at home, (2) English language proficiency level, (3) educational history in the home country and in the United States, (4) length of time in the United States, (5) reason for immigration, (6) number of siblings, and (7) parents' educational history, employment, and proficiency in English and other languages. The ELL student profile can be used to help gather and analyze this important information (ELL Profile, form).

Box 1.4

Need for Bilingual Citizens

The following headlines appeared in newspapers around the country. What do these headlines indicate about the need for bilingual citizens in the United States? How are the educational policies and programs in your community's schools addressing this growing need?

Bosses Learn Español to Boost Effectiveness — Baltimore Sun
Spanish Course Helps Managers and Workers Communicate — Associated Press
Alameda County Looking for Spanish-Speaking Teachers — San Francisco Chronicle
Immigration Creating Demand for Bilingual Assistance — Associated Press
Board OKs Pay for Bilingual Teachers — Albuquerque Journal
Language Linked to Medical Mistakes — Milwaukee Journal Sentinel
Demand Rising for Advanced Spanish — Herald-Sun (North Carolina)
Police Officers Will Immerse Themselves in Mexico — Oregonian
Language Is a Barrier for Foster Families — Atlanta Journal and Constitution
Shabazz's First Latino Student Fills Dual Roles—Stylist, Interpreter — Herald (South Carolina)
Bilingual Help; Hmong Tutor Lowers Barriers for Mountain View Students — Anchorage Daily News
Help Still Wanted: Arabic Linguists — Washington Times

Source: Wright, 2003

How can teachers obtain this information, some of which may be considered private and very personal? Much of it may be found in students' enrollment papers, academic files, and school emergency cards. Students' academic files should contain a copy of a home language survey that indicates the languages used at home, and the results of any English language proficiency testing (and sometimes native language proficiency testing) conducted at the time of enrollment or at the end of the previous school year. School enrollment papers and the school emergency cards that parents typically fill out each year may list parents' occupations and work phone numbers, as well as school-age siblings. A teacher could also obtain much of this information simply by asking the parents, in a sensitive way, at a back-to-school program or during parent conferences. Teachers can also obtain this information from the students in appropriate ways. For example, at the beginning of the school year, students can provide some of this information as part of an "All About Me" unit.

Once teachers have basic information about the home countries, ethnic and cultural groups, and languages of their students, they can obtain further information by searching the Internet. For example, teachers can learn about the history and educational system of the home country of a student born outside of the United States, as well as any difficulties there that may have caused the student's family to leave their country and come to the United States. Information about the student's ethnicity and culture may help explain some of the student's behaviors in class and suggest things the teacher can do to be sensitive to his or her culture and incorporate aspects of that culture into the classroom. A search for information about the student's language may reveal some important similarities and differences between the native language and English that can help the teacher plan effective ESL instruction.

Another important use of this information is for teachers to identify appropriate supplemental education materials for use in the classroom, such as bilingual (or bilingual picture) dictionaries, and fiction and nonfiction books in the students' native languages, including, if appropriate, bilingual versions with English and another language. Teachers can also identify multicultural literature that may be interesting and motivating to ELL students in learning to read and could help other students in the class learn about and appreciate an ELL student's country and culture. These ideas and additional suggestions are discussed in more detail in other chapters.

SUMMARY

ELL students are a diverse group, despite the misleading unifying label. ELLs come from a wide range of ethnic, cultural, linguistic, educational, and socioeconomic backgrounds. While many are foreign born, the majority are U.S.-born citizens. Procedures for identifying and redesignating ELLs can vary across schools, districts, and states. Many different labels are used to describe students who are learning English, and each has its own positive and negative aspects. *ELL* is used in this book because it focuses on the students as active learners who are on their way to attaining proficiency in English.

Immigration to the United States is occurring at rates similar to those of the early 1900s, but today's immigrants come primarily from Latin American and Asian countries rather than European countries. The growth rate of the ELL student population far surpasses that of the total student population. Nationwide, ELLs make up about 10% of the total population, and the number of ELLs is growing rapidly, including in states not known for their ethnic diversity. In addition to language and academic learning challenges, ELLs also face cultural adjustment challenges, including pressure to assimilate. The melting pot is an outdated metaphor that never accurately captured the reality of diversity in the United States. Students' acculturation, however, may not necessarily be full acceptance of either the home or the dominant culture, but instead students may develop a new, hybrid type of cultural identity. Teachers must get to know their students by obtaining information about their sociocultural background. This information will help teachers make the best possible decisions for providing effective instruction for their ELL students.

Discussion Questions

1. Review the profiles of the students at the beginning of the chapter. Which students are likely to face the greatest challenges in learning English and academic content? Which ones might have fewer challenges? Why?

2. **On-Line Discussion Board** Consider the different labels that have been used to describe students who are not yet proficient in English. Which ones have you heard used in your school or program? Which do you prefer? Why?

3. Compare immigration to the United States at the beginning of the 20th century with immigration today. Next, compare the growth in the number of ELL students with the growth of overall student enrollment. What are the implications of these demographic trends for preparing teachers to work with ELL students?

4. **On-Line Discussion Board** How can poverty affect the teaching and learning of ELLs? What is the danger in attributing students' underachievement to cognitive deficits rather than seeking to understand sociocultural factors that

can affect students' opportunities to learn? Describe your own experiences or observations related to this issue.

5. Why is it so important for teachers to know their ELL students' backgrounds? Give examples of the kinds of decisions teachers need to make that are based on this knowledge.

Research Activities

1. **Wiki This**   Complete the student profile for an ELL student, then answer the following questions:

   a. Which factors may positively influence this student's acquisition of English? Why?

   b. Which factors may be obstacles to this student's acquisition of English? Why?

   c. How easy or difficult do you think it will be for this student to develop literacy skills in English? Why?

   d. What are some particular things the teacher should do to address this student's unique needs as revealed in your answers to (a) through (c)?

2. **Wiki This**   School-level demographics typically report only broad categories of students—Asian, Hispanic, White, Black, and Native American. Create a more detailed demographic profile of your school that includes information on each student's country of origin, ethnicity or ethnicities, language or languages spoken, and level of English language proficiency. Discuss the implications of your findings for the school's instructional programs.

3. Find out what processes your state, district, and school use to identify ELL students. Then find out how ELL students are redesignated (i.e., reclassified as fluent English proficient). How consistently are these processes applied across schools and districts in your state? How do they compare with the processes in other states? What concerns, if any, do you have about these processes?

Recommended Reading

Baker, C., & Jones, S. P. (1999). *Encyclopedia of bilingualism and bilingual education*. Clevedon: Multilingual Matters.

A definitive international work with entries on a wide variety of topics related to bilingualism and bilingual education.

Berliner, D. C. (2006). Our impoverished view of educational reform. *Teachers College Record, 108*(6), 949–995.

The renowned education scholar David Berliner describes the relationship between poverty and academic achievement and argues that poverty places severe limits on what can be accomplished through school-reform efforts.

Capps, R., Fix, M., Murray, J., Ost, J., Passel, J. S., & Herwantoro, S. (2006). *The new demography of America's schools: Immigration and the No Child Left Behind Act*. Washington, DC: Urban Institute.

This report from the Urban Institute notes the potential of NCLB to improve education for immigrant students but also documents a number of substantial challenges NCLB poses for schools with large LEP and immigrant populations.

Hamayan, E., Marler, B., Sanchez-Lopez, C., & Damico, J. (2006). *Special education considerations for English language learners: Delivering a continuum of services*. Philadelphia: Caslon.

Provides a useful framework for the identification of ELLs who are also learning disabled, for developing appropriate interventions, and for evaluating the students' responses to these interventions.

Second Language Learning and Teaching

The more you know about SLA (its processes and products), the better you can gauge what instructional efforts are worth your while and what method or methods work best for teaching and learning languages

Bill VanPatten (2003)

KEY TERMS

- phonology
- morphology
- syntax
- semantics
- pragmatics
- lexicon
- academic language proficiency
- communicative competence
- register
- comprehensible input
- affective filter
- comprehensible output
- zone of proximal development (ZPD)
- scaffolding
- communicative language teaching (CLT)
- content-based instruction (CBI)

GUIDING QUESTIONS

1. What do teachers need to know about language, and why do they need to know it?
2. What does it mean to "know a language"?
3. How do people acquire language?
4. What do different theories of second language acquisition tell us?
5. How would you describe your approach to second language teaching?

As we begin our discussion of second language learning and teaching, consider the following questions teachers might ask about language issues that arise in their classrooms.

1. Vihn has difficulty pronouncing *th* words. Does he have a speech impediment?
2. Chanyoung always leaves off the final *s* when she reads. I've told her a million times that plural words end with an *s*. Why is she refusing to read the words correctly?
3. Rosa always switches words around in the sentence, saying and writing things like "car red" instead of "red car." Is she dyslexic?
4. Suling always mixes up the gender-specific pronouns, calling girls *he* or *him* and boys *she* or *her*. I keep correcting her, but she just doesn't get it. And if she calls me *Mrs.* Wright one more time I'm going to scream! Can't she tell the difference between boys and girls? Should I refer her to special education?

5. Reading time was over and students were supposed to put their books away and start working on their math worksheets. But Thanawan, just kept right on reading. I said to her, "Why are you still reading instead of doing your math?" She smiled and said, "Oh, because I not finish yet," and she just kept on reading. Why did she disobey me so rudely?

6. Our school puts most of the ELLs in a bilingual program. Everyone knows young children learn new languages quickly. So shouldn't the students be placed in an English-only classroom before it's too late for them to learn English?

7. My principal just bought us a software program that drills the ELL students in English. It's really neat. If they get 30 drills in a row right they get rewarded with a little animation where a bunny pops out of the tree and does a little dance. The box the software came in says the students will be speaking English in 3 or 4 weeks. Does this mean our ELLs will be ready for the poetry analysis unit we're starting next month?

8. Roberto keeps saying, "I have 6 years old" when people ask him how old he is. We've done grammar worksheets and drills on *am*. And I keep correcting him. Why isn't he learning it? Is he a slow learner?

9. While students were supposed to be working independently at their desks, I noticed one of my African American students was digging around in his backpack. I prompted him, "William, get to work please." He responded politely, "I be doin' mah work, I jus' gitten' a pencil." I just don't understand why he speaks such poor English.

One goal of this chapter is to help you answer questions like these and address similar issues with informed confidence. We begin by exploring what language is and then dig deeper into why teachers need to know about language. Next we focus on the subsystems of language (phonology, morphology, syntax, semantics, and pragmatics), vocabulary, spelling, and language variation. We briefly discuss what it means to know a language and then take a look at different ideas about first and second language acquisition and some of the approaches and methods in second language teaching that have been influential in K–12 education. We conclude with a discussion about how teachers can move beyond traditional approaches and methods and develop their own approach grounded in an understanding of language and second language acquisition. In our discussion, the preceding questions are referred to as "situation #1," "situation #2," and so on.

What Is Language?

One of the characteristics of being human that separates us from other species on earth is the ability to use language. As humans we tend to take this amazing ability for granted. And because language is ubiquitous, we rarely stop to think about what it actually is. How you would define language?

David Crystal (2001), a renowned linguist, defines language as "the systematic, conventional use of sounds, signs, or written symbols in a human society for communication and self-expression" (p. 184). Linguists study language as an act of speaking (or signing) and writing in different situations. They examine different aspects of communication, including the context, the background of speakers, the interactive nature and purpose of communication, and language variation. They also study the underlying system of language, which includes the properties of words and how words are combined to form sentences. Linguists also study how language is acquired. Providing effective language and content instruction for ELLs requires an understanding of language at these different levels of abstraction.

Why Teachers Need to Know About Language

Lily Wong Fillmore and Catherine Snow (2000) identify five functions that teachers perform that have consequences in their work with ELLs. For teachers to perform each of these functions, they must have a thorough understanding of language.

Teacher as communicator. Teachers must know enough about the structure of language to speak and write so their students can understand them and they must be able to understand what their students are saying. Understanding student talk is essential to teachers' ability to analyze what students know, how they understand, and what teaching methods would be most useful. Effective communication with linguistically and culturally diverse students includes recognizing, valuing, and drawing on their home languages (languages other than English and nonstandard varieties of English) as resources in teaching and learning.

Teacher as educator. Teachers need to know which language problems will resolve themselves and which problems need attention and intervention. Teachers need to select or modify the language used in instruction (written and oral) to make complex content-area concepts comprehensible to ELLS at different English proficiency levels.

Teacher as evaluator. Teachers frequently make judgments based on language behaviors of students that have enormous consequences for the students' lives. These include everyday judgments and responses that affect students' sense of themselves as learners, as well as decisions about reading group placement, promotion, and referral for evaluation. For example, when educators mistake language differences or language development issues for cognitive deficiencies, many ELL students and speakers of nonstandard varieties of English are inappropriately placed in special education. Assessment instruments designed for monolingual standard English speakers may not provide valid indicators of the growth and achievement of ELLs or speakers of nonstandard varieties of English.

Teacher as an educated human being. Teachers should understand the role of language in education and know something about the differences between the structure of English and that of other languages. Public ignorance about language and language issues has resulted in damaging policies (e.g., restrictions on bilingual education programs for ELLs in California, Arizona, and Massachusetts), public debates about challenging issues involving people who are uninformed and ill-prepared to participate (e.g., the Ebonics controversy in Oakland, California, discussed later in this chapter), and pedagogically unsound decisions in schools (e.g., about methods for teaching English or reading).

Teacher as agent of socialization. Students from immigrant and minority homes may find the culture of the school vastly different from the culture of their home, and the teacher may be their first contact with the social world outside the home and even, among ELLs, their first contact with English. Thus, the ways teachers organize their programs and practices helps students adjust to the everyday practices, the system of values and beliefs, and the means and manners of communication at school and in society. In this role, as in their role as communicators, teachers who respect their students' home languages and cultures can be most effective in helping students make the necessary transitions without undercutting the role that parents and families must continue to play in their education and development.

All classrooms are language environments, and language is at the heart of teaching and learning. To help students succeed in the classroom and in school, teachers need to "think linguistically," that is, teachers need to "understand language as an integral element in the content they teach, the contributions that their students make in the classroom, and how these students participate in lessons and activities" (Bailey, Burkett, & Freeman, 2008, p. 609).

What Teachers Need to Know About Language

In this section we look briefly at five subsystems of language—phonology, morphology, syntax, semantics, and pragmatics—and vocabulary, spelling, and language variation.

Phonology

Phonology is the study of the sound systems of languages. Segmental phonology focuses on the discrete sounds within a language, called phonemes; suprasegmental phonology focuses on intonation, stress patterns, and other features that occur across phonemes.

Phonemes are the smallest units of sound in a language. A change in phoneme causes a change in meaning; for example, a slight difference in vowel sound changes the word *bit* to *bet*. Allophones are the manifestations of a single phoneme in speech; for example, *peak* and *speak* include the phoneme /p/, but the manifestation of the *p* sound is slightly different. In *peak,* the *p* is aspirated (a small puff of air is released when you say it), whereas in *speak,* the *p* is unaspirated. (Say both words with the back of your hand in front of your mouth to feel the difference.) Thus, the phoneme /p/ is manifested in these words by its allophones [p^H] (aspirated) and [p] (unaspirated). Note that saying *speak* with an aspirated *p* [p^H] does not change the meaning of the word; it just sounds a bit funny. In some languages, however, such as Khmer and Thai, a change in aspiration changes the meaning of the word. In these languages, the aspirated and unaspirated *p* would actually be two separate phonemes.

Phonology also addresses syllable structure and the sequence of sounds in a word. For example, English words use several different patterns of constants (C) and vowels (V)—V (*I*), VC (*it*), CCV (*spy*), CV (*hi*), CVC (*mat*), CVCC (*best*), CVCCC (*burned*), CCVC (*quit*), and CCCVCCC (*squints*). Our knowledge of phonology and of these patterns helps us recognize words that could be English words even though they are not (e.g., *gub, tricand, subgrased*), and words that could not be English words (e.g., *ntrgn, aeouiv, pmuououeg*). Note that you can read the first set of words but not the second.

Knowledge of phonology helps teachers understand issues related to pronunciation, accents, and regional varieties of English. Student difficulties in pronunciation often have to do with the fact that some English phonemes may not exist (or may vary slightly) in a student's native language, and vice versa. Also, some of the sequences of sounds allowed in English are not allowed in other languages, and vice versa. A foreign-sounding accent is usually a result of small differences in phonology between English and the speaker's native language. For example, in situation #1 at the beginning of the chapter, Vihn may have difficulty pronouncing the *th* sound because this phoneme does not exist in her native Vietnamese language. She does not need to be sent to the speech therapist, and in time she will likely acquire the *th* sound on her own, especially if she is a younger student. If not, and if the teacher or student feels it is necessary, activities such as using minimal pairs (e.g., *thing/ding*) can help her improve her pronunciation.

Morphology

Morphology is the study of the structure of words. Every word is made up of one or more morphemes. Morphemes are the smallest units that carry meaning or have a grammatical function. For example, the word *books* has two morphemes: *book* conveys the content meaning of a bound text that can be read, and -*s* conveys the grammatical meaning of plurality, indicating that there is more than one book. *Book* is a free morpheme, because it can stand as a word by itself; -*s* is a bound morpheme, because it cannot stand on its own and must be bound to a free morpheme.

Linguists divide morphology into two subcategories: inflectional morphology and derivational morphology. Inflectional morphology addresses the way bound morphemes make inflectional changes to a word, such as changes related to number (e.g., *book/books*), tense (e.g., *jump/jumps/ jumped/jumping*), and degree (e.g., *fast/faster/fastest*). Derivational (or lexical) morphology addresses word formation, that is, the way words are derived from other words, and includes the use of prefixes (a bound morpheme affixed in front of a free morpheme; e.g., *mis-* in *misrepresent*) and suffixes (a bound morpheme affixed after a free morpheme; e.g., -*ation* in *mispresentation*). Bound morphemes can change the lexical category (noun, verb, adjective, etc.) of a word. For example, *teach* is a verb, but the addition of the suffix -*er* changes it to a noun—*teacher*. Bound morphemes can also change a noun to a verb (e.g., *idol/idolize*), a noun to an adjective (e.g., *sin/sinful*), an adjective to a verb (*tight/tighten*), or an adjective to an adverb (*quiet/quietly*). New words can also be derived without changing the lexical category, for example, *tie/untie, representation/misrepresentation, test/pretest, wife/ex-wife.*

Morphology also addresses the creation of new vocabulary through techniques such as compounding (e.g., *sunroof*), borrowing from other languages (e.g., *karaoke* from Japanese, *algebra* from Arabic, *patio* from Spanish), shortening (e.g., the *fed*, from *federal government)*, and blending (e.g., *smog* from *smoke* and *fog*). New vocabulary is also created through the use of acronyms (abbreviations that can be pronounced as a word, e.g., *NASA*), and initialisms (abbreviations in which each letter name is pronounced, e.g., *ESL*). The proliferation of "net-speak" or the acronyms and initialisms used in on-line communication (e-mail, chat, text-messaging) also falls within the venue of morphology; acronyms such as LOL (laughing out loud) and BFF (best friends forever), once constrained to these on-line text environments, are now creeping into oral speech and even students' schoolwork.

Teachers can use their knowledge of how words are structured to help students understand how to change verb tenses, how to make compound words, plurals and possessives, and comparatives and superlatives, and how to use contractions. Through word study lessons, teachers can help students use morphemes to create new words. For example, if students know the meaning of *record* they can figure out *records, recorded,* and *recording.* They can also learn how new words are formed in English (e.g., *thumbdrive, ringtone, supersize*).

One of the challenges of teaching a new language is that the rules of morphology differ across languages. For example, many languages do not use inflectional morphemes to indicate number or tense, such as -*s* or −*ed* in English, but instead use a stand-alone morpheme, a separate word, to indicate number or tense. Thus, Chanyoung's problem reading words with a final −*s* in situation #2 may not be a reading problem. Instead, it may be related to morphological differences between how plurality is marked in Korean and English.

Syntax

Syntax is the study of the rules governing the way words are combined to form sentences and the rules governing the arrangement of sentences in sequences. Syntax is what most teachers think of as grammar. Once we understand the basic rules of grammar, we can produce an unlimited number of sentences. Think about how many new phrases or sentences you speak or write every day that you have never uttered before; your knowledge of syntax allows you to do this.

Syntax is about the relationships between words. You can think of syntax as helping us understand who did what to whom when, where, and how. For example, our knowledge of syntactic rules in English helps us understand the difference between *Dad gave my book to Mom* and *Mom gave my book to Dad*. Even if we are not able to articulate the rules, our underlying knowledge of word order in English (which has a relatively strict subject-verb-object word order) tells us that *Dad* is the subject and *Mom* is the object of the first sentence, while *Mom* is the subject and *Dad* is the object of the second sentence. Our knowledge of syntax also tells us that *To book my gave Dad Mom* is not an acceptable English sentence. Knowing the meaning of these individual words is not sufficient to understand the different meanings conveyed by these sentences. Knowledge of the syntactic rules governing word order in English is necessary to comprehend the meaning.

For ELLs, producing grammatically correct phrases and sentences can be a major challenge, because the rules for syntax vary across languages. For example, *Tomorrow I go house friend* is acceptable according to syntactic rules governing word order in Khmer, but the syntactic rules in English would require *Tomorrow I am going to my friend's house*. Like Rosa in situation #3, Spanish speakers who are beginning to learn English may produce utterances like *car red, house big,* and *friend good* because according to the syntactic word order rules in Spanish, the adjective generally follows the noun it modifies. Thus the teacher can rest assured that Rosa is not dyslexic. Errors like these are normal at the beginning stages of English language acquisition.

Semantics

Semantics is the study of the meaning of words, phrases, and sentences. Individual words have semantic features that indicate various properties or meanings inherent in the word. For example, the word *woman* contains the following semantic features: animate, human, female, adult; the word *girl*, in contrast, has only three of these semantic features: animate, human, female. Our understanding of semantic features helps us recognize the oddity of a sentence such as *My poodle is an excellent cook*. Although the syntax of the sentence is acceptable, the semantic features of *poodle* do not include *human*, and only humans get to cook.

Semantics also helps us understand the relationships between words, using the following terms:

- *Synonym*s. Words that have the same linguistic meaning (*evil/wicked; cold/freezing; large/huge*)
- *Antonyms*. Words that are opposite in meaning (*rich/poor; happy/sad; hot/cold*)
- *Homophones*. Words that sound the same but have different meanings (*bear/bare; to/two/too; meat/meet*)
- *Homonyms*. Words that have two or more different meanings (*chair:* an object to sit on; leader of a committee or a department).
- *Hyponym*s. Words that are included in the meaning of another word (*dog* is a hyponym of *animal; rose* is a hyponym of *flower*). Hyponyms can be arranged in a hierarchical relationship: *pit bull → dog → mammal → animal → creature → living thing.*
- Converseness. Refers to a reciprocal semantic relationship between words (husband/wife; child/parent; grandchild/grandparent; buy/sell; give/receive)
- *Polysemy*. Refers to two or more related meanings that a word can have (*plain:* 1. easy, clear (*plain English*); 2. undecorated (*plain white shirt*); 3. not good looking (*plain Jane*).
- *Part/whole relationships.* Refers to the relationship between words in which

one or more words are part of another word (*hand* → *arm; second* → *minute; hand, elbow, forearm, wrist* → *arm; second, minute, hour* → *day*).

Semantics also addresses issues such as modality (mood), which enables us to distinguish between a command (*Bring your homework tomorrow*), a statement (*He will bring his homework tomorrow*), permission (*You may bring your homework tomorrow*), and probability (*He will probably bring his homework tomorrow*). Semantics includes the way we can refer to real-world entities including the use of personal pronouns (*I, you, her*) and words that provide orientation or points of reference (deixis) (*here, there; now, then*).

Teachers can use their understanding of semantics to develop vocabulary lessons that are based on lists of semantically related words, which are much easier to learn than lists of semantically unrelated words. An understanding of semantics can also inform the teaching of cognates—words that are similar in English and a student's native language because they come from the same root (e.g., *important* in English and *importante* in Spanish).

Not all cognates, however, are fully equivalent. For example, in English *parents* has a specific meaning (birth mother and father), but in Spanish *parientes* refers to relatives in general. We also find false cognates across languages (e.g., *éxito* in Spanish means "success," not "exit," as it appears). Direct translation can be complicated because the "same" word may not contain the same semantic features across languages. For example, a Khmer speaker may say "open the light" or "open the radio" because the semantic properties of *open* in Khmer include the turning on of electrical items. Suling's confusion with English gender pronouns in situation #4 is a semantic issue. Her teacher should understand that Suling knows the difference between boys and girls; but because most third person pronouns are not marked for gender in her native Khmer, it may take a little time for Suling to figure out the semantic properties of gender in pronouns such as *he/she, him/her*, and *his/hers* in English.

Pragmatics

Pragmatics is the study of language in use, including the study of "invisible" meaning or how we recognize what is meant even when it is not actually stated. A lot more is communicated in conversation than is actually said. Recognizing the "invisible," or beneath-the-surface, meaning depends on certain socially constructed assumptions and expectations that the speaker shares with the listener.

Pragmatics can help us understand how language users interpret speech acts, such as requests, commands, questions, and statements. Speech acts can be direct or indirect. For example, my wife frequently asks me (in a harsh tone), "Why did you leave the door open?" My understanding of pragmatics tells me that although this utterance has the surface structure of a question, it is actually an indirect request or command for me to close the door. An understanding of the difference between direct and indirect speech acts can help us explain the miscommunication that arose in situation #5. If Thanawan interpreted the teacher's utterance, "Why are you still reading instead of doing your math?" as a simple question, then her response, "Oh, because I not finish yet" is an appropriate answer. But the teacher's interpretation of Thanawan's response as rude and an act of disobedience suggests that the teacher's utterance was not meant as a question but rather as an indirect request to stop reading and start doing math.

Pragmatics also helps us understand how we use language to start, maintain, and end conversations, take turns, express opinions, agree and disagree, negotiate social status in relationships, save face, and make excuses. From pragmatics, we understand that it's not just what we say but often how we say it that conveys the intended meaning (or how the listener interprets what was said). And because these ways of speaking vary cross-culturally, what is considered an appropriate way, for example, to agree or disagree in one speech community may be considered inappropriate in another. As research on cross-cultural differences in ways of speaking has demonstrated, these differences can lead to miscommunication, stereotyping, and discrimination.

Susan Philips's (1983) classic ethnographic study of cross-cultural communication at school provides an excellent example of how cultural differences can cause miscommunication. Philips found that students from the Warm Springs Indian Reservation in Oregon tend to pause longer than standard English-speaking White middle-class students before responding and that the Anglo teacher often interprets the longer pause as an indication that the child does not know the answer or is being intentionally uncooperative. As a result of this miscommunication, the Anglo teacher calls on the Anglo students more often, and positions the Warm Springs Indian students as invisible in the classroom interaction. Philips argues that this ongoing positioning at school socializes the Warm Springs Indian students into seeing themselves as invisible relative to Anglo students and helps explain the subordinate status of Warm Springs Indians in the larger society.

Invisible meaning that is based on certain assumptions and expectations can pose serious challenges to ELLs who do not share the assumptions and expectations of standard English-speaking students and teachers. Even those who quickly learn vocabulary and grammar may continue to struggle with issues related to pragmatics. Thus, it is necessary for teachers to have a strong understanding of this important area of language use so they can make the invisible visible for their students.

Lexicon

The vocabulary of a language is its lexicon. To use a word from the lexicon, a speaker needs four kinds of information:

- its sounds and their sequencing (phonology),
- its meanings (semantics),
- its category (e.g., noun or verb) and how to use it in a sentence (syntax), and
- how related words such as the plural (for nouns) and past tense (for verbs) are formed (morphology). (Finegan, 2004, p. 40)

Children growing up in English-speaking families acquire vocabulary very rapidly and usually with little direct assistance. They pick up words in conversation and by reading and being read to. On average, children between the ages of 1 and 17 add 13 words a day to their growing vocabulary, and by the time they are 17, they know about 80,000 words (Fillmore & Snow, 2000, p. 18). Teachers can help ELL students acquire new words in the same natural, noninstructional ways, by understanding that vocabulary acquisition happens most easily in context and related to topics that the students care about. Thus, talk about mothers and fathers should include talk about brothers, sisters, grandfathers, grandmothers, aunts, uncles, and cousins; talk about food should include talk about eating, cooking, utensils, and kitchen appliances.

Spelling

Teachers who have some knowledge of the history of the English language can help ELL students understand the often confusing English spelling system. Between the 11th and 15th centuries Middle English was spoken and there was a much closer relationship between English spelling and English pronunciation. In the past 600 years, however, English has changed considerably. David Freeman and Yvonne Freeman (2004) note that modern American English is more logical and systematic than it may seem. The spelling system, they point out, is not based simply on spelling words the way they sound. Two words may be spelled similarly because they are related in meaning rather than sound and words borrowed from other languages may be spelled to reflect their origin (p. 149). Thus words such as *know* and *acknowledge* or *sign* and *signify* have spellings that are semantically related, but with roots that are pronounced differently. Words such as *croissant, tamale,* and *jaguar* are spelled the way they are to reflect their origin (French, Spanish, and Guarani, respectively).

Language Variation

Standard English is the variety of English spoken by members of the dominant society in the United States, and it is the variety taught and assessed in school. Many students, however, in their homes and communities speak regional or nonstandard varieties of English that differ in phonology, morphology, syntax, semantics, pragmatics, and vocabulary. Teachers need to understand that these nonstandard varieties are not "bad English." Rather, they are rule-governed and legitimate varieties of English. But because standard English is the variety spoken by the dominant and powerful group in U.S. society, it is taken for granted as the norm. It is elevated to the role of "proper English," and all other varieties are deemed "substandard."

A controversy in 1996, for example, over a proposal by the Oakland Unified School District to recognize African American Vernacular English (AAVE) or Ebonics, as a legitimate variety of English for instructional purposes at school was based on the stigma attached to Ebonics because it is a nonstandard variety of English. The district's proposal resulted in an emotional national debate and even mockery on late-night television. Lost in the debate, however, was the objective of the proposal: to help African American students, who spoke Ebonics at home and who were doing poorly in school, to learn standard English—the variety needed to succeed academically and in society. In other words, the district planned to use Ebonics to help students learn standard English (Rickford, 2005). Although this approach is grounded in research on language teaching and learning, public outrage over Oakland's efforts to recognize the legitimacy of Ebonics dominated the debate. Discrimination against a person's language or way of speaking is rarely based on the language itself. As the controversy over Ebonics suggests, the discrimination may be less about the language and more about the people who speak it.

In situation #9, William's speech is not "poor English," rather, it is proper AAVE, a legitimate nonstandard variety of English. Teachers should also be aware that ELLs growing up in areas where nonstandard varieties of English are spoken will likely pick up features of these varieties. To provide the best education possible for students like William and other nonstandard variety speakers, educators need to learn pedagogically sound and culturally sensitive methods for helping students learn standard English without delegitimizing the variety of their homes and communities.

What Does It Mean to "Know" a Language?

We frequently hear people ask questions such as, "Do you speak English?" "Do you know Spanish?" or "Are you fluent in Vietnamese?" But what it means to speak, know, or be fluent in a language depends first on how language and language proficiency are conceptualized. Earlier approaches to second language learning viewed language as a set of discrete skills, including reading, writing, listening, and speaking. Knowing a language meant mastering these skills, including attaining a basic vocabulary and understanding of grammar. Such a narrow view of language and language proficiency, however, has proven insufficient for our understanding of how ELLs acquire the English they need to participate and achieve across content areas at school and in society. This section reviews recent developments in and challenges to our understanding of what it means to know a language.

Conversational Fluency and Academic Language Proficiency: BICS and CALP

Jim Cummins has had a significant influence on K–12 educators' understanding of what it means to know a language and how long it takes ELLs to become proficient in English.[1] A key component of Cummins's frameworks is the distinction between what he calls basic interpersonal communication skills (BICS) and cognitive academic language proficiency (CALP). BICS, Cummins (2008a) explains, refers to "conversational fluency in a language while CALP refers to students' ability to understand and express, in both oral and written modes, concepts and ideas that are relevant to success in school" (p. 71). Cummins later elaborated his original BICS/CALP distinction into a "quadrants" framework to highlight the range of cognitive demands and contextual support for particular language tasks and activities. He now distinguishes three different aspects of language proficiency, which he calls *conversational fluency, discrete language skills,* and *academic language proficiency.* Cummins (2006) argues that conversational fluency takes about 1 to 2 years for ELLs to develop, but that it takes 5 years or longer for ELLs to catch up to native English speakers in academic English.

Cummins's work has had significant impact on policy and practice in K–12 ELL education. An understanding of how long it takes for ELLs to acquire academic English can inform our response to the claim that accompanies the software in situation #7 (see Box 2.1). Clearly, no software program, no matter how engaging, will prepare a beginning ELL for participation in a mainstream poetry analysis unit in just a few weeks.

Cummins's work has been subject to substantial criticism, including the charge that the BICS/CALP constructs are an oversimplification of the complex construct of language proficiency, and that the use of these terms leads to misunderstandings about language.[2] One of these critics, Terrence Wiley (2005a), taking a sociocultural perspective, argues that the focus should be on the communicative functions of language and the heavily contextualized language used in the teaching of academic subjects. He points out that language and literacy development always takes place in specific social contexts (e.g., a high school science classroom). There are specific literacy practices in these contexts (e.g., lab reports), and each student's motivation, involvement, and success will depend on the manner in which these literacy practices build on their prior knowledge. Wiley notes that much of what falls under academic language proficiency is really just academic socialization to specific literacy practices. Thus, he argues, the focus should be on understanding what these specific practices are, rather than on achieving a general

---

1: For the development of Cummins's work, including his response to some of his critics, see Cummins 1979, 1981, 1984, 1992, 2000, 2006, 2008a.

2: For criticisms of Cummins's frameworks, see Edelsky et al., 1983; MacSwan, 2000; MacSwan & Rolstad, 2003; MacSwan, Rolstad, & Glass, 2002; Rolstad, 2004; Romaine, 1995; Valdés, MacSwan, & Martinez, 2002; Wiley, 2005a.

Box 2.1

How Long Does It Take for ELLs to Attain Proficiency in English?

Estimates vary, but the quick answer to this question is that it takes about 4 to 7 years for an ELL student to attain proficiency in English (Hakuta, Butler, & Witt, 2000). But stating it in these simple terms can be misleading. Analyses of state assessment and redesignation data reveal that it may take only 2 to 4 years for ELLs to develop oral language skills in English to a level similar to that of native English-speaking peers, but it can take from 5 to 8 years for ELLs to catch up to native speakers in the English language proficiency required for academic purposes, which includes grade-level literacy skills in English (Crawford & Krashen, 2007; Hill, 2004, 2006).

English proficiency that is not specific to any particular context. In other words, the construct of academic language proficiency is too general. It is too simplistic and unhelpful to claim that there is a single construct called "academic language" and that once students learn it they can master any academic content area.

Language for Academic Success in Language Arts, Math, Science, and Social Studies

Despite its inadequacies, language experts have attempted to unpack the term *academic language proficiency*. Anna Uhl Chamot (2009), for example, identifies the following academic language functions: seek information, inform, compare, order, classify, analyze, infer, justify and persuade, solve problems, synthesize, and evaluate. For the academic language function *order*, for example, students use language to sequence objects, ideas, or events by creating a timeline, continuum, cycle, or narrative sequence. Chamot's cognitive academic language learning approach (CALLA), discussed later in this chapter, shows teachers how they can structure their classes to help ELLs learn to use English for these academic purposes. But note, however, that Chamot's list of academic language functions is no different from the social language functions a group of students might use as they organize, play, and discuss a soccer match on the playground. Look at each function in Chamot's list and think about how it would be used in this context. You will see that these functions are not unique to academic contexts.

The TESOL (Teachers of English to Speakers of Other Languages) English language proficiency (ELP) standards reflect a national effort to delineate what academic language proficiency means for ELLs. According to the TESOL ELP standards, academic language proficiency includes being able to communicate for social, intercultural, and instructional purposes within the school setting and being able to communicate information, ideas, and concepts necessary for academic success in language arts, mathematics, science, and social studies (see Table 2.1). Although the TESOL ELP standards reflect the traditional view that divides language into the four discrete skill areas of listening, speaking, reading, and writing, TESOL has taken a step toward a more current view of language that delineates the different kinds of language demands associated with the different academic content areas.

Communicative Competence

From a sociocultural perspective, knowing a language means being able to use it to communicate effectively and appropriately with other speakers of the language.

Table 2.1	**TESOL's English Language Proficiency (ELP) Standards**
Standard 1:	English language learners **communicate** for **social, intercultural, and instructional** purposes within the school setting.
Standard 2:	English language learners **communicate** information, ideas, and concepts necessary for academic success in the area of **language arts**.
Standard 3:	English language learners **communicate** information, ideas, and concepts necessary for academic success in the area of **mathematics**.
Standard 4:	English language learners **communicate** information, ideas, and concepts necessary for academic success in the area of **science**.
Standard 5:	English language learners **communicate** information, ideas, and concepts necessary for academic success in the area of **social studies**.

Source: TESOL, 2006a.

This ability is referred to as communicative competence, a term introduced by Dell Hymes (1972), one of the founders of sociolinguistics, in the late 1960s. Michael Canale and Merrill Swain (1980) identify four components of communicative competence that are interrelated:

1. *Grammatical competence.* The ability to recognize the lexical, morphological, syntactic, and phonological features of a language and use them to interpret and form words and sentences.
2. *Discourse competence.* The ability to connect a series of utterances, written words, or phrases to form a meaningful whole.
3. *Sociolinguistic competence.* The ability to understand the social context in which language is used, including the roles of the participants.
4. *Strategic competence.* The ability to use coping strategies in unfamiliar contexts when imperfect knowledge of rules (or factors that limit their application) may lead to a breakdown in communication.

We typically hold up the "native speaker" as the model of communicative competence to which all second language learners should strive. But many linguists view the existence of the native speaker as a myth. The concept of a native speaker is one most of us take for granted, agreeing that the term describes a person who acquires a particular language naturally, beginning at birth, through interaction with other people rather than by formal instruction. As noted earlier, however, there can be different varieties within a language, and even within the standard variety of English, native speakers vary widely in how they use language and how skilled they are in language-related tasks. The notion of native speaker also fails to account for children who grow up with two or more languages. Sandra Savignon (2001) stresses that "the 'ideal native speaker,' someone who knows a language perfectly and uses it appropriately in all social interactions, exists in theory only" (p. 18). Thus, communicative competence is a relative, not an absolute, concept.

Register, Genre, and Discourse

The degree to which one knows a language or is communicatively competent depends on the social setting in which the language is used. Linguists use the term register to refer to the variations in language, including the choice of words and grammar, that reflect the social setting in which it is used. Think about the difference between the way you speak in a formal setting, such as a class at the university, and in an informal setting, such as when hanging out with close friends. Or think about the difference between the writing style you use for an academic paper and the style you use in an e-mail or text message. These are examples of formal and informal registers.

M. A. K. Halliday's (1994) theory of systemic functional linguistics (SFL) can be useful to teachers in understanding the linguistic challenges ELLs face with advanced language and literacy tasks at school. In SFL, the notion of linguistic register is employed to understand how language is related to the context in which it is used. What makes a register unique is the range of lexical and grammatical features that create the specific context. In SFL theory, a genre is a goal-directed activity, such as the creation of a particular kind of text to achieve a particular cultural purpose. The meaning of a text (either spoken or written) is based on the lexical and grammatical choices that the speaker or writer makes. Thus, through SFL theory, it is possible to identify the lexical and grammatical features that make a particular genre the kind of text is. In other words, SFL allows teachers to pinpoint what makes a personal narrative a personal narrative, a persuasive essay a persuasive essay, a science lab report a science lab report, a history report a history report, and so on. Once teachers are able to identify the lexical and grammatical features of these genres, they can make them more explicit to their ELL students and enhance their learning of these genres.

James Paul Gee (1996) takes language even further into its sociocultural context by making a distinction between discourse ("little d") and Discourse ("Big D"). "Little d" discourse refers to stretches of language beyond a single phrase or sentence (such as conversations or stories) that are used in a particular context to enact activities and identities. These discourses include, for example, the ways that a doctor uses oral and written language within the context of an appointment with a patient, or the ways that a scientist uses oral and written language within the context of a scientific experiment. In contrast, according to Gee, "'Big D' Discourses always includes language plus "other stuff" (p. 17). "Big D" Discourse refers to:

> different ways in which we humans integrate language with non-language "stuff," such as different ways of thinking, acting, interacting, valuing, feeling, believing, and using symbols, tools, and objects in the right places and at the right times so as to enact and recognize different identities and activities, give the material world certain meanings, distribute social goods in a certain way, make certain sorts of meaningful connections in our experience, and privilege certain symbol systems and ways of knowing over others. (p. 13)

The doctor referred to above draws on medical Discourses as she participates in the doctor-patient interaction, which in turn helps construct her identity as a doctor, the patient's identity as a patient, and the meaningfulness of their doctor-patient relationship.

Kellie Rolstad (2004) argues schools need to help students learn many registers or Discourses. She writes:

> Students need to learn all the registers of the subjects they study in school, each with its peculiar vocabulary and whatever other linguistic features that inhere. At the same time, they must also learn those registers that are necessary for their social success in school as well as in other areas of their lives. Social, communicative competence requires the acquisition of myriad registers, or Discourses, ways of talking to other students, inside and outside of class, and ways of talking to teachers, each of whom may have his or her own preferences for interaction. (pp. 1997–1998)

Thus, instead of focusing on "academic language" as an isolated construct, the focus should be on how language and literacy are actually used in the classroom for teaching and learning specific academic subjects, and on finding ways to help ELLs learn and use these correctly and appropriately in academic settings.

As a conceptual alternative to "academic language," Jeff MacSwan and Kellie Rolstad (2003) introduced the concept of "second language instructional competence" (SLIC), which they define as "the stage of second language (L2) development at which the learner is able to understand instruction and perform grade-level school activities in the L2 alone, in the local educational context" (pp. 329–330). The concept of SLIC helps us to focus more clearly on the specific subject-matter or task at hand. Teachers can ask themselves, What is "the amount and type of linguistic proficiency that is required for that student to engage the subject matter at hand?" or, What level of oral and written language is required for students to "understand the language of instruction sufficiently well at that moment, in that context, to participate in that lesson and learn from it"? (Rolstad, 2004, p. 1998). The amount of SLIC needed will vary from subject to subject, and from task to task, depending on the language demands of the specific task within a given content area.

Language Acquisition

Newborn babies are unable to speak, but by the time they are 5 years old (assuming no cognitive or developmental disorders) they have a fully developed language system. Two major theories have evolved to explain this amazing achievement. In the behaviorist perspective, the well-known psychologist B. F. Skinner and others hypothesized that children learn their first language through imitation and positive reinforcement. Young children imitate the speech they hear around them, and adults positively reinforce their meaningful utterances, helping them develop habits of correct speech. This view was prominent throughout the 1940s and 1950s but was challenged by Noam Chomsky in 1959.

Chomsky, widely recognized as one of the world's most influential linguists, demonstrated that children are able to produce language and unique utterances that go well beyond what they could reasonably have been exposed to and imitated. He hypothesized that children have an innate ability—they are prewired—to learn language. Chomsky's theories, often referred to as the innatist perspective, suggest the presence of a language acquisition device (LAD) that enables children to figure out the underlying rules of the language on their own because of their exposure to samples of natural language. He refers to these underlying rules as Universal Grammar. Once the LAD is activated and children internalize the rules for the structure (syntax) of their language or languages, they can generate an infinite number of unique, grammatically correct utterances.

Chomsky's theories were revolutionary and they led to a rejection of the behaviorist perspectives on language acquisition. Although his work remains influential, with most linguists agreeing that children have some form of genetic predisposition for language learning, new research is emerging from within linguistics and other academic fields. Those who accept Chomsky's ideas at some level vigorously debate exactly how they work, while others challenge the core of his ideas.

Two important developments in different branches of linguistics have influenced the second language acquisition research we discuss in the next section. Hymes challenged Chomsky's exclusive focus on linguistic competence when he introduced the concept of communicative competence. His work stimulated ethnographic research that describes and explains how social context influences the ways languages are learned and used. Recent work in linguistic anthropology fol-

Box 2.2

The Critical Period Hypothesis

*Do Younger Students Learn a Second Language
Better and Faster Than Older Students?*

The critical period hypothesis holds that language learning must take place during early childhood if an individual is to attain native-like proficiency. This hypothesis has supported the popular view that young children have cognitive advantages that enable them to learn languages better and faster than adults.

Research has challenged this view with evidence that adults can and do learn languages successfully and even attain native-language proficiency (Birdsong & Park, 2008). Research has shown, however, that younger students do have some advantages over adult learners of a second language, and vice-versa, though these advantages have nothing to do with the brain.

Advantages of Young Children in Language Learning

- Young school-age children often have greater motivation, pressure, needs, and opportunities to develop second language proficiency than adults.
- Younger students receive a much greater amount of instructional time in the K–12 educational systems to learn a language (e.g., 6 hours a day, 5 days a week) than the typical adult learner, who may receive only a few hours of instruction a week.
- Younger learners may have a lower affective filter than older students; thus, they may feel more comfortable using their new language.

Advantages of Older Students and Adults in Language Learning

- Older learners may be literate in their first language and have other knowledge and skills that can readily transfer to a second language.
- Older learners may have learning strategies they developed in the first language that will help them as they learn a second language.

lows this tradition, investigating how children are socialized into their respective speech communities across a wide range of sociocultural contexts. Efforts have been made within the field of cognitive and developmental psychology since the 1970s to focus more on the developmental aspects of language acquisition with greater attention to the environment in which children are exposed to language and the interactions that occur in that environment.

Second Language Acquisition Theories

Since we do not know exactly how people learn their first language, it is no surprise that there are many competing theories and much debate over how people learn a second (or third or more) language (see Box 2.3). Nonetheless, excellent research in the field of second language acquisition (SLA) has led to the development of several plausible theories that have important implications for second language teaching and learning. Patsy Lightbrown and Nina Spada (2006) identify four major perspectives from which theories about SLA have emerged: behaviorism, the innatist perspective, the cognitive/developmental perspective (psychological theories), and sociocultural perspectives. Each of these is briefly outlined in the sections that follow.

> **Box 2.3**
>
> **English May Not Be the Second Language**
>
> Although we use the terms *second language acquisition* and *second language teaching,* for some ELLs, English is not their second language but their third, fourth, or even fifth or higher language. Much of what we talk about under the label *second language acquisition* still applies to these students' efforts to learn English. Researchers, however, are just now beginning to explore the many factors that may be unique to the acquisition of a third language, a fourth language, and so on.

Behaviorism

The behaviorist perspective in SLA mirrors that of first language acquisition described earlier. B. F. Skinner's theories of learning as habit formation through stimulus and response with negative and positive reinforcement greatly influenced second language teaching from the 1940s to the 1970s. Classes taught from the behaviorist perspective focused mainly on memorization and language drills. Although by the end of the 1970s most SLA researchers had rejected the behaviorist perspective, methodologies connected with behaviorism can still be found in many language classrooms and textbooks.

The Innatist Perspective

Although Chomsky's work focuses on first language acquisition, his theories have been highly influential on SLA researchers and theories. Many researchers argue that we learn a second language in much the same way we learn our first language, and that second language learners also access the Universal Grammar to form internal rules about the language that are based on the input they receive.

One of the most influential models of SLA from the innatist perspective includes five interrelated hypotheses developed by Stephen Krashen (1982, 1985, 1992, 2004a). Krashen asserts that these hypotheses support Chomsky's claims and he extends them to SLA.

1. *The acquisition-learning hypothesis.* There is a fundamental difference between learning a language and acquiring a language. Language acquisition is a subconscious process. We are not aware that it is happening, and we are not even aware that we possess any new knowledge that is subconsciously stored in our brains. Language learning, in contrast, is a conscious process; it is what we do in school. When we are learning, we know we are learning and the learned knowledge is represented consciously in our brains. Learning results in just knowing *about* the language, rather than actually *knowing* the language (i.e., able to use it for authentic communicative purposes). Krashen argues that because of the complexity of language, the vast majority is acquired, rather than consciously learned.

2. *The natural order hypothesis.* We acquire the parts of a language in a predictable order. The order for SLA is similar, but not identical, to the order for first language acquisition. For example, the *–ing* marker in English (the progressive) is acquired fairly early, whereas the third person singular *–s* is acquired much later or may not be acquired at all by older ELLs. Because the natural order appears to be immune to teaching, drilling a student on a grammatical item before he or she is ready

to acquire it will be of little use. This hypothesis could explain, for example, why Roberto in situation #8 is not using *am* correctly despite the worksheets and drills.

3. *The monitor hypothesis.* Although most language is acquired, we can use learned language to monitor or inspect what we acquire and then correct errors. Sometimes we make a correction internally before we actually say or write something; other times we self-correct after producing a sentence. The monitor is like a little language teacher in our heads reminding us of the rules. Krashen asserts that the monitor can make a small contribution to accuracy but acquisition is responsible for fluency and most of our accuracy.

4. *The input (comprehension) hypothesis.* This is Krashen's most important hypothesis because it directly addresses how language acquisition occurs. He originally called it the input hypothesis but renamed it the comprehension hypothesis to more accurately reflect what it says (Krashen, 1985, 2004a). According to this hypothesis, we acquire language when we understand messages or obtain comprehensible input. That is, we acquire language when we understand the things we hear or read. Krashen uses the formula *i*+1 to explain comprehensible input; *i* represents a student's current level of proficiency, and +1 represents input that is just slightly above that level (in line with the natural order hypothesis). He suggests that we move from *i* to *i*+1 by understanding input containing *i*+1. We are able to do this, "with the help of our previously acquired linguistic competence, as well as extra-linguistic knowledge, which includes our knowledge of the world and our knowledge of the situation. In other words, we use context" (Krashen, 1985, p. 5). Thus, *i*+1 is the key to providing comprehensible input that enables further acquisition to take place. Krashen argues that we acquire language and develop literacy by understanding messages, not by consciously learning about language and not by memorizing grammar rules and vocabulary.

5. *The affective filter hypothesis.* The affective filter controls how much comprehensible input gets through to the learner. Even though the language acquirer understands certain input, anxiety, low-self esteem, or a sense that he or she is not a potential member of the group that speaks the language—the affective filter—will keep it out. Thus, a major goal in language teaching and learning is to "lower" the affective filter to maximize comprehensible input. This hypothesis has been useful in explaining why individual students make different amounts of progress when presented with the same input.

Comprehensible input, Krashen (1985) points out, is the essential ingredient for SLA. He summarizes the five hypotheses with a single claim: "People acquire second languages only if they obtain comprehensible input and if their affective filters are low enough to allow the input 'in.' When the filter is 'down' and appropriate comprehensible input is presented (and comprehended), acquisition is inevitable. It is, in fact, unavoidable and cannot be prevented" (p. 4).

Although Krashen's hypotheses have been and continue to be highly influential, they have been criticized for their emphasis on acquisition over learning and, in their application to classroom teaching, what seems to be the lack of direct instruction on grammatical and other language forms. Research shows, however, that despite the considerable progress students can make through exposure to comprehensible input without direct instruction, they "may reach a point from which they fail to make further progress on some features of the second language unless they also have access to guided instruction" (Lightbrown & Spada, 2006, p. 38).

Krashen does acknowledge a role for some direct teaching, as addressed in the monitor hypothesis (see also Krashen & Brown, 2007), but his theories do not necessarily provide guidance about what should be directly taught and what students will naturally acquire on their own.

Critics of the natural order hypothesis point out that no one has been able to identify a strict order in which different grammatical forms and other components of a language are acquired. Another criticism is that the constructs *i* and +1 from the comprehension hypothesis cannot be put into operation. Because of the complexity of language and the limitations we have in determining a student's actual language proficiency through language proficiency tests, we cannot obtain a precise measure of a student's *i*. Assuming we could measure *i*, exactly how much is +1?

Of greater concern to Krashen's critics, however, is his oversimplification of complex processes in SLA and his downplaying of the importance of production (i.e., speaking and writing) in SLA. It may strike some as counterintuitive that one can acquire a new language without ever having to speak it. But Krashen (1985) asserts, "Speaking is a *result* of acquisition and not its *cause*. Speech cannot be taught directly but 'emerges' on its own as a result of building competence via comprehensible input" (p. 2; emphasis added). He adds, however, that speaking can be an indirect aid to language acquisition. Speaking results in conversation, and what the other person says is an excellent source of comprehensible input. Speaking can also help by making the learner feel more like a user of the second language, and this feeling helps lower the affective filter.

Despite the criticisms, Krashen's theories have inspired a considerable amount of research, much of it by scholars in psychology whose work has led to a number of psychological theories of SLA. We now turn to these.

The Cognitive/Developmental Perspective (Psychological Theories)

Cognitive and developmental psychologists believe that there is no distinction in the brain between learning and acquisition and that therefore general theories of learning can account for language learning. Among these are the information-processing model, connectionism, and the competition model.[3] Bill VanPatten (2003), a psycholinguist, argues, however, that language acquisition involves processes and mechanisms that are unique to language. He and other psycholinguists are interested in understanding the processes and mechanisms that enable a learner to comprehend and produce language.

In this section we look at the following SLA hypotheses, theories, and models from within the cognitive/development perspective: the interaction hypothesis, the comprehensible output hypothesis, the noticing hypothesis, processability theory, and input processing.

The Interaction Hypothesis

Researchers have argued that interaction is essential for SLA to occur,[4] and thus they have studied the ways in which speakers modify their speech and their interaction patterns to help learners participate in conversation. Michael Long (1983, 1996), who developed the interaction hypothesis, agrees that comprehensible input is needed, but he focuses on how input can be made comprehensible through modified interaction, arguing that learners need opportunities to interact with other speakers and reach mutual comprehension. In modified interaction, particularly interactions between a language learner and a native speaker, the speakers may

---

3: See Lightbrown & Spada, 2006, for summaries of these theories.

4: See, e.g., Gass, Mackey, & Pica, 1998; Pica, 1994.

make several modifications as they converse to get their meanings across (Swain & Suzuki, 2008). Some of these modifications may include simplifying the language, reducing the rate of speech, and using gestures. Native speakers might repeat or paraphrase what they say and use "comprehension checks," asking the learner during the conversation, "Do you understand?" The learner may make "clarification requests" with questions such as, "Can you repeat that please?" or "I'm sorry, what did you say?" or even a simple, "Huh?" along with a puzzled look. The native speaker also provides "corrective feedback," which may take the form of direct correction or indirect correction through more subtle means, such as repeating what the learner said but recasting it in the correct form. All these corrections are made within the natural flow of the conversation. For example, if the learner says "I go to doctor yesterday," the native speaker might respond, "You went to the doctor yesterday? Why? Are you sick?"

The Comprehensible Output Hypothesis

Merrill Swain (1985, 2000) brought attention to the importance of output in SLA through her comprehensible output hypothesis. Swain argues that when learners are in conversation, making an effort to produce language that the person with whom they are conversing can understand, they are most likely to see the limits of their second language ability and the need to find better ways to get their meaning across. Knowing they have to speak forces them to pay more attention to what they are saying. Thus, creating comprehensible output facilitates their language acquisition. VanPatten (2003) notes that "it is theoretically possible that some aspects of the input would not be processed or noticed if learners did not have experience making output" (p. 69).[5]

The Noticing Hypothesis

Richard Schmidt (1990, 2001) points out in his noticing hypothesis that learners cannot acquire specific language features in the input unless they notice them. Learners may notice language features when, for example, their teachers bring them to their attention in class or when something in the input is different from what they expected. Psycholinguists continue to debate the importance of awareness and attention in SLA, and research on these issues is ongoing.

Processability Theory

Manfred Pienemann argues in his processability theory that the sequence in which learners acquire certain language features depends on how easy they are to process (Lightbrown & Spada, 2006). Part of this ease depends on where features occur within a sentence in the input, with those at the beginning or end being easier to process than those in the middle. He also theorizes that learners acquire some linguistic features in the same sequence, even if they progress at different rates, while other linguistic features vary in terms of when they were processed.

The Input Processing Model

VanPatten (2004) developed the input processing model, which looks at how learners make sense out of input and how they get linguistic data from it. He defines input as the language learners hear or read and then process for meaning, and he stresses that to be successful, learners must have access to input and interaction with other speakers of the second language they are learning. In his model, VanPatten accepts the processability theory and adds the following:

5: Krashen, of course, disagrees. See his critique of Swain's output hypothesis in Krashen, 1998.

- Learners always process input for meaning first and rely on content words before anything else to get that meaning.
- When a content word and a grammatical form encode the same meaning (e.g., pastness is encoded both by a time reference such as "yesterday" and a verb inflection such as –*ed*), learners rely on the content word and "skip" the grammatical form.
- Learners rely on a first-noun strategy to understand "who did what to whom." (p. 41)

VanPatten (2003) also addresses how newly processed input leads to changes in the learner's developing linguistic system. He explains that this system change involves two subprocesses. The first, *accommodation*, describes the process by which learners actually incorporate a grammatical form or structure into the "mental picture" of the language they are creating. The second, *restructuring*, describes the process by which the incorporation of a form or structure makes other things change without the learner's ever knowing. Finally VanPatten addresses *output processing* to explain "how learners acquire the ability to make use of the implicit knowledge they are acquiring to produce utterances in real time, e.g., during conversation" (p. 15).

To summarize, VanPatten (2003) says: "Language acquisition happens in only one way and all learners must undergo it. Learners must have exposure to communicative input and they must process it; the brain must organize data. Learners must acquire output procedures, and they need to interact with other speakers. There is no way around these fundamental aspects of acquisition; they are the basics" (p. 96).

Sociocultural Perspectives

Sociocultural perspectives stem from the pioneering work of Lev Vygotsky (1978), a Russian psychologist who studied child development in the 1920s and 1930s. Vygotsky died in 1934 at the young age of 38 from tuberculosis, and some of his most influential work was published only after his death. English translations of his work did not appear until the late 1960s, but since then they have been highly influential in the West in psychology and education (see, e.g., Moll, 1992). Vygotsky's influence on SLA began gaining momentum in the 1990s.

According to Vygotsky, learning is a social activity, and knowledge is constructed through interaction and collaboration with others. Children's learning takes place when they interact and collaborate with adults or more skillful peers. Thus, children's language, a form of knowledge in Vygotsky's view, develops primarily from interactions (conversations) in social settings, especially in a supportive interactive environment. Through these "processes of meaning-making in collaborative activity . . . language itself develops as a 'tool' for making meaning" (Mitchell & Myles, 2004, p. 200). Second language researchers who accept Vygotsky's sociocultural theory believe these same ideas apply to second language learning.

Vygotsky identified the zone of proximal development (ZPD) as a domain or metaphoric space where children can reach a higher level of knowledge and performance with the support of an adult or other more knowledgeable person. He refers to this assistance within the ZPD as scaffolding, evoking a construction metaphor, where scaffolding is temporarily used to build something and removed once the building is completed. As with the rest of Vygotsky's theory, researchers apply the concepts of ZPD and scaffolding to the process of SLA.

Teachers, however, often incorrectly view Vygotsky's ZPD as essentially the same principle as the *i* + 1 in Krashen's input hypothesis. Although it is tempting to view them as the same, since both appear to be addressing the issue of providing something just above a learner's current level of proficiency, the two concepts depend on very different ideas about how development occurs. Krashen's theory focuses on the acquisition of a second language and the provision of comprehensible input that contains linguistic forms and structures that are just beyond the student's current level and that they are ready to acquire. Vygotsky's theory is about knowledge development in general, with an emphasis on how learners co-construct knowledge based on their interactions with others in a given sociocultural context.

Vygotsky's emphasis on interaction seems closely related also to Long's psycholinguistic interaction hypothesis, because Vygotsky and Long both highlight the importance of meaningful interactions. Long and other psycholinguists, however, are more interested in the cognitive processes initiated by input and output in the conversations, whereas in the sociocultural perspective the focus is on the conversations themselves, with learning occurring through the social interaction.

Sociocultural theory, then, gives much greater emphasis to the role of speaking in learning a second language and thus has opened the way for researchers to focus on collaboration and interaction as key to SLA. Swain, for example, has been able to use sociocultural theory to extend the work on her comprehensible output hypothesis by focusing on collaborative dialogues through which language use and language learning co-occur (see Swain & Suzuki, 2008).

Vygotsky's ideas have also been widely embraced by educators, who appreciate the important role given to teachers and to classroom interaction in sociocultural theory (Mitchell & Myles, 2004). Teachers are elevated from mere facilitators of comprehensible or modified input to knowledgeable, skilled experts who interact and collaborate with students, scaffolding instruction within the ZPD to co-construct knowledge with their students.

Language socialization theory, stemming from the early work of Elinor Ochs and Bambi Schieffelin (1984), is grounded in the sociocultural perspective of SLA. Language socialization "refers to the process by which individuals acquire the knowledge and practices that enable them to participate effectively in a language community" (Langman, 2008b, p. 489). In addition, language and cultural learning are considered inseparable. As students learn the new language they also gain knowledge about how to use the language in sociocultural contexts. This theory helps make teachers aware that when they work with ELL students they are not just teaching them a new language but are also socializing their students into a community of English language speakers.

Transfer from L1 to L2

Students are able to take much of the content-area knowledge and literacy skills they gained in their first language (L1) and transfer them to their second language (L2). This ability to transfer knowledge and skills means that students who have literacy skills in their native language will likely make rapid progress in learning to read and write in English.[6] Likewise, students who have developed substantial content-area knowledge through their native language do not need to relearn the same concepts in English. ELL students who have advanced skills in math, for example, do not need to relearn these concepts in English; they just need to learn the language necessary to demonstrate what they already know.

Although linguists and language educators recognize that much of what trans-

---

6: For more information on transfer from L1 to L2, see August & Hakuta, 1997; August & Shanahan, 2006a; Cummins, 1992.

fers from one language to another is beneficial (i.e., positive transfer), in some instances, transfer from the native language may cause interference (i.e., negative transfer). Students may attempt, for example, to apply their knowledge of the syntax of their native language to English (e.g., a Spanish speaker saying "house of friend" rather than "friend's house"). Although more research is needed to determine precisely what does and does not transfer, teachers can be assured that a student's knowledge and literacy skills in an L1 is a strength that will facilitate his or her academic and English language development. Effective teachers recognize and value the vast store of knowledge students have in their L1 and provide instruction that enables students to draw on this knowledge—an approach Jim Cummins (2008b) calls "teaching for transfer".

Second Language Teaching Approaches and Methods

The approaches and methods used in teaching a second language have evolved along with, and been influenced by, the theories about SLA. Approaches refers to an overarching philosophy of second language instruction; methods refers to a set of procedures for delivering second language instruction. Jack C. Richards and Theodore S. Rodgers (2001) have identified and described over a dozen different approaches and methods that have been used since the 19th century. Some have come and gone and some overlap. In reviewing ESL curricular materials or visiting the classrooms of effective ESL teachers, you will likely see a mixture of approaches and methods in use. Let us briefly look at some of the more common approaches and methods that continue to have an influence today on instruction for K–12 ELLs.

The Grammar-Translation Method

The grammar-translation method, based to a large extent on the way Latin was taught, was predominant from the 1840s to the 1940s. Students were required to analyze and memorize rules of grammar, then translate sentences between the two languages. This approach is not based on any theory and has no advocates, but it continues to be used widely among teachers with little training or experience. When opposition to grammar-translation developed and language educators and researchers began questioning why methods for teaching Latin—no longer a spoken language—were being used to teach modern languages, new methods were developed.

The Audiolingual Method

The audiolingual method grew out of the need for foreign language proficiency in the U.S. military after the United States entered World War II. Its appearance coincided with other efforts in the late 1930s and early 1940s to apply principles of structural linguistics to language teaching. The audiolingual method was highly influenced by behaviorism, the dominant view of second language learning at the time. Language learning was viewed as mechanical habit formation accomplished through dialogue memorization and drills focused on particular language structures. Audiolingualism fell out of favor by the 1970s, after publication of Chomksy's challenge to behaviorist theories of language learning. Also, many language teachers, and students themselves, were frustrated when students had difficulty moving from their memorized dialogues and drills to real-life communication. While audiolingualism is no longer the dominant method, vestiges of it are still apparent in many textbook dialogues and drills, language labs, and even in commercial language learning audio and software programs.

The Natural Approach

Tracy Terrell (1977), a language educator, developed the natural approach. Later, in collaboration with Stephen Krashen, they elaborated the approach further and provided it with a theoretical base (Krashen & Terrell, 1983). The natural approach essentially applies Krashen's five hypotheses to the communicative language learning classroom. In contrast to audiolingualism and other methods with a focus on grammar, the natural approach emphasizes the use of comprehensible input in the classroom so that students can acquire the language and its structures naturally as they use it for meaningful communication. The teacher's job is to provide comprehensible input in a safe and enjoyable classroom environment. Such an environment helps to lower the affective filter and thus maximize comprehensible input. The teacher uses a wide variety of techniques, such as total physical response (TPR), ample use of visuals and realia, small-group work, and any other activities involving meaningful communication that can facilitate the provision of comprehensible input. Krashen and Terrell also outlined five stages of language acquisition: preproduction, early production, speech emergence, intermediate, and advanced (reviewed in Chapter 1). Using these stages, teachers can identify appropriate activities and expectations for students that facilitate the provision of comprehensible input ($i + 1$) and enhance SLA. Because students acquire vocabulary and grammar naturally, there is little need for direct instruction and practice though the use of memorized dialogues or drills.

The natural approach, like Krashen's theories on which the approach is based, has been highly criticized for lacking a clear focus, providing too little guidance for teachers, and leaving too much to chance in terms of students' learning needed vocabulary and grammatical forms. Many educators who have seen students succeed in learning languages with the natural approach continue to use it. But criticisms of it have led to increased attention to form in communicative language teaching.

Communicative Language Teaching

Communicative language teaching (CLT) emerged in the 1980s and remains the approach favored by most experienced language teachers and researchers today. CLT grew out of dissatisfaction with audiolingualism, which produced students who could memorize dialogues and respond to drills but who had difficulty actually communicating with other speakers of the target language. CLT draws on Hymes's notion of communicative competence; thus, the focus is on learning language to actually use it to communicate in the target language with other speakers. CLT, however, is not a singular teaching method but a set of core principles that can be applied and interpreted in a variety of ways. These principles include the following:

- Learners learn a language through using it to communicate.
- Authentic and meaningful communication should be the goal of classroom activities.
- Fluency is an important dimension of communication.
- Communication involves the integration of different language skills.

■ Learning is a process of creative construction and involves trials and error. (Richards & Rodgers, 2001, p. 172)

In recent years, there has been an increasing push in communicative class-rooms to have some focus on form. That is, there has been an emphasis on providing grammar instruction within the communicative context of a particular academic subject or field. Thus, the goal of grammar instruction is not simply to memorize a rule but to develop the ability to effectively comprehend and convey intended meanings when reading books or other texts, making an oral presentation, writing a science or history report, or collaborating with peers to conduct a scientific experiment.

Content-Based Instruction

Content-based instruction (CBI) is an approach to second language teaching in which instruction is centered on a particular content area. The content area provides a meaningful context for authentic communication as learners collaborate to complete carefully designed academic tasks. This approach is consistent with the goal of most K–12 ELL programs, which is to prepare students for mainstream content area classrooms.

When CBI was introduced, ESL teachers used content areas such as math, science, and social studies as vehicles for language instruction, though their instructional and assessment focus was on English language development rather than content. Few ESL teachers, however, were properly trained to teach such content areas, and the ELL population was growing rapidly in schools. One solution was to train content-area teachers to help ELLs learn the content area while supporting their English language development. This type of instruction is called sheltered instruction, or specially designed academic instruction in English (SDAIE). CBI can now be thought of as a cover term for a continuum of approaches that integrate content and language instruction. On one end is content-area instruction by ESL teachers who focus on language development, on the other is sheltered instruction by content-area teachers who are trained to make complex content-area concepts comprehensible to ELLs at different English language proficiency levels.

Bilingual, ESL, and content-area teachers with ELLs in their classes receive training in sheltered instruction. The cognitive academic language learning approach (CALLA) developed in the 1980s and the sheltered instruction observation protocol (SIOP) model developed in the 1990s remain popular models for providing content-based instruction for ELLs in K-12.[7]

Whole Language, Multiple Intelligences, and Cooperative Learning

Whole language, multiple intelligences, and cooperative learning were not designed specifically for language teaching and learning, but teachers of ELLs have found them well suited for use in language learning classrooms. Whole language is a philosophy of literacy instruction that places emphasis on teaching reading strategies and skills within the meaningful context of whole stories, poems, and other texts (a top-down approach). Although the term *whole language* is now used infrequently because of political controversy over what some perceived to be its rejec-

---

7: For recent work on CALLA, see Chamot, 2009; for recent work on the SIOP model, see Echevarria, Vogt, & Short, 2010a, 2010b.

tion of training in basic skills such as phonics, the strategies and practices associated with whole language are still in common use. Multiple intelligences, a theory proposed by Howard Gardner (1999), asserts that intelligence is multidimensional; thus, classroom instruction should be designed to maximize learning according to the particular set of intelligences a child may have. These intelligences include linguistic, logical/mathematical, spatial, musical, kinesthetic, interpersonal, intrapersonal, and naturalistic. Teachers have found that multiple intelligences approaches to teaching help them identify and teach to their ELL students' strengths in both language and content-area instruction. Cooperative learning focuses on the use of small groups within which students collaborate to solve problems or complete academic tasks. Cooperative learning appeals to language teachers because it offers rich opportunities for students to engage in meaningful communication and obtain comprehensible input as they interact to complete academic tasks.

Critical Pedagogy

Paulo Freire, a Brazilian educator, developed critical pedagogy in the 1960s while seeking ways to offer an education to impoverished and illiterate adult students in his country that would help them improve their situation and thus transform their lives and the society in which they lived. Although it is not presented as an approach to teaching second languages and is not included in Richards and Rodgers's list of influential methods and approaches, many educators in the field of language education have recognized its importance in helping ELL students understand and confront unequal power relations as they attain English proficiency and learn academic content.

Freire (1993) decried what he refers to as the "banking" concept of education, according to which teachers simply make deposits of essential knowledge and skills into the heads of students. In the banking concept of education, the assumption is that "the teacher knows everything and the students know nothing" (p. 54). Freire called for a transformative education that would "liberate" impoverished students from their oppressed status. To accomplish this, Freire called for a process that encourages students to confront the social issues that contribute to their oppression in the dominant society. Critical pedagogy involves "problem posing, reflective thinking, knowledge gathering, and collaborative decision making," and it helps students and teachers "find and express their voice, in oral and written form" (Ovando, Combs, & Collier, 2006). Critical pedagogy calls for teachers to take some risks by exploring new knowledge and being open to new ways of perceiving the world, including thinking about ways to transform power relations that exist within and outside of schools. Freire's concepts are central to levels 3 (transformative) and 4 (social action) of James Banks's levels of multicultural education discussed in Chapter 1.

Beyond Approaches and Methods

Richards and Rodgers acknowledge that while it is useful to study and understand different approaches and methods, teachers should keep in mind that adherence to a specific method may restrict a teacher's creativity and professional judgment. Current knowledge is always changing, and no one method or approach is applicable to every language classroom, everywhere in the world. The context of the classroom and the needs of the students should be the starting point, rather than any given method.

Teachers can use the following questions to guide their decisions about what strategies to use to promote ELLs' content-area learning through English, their second language development, and cultural integration into the classroom and school community:

1. What are the students' strengths and needs?
2. What are the instructional goals?
3. What is likely to be challenging about these goals for these students?
4. What strategies can help address these challenges?
5. How will you know whether these strategies are effective?

Once teachers know their ELL students' language, literacy, content, and culture strengths and needs and can compare them to the their language, literacy, content, and culture instructional goals, they can determine what is likely to be challenging about a particular activity, lesson, or unit for those ELLs and select appropriate instructional and assessment strategies. The chapters that follow will introduce you to a wide range of strategies and techniques that promote listening, speaking, reading, and writing across the content areas that are consistent with what we know about second language teaching and learning.

Richards and Rodgers (2001) suggest that teachers should try out different methods and approaches. In doing so they should be flexible and creative, drawing on their own beliefs, values, principles, and experiences to adapt the methods and approaches they use to the realities of the classroom. They refer to this process as the development of a "personal approach" to teaching and a set of core principles to draw on when teaching. They offer the following examples:

- Engage all learners in the lesson.
- Make learners the focus of the lesson.
- Provide maximum opportunities for student participation.
- Be tolerant of learners' mistakes.
- Develop learners' confidence.
- Respond to learners' difficulties and build on them.
- Use a maximum amount of student-to-student activities
- Promote cooperation among learners.
- Address learners' needs and interests. (p. 251)

The methods and approaches highlighted in this book reflect these principles and are grounded in our current understanding of second language learning and teaching.

SUMMARY

Knowledge of language is relevant to the many roles teachers play as communicators, educators, evaluators, educated human beings, and agents of socialization. Teachers need to know about phonology, morphology, syntax, semantics, pragmatics, and how the lexicon is structured and acquired. They need to know about language variation and be able to recognize and value nonstandard varieties of English, while helping students acquire standard English. With experience, teachers develop their own approaches to teaching ELLs. To be effective, their approaches must be grounded in an understanding of language and SLA.

While the linguists continue to conduct research to determine how exactly one learns a language, we can focus on the areas of consensus that have important implications for teaching and learning. Whether one takes an innatist, interactionist, or sociocultural view of SLA, researchers and educators agree on the need for students to receive comprehensible input and to engage in meaningful interactions with other speakers of the target language. Thus, teachers need to find ways to make their instruction comprehensible for ELLs, and they need to provide ample opportunities for meaningful interactions in the classroom. Teachers' experiences and classroom-based research have given us a good sense of what does and does not work.

We can look at constructs of comprehensible input, such as the formula $i + 1$, and we can consider a student's ZPD. These concepts may be impossible to operationalize, however, teachers interact with their students every day—talk to them, listen to them talk, read with them, listen to them read, write with them and read what they write. Those teachers will have a sense of what is and is not comprehensible for their students, and what type and amount of scaffolding is needed to help them succeed.

When teachers know their students well, they can provide the type of learning environment that builds on their students' strengths and addresses their unique needs. They can provide appropriate instruction, activities, and opportunities for meaningful interaction to help their students continue to make progress in developing proficiency in English.

Discussion Questions

1. Fillmore and Snow identify five functions that teachers perform for which they need to know about language. Are these functions relevant only for teachers of ELLs, or are they important for all teachers? Of the teachers you know, how many do you think have the kind of knowledge Fillmore and Snow deem essential? In what ways might their lack of such knowledge affect their instruction?

 2. **On-line Discussion Board**   Go back to the situations at the beginning of this chapter. For each one, discuss what misunderstanding the teacher may have, and discuss how an understanding of language and SLA can help these teachers pinpoint the issues and address them in an appropriate manner. What other examples have you run across where misunderstandings about language and SLA led to problems?

3. Of the SLA theories discussed in this chapter, which one do you most agree with? Do you feel these different theories are incompatible? If not, discuss some ways different theories could help inform your instruction.

4. Describe the English language communicative competence that may be needed in each of the following domains where English is the dominant language: (a) a fast-food restaurant; (b) church; (c) a game of soccer among friends; (d) television or movies, (e) a 1st grade classroom; (f) a high school biology classroom; (g) a university classroom discussing teaching ELLs.

 5. **On-line Discussion Board**   Describe your experiences with the various methods and approaches presented in this chapter, either learning under them or putting them into practice in your own classroom. Which one did you find to be the most effective?

6. Identify the level of English proficiency (or amount of second language instructional competence) that students may need to succeed in the following academic tasks: (a) listen and take notes during a high school class lecture on U.S. history; (b) solve 50 2-digit addition and subtraction facts; (c) read a chapter in a 5th grade science book and answer the questions at the end; (d) sing along and do movements to a song; (e) listen to a book read aloud by a 1st grade teacher and draw a picture of your favorite part; (f) practice for an 8th grade reading comprehension test (reading text passages and answering multiple-choice questions); (g) work cooperatively with a group of peers to carry out a science experience; and (h) write a persuasive essay. For each of these, discuss the linguistic skills students would need to succeed.

Research Activities

1. Interview a teacher of ELL students and ask what he or she knows about linguistics and how this knowledge helps him or her address language-related issues that arise in the classroom. Ask for specific examples.

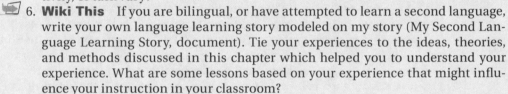 2. **Wiki This**   Observe one or more ESL lessons in a classroom. Which approaches or methods does the teacher's instruction seem to align with most closely?

3. Interview a teacher of ELL students and ask what approaches or methods he or she uses in the classroom. Ask why he or she has chosen to use these and how effective they are in helping the students learn English.

4. Obtain a set of ESL textbooks or other curricular materials for ELLs. What approaches or methods are apparent in the materials? Which ones do you think would be most effective for their target audience?

5. Observe a classroom with ELL students. Make a list of the academic lessons, activities, and tasks you observe. Describe the linguistic skills students needed to participate or complete each one of these successfully. Did each one require the same level of proficiency in English? How did the amount of second language instructional competence (SLIC) students needed to complete each lesson, activity, or task vary?

6. **Wiki This**   If you are bilingual, or have attempted to learn a second language, write your own language learning story modeled on my story (My Second Language Learning Story, document). Tie your experiences to the ideas, theories, and methods discussed in this chapter which helped you to understand your experience. What are some lessons based on your experience that might influence your instruction in your classroom?

Recommended Reading

Freeman, D. E., & Freeman, Y. S. (2004). *Essential linguistics: What you need to know to teach reading, ESL, spelling, phonics, and grammar.* Portsmouth, NH: Heinemann.
An excellent introduction to linguistics for teachers.

Krashen, S. D. (2003). *Explorations in language acquisition and use.* Portsmouth, NH: Heinemann.
A concise and readable overview of Krashen's hypotheses of language acquisition.

Lightbrown, P. M., & Spada, N. (2006). *How languages are learned* (3rd ed.). New York: Oxford University Press.
An excellent and easy-to-read introduction to second language acquisition theories.

Richards, J. C., & Rodgers, T. S. (2001). *Approaches and methods in language teaching* (2nd ed.). Cambridge: Cambridge University Press.
An excellent overview of the history, theory, and practices of language teaching approaches and methods.

VanPatten, B. (2003). *From input to output: A teacher's guide to second language acquisition.* Boston: McGraw Hill.
A concise and easy-to-read overview of VanPatten's views on second language acquisition.

3

Language and Education Policy for ELLs

Above all, we should resist the idea of having the federal government define what constitutes high quality programs of bilingual education. That can only come from practitioners and researchers in the field; it cannot be negotiated in the back offices of Congressmen and Senators.

—Josué M. González (2002)

KEY TERMS

- Elementary and Secondary Education Act (ESEA)
- Bilingual Education Act (Title VII)
- No Child Left Behind Act of 2001 (NCLB)
- annual measurable achievement objectives (AMAOs)
- adequate yearly progress (AYP)
- English for the Children initiatives (Proposition 227, Proposition 203, and Question 2)
- 14th Amendment
- Lau Remedies
- Equal Educational Opportunities Act of 1974 (EEOA)

GUIDING QUESTIONS

1. How has the policy context surrounding the education of ELLs changed in the United States?
2. How do federal and state policies influence the education of ELLs on the local district and school levels?
3. How have the courts influenced the education of ELLs?
4. How can educators use their understanding of the policy and legislative context surrounding ELL education to enhance their ELLs' access to educational opportunities?

Language and education policy for ELLs in the United States is complicated by the absence of a centralized education system. Policies that outline rules, regulations, and procedures related to educating ELL students may come from the federal government, state governments, voter initiatives, or court decisions. Policies are set by powerful institutions usually controlled by members of the dominant group. Some policies have had a discriminatory impact on minorities. Other policies may have been designed to ensure the protection of minority rights. Sometimes the various stakeholders have reached compromises through the democratic process to ensure fairness to all involved. Other times, those negatively impacted by policies have turned to the courts for assistance, with these efforts resulting in orders that either uphold or require changes to existing policies. As we see in this chapter, the pendulum swings between discourses of relative tolerance or support for linguistic diversity and discourses of increased language restrictionism and English-only efforts. These discourses have serious implications for the education of ELLs.

Educators who work with ELLs need to understand the history and the current language and education policies and legislation that affect their students and classrooms. We begin with a brief history of bilingual education and policy regarding language use in the United States. Then we review federal and state policies regarding ELLs and look at the important role the courts have played in guiding policies for these students. The chapter concludes by emphasizing how educators can draw on their understanding of the larger policy context to develop sound policies on the local district and school levels that ensure equal educational opportunities for their ELLs.

A Historical Perspective

Many people believe that the challenge of educating ELL students and the need for special programs for them are relatively recent phenomena. Many also believe that in the past immigrants and their children quickly gave up their native languages and cultures to become Americanized monolingual English-speakers. These assumptions are false. The United States is now, always has been, and will continue to be a multilingual and multicultural country. Heinz Kloss (1998) provides a thorough sociohistorical analysis of the role languages other than English have played in government, education, and U.S. communities since the founding of the country in his book *The American Bilingual Tradition*. James Crawford's (1992) edited collection *Language Loyalties* provides a rich source of historical documents that re-

Figure 3.1
Front page of the *Philadelphische Zeitung*, June 24, 1732. This was America's first German-language newspaper, printed by Benjamin Franklin. Image retrieved from Library of Congress, www.loc.gov/rr/european/imde/images/zeitung.jpg

veal that since its founding the United States has faced issues related to language and cultural diversity, particularly in the area of education.

Many people assume also that English is the official language of the United States. But the founding fathers never declared any language as an official language, and the U.S. Constitution has never been amended to declare English as the official language. To the founders, declaring an official language would have been unnecessary. By the time the Constitution was ratified, English was well established as the dominant language. Also, the founders respected diversity among those who had fought for independence and were hesitant to offend them by restricting their languages or in any way implying their inferiority. Throughout U.S. history English has functioned as if it were the official language and therefore there has never been a need for an official designation.

Bilingual education has been referred to it as a "30-year experiment" that began with the passage of the federal Bilingual Education Act of 1968. Three centuries ago, however, native language instruction and bilingual education were common in those areas of the United States where non-English-speaking immigrant groups settled and made up a major portion of the local population (see Figure 3.1 and Box 3.1). For example, German bilingual education was offered in the 17th century and continued to be common in German communities throughout the United States up to the time of the U.S. entrance into World War I (see Figure 3.2). Spanish bilingual education programs were common throughout the Southwest in the 19th century. Carlos Kevin Blanton (2004) documents the history of bilingual education in Texas

---

Box 3.1

The American Bilingual Tradition: Education

1800s
- French was a compulsory subject in Massachusetts high schools.
- Dutch was taught in the district schools of seven communities in Michigan.
- German was taught in Washington, DC elementary schools.
- Many midwestern high schools were bilingual German-English.

Early 1900s
- In some towns in New Jersey, Missouri, Texas, Minnesota, and Indiana, nearly all elementary school students received German instruction.
- Swedish, Norwegian, and Danish were taught in many high schools and elementary schools in Iowa, North Dakota, South Dakota, Minnesota, Wisconsin, Illinois, Iowa, Nebraska, and Washington.
- Czech taught in some schools in Texas and Nebraska and was likely taught in other elementary schools throughout the Midwest.
- Polish was taught in public schools in Milwaukee, and Italian was taught in all grade levels in elementary school.
- Spanish was a compulsory subject in New Mexico public high schools.
- The French, Russian, Hungarian, and Italian governments provided support to public and private schools for the teaching of French in New Orleans, Russian in Alaska, Magyar in Connecticut, and Italian in schools throughout the country, respectively.

Mid 1900s
- Spanish was taught in elementary schools in several cities, including Corpus Christi, San Antonio, and El Paso, TX; Los Angeles and San Diego, CA; and Gainesville and Miami, FL.

Source: Kloss, 1998.

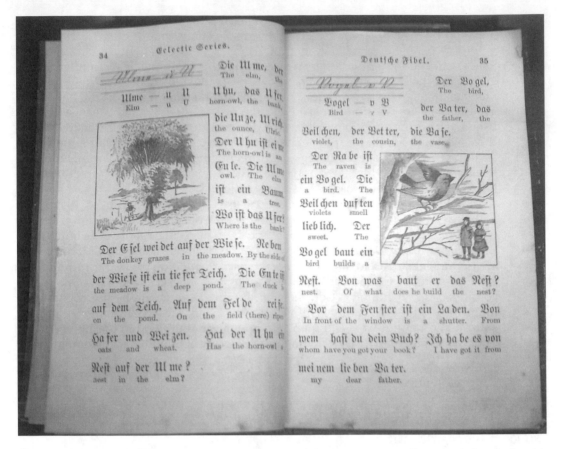

Figure 3.2 Bilingual German primer used in Texas and other German schools in the United States in the early 1900s. Published by the American Book Company, New York.
Photo used by permission from UTSA's Institute of Texan Cultures, San Antonio

beginning in 1836. And in 1848 the territory of New Mexico, which included modern-day Arizona and parts of Colorado, Utah, and Nevada, had a law calling for Spanish-English bilingual programs, and other schools in the United States offered instruction in Chinese, Japanese, French, Cherokee, Swedish, Danish, Norwegian, Italian, Polish, Dutch, and Czech (Crawford, 2004). In Texas, for example, in the small community of Danevang, founded by settlers from Denmark, students were taught Danish language and history at the Danevang School, which was established around 1895 (Davis, 2008) (see Figure 3.3).

In 1858 the *American Journal of Education* published an article, translated from German, describing the work of the German scholar Wolfgang Ratich, who in 1612 developed a new method by which languages, he said, "may be easily taught and learned both by young and old, more thoroughly and in shorter time" (von Raumer, 1858, p. 229). Ratich decried the sink-or-swim method of throwing German children into Latin before they could understand anything in the language. He proposed that young students to be instructed in their native language first and attain sufficient literacy skills before they were transitioned to other languages. As Ratich stated, "After the mother tongue, then the other languages." Ratich had many critics at the time who, like present-day critics of bilingual education, found his ideas to be radical and scandalous. Ratich died before he was given a fair chance to prove his ideas, but others carried on his work. Among them was a language teacher

Figure 3.3   Danevang School, 1908. Photo no. 072–0724 from UTSA's Institute of Texan Cultures. Courtesy of Ella Hansen.

named Hedwig who put Ratich's methods to work in Germany shortly after his death and "was considered one of the most skillful teachers of his day" (p. 251).

Language minorities have always been a part of the American landscape, but their unique languages and cultural practices have not always been warmly welcomed by the broader society. Although there are many instances in the country's history in which languages other than English were tolerated or even promoted, there also have been waves of linguistic restrictionism, that is, policies and practices that attempted to limit or outlaw the use of languages other than English. Such language restrictions by the dominant group in society against language-minority communities were most often imposed for purposes of social control, not to help immigrants (and non-English-speaking native-born Americans) learn English. For example:

■ Enslaved Africans were prohibited from using their native tongues for fear their doing so would facilitate resistance or rebellion.

■ In the 1740s, southern colonies institutionalized "compulsory ignorance" laws, which prohibited enslaved Africans from acquiring English literacy. These slave codes remained in force until the end of the Civil War in 1865.

■ English proficiency was made a requirement for naturalization and citizenship at the turn of the 20th century.

■ The Americanization movement during and after World War I pushed the belief that to be American means to speak only English.

■ Coercive assimilation policies targeted Native Americans through the establishment of English-only Indian boarding schools. These schools were designed to eradicate Indian languages and cultural practices, and facilitated the taking of Native American land.

- After World War I, heavy restrictions were placed on German-language instruction in schools.
- After World War II, Japanese-language schools in California and Hawaii were closed. (Wiley & Wright, 2004)

Restrictions on languages other than English tend to come in waves. Before 1900, several states and local school districts had laws or policies that allowed bilingual education, or at least did not restrict schools from offering such programs (see the examples in Box 3.1). By the late 1880s and early 1900s, however, several states implemented laws requiring that English be used as the language of instruction in schools.

The legal expert and scholar Arnold Leibowitz (1971, 1974, 1976) observed in the 1970s that language restrictionism is usually tied to other forms of discrimination. Thus, attempts at language restrictionism are rarely about concerns over the languages themselves but, rather, about the individuals who speak them. The recent calls for language restriction coincide with mounting concerns by the majority about changing demographics with a large and growing Latino population. Debates over bilingual education take place in the context of larger debates over issues of immigration (see Box 3.2).

In 2006 a proposal in Congress to make it a felony to be in the United States illegally led to massive immigrant rights marches in major cities throughout the country. In the aftermath of these demonstrations much of the immigration debate turned to issues of language. For the first time in history, the U.S. Senate approved an amendment (to the proposed immigration bill) that would declare English to be the official language of the United States. In a later version of the bill the "official language" status of English was downgraded to simply declaring it the "common and unifying" language of the United States. No bipartisan consensus, however,

---

Box 3.2

Waves of Tolerance and Restrictionism

Prior to the 1920s
Colonizing of America, westward expansion, large European immigration: general tolerance for community-run bilingual programs.

1920s–1950s
World War I, Great Depression, World War II: Americanization campaign, language restrictionism.

1960s–1970s
Civil rights movement, loosened immigration leading to an influx of Latin American and Asian immigrants: first federal involvement in public education, Bilingual Education Act.

1980s
Reagan Revolution: resurgence of English-only, anti-bilingual rhetoric and legislation.

1990s
Clinton era: increased attention to and funding for dual-language programs.

2000s
George W. Bush era and NCLB: resurgence of anti-immigrant, English-only, anti-bilingual rhetoric and legislation.

was reached over the controversial immigration bill by the time the legislative session ended.

Evolution of Federal Policy for ELLs

Although the United States has a long history of language diversity, federal involvement in education is a fairly recent endeavor. Education is not addressed in the U.S. Constitution. The United States did not have a Department of Education until 1980. Before that, federal interests in education were handled through the Department of Health, Education, and Welfare, created in 1953. Thus, education has been primarily the responsibility of each state.

The federal government has great interest in ensuring that the country has well-educated citizens who are able to earn a living (and are thus able to pay taxes), and who are able to fully participate in our democratic society. But because of the lack of jurisdiction the federal government has over schools, the best it can do is to offer funding to supplement state and local funding for schools. The catch is that if states accept federal education funding, they must follow federal education policies. Currently, all 50 states accept federal funding and thus are subject to federal education law.

Before 1968, there were no federal educational language policies for ELLs. Too often, schools ignored the needs of language-minority students and simply placed them in regular (often segregated) classrooms, where they were left to "sink or swim." Education for language-minority students began to improve during the civil rights movement and President Lyndon B. Johnson's War on Poverty, which emerged from the civil rights movement. In 1965 Congress passed the Elementary and Secondary Education Act (ESEA). Some of the key components of the ESEA are funds, policies, and procedures that target students from low-income families.

Title VII Bilingual Education Act

Within the context of the civil rights movement, educators and policymakers became more sensitive to the needs of the rapidly growing language-minority student population in the United States. Concerned educators noted a high drop-out rate among Mexican American students. According to the 1960 U.S. Census, White students on average completed 14 years of schooling; in contrast, Mexican American students on average completed less than 5 years.

In an attempt to address this and other issues, the National Education Association sponsored a conference in 1966 in Tucson, Arizona, on the education of Spanish-speaking children. One result of this conference was an influential report titled *The Invisible Minority . . . pero no vencibles* [but undefeatable]. This report outlines areas of concern and describes innovative education programs in southwestern states that have made use of students' native languages. A successful two-way bilingual program for Cuban refugee students at Coral Way Elementary School in Florida also garnered much attention. The report calls for the repeal of state English-only instruction laws and includes the following recommendations: "Instruction in pre-school and throughout the early grades should be in both Spanish and English" and "English should be taught as a second language" (National Education Association, 1966, p. 6).

Soon after the release of the *Invisible Minority* report, Senator Ralph Yarborough of Texas introduced a bill to provide federal funding for school districts to support bilingual education programs. His bill eventually became the 1968 Bilingual Education Act and entered into federal law as Title VII of the ESEA. The Bilingual Education Act provided grants to school districts and other eligible entities through a competitive grant process. Thus, most of the regulations associated with Title VII applied only to those programs that submitted grants and were awarded funding.

Yarborough's original bill applied only to Spanish-surnamed students, but 37 similar proposals introduced by other legislators were ultimately merged into the final bill, which called for the inclusion of all children whose native tongue is not English. These students were referred to in the law as "children of limited-English speaking ability" (LESA), defined as "children who come from environments where the dominant language is other than English." A requirement was also added that reserved these funds for LESA students who were living in poverty. The original proposal identified students by the language they spoke at home. The LESA label and poverty criteria stressed that the population to be served was deficient in English and very poor and thus needed remediation. This deficit view of students is apparent in the findings section of the Bilingual Education Act (§701), which describes the presence of "millions of children of limited English-speaking ability" as "one of the most acute educational problems in the United States" and as a "unique and perplexing educational situation."

The law identified a problem but was quite vague about solutions. It noted the need for "adequate and constructive solutions" and called for "forward-looking approaches" and "new and imaginative elementary and secondary school programs" designed to meet the "special needs" of LESA students. The law provided a brief list of "activities," which included bilingual education, programs that impart knowledge of the history and culture associated with their languages, home-school collaborations, adult education for parents of children in the Title VII programs, and dropout-prevention programs.

Ironically, the original version of the Bilingual Education Act did not include a definition of bilingual education. This omission resulted in a great deal of confusion for educators and policymakers. There was little agreement among them on the purpose and goals of Title VII and many had questions about how students would benefit from instruction in their native language. They disagreed over whether Title VII was meant to be an antidiscrimination measure or an antipoverty measure and argued over whether Title VII programs were supposed to help students become proficient bilinguals or if they were simply to transition students to all English instruction as quickly as possible. Although the programs receiving Title VII funds were called "bilingual education" programs, they were not consistent in the way they used the students' native languages. The passage of the Bilingual Education Act led to the adoption of similar policies in several states. By the early 2000s, 32 states had statutes allowing native language instruction, and 7 states mandated it under certain conditions; 7 other states stopped enforcing their laws prohibiting native language instruction.[1]

Since 1968, the ESEA has undergone six reauthorizations (1974, 1978, 1984, 1988, 1994, 2001). Each reauthorization resulted in changes to the Bilingual Education Act. By 1994, after five reauthorizations and numerous debates and compromises between advocates and opponents of bilingual education, the goals of Title VII were clarified, definitions of the target population and the programs to serve them were made more explicit, and lists of the purposes and benefits of bilingual education, bilingualism, and multicultural understanding were expanded and clarified. Each reauthorization resulted in greater recognition of the personal and

---

1: For more details on the history and content of the Bilingual Education Act and the politics surrounding it, see Crawford, 2000 2004; Leibowitz, 1971, 1980; Lyons, 1995; Stewner-Manzanares, 1988.

societal benefits of bilingualism and bilingual education. The focus on helping LEP students achieve fluency in English remained constant. Each reauthorization, however, expanded the types of programs that were eligible for federal support through Title VII funding. Transitional bilingual education programs were the most likely to receive Title VII funding. And though compromises led to some funding for nonbilingual approaches, the majority of funds were reserved for programs that provided at least some native language instruction. In addition, there was increasing support for developmental and dual language programs. Many saw this support as key to changing the public's view of bilingual education as a compensatory program (i.e., compensating for student's "lack" of English) to the view of bilingual education as an enrichment program (i. e., enriching students by helping them become proficient bilinguals). The Bilingual Education Act was reauthorized for the final time in 1994 and remained in effect until the beginning of 2002. (Reauthorizations to Title VII, document)

No Child Left Behind

Federal policy for language-minority students learning English changed dramatically with the passage of the No Child Left Behind Act of 2001 (NCLB) (Public Law 107–110), President George W. Bush's plan for the reauthorization of the ESEA. The Bilingual Education Act was replaced by a new Title III, "Language Instruction for Limited English Proficient and Immigrant Students." The Office of Bilingual Education and Minority Language Affairs (which had been responsible for administering Title VII grants) was changed to the Office of English Language Acquisition, Language Enhancement, and Academic Achievement for Limited English Proficient Students, and the National Clearinghouse for Bilingual Education was changed to the National Clearinghouse for English Language Acquisition and Language Instruction Educational Programs. LEP student issues are also featured prominently in changes to Title I, "Improving the Academic Achievement of the Economically Disadvantaged," which addresses issues of accountability and high-stakes testing. Let us now take a closer look at mandates of NCLB for ELLs in Title III and Title I.

Title III: Language Instruction for Limited English Proficient and Immigrant Students

Whereas grants under the former Title VII Bilingual Education Act were competitive, Title III provides formula grants to state education agencies. These agencies, in turn, make subgrants to eligible local education agencies (i.e., school districts and charter schools) that apply to the state for the funds. Under Title III, funding for LEP students nearly doubled, and for the first time federal funds for LEP students went to nearly all eligible schools. But because these federal funds are now spread more thinly, fewer dollars are available for each eligible LEP student.

Unlike recent versions of the Bilingual Education Act, Title III does not make any distinctions between bilingual and nonbilingual programs. The federal law now requires only that LEP students be placed in "language instruction education programs," defined as an instructional course:

(A) in which a limited English proficient child is placed for the purpose of developing and attaining English proficiency, while meeting challenging State academic content and student academic achievement standards; and

(B) that may make instructional use of both English and a child's native language to enable the child to develop and attain English proficiency, and may include the participation of English proficient children if such course is designed to enable all participating children to become proficient in English and a second language. (NCLB §3301(8))

Thus, any program for LEP students must meet only two requirements: teach English, and teach academic content, as outlined in state English language proficiency (ELP) and academic standards. Instruction in the native language is optional. This option, without referring to transitional bilingual education or dual language programs by name, nonetheless makes allowances for these types of programs. Title III gives the ultimate authority to each state to determine what programs it will and will not support.

To receive Title III funds, school districts must submit plans to the state, which in turn must submit plans to the U.S. Department of Education. In these plans, school districts and their states must describe how they are "using a language instruction curriculum that is tied to scientifically based research on teaching LEP children and that has been demonstrated to be effective . . . in the manner the eligible entities determine to be the most effective" (NCLB §3301(b)(6)). The law also stipulates that none of the requirements of Title III "shall be construed to negate or supersede State law" (NCLB §3126). As a result, in states with laws restricting bilingual education, schools cannot use the allowances for bilingual education in Title III to offer such programs unless they meet their state law's waiver requirements. At the same time, states that mandate bilingual programs may continue to provide those programs.

Also unlike Title VII, Title III includes no recognition of the personal and societal benefits of bilingual education and bilingualism. Nor is there any acknowledgment of the factors that have negatively impacted the education of LEP students, such as segregation, improper placement in special education, and underrepresentation of LEP students in gifted and talented education and shortages of bilingual teachers. Not addressed are issues of cultural differences or the need for multicultural understanding.

The sole focus of Title III is English. The list of purposes stresses repeatedly that Title III funds and programs are to "ensure that LEP students attain English proficiency, develop high levels of academic attainment in English, and meet the same challenging State academic content and student academic achievement standards as all children are expected to meet" and to assist state and local education agencies in creating "high quality instructional programs" that prepare LEP students to "enter all-English instruction settings" (NCLB §3102). Another stated purpose of Title III is "to hold State educational agencies, local educational agencies, and schools accountable for increases in English proficiency and core academic content knowledge" of LEP students by requiring "demonstrated improvements in the English proficiency" and "adequate yearly progress" on state academic achievement tests (NCLB §3102(8)).

Before the passage of NCLB, each state set its own policies on how to identify LEP students. In most states, at the time of initial school enrollment, schools would administer a home language survey to determine whether students come from a household with a "primary home language other than English" (PHLOTE). School districts were then required to assess PHLOTE students with an ELP test to identify LEP students. Decisions about which test to use among many on the market were frequently made at the district level. There is great variability among the tests and from one district to the next and one state to the next in assessments used and procedures followed to identify and report the number of LEP students. Even at the national level, attempts to measure the national LEP student population accurately prove problematic because of the lack of data and inconsistencies among data sets.

NCLB requires each state to develop ELP standards and ELP assessments designed to measure LEP students' progress in meeting those standards (NCLB §3102

(8)). The standards and assessments must be based on "the four domains of speaking, reading, listening, and writing," and assessments must also include the domain of "comprehension" as exhibited through listening and reading (U.S. Department of Education, 2003a, p. 5). In addition, the standards established for each grade level must identify benchmarks for ELL students at different levels of English proficiency. Each state's ELP standards must have the following components (p. 8):

1. A label for each level (e.g., Beginning, Intermediate, Advanced)
2. A brief narrative description that suggests the defining characteristics of the level
3. A description of what students can do in content at this level of English language proficiency
4. An assessment score that determines the attainment of the level

Most of the language proficiency assessments that states and school districts were using when NCLB went into effect did not meet these requirements, and thus new statewide ELP standards and assessments had to be developed. Many states struggled to fully comply with the requirements by the deadlines.

Just as other professional content-area organizations, such as the National Council of Teachers of Mathematics, the National Science Teachers Association, and the National Association for Music Education have created their own set of model content-area standards that states adopted or adapted, Teachers of English to Speakers of Other Languages (TESOL) had created its own set of model standards in 1997. TESOL educators, however, recognized the need to substantially modify its original standards to meet the NCLB mandates, particularly the requirement for ELLs to meet the same academic content standards as native English speakers. TESOL's new ELP standards were completed in 2006 (TESOL, 2006a).

The result is the set of five standards, discussed in Chapter 2, that address the teaching of ESL and the teaching of the academic content-areas of language arts, mathematics, science, and social studies to ELLs. As required of each state by NCLB, the TESOL standards identify and label each level of ELP and list the defining characteristics of each level. TESOL identifies five levels of English language proficiency (levels 1–5) with the following labels: Starting, Emerging, Developing, Expanding, and Bridging. The description of each level appears in Table 3.1. (Compare these with the labels and descriptions of the five stages of second language acquisition outlined in Chapter 1.)

The TESOL ELP standards are further organized into five grade clusters: pre-K–K, 1–3, 4–5, 6–8, and 9–12. Each of the proficiency standards is organized along the four traditional language domains—listening, speaking, reading and writing—with sample performance indicators. While TESOL's new ELP standards share many of the same problems as those for the content-area standards described later in this chapter, they can be of great benefit as a general guide to content-area teachers as well as traditional ESL teachers. In particular, these standards are useful in helping teachers to understand what can reasonably be expected of ELLs at various levels of English proficiency.

The demands of NCLB for the creation of aligned ELP standards and assessments have been especially difficult for smaller and less populated states with relatively low numbers of ELL students. Nineteen of these states—Alabama, Delaware, Georgia, Hawaii, Illinois, Kentucky, New Hampshire, New Jersey, Maine, Mississippi, North Carolina, North Dakota, Oklahoma, Pennsylvania, Rhode Island, South Dakota, Vermont, Virginia, and Wisconsin, as well as the District of Columbia—have formed the World-class Instructional Design and Assessment (WIDA) consortium for the joint development of resources to comply with the demands of NCLB.

| Table 3.1 | TESOL ELP Standards: Levels of English Language Proficiency |

Level 1 Starting

Students initially have limited or no understanding of English. They rarely use English for communication. They respond nonverbally to simple commands, statements, and questions. As their oral comprehension increases, they begin to imitate the verbalizations of others by using single words or simple phrases, and they begin to use English spontaneously. At the earliest stage, these learners construct meaning from text primarily through illustrations, graphs, maps, and tables.

Level 2 Emerging

Students can understand phrases and short sentences. They can communicate limited information in simple everyday and routine situations by using memorized phrases, groups of words, and formulae. They can use selected simple structures correctly but still systematically produce basic errors. Students begin to use general academic vocabulary and familiar everyday expressions. Errors in writing are present that often hinder communication.

Level 3 Developing

Students understand more complex speech but still may require some repetition. They use English spontaneously but may have difficulty expressing all their thoughts due to a restricted vocabulary and a limited command of language structure. Students at this level speak in simple sentences, which are comprehensible and appropriate, but which are frequently marked by grammatical errors. Proficiency in reading may vary considerably. Students are most successful constructing meaning from texts for which they have background knowledge upon which to build.

Level 4 Expanding

Students' language skills are adequate for most day-to-day communication needs. They communicate in English in new or unfamiliar settings but have occasional difficulty with complex structures and abstract academic concepts. Students at this level may read with considerable fluency and are able to locate and identify the specific facts within the text. However, they may not understand texts in which the concepts are presented in a decontextualized manner, the sentence structure is complex, or the vocabulary is abstract or has multiple meanings. They can read independently but may have occasional comprehension problems, especially when processing grade-level information.

Level 5 Bridging

Students can express themselves fluently and spontaneously on a wide range of personal, general, academic, or social topics in a variety of contexts. They are poised to function in an environment with native speaking peers with minimal language support or guidance. Students have a good command of technical and academic vocabulary as well of idiomatic expressions and colloquialisms. They can produce clear, smoothly flowing, well-structured texts of differing lengths and degrees of linguistic complexity. Errors are minimal, difficult to spot, and generally corrected when they occur.

Source: TESOL, 2006a.

The WIDA consortium designed and implemented ELP standards and an accompanying language proficiency assessment, marketed as ACCESS for ELLs, which has been touted as a model for the rest of country. Indeed, TESOL's ELP standards build on the work of the WIDA consortium and are officially subtitled "An Augmentation of the WIDA English Language Proficiency Standards" (TESOL, 2006a). The WIDA consortium has also developed Spanish language arts standards and is developing alternate academic assessments for beginning ELLs that meet the mandates of NCLB. It is at the forefront of efforts to make the accountability demands of NCLB feasible for ELLs and is breaking new ground in the area of standards and testing for ELLs. The consortium's Web site, www.wida.us, provides detailed information on these efforts.

According to NCLB, ELP assessments must be given annually to all LEP students enrolled in schools in every state. Local school districts receiving Title III funds are required to submit an evaluation of their programs for LEP students every 2 years to the state indicating each student's current status and progress in learning English, attaining proficiency in English, and passing the state's content-area tests.

Results of the ELP assessments are a part of each state's accountability system. Each state must establish baseline data and then set annual measurable achievement objectives (AMAOs) to hold school districts accountable for the progress of LEP students in attaining proficiency in English. School districts' adequate yearly progress (AYP) in achieving Title III AMAOs is determined by "annual increases in the number or percentage of children making progress in learning English" and "annual increases in the number or percentage of children attaining English proficiency by the end of each school year" (NCLB §3122(a)(3)). In addition, AMAOs under Title III includes LEP students meeting the AYP requirements under Title I. Title III outlines serious consequences for districts that fail to make AYP related to LEP student's progress and attainment of ELP. These consequences range from requiring districts to develop and follow an improvement plan to replacing district educators and cutting off Title III funding.

Title I: Improving the Achievement of the Economically Disadvantaged

The purpose of Title I is "to ensure that all children have a fair, equal, and significant opportunity to obtain a high quality education and reach, at a minimum, proficiency on challenging State academic achievement standards and State academic assessments" (NCLB §3122(b)). Thus, Title I mandates annual testing of all students in grades 3 through 8, and once while in high school. Title I requires each state to create its own academic content and achievement standards and assessments to measure those standards and use the results to hold schools, districts, and the state itself accountable. Students must be tested every year in math and reading/language arts, and three times between grades 3 and 12 in science. Every year (beginning in the 2002–2003 school year) the state must issue individual student reports and detailed school and district progress reports ("report cards") that include the results of the student achievement assessments.

Under NCLB all students are expected to meet or exceed the state's academic standards as measured by state standardized tests by 2014. Test score data must be disaggregated into the following subgroups: male and female, major racial and ethnic groups, students with disabilities, students with limited English proficiency, and students who are economically disadvantaged (NCLB §1111(a)(2)(C)(v)(II)). When NCLB was first passed, states were required to establish AMAOs that articulate how all subgroups would eventually pass the state content achievement test by 2014. For example, Arizona's AMAO for 3rd grade reading in the 2009–2010 school year is that 62.6% of all students in each subgroup will meet the passing standards for the test. A subgroup is deemed to have made AYP if it meets or exceeds that year's AMAO. Thus, in the Arizona example, at least 62.6% of 3rd grade ELLs would need to pass the reading test for the LEP subgroup to be deemed as having made AYP.

Each state must submit its annual "report cards" on its schools and districts to the U.S. Department of Education. If any subgroup does not make AYP, then the entire school or district is designated as failing. AYP designations are also made at the district and state level. If a school fails to make AYP for 2 consecutive years, it must develop and submit an "improvement plan" to the state. The state is required to provide technical assistance to the school. After a school has been deemed as "failing" to make AYP for 2 or more consecutive years, it faces a series of sanctions that become more severe each additional year the school fails to make AYP, beginning with the school's allowing students to transfer to a nonfailing school and paying for supplemental instruction (i.e., tutoring) from an outside provider. The most severe sanction is state or private takeover of the school. If the school fails to make AYP after 4 consecutive years, the state may (1) require the school to modify its curriculum program or method of instruction, (2) withhold Title III funds, or (3) replace educational personnel in the school (NCLB §11113122(b)). The complete list of sanctions appears in Box 3.3.

Before passage of NCLB, states and school districts had the flexibility to set their own mandates for statewide testing and how and when to include LEP students. Many states, for example, excluded LEP students from statewide tests in English if they had been in the country for less than 4 years, according to the rationale that students need time to learn English before taking the same tests as native English speakers. Title I of NCLB, however, requires LEP students to take the mandated state assessments regardless of their ELP and regardless of how long they have attended school in the United States. Two exceptions were added to this mandate after the law went into effect. The first exception (added in 2002, a year after NCLB was passed) allows ELLs to be excluded from state reading/language arts assessments if they have attended schools in the United States for less than 12 months. The second exception, which went into effect in the 2006–2007 school year, concerns the math assessment. All LEP students are still required to take their state's math assessment, but their scores may be excluded from school AYP calculations if they have attended U.S. schools for less than 12 months (U.S. Department of Education, 2006a).

States are required to assess LEP students "in a valid and reliable manner" and must also provide "reasonable accommodations." Guidelines issued by the U.S. Department of Education (2003b) suggest that these accommodations might in-

---

Box 3.3

NCLB's Sanctions for Failing to Make Adequate Yearly Progress

Failing to Make AYP for 2 Consecutive Years
School is identified by the state for "school improvement"
School is designated as a "targeted assistance school"
The school must
> Notify parents of the designation
> Provide students the opportunity to transfer to a nonfailing school and cover the transportation costs
> Develop and implement a 2-year school improvement plan

Failing to Make AYP for 3 Consecutive Years
The school must provide "supplemental educational services" to students from an outside provider
The district must take "corrective action," which could include:
> Appointing outside experts to advise the school
> Decreasing the authority of the school's management

Failing to Make AYP for 4 Consecutive Years
School is subject to state take-over. This may entail:
> Replacing the entire staff
> Converting the school into a charter school
> Turning the school over to a private company

clude extra time to take a test, testing in small groups, flexible scheduling, simplified instructions, audio-taped instructions in the native language or English, additional clarifying information, and assessments in the language and form that are most likely to yield accurate data on what students know and can do in academic content areas.

A Critical Look at Federal Policy

Federal policy for language-minority students began in 1968 with passage of the Bilingual Education Act. This act was created out of recognition of the dismal educational attainment of LEP students and the failure of schools to address the linguistic, cultural, and educational needs of this rapidly growing student population. Although the initial goals and purposes were ambiguous, a constant theme throughout the five reauthorizations was the recognition of the importance of providing instruction to LEP students in the language they understand the most, and the recognition that bilingual education programs and techniques help students learn English and attain academic success. As the act evolved, the need for flexibility was recognized, but so too was the need for developmental and dual language programs that promote bilingualism and biliteracy for LEP and native English speakers. There was also recognition that bilingual programs serve societal and national interests.

Title III, unlike its predecessor, Title VII, the Bilingual Education Act, has an exclusive focus on English. It makes clear that "language instruction educational programs" are to teach LEP students English and move them into mainstream English-only classrooms as quickly as possible. Although allowances are made for bilingual education programs, the Title III legislation does not use the term *bilingual*, and the federal offices responsible for ELL education have stopped using it, demonstrating that developing and promoting bilingualism is no longer a federal goal. The recognition of the linguistic resources ELL students bring to school and the benefits of bilingualism to society so apparent in the 1994 reauthorization of Title VII have been stripped from the federal law.

Although the flexibility afforded state and local education agencies to define their own approaches to teaching LEP students potentially creates opportunities for funding bilingual programs, such funding is less likely in the current sociopolitical climate. State education agencies have been given unprecedented power to decide which programs they deem "scientifically based" and thus eligible for funding.

Title III testing requirements for English proficiency and Title I testing requirements for academic content tend to discourage the use of bilingual education programs. Despite allowances for testing in the native language, the vast majority of ELL students in the country take state assessments in English. Schools with large ELL populations are under immense pressure to ensure that the LEP subgroup makes AYP at the risk of the entire school being labeled as failing. Research from California has shown that pressure to raise LEP student scores on an English-only test have also been influential in ending bilingual education programs.[2]

NCLB makes it clear that ELL students are held to the same language arts, math, science, and other content-area standards as their native English-speaking peers. These standards help teachers by providing guidelines about what they should teach and what students should know and be able to do. Furthermore, having "rigorous" academic content standards addresses the problem in many schools where teachers may have low expectations for their students. Content standards,

---

2: See, e.g., Alamillo & Viramontes, 2000; Dixon, Green, Yeager, Baker, & Franquiz, 2000; Gandara, 2000; Wright, 2003b, 2007.

however, that merely outline what each state feels its students should know and be able to do have been very controversial.[3]

By focusing narrowly on isolated standards that break schooling into discrete measurable units and focus solely on individual student performance, teachers may lose sight of the holistic view of educating the whole child (Wiley & Hartung-Cole, 1998). Debates in education about what the curriculum should include and how it should be taught to students continue unresolved. These include disagreements over whether creationism has a place in science classes, whether multicultural literature should be taught in language arts classes, and whether diverse perspectives on history should be included in social studies classes. Since standards are created by state governments and reflect the dominant group's beliefs about what is and what is not important for children to know, the standards tend to privilege children of the dominant group from middle- and upper-class homes; the knowledge and skills of minority children are typically not reflected or valued. ELLs are especially disadvantaged, because content standards are designed for and thus privilege students who are fluent in English. In short, content standards create a one-size-fits-all situation, but not all students fit—particularly ELL students.[4]

Nearly all of the problems and issues related to academic content standards apply equally to standards for ELP. ELP standards, however, have a unique set of problems. As discussed in Chapter 2, the construct of language proficiency is highly complex and multidimensional, making it nearly impossible to organize language into neat lists of specific knowledge and skills. Also, it is very difficult to identify and work with generic levels of proficiency in English. Federal guidelines do not specify how many levels of English proficiency states must identify and track. Thus, some states have only three levels (e.g., beginning, intermediate, or advanced), while other states have four or five levels. Moreover, states use different labels for their levels, and descriptions of these levels vary from state to state. This variability reflects the complexity of the task and makes it difficult to compare proficiency and progress of ELLs across different states.

As states began to develop their ELP standards, confusion arose in some states over how ELP standards differ from the reading/language arts standards required by NCLB. The U.S. Department of Education's (2003a) guidance document states: "Reading/language arts standards are not the same as English language proficiency standards" and "English language proficiency standards should be specifically developed for limited English proficient students and define progressive levels of competence in the acquisition of the English language" (p. 8). And because the guidelines also stress that there should be a clear link between ELP standards and reading/language arts standards, many states have struggled to create "different" but "linked" standards.

Despite the challenges, critics and proponents of NCLB agree that it has brought renewed attention to the needs of ELL students. Districts and schools that have long neglected their ELLs can no longer afford to do so. As one NCLB proponent declared:

> The biggest benefit of all? There are no more invisible kids. NCLB has shone a spotlight on the academic performance of poor and minority students, English language learners, and students with disabilities—students whose lagging achievement had previously been hidden. As a result, schools are now focusing more attention on these students' education. (Haycock, 2006, p. 38)

Districts and schools are now held accountable for ELLs' attainment of ELP and the mastery of academic content as articulated in state ELP and academic content standards. Indeed, an entire school or district could be deemed as "failing" to

---

3: See Meier, 2000, for a critique of the standards movement.

4: The veteran educator Susan Ohanian (1999) makes a strong case, arguing that when it comes to educational standards, one size fits few.

make AYP and subject to state sanctions based on the test scores of the LEP subgroup alone. Some reports from the field indicate that educators with experience and expertise in teaching LEP students are now finding their knowledge and skills in demand from their colleagues in their schools and districts as never before. But despite this positive aspect of NCLB, there is widespread evidence that technical flaws, unrealistic expectations, and overreliance on high-stakes tests are causing much more harm than good.[5]

The Obama Administration and Federal Education Policy

Barack Obama was sworn in as the 44th President of the United States on January 20, 2009. Although education reform has taken a back seat to other pressing national concerns, particularly the economy, Obama has been critical of NCLB and its emphasis on high-stakes testing. The President has also spoken out in support of bilingual education. At the time of this writing, the Obama administration has not offered any concrete proposals for legislative changes to the ESEA, which is now due for reauthorization.

The Obama administration, however, is setting the stage for major education reforms through the American Recovery and Reinvestment Act of 2009 (ARRA), which is designed to turn the struggling economy around. The ARRA includes over $44 billion in stimulus funding for education, $10 billion of which is reserved for Title 1 schools (i.e., schools that receive funding through Title 1 of NCLB to serve socioeconomically disadvantaged students). In addition, in July 2009 President Obama announced a new program as part of the ARRA called Race to the Top, which provides $4.3 billion in competitive grants states can apply for to begin education reform efforts. States receiving the stimulus funding and states that apply for the Race to the Top grants must adhere to four general requirements for the use of the funds (U.S. Department of Education 2009a, 2009b):

1. Adopting internationally benchmarked standards that prepare students for success in college and the workplace, and high-quality assessments that are valid and reliable for all students, including English language learners and students with disabilities
2. Recruiting, developing, rewarding, and retaining effective teachers and principals
3. Increased transparency by building data systems that measure student success and inform teachers and principals how they can improve their practices
4. Supporting effective intervention strategies to turn around the lowest-performing schools

Because these funds had just been released at the time of this writing, it is not yet clear what the impact will be on ELL students.

ELL advocates and others, however, are deeply concerned that the emphasis on high-stakes testing remains. Of greatest concern is a requirement that teacher performance be tied to their students' test scores. Without substantial change to the testing mandates of NCLB, this means that teachers of ELLs will be held accountable for test scores of questionable validity and thus may be unfairly penalized. Educators who were hopeful that the administration would relieve schools of the heavy focus on high-stakes testing are protesting that this new requirement makes the problem even worse. The National Education Association (NEA) issued a formal letter to Secretary of Education Arne Duncan in August 2009 that applauds the overall goals of Race to the Top but outlines a number of concerns, among

5: For the results of research on the negative impacts of NCLB on the education of ELLs, see Menken, 2008; Nichols & Berliner, 2007; Valenzuela, 2004; Wright, 2005a, 2005b, 2006a, 2008.

them: "We should not continue the unhealthy focus on standardized tests as the primary evidence of student success."[6] James Crawford, executive director of the Institute for Language and Education Policy (ILEP), issued a similar letter to Duncan that same month addressing the harm the administration's mandate may have on ELL students and their teachers.[7] It remains to be seen whether or how the administration will address these issues.

Despite these valid concerns, the federal stimulus funds, in addition to other funding for assessment reform, may in fact provide an opportunity for states to make major changes to when and how ELLs are assessed. There is also the potential for an expansion of high quality language education programs. Whatever happens through these initial reform efforts will likely be key in informing the administration's proposed changes to the ESEA.

State Policies for ELLs

Bilingual education, as discussed earlier, was once common in this country, particularly in isolated areas where immigrants from non-English-speaking countries settled and were the dominant groups and in areas of the Southwest where Spanish speakers were long the dominant group. As state governments began assuming more responsibility for public schooling and as pressure built during the Americanization movement, many states passed English-only instruction laws. After the passage of the Bilingual Education Act in 1968 and the *Lau v. Nichols* decision by the U.S. Supreme Court in 1974 (discussed in the next section), many state governments repealed these laws and many others also created their own bilingual education mandates.

The policy scene changed dramatically after voters in three states with large ELL student populations—California, Arizona, and Massachusetts—approved English for the Children initiatives, which placed severe restrictions on bilingual education programs. In 1998 California voters approved Proposition 227, in 2000 Arizona voters approved Proposition 203, and in 2002 Massachusetts voters approved Question 2. An attempt to pass a similar initiative in Colorado (Amendment 31) failed.[8]

Ron Unz, a California millionaire software developer from Palo Alto, authored these initiatives and provided nearly all the funding and leadership for the campaign. Ignoring the history, purpose, and design of bilingual programs, Unz claimed that bilingual education programs are a violation of immigrant children's right to learn English. Unz also used misleading statistics and data in making the case for eliminating bilingual education programs.

He claimed, for example, that bilingual education in California had a 95% failure rate. He constructed this figure by looking at annual redesignation rates of ELLs in California, that is, the number of ELLs each year determined to have reached a level of proficiency in English (based on language proficiency tests and other measures) to be exited from the ELL category and redesignated as fluent English proficient. Unz claimed that because only 5% of ELLs had been redesignated (actually, it was 7%), bilingual education had a 95% failure rate (Crawford, 2003). Unz's figure fails to account for the progress ELLs make in learning English each

---

6: For the NEA statement, see www.nea.org/home/35447.htm

7: For the ILEP statement, see www.elladvocates.org/documents/federal/ILEP%20comments%20on%20Race%20to%20the%20Top.pdf

8: For the story of how Unz was defeated in Colorado, see Escamilla, Shannon, Carlos, & Garcia 2003; for a critique of this victory, see Crawford 2003.

year. It also creates an unrealistic expectation—if ELLs do not become fluent in English after just 1 school year (9 months or less of instruction), then the program serving them failed. Unz dismissed the findings from scientific research that it takes much longer than a year to develop fluency in a second language. And whereas his use of this 95% figure was misleading, his attributing the failure to bilingual education programs was outright dishonest. Unz's figure included all ELL students, 70% of whom were already in the types of English-only programs his initiative mandates. Despite its flawed logic and misrepresentations, the "95% failure rate" was such an effective campaign sound-bite that Unz used it in his subsequent campaigns in the other states.

Another misleading but influential use of data that proved effective in helping Unz's initiatives pass in Arizona and Massachusetts was his claim that Proposition 227 and the elimination of bilingual education in California led to increases in test scores of ELLs. In other words, Unz argued that English-only instruction was working for ELLs in California, and the test scores proved it. This claim was so compelling it made the front page of the *New York Times* (Steinberg, 2000). From there it was picked up by major newspapers throughout the country and was cited as an authority on the issue in 56 editorials and letters to the editor (Thompson, DiCerbo, Mahoney, & MacSwan, 2002). Despite this wide coverage, the claim that Proposition 227 led to higher ELL test scores is not supported by the data. Researchers who examined Unz's claim all found that his analysis was so deeply flawed that his claims were completely unfounded (Butler, Orr, Gutierrez, & Hakuta, 2000; Thompson, DiCerbo, Mahoney, & MacSwan, 2002). What the data did reveal, these researchers found, is that test scores rose for all students, including schools that maintained their bilingual education programs. Even more significant, they found that the gap between ELLs and non-ELLs had not decreased. Furthermore, as these researchers noted, the norm-referenced state test was not designed for program evaluation, and thus, it really could not be used to show the superiority of one approach to teaching ELLs over another.

Although English for the Children initiatives were passed only in California, Arizona, and Massachusetts, the influence of Unz's campaign extends beyond these states' boundaries. Since the defeat of Amendment 31, some Colorado lawmakers have attempted to pass similar legislation restricting bilingual education. Some policymakers in Texas, where bilingual education remains strong, desire to put restrictions on bilingual programs and push structured English immersion programs. Anti-bilingual education advocates from out of state were invited by a state Board of Education member to testify to the board in February 2006, though a previous report commissioned by the board documented the success of Texas bilingual programs (Texas Education Agency, 2000). Other states are considering legislating or creating voter initiatives to restrict bilingual programs.

Analyses of the impact of Proposition 227 between 2004 and 2006, including studies of English language proficiency data by California's Legislative Analyst's Office, and a 5-year evaluation study of Proposition 227, commissioned by the state and conducted by the American Institutes for Research and WestEd, found no evidence that the replacement of bilingual education programs with mandates for structured (or sheltered) English immersion had helped ELL students learn English faster, or perform at higher levels on state achievement tests (American Institutes for Research & WestEd, 2006; Hill, 2004, 2006). Analyses conducted in Arizona on the impact of Proposition 203 have found similar results (Mahoney, Thompson, & MacSwan, 2004, 2005). In fact, in Arizona, test scores of elementary school ELL students actually declined in reading and math on both the SAT-9 and the Arizona Instrument to Measure Standards (AIMS) test the year following strict enforcement of Proposition 203 (Wright & Pu, 2005).

Despite the voter initiatives that have severely limited bilingual education in three states, the weakening of support for bilingual education at the federal level, and the stirring of anti-bilingual-education sentiment in other states, bilingual education is thriving, even in the three states that passed the English for the Children initiatives. Several schools in California, Arizona, and Massachusetts have used the waiver provisions of the law to continue bilingual programs, because they are effective and parents want them for their children. In Massachusetts, dual language programs were exempted from the law altogether.[9] Several states still have bilingual education policies that require schools to offer bilingual programs when there are a certain number of ELL students at a given grade level who speak the same language. And in most other states, bilingual education is neither restricted nor required but remains a viable option for many schools. The fact that nearly half of the states in the country have professional organizations for bilingual education provides evidence that many schools are indeed continuing to provide bilingual programs because they have found them to be effective in meeting the language and academic needs of their ELL students.

Important Court Decisions and Legislation

Historical reluctance by many states throughout the country to provide equitable educational opportunities to ELL and other minority students and controversies over the use of languages other than English in public schools have sparked a large number of lawsuits that address these issues. The court decisions that grew out of these lawsuits have led to legislative changes that have helped to shape the policy climate of today. In this section we briefly review some of these cases and related legislation.

First, however, we must consider the 14th Amendment to the U.S. Constitution. This amendment, ratified in 1868 after the Civil War, declares in part: "No State shall make or enforce any law which shall abridge the privileges or immunities of citizens of the United States; nor shall any State deprive any person of life, liberty, or property, without due process of law; nor deny to any person within its jurisdiction the equal protection of the laws." Many of the cases discussed in this section are based on the due process and the equal protection clauses of the 14th Amendment.

Addressing Segregation

In 1896 the U.S. Supreme Court issued its now infamous decision in *Plessy v. Ferguson* that "separate but equal" public facilities, including school systems, are constitutional. Although the decision was related to the segregation of African American students, in many parts of the country Native American, Asian, and Hispanic students were also routinely segregated. The Supreme Court unanimously reversed *Plessy v. Ferguson* 58 years later in 1954 in *Brown v. Board of Education*. A few lesser known lower-level cases concerning the segregation of Hispanic student predate *Brown*. In *Independent School District v. Salvatierra* (1930), Mexican American parents in the small border town of Rio, Texas, brought suit against the school district over segregation. The court sided with the school district that argued the segregation was necessary to teach the students English. This argument did not hold, however, for two similar cases in California: *Alvarez v. Lemon Grove* (1931) and *Méndez*

9: For details, see Combs, Evans, Fletcher, Parra, & Jiménez, 2005; de Jong, Gort, & Cobb, 2005; García & Curry-Rodriguez, 2000; Palmer & García, 2000; Wright, 2005b.

v. Westminster School District (1947). The judge in *Alvarez* noted that segregation was not beneficial for the students' English language development (Trujillo, 2008), and the success of the *Méndez* case helped set the stage for *Brown*.

Like *Plessy, Brown v. Board of Education* focused on the segregation of African American students. But by ruling that states are responsible for providing "equal educational opportunities" for all students, *Brown* made bilingual education for ELLs more feasible. In some instances, however, desegregation efforts made it more difficult. In San Francisco, for example, Chinese Americans fought a desegregation order that would force students out of neighborhood schools that provided bilingual English-Chinese programs for newcomer Chinese ELL students. The Chinese community took the case to court in 1971 in *Guey Heung Lee v. Johnson*, and it was appealed to the 9th Circuit Court of Appeals in *Johnson v. San Francisco Unified School District*. In 1974, the court ruled against the Chinese community, declaring simply *Brown* applies to races.

Despite significant progress in the half century since *Brown*, the practice of segregation in public schools remains widespread (Kozol, 2005). School districts that provide bilingual education and ESL programs constantly struggle to balance the need for separate classes where the unique needs of ELL students can be addressed against the need to avoid prolonged segregation of ELLs from other students.

The Right of Communities to Teach Their Native Languages to Their Children

Three important cases have addressed the issue of private language-schooling for language-minority students. In the early 1900s, German communities typically ran their own private schools where students received instruction in both German and English. Then, in 1919, Nebraska passed the Siman Act, which made it illegal for any school, public or private, to provide any foreign language instruction to students below the 8th grade. Roman Catholic and Lutheran German parochial schools joined together to file suit against the act under the 14th Amendment. The state court ruled that the act could not prevent schools from providing German language instruction outside of the hours of regular school study. In response, the parochial schools taught German during an extended recess period. Language restrictionist policymakers sought to close the loopholes in the law and fined Robert Meyers $25 fine for teaching Bible stories to 10-year-old children in German. The case, *Meyer v. Nebraska* (1923), went to the Supreme Court, which consolidated this case with similar cases from Ohio and Idaho.

In a major victory for language-minority parents and communities, the Supreme Court struck down the states' restrictive legislation, ruling, in essence, that whereas state governments can legislate the language used for instruction in schools, states may not pass laws that attempt to prevent communities from offering private language classes outside of the regular school system. *Meyers* is an important case because it makes clear that the 14th Amendment provides protection for language minorities. As the legal expert Sandra Del Valle (2003) points out, however, this decision did not give language minorities additional rights and privileges but simply ensured that "laws not be used as a rationale for denying them the same rights accorded others" (p. 39). Furthermore, because the focus of this case was on parochial schools, the decision was not an endorsement of bilingual education. In a similar case handed down in Hawaii in 1927, *Farrington v. Tokushige*, the court offered further protections of after-school community language programs after attempts by education authorities to put restrictions on Japanese and Chinese heritage language programs.

Despite these victories, as Del Valle observes, these cases were essentially about parents' rights rather than language rights. In addition, within the court's decision there were still signs of negative attitudes toward the "foreign population." Indeed, Hawaii tried yet again to limit private foreign language instruction. When the Chinese communities after World War II sought to restart their private language schools, the state passed the "Act Regulating the Teaching of Foreign Languages to Children." Part of the state's rationale was the need to "protect children from the harm of learning a foreign language" (Del Valle, 2003, p. 44). In *Stainback v. Mo Hock Ke Kok Po* (1947), the state court struck down the statute, rejecting the state's claim and arguing that, at least for "the brightest" students, study of a foreign language can be beneficial. The case was decided on the basis of *Farrington* and, once again, had more to do with parents' rights in directing the education of their children than with language rights.

Xenophobia toward German and Japanese Americans during World War I and World War II succeeded where attempts at language restrictive legislation failed. When Germany and later Japan became war enemies of the United States, the number of U.S. schools that provided instruction in these languages dropped dramatically, largely because of fears by members of these communities that such instruction would lead others to question their loyalty to the United States (Tamura, 1993; Wiley, 1998).

Nevertheless, the legacy of these cases, despite agreement in the courts about the need for states to Americanize minorities and their right to control the language used for instruction in public schools, is that minority communities have a clear right to offer private language classes in which their children can learn and maintain their home languages. Thus, the common practice of language-minority communities today in offering heritage language programs after school and on weekends is protected by the U.S. Constitution.

Addressing the Linguistic and Educational Needs of ELL Students

Case law concerning the linguistic and educational needs of ELL students has had a major impact on federal and state policy for ELL students, their families, and their communities. Since the early 1970s, conflict and controversy have surrounded the issue of what constitutes an appropriate education for ELLs. Some rulings provide support for bilingual education; others erode that support. Some cases involve suits filed against bilingual education; others involve suits filed against anti-bilingual education voter initiatives.

Equal Educational Opportunities for ELLs

The 1974 Supreme Court case *Lau v. Nichols* resulted in perhaps the most important court decision regarding the education of language-minority students. This case was brought forward by Chinese American students in the San Francisco Unified School District who were placed in mainstream classrooms despite their lack of proficiency in English, and left to "sink or swim." The district had argued that it had done nothing wrong, and that the Chinese American students received treatment equal to that of other students. Justice William Douglass, in writing the court's opinion, strongly disagreed, arguing:

> Under these state-imposed standards there is no equality of treatment merely by providing students with the same facilities, textbooks, teachers, and curriculum; for students who do not understand English are effectively foreclosed from any meaningful

education. . . . We know that those who do not understand English are certain to find their classroom experiences wholly incomprehensible and in no way meaningful.

The influence of *Lau* on federal policy was substantial. After the court's decision, the U.S. Department of Education's Office of Civil Rights created the Lau Remedies. Whereas Title VII Bilingual Education Act regulations applied only to funded programs, the Lau Remedies applied to all school districts and functioned as de facto compliance standards. The Office of Civil Rights used the *Lau* decision to go after districts that, like San Francisco, were essentially ignoring the needs of its LEP students. Even though the court decision does not mandate any particular instructional approach, the Lau Remedies essentially require districts to implement bilingual education programs for LEP students. James Lyons (1995), former president of the National Association for Bilingual Education, explains further:

> The *Lau Remedies* specified proper approaches, methods and procedures for (1) identifying and evaluating national-origin-minority students' English-language skills; (2) determining appropriate instructional treatments; (3) deciding when LEP students were ready for mainstream classes; and (4) determining the professional standards to be met by teachers of language-minority children. Under the *Lau Remedies,* elementary schools were generally required to provide LEP students special English-as-a-second-language instruction as well as academic subject-matter instruction through the students' strongest language until the student achieved proficiency in English sufficient to learn effectively in a monolingual English classroom. (pp. 4–5)

The essence of *Lau* was codified into federal law though the Equal Educational Opportunities Act of 1974 (EEOA), soon after the case was decided. Section 1703(f) of this act declares: "No state shall deny educational opportunities to an individual on account of his or her race, color, sex, or national origin by . . . (f) the failure of an educational agency to take appropriate action to overcome language barriers that impede equal participation by its students in its instructional programs." At the time of its passage, this section of the EEOA was viewed as a declaration of the legal right for students to receive a bilingual education, under the assumption that this is what *Lau* essentially mandated (Del Valle, 2003). Although other legal actions have since made it clear that the Supreme Court never did mandate bilingual education, the EEOA remains in effect and several subsequent lawsuits have been based on this important legislation.

Rulings that Support Bilingual Education

United States v. Texas (1971, 1981) includes mandates that affect all Texas schools. The court ordered the district to create a plan and implement language programs that would help Mexican American students learn English and adjust to American culture and also help Anglo students learn Spanish. The court relied heavily on the testimony of José Cardenas and his theory of incompatibilities, which blames the educational failure of students on the inadequacies of school programs rather than on students themselves.[10]

Serna v. Portales (1974) was the first case to raise the issue of bilingual education outside of the context of desegregation (Del Valle, 2003). The case dealt with a White-majority school in New Mexico that failed to meet the unique needs of "Spanish-surnamed students." It was argued under Title VI of the Civil Rights Act of 1964, which prohibits discrimination on the basis of "race, color, or national origin" in any program that receives federal funding. The court found the school's program for these students to be inadequate. The judge declared, "It is incumbent on the school district to reassess and enlarge its program directed to the special-

---

10: For a complete discussion of the theory, see Cardenas & Cardenas, 1977.

ized needs of the Spanish-surnamed students" and to create bilingual programs at other schools where they are needed. This case was first decided in 1972. Later it was appealed to the 10th Circuit Court of Appeals and decided in 1974 just six months after *Lau*. Like *Lau*, it makes clear that schools cannot ignore the unique language and educational needs of ELL students.

Legal action taken by Puerto Rican parents and children in New York in *Aspira v. New York* (1975) resulted in the Aspira Consent Decree, which mandates transitional bilingual programs for Spanish-surnamed students found to be more proficient in Spanish than English. The Aspira Consent Decree is still in effect and has been a model for school districts across the country, though it is frequently under attack by opponents of bilingual education.

Bilingual education in New York received a further boost a few years later in *Rios v. Reed* (1978). The case was argued under Title VI of the Civil Rights Act and the EEOA. Puerto Rican parents brought suit claiming that many so-called bilingual education programs were not bilingual but based mainly on ESL. The federal court found the district's bilingual programs to be woefully inadequate, pointing to the lack of trained bilingual teachers and the absence of a clearly defined curriculum, clear entrance and exit criteria, and firm guidelines about how much instruction should be in the native language of the students. Although the court issued no specific remedies, the federal Office of Civil Rights came in to ensure that the district made improvements. This case is significant because it made a strong case for offering bilingual education and for doing it right.

Rulings That Erode Support for Bilingual Education

Another Texas case, *San Antonio Independent School District v. Rodriguez* (1973), although not directly related to bilingual education, had some serious implications for it. It dealt with inequalities in school funding, with the plaintiff charging that predominantly minority schools received less funding than schools that served predominantly White students. The case was argued under the Equal Protection Clause of the 14th Amendment, but the U.S. Supreme Court ruled that there is no fundamental right to an education guaranteed by the Constitution. Indeed, if there is no constitutional right to an education under the 14th Amendment, as Del Valle (2003) points out, "there is clearly no constitutional right to a *bilingual* education" (p. 234, emphasis in original).

Because of this case, all subsequent cases over inadequacies in school funding have had to be argued under state constitutions. Some of these cases, such as *Flores v. Arizona* (2000) and *Williams v. California* (settled in 2004), include or specifically address inadequacies related to the education of ELL students. But despite court orders in *Flores* to increase funding for ELL students, state legislators and educational leaders have used a wide variety of stall tactics and legal maneuvering to avoid fully complying with the court's order. In 2009 the Arizona legislature and the state superintendent of public instruction appealed the case to the U.S. Supreme Court. The high court essentially agreed with the state leaders that the situation in Arizona for ELLs had changed substantially since the original lower court ruling, and thus the lower courts must take these changes into consideration. Although the ruling was disappointing to the plaintiffs, it nonetheless keeps the legal battle alive. The attorney and advocates in the state are gathering new evidence of the harm caused by recent state policies and the underfunding of ELLs' education. This case demonstrates that even when courts issue decisions with specific mandates, changes do not happen immediately and are often resisted by political figures who disagree with the decision.

In the 1980s, in the wake of *Lau,* support for bilingual education was eroded by the courts. For example, a case in Colorado, *Otero v. Mesa County Valley School District* (1980), failed in the plaintiffs' attempt to obtain a court order for bilingual education. The plaintiffs wanted a plan for its Mexican American students like the one based on the testimony of Cardenas that was recommended by the court in *United States v. Texas* (1971) even though they made up a small number of students in the district, and less than 3% could even speak or understand Spanish. As in *United States v. Rodriguez,* the court's decision made it clear that despite *Lau,* there is no constitutional right to bilingual or bicultural education (Del Valle, 2003).

In another Colorado case, *Keyes v. School District No. 1* (1983), the court also rejected a Cardenas-like plan on the basis that *Lau* did not mandate bilingual education and that according to the decision in *Rodriguez* there is no constitutional right to education. The bilingual education component was just one part of this complicated desegregation case. Del Valle suggests that the court seemed content that the district was simply offering a "number of programs" for ELLs, without examining the adequacy of these programs. This issue of program adequacy, however, was addressed in subsequent lawsuits.

The right to bilingual education suffered a further blow in 1981 in *Castañeda v. Pickard.* The case originated in Texas, where plaintiffs charged that the Raymondville Independent School District was failing to address the needs of ELL students as mandated by the EEOA. The federal court ignored the old assumption that *Lau* and the EEOA mandated bilingual education. Nevertheless, it did find that Raymondville fell far short of meeting the requirements of the EEOA. A major outcome of this case is a three-pronged test to determine whether schools are taking "appropriate action" to address the needs of ELLs as required by the EEOA. The Castañeda standard mandates that programs for language-minority students must be (1) based on a sound educational theory, (2) implemented effectively with sufficient resources and personnel, and (3) evaluated to determine whether they are effective in helping students overcome language barriers (Del Valle, 2003). Since the U.S. Supreme Court decision in Lau, two other lawsuits have been decided in the high court that, while not related to bilingual education, nonetheless undermine the original legal argument of *Lau.*[11] Thus, the Castañeda standard, which encapsulates the central feature of *Lau*— that schools do something to meet the needs of ELL students—has essentially become the law of the land in determining the adequacy of programs for ELLs.

Del Valle (2003), however, points out the shortcomings of the Castañeda test. Referring to prongs 1 and 2, she notes that nearly any program can be justified by an educational theory and that some approaches require very little in the way of staff or funding. Of even greater concern is that, under prong 3, a certain amount of time must pass before a determination can be made about the adequacy of the programs. Thus, many students may be harmed before inadequate programs are identified and rectified.

Despite these shortcomings, a case 6 years after *Castañeda—Gomez v. Illinois State Board of Education* (1987)—demonstrated the value of the Castañeda test in legal efforts to rectify inadequate programs. The U.S. Court of Appeals for the 7th Circuit relied heavily on *Castañeda* in its decision and gave state boards of education the power to enforce compliance with the EEOA. The court declared, in a ruling much like *Lau,* that school districts have a responsibility to serve ELL students and cannot allow children to just sit in classrooms where they cannot understand instruction. However, as in *Lau,* the court did not mandate any specific program models.

11: These two cases are *Regents of the University of California v. Bakke* (1978) and *Alexander v. Sandoval* (2001).

Recent Lawsuits

Between 1995 and 2001, opponents of bilingual education in a few communities filed lawsuits against their school districts (e.g., *Bushwick Parents Organization v. Mills* [1995] in New York). Del Valle (2003) suggests that through these cases opponents of bilingual education attempted to turn the original purpose of bilingual education on its head by charging that a program that was developed to ensure that ELL students have the same educational opportunities as all other students was actually preventing equal educational opportunities for ELL students. These cases also illustrate that attacks on bilingual education are rarely grass-roots efforts by Latino parents but rather are orchestrated by powerful outsiders who mislead parents into joining their cause and in the process often create divisions within Latino communities. Although these legal attacks on bilingual education failed, opponents of bilingual education have scored major victories in the court of public opinion through the English for the Children voter initiatives described earlier.

These voter initiatives, however, have not gone uncontested. Five cases in California were based on challenges to Proposition 227: *Quiroz v. State Board of Education* (1997); *Valerie G. v. Wilson* (1998); *McLaughlin v. State Board of Education* (1999); *Doe v. Los Angeles Unified School District* (1999); *California Teachers Association v. Davis* (1999). At least two cases in Arizona were based on challenges to Proposition 203: *Sotomayor and Gabaldon v. Burns* (2000) and *Morales v. Tucson Unified School District* (2001). Although some of these resulted in small victories, none has succeeded in overturning the voter initiatives. (Anti-bilingual Education Court Cases, document)

Case law has had a major impact on federal and state policy for ELL students and their families and communities. While the courts have been reluctant to mandate a particular educational model or approach or to give language minorities fundamental rights directly related to the use of their native languages, the courts have nonetheless made it clear that schools may not ignore the unique needs of ELL students.

Any program for ELLs, regardless of the language of instruction or the models used, must do two very important things: teach English and teach academic content. Schools must provide instruction in English for ELLs because they are not yet proficient in English, and because they need fluency in English to succeed in mainstream classrooms and to be successful in life in general in the United States. At the same time, schools cannot focus just on teaching English. Students must also learn the same academic content their English proficient peers are learning, in such subjects as language arts, math, science, social studies, music, art, and physical education. In Chapter 4 we review the different program models for ELL students and how these programs address the legal requirements for teaching English and the content areas.

Language Policy at the Local Level

Federal and state policies for ELLs have raised awareness that schools are responsible for meeting the needs of ELL students. An important first step in assuming that responsibility is to articulate a school or district language policy. David Corson (1999) defines a school language policy as follows:

> A document compiled by the staff of a school, who are often assisted by other members of the school community, to which the staff give their assent and commitment. It identifies areas in the school's scope of operations and programs where language problems exist that need the commonly agreed approach offered by a policy. A language policy sets out what the school intends to do about these areas of concern and includes provi-

sions for follow-up, monitoring, and revision of the policy itself in light of changing cir-cumstances. It is a dynamic action statement that changes along with the dynamic con-text of a school.

Corson asserts that in multilingual settings like the United States three policy principles are necessary:

1. Children have the right to be educated in their home language.
2. If the first principle cannot be met, children have the right to attend a school that respects and values their home language,
3. Children have the right to learn the standard language variety (e.g., standard English in the United States) to the highest level of proficiency possible.

These three principles should be a starting point for schools in developing their own language policies. A school's language policy, along with an accompanying implementation manual or guide, provides the necessary structure for ensuring that ELLs have equal access to educational opportunities on the local level. The programs for ELLs that are based on the policy reflect the mission and vision of the school and the district for all students, including ELLs.

Endorsed programs are based on the strengths and needs of the students and community and on second language/bilingual teaching and learning. While the programs must be in compliance with all federal and state mandates and account-ability requirements, measures should be taken to minimize any harm ill-informed policies may have on the students. Programs must also be aligned with court find-ings regarding equitable education for ELLs. To ensure that everyone responsible for the education of ELLs at school (coaches, administrators, literacy specialists, and general education, bilingual, ESL, and special education teachers) under-stands his or her role in educating ELLs, endorsed programs for ELLs must be clearly defined, and the policies and procedures ensuring effective implementa-tion must be outlined. In this era of accountability, districts and schools must have a valid and reliable means of assessing ELLs, and the policy and implementation guide must lay out the specifics of that assessment plan with attention to what data are collected, when, by whom, and for what purposes. All policies, procedures, and forms regarding the education of ELLs, from placement to proficiency, should be included in the implementation guide, which is reviewed and revised regularly.

The language policy and implementation guide provides a vehicle for creating a coherent vision of ELL education and for the institutionalization of effective pro-grams districtwide. When every educator who is responsible for the education of ELLs on the local level shares a common understanding, a common language, and a common practice committed to the equal access to educational opportunities for ELLs, programs improve, instruction improves, and ELL performance improves.

Rebecca Freeman has helped schools in multilingual communities put Cor-son's principles into practice. In her book *Building on Community Bilingualism,* she documents the efforts of school districts to develop school language policies that promote multilingualism for students from diverse language backgrounds. She provides substantial evidence that even within this age of accountability there is "room for language policies and bilingual programs that promote multilingual-ism" (Freeman, 2004, p. 28). Freeman argues that "in multilingual communities, educators can build on the linguistic and cultural resources that students bring with them to school and/or that are available in the local community to address students' language education needs" (p. 325). She further argues: "Schools located in multilingual communities have a responsibility to build programs that encour-age ELLs and heritage language speakers to maintain and develop their native and/or heritage languages, and this work can begin to challenge the assimilation strat-egy that has been dominant in the United States over the last century" (p. 348).

Summary

Although the United States has a long history of bilingual education, the federal government has had direct involvement in the education of ELLs only since the late 1960s, beginning with the Title VII Bilingual Education Act of 1968. During the next three decades, the Bilingual Education Act was revised many times, each time providing greater clarity about the goals of the program, the students to be served, and the programs eligible for federal funding. Though nonbilingual programs were afforded greater flexibility, the final version of the Bilingual Education Act revealed that the federal government fully recognized the value of bilingualism and the need for bilingual citizens and marked its commitment to bilingual education.

Federal commitment to these values and programs came to an abrupt end with the passage of the No Child Left Behind Act of 2001. The Bilingual Education Act was replaced with Title III, "Language Instruction for Limited English Proficient and Immigrant Students." Title III focuses exclusively on English. Bilingual education—while not mentioned by name—is still allowed, but NCLB makes it clear that whatever programs districts choose to offer, they must ensure that ELLs learn English as quickly as possible. Bilingualism is no longer a goal of interest to the federal government. Other aspects of NCLB, including its heavy reliance on high-stakes testing, indirectly discourage schools from providing bilingual programs.

NCLB has brought increased attention to the linguistic and academic needs of ELL students by holding schools accountable for ensuring that students in the LEP subgroup make AYP in learning English and academic content. Because of NCLB, schools can no longer afford to ignore the needs of ELLs. However, the one-size-fits-all standards, testing, and accountability requirements mandated by NCLB are not appropriate for the diverse ELL student population in U.S. schools. The administration of President Barack Obama has acknowledged problems with NCLB and has promised change, but as of this writing, the work on reauthorizing the ESEA has yet to begin. Early efforts at school reform through economic stimulus funding continue the focus on high-stakes testing. Mandates to tie student test results to teacher evaluations threaten to make the situation with high-stakes testing worse than ever before. However, there is also potential for major changes to when and how ELL students will be tested.

State policies for ELL students have also varied widely, though since 2002, state education policies have been driven largely by NCLB. Bilingual education remains a viable option in most states, even in the three states with large ELL populations that have placed restrictions on bilingual education for ELLs as a result of voter initiatives—California, Arizona, and Massachusetts. In those states bilingual education is still possible through the waiver process. Nonetheless, even in states like Texas that have strong commitments to bilingual education, the accountability requirements of NCLB make it difficult for schools to continue to offer strong bilingual program models that promote bilingualism, biliteracy, and biculturalism.

The courts have played (and continue to play) a significant role in the development of policy for ELLs. Through a variety of decisions in important cases, the courts have made it clear that language minorities in the United States have the same rights as other Americans under the U.S. Constitution. Language minorities have the right to teach their children their native language through private language classes. And though the courts have made it clear that there is no constitutional right to bilingual education in the public schools, the courts have stipulated that schools cannot ignore the linguistic and academic needs of ELL students. Programs for ELLs must be based on sound educational theory, they must be provided with adequate resources and properly trained teachers, and they must be evaluated to ensure that they are sufficient in meeting the needs of the students. School districts and schools have begun to develop language policies and procedures to ensure that their programs for ELLs comply with all federal and state policies and meet the needs of the students and community they serve.

Discussion Questions

 1. **On-Line Discussion Board** What efforts are being made in your state, in relation to the economic stimulus funding for education or Race to the Top grants, to reform assessment and school accountability for ELL students? Do you feel these are positive changes that will benefit ELL students and their teachers? Why or why not?

2. **On-Line Discussion Board** How has federal policy for ELLs changed since 1968? How does Title III of NCLB compare to the Bilingual Education Act it replaced? What are the current proposals or recent changes to the ESEA with regard to ELLs? Do you feel these have been positive or negative changes? Why?

3. What are academic content standards? Why are they controversial? Discuss some of the issues of standards as they relate to language and content instruction for ELLs. Describe your own experiences related to these standards.

4. How can state ELP standards help teachers modify their language and content instruction to the appropriate levels of their ELL students?

5. **On-Line Discussion Board** Standards are supposed to help teachers know what to teach (i.e., drive instruction), and statewide assessments (as mandated by NCLB) are supposed to measure students' attainment of these standards. But many educators are concerned because the high stakes of state assessments appear to be driving instruction instead. Why is this a problem? Describe any personal experiences or observations related to this issue. What are some ways teachers can ensure that tests do not narrow the curriculum?

6. What are annual measurable achievement objectives (AMAOs)? What is adequate yearly progress (AYP)? What are the consequences for a school if each of its subgroups does not meet the AMAOs? Do you believe this is a fair system for holding schools accountable? Why or why not?

7. What has been the role of the courts in guiding federal policy for ELL students? What has case law identified as the main responsibilities of schools in meeting their needs? Which case set forth a test for determining the adequacy of an ELL program, and what are the three prongs of this test? What are the shortcomings of this test in ensuring high quality programs for ELLs?

Research Activities

 1. **Wiki This** Interview a teacher of ELL students. Ask what impact NCLB has on his or her classroom and whether the law's focus on standards and high-stakes testing has been beneficial or harmful to the ELL students.

 2. **Wiki This** Obtain school achievement and accountability data for your own school or for a school with which you are familiar. Data should include test scores for each tested grade level and each test mandated by NCLB and the AMAOs and AYP designations. What are the AMAOs for the previous school year? Did each subgroup meet the AMAO? Did each subgroup meet the 95% testing requirement and the other achievement indicator? Was the school as a whole designated as making AYP? What are the AMAOs for the next 3 years? How likely do you think it will be for the LEP and other subgroups to make AYP in the next 3 years?

3. Collect articles from your local newspaper on language and education policies

for ELL students. What are the controversial issues being discussed, and how do they relate to the issues covered in this chapter or other chapters of this book? What are your own views on these issues?

Recommended Reading

Corson, D. (1999). *Language policy in schools: A resource for teachers and administrators.* Mahwah, NJ: Lawrence Erlbaum.

An excellent overview of the rationale and importance for schools to develop their own language policies. Includes numerous resources to help teachers and administrators develop such policies.

Crawford, J. (2004). *Educating English learners: Language diversity in the classroom* (5th ed.). Los Angeles: Bilingual Education Services.

James Crawford, a well-known expert in the field of bilingual education, gives a thorough overview of history, politics, theory, and practice in educating ELLs.

Del Valle, S. (2003). *Language rights and the law in the United States: Finding our voices.* Clevedon, UK: Multilingual Matters.

Sandra Del Valle, a civil rights lawyer with over a decade of experience with cases dealing with the rights of language-minority groups, provides an in-depth look at historical and contemporary cases that have shaped policy. One chapter is devoted to bilingual education policy.

Ohanian, S. (1999). *One size fits few: The folly of educational standards.* Portsmouth, NH: Heinemann.

Susan Ohanian, a veteran educator, makes a strong case against the over-emphasis on standards in school reform efforts. Her engaging writing style and gift for storytelling with a sting will have readers laughing out loud on some pages and crying on others.

TESOL (Teachers of English to Speakers of Other Languages). (2006a). *PreK–12 English language proficiency standards.* Alexandria, VA: Author.

TESOL's official publication of its ELP standards. Includes an overview of the rationale for the standards, the theoretical framework of the standards, a broad range of sample performance indicators across grade levels for each of the standards, and instructions for teachers to create their own performance indicators.

4

Program Models for ELLs

There is no equality of treatment merely by providing students with the same facilities, textbooks, teachers, and curriculum; for students who do not understand English are effectively foreclosed from any meaningful education.

—*Lau v. Nichols* (1974)

KEY TERMS

- English as a second language (ESL)
- English language development (ELD)
- native language (L1) instruction
- sheltered instruction
- specially designed academic instruction in English (SDAIE)
- Sheltered Instruction Observation Protocol (SIOP)
- transitional bilingual education (TBE)
- developmental bilingual education (DBE)
- dual language programs
- bilingual immersion programs
- heritage language programs
- pull-out ESL
- sheltered English immersion (SEI)
- newcomer programs
- submersion

GUIDING QUESTIONS

1. What are the essential components of any instructional program for English language learners?
2. What is the difference between ESL and sheltered instruction?
3. What are the pros and cons of each of the English-medium and bilingual education program models that we find in the field today?
4. How can educators determine what type of program is appropriate for their context?

Language and education policies for ELLs are realized at the classroom level through a variety of instructional programs. As we saw in the Chapter 3, federal policy holds states accountable for the academic achievement and English language proficiency development of ELLs and grants each state the flexibility to identify what program models are eligible for funding. Some states have mandates for bilingual education; a few have passed laws placing restrictions on bilingual education. Educators who work with ELLs determine what instructional programs are appropriate for their school. Their decisions are based on their consideration of federal and state policies, the research base, and the characteristics of their students and community.

We begin this chapter with a discussion of the essential components of ELL programs, as well as English as a second language and content-area instruction, and the differences between the two. We then examine the relationship between

English as a second language and English language arts. Finally, we take a close look at the different program models for ELLs.

Essential Components of Instructional Programs for ELLs

All effective instructional programs for ELLs have three essential components: English as a second language instruction, content-area instruction, and primary language support (see Table 4.1). We discuss primary language support in Chapter 10.

ESL Instruction

English language instruction for students who have been identified as ELLs is called English as a second language (ESL). Along the East Coast and elsewhere, the term *English for speakers of other languages* (ESOL) is often used. Because there are many students for whom English is a third, fourth, or even higher-number language, it is a more accurate label. In California and other states ESL—particularly at the elementary school level—is frequently referred to as English language development (ELD). Since these terms are essentially synonymous, for the sake of simplicity, we use the more common term, ESL, from here on.[1] The purpose of ESL programs is to enable ELL students to master the skills of listening, speaking, reading, and writing in English to the extent that they are able to use the English language appropriately and effectively for authentic communicative purposes and to achieve academic success in English-language mainstream classrooms.

ESL is a separate content-area, just like math, science, social studies, and language arts. It has its own set of content standards (the English language proficiency standards mandated by Title III as described in Chapter 3), its own set of curricular materials, and its own separate time slot within the daily teaching schedule.

Many schools that provide daily ESL instruction for ELLs typically do so only for students at the beginning stages of English proficiency and stop once the students reach the intermediate level. This approach is a mistake based on the false assumption that these ELL students no longer need ESL because they can develop fluency in English by working with content-area teachers who are trained to help ELLs learn the content area while supporting their English language development. Data collected for the State of California to study the impact of Proposition 227 show that ELL students move up to the intermediate levels within 2 to 3 years but then most get stuck at the intermediate and advanced levels, often for several years (American Institutes for Research & WestEd, 2006; Hill, 2006). These studies reveal that ELLs at the intermediate and advanced levels need high quality ESL instruction in order to reach the "fluent" level.

ESL instruction at the intermediate and advanced levels should provide more emphasis on increasing vocabulary and developing skills in advanced literacy. Many teachers report that ELLs at these higher levels have good listening and speaking skills (often described as "native-like"), and sound fluent when they read text aloud. The problem is often that ELLs do not fully comprehend what they read because they lack higher-level vocabulary, knowledge of more complex sentence structures, understanding of the more subtle uses of languages, and enough back-

---

1: Some educators consider ELD a broader concept than ESL, because, traditionally, ESL tended to focus on oral language development, whereas ELD includes a strong focus on English literacy development. Now, however, ESL also includes this literacy focus.

Table 4.1   Essential Components of Effective Programs for ELL Students

Standards-based ESL		Standards-based content-area instruction		Primary language support
Pull-out ESL	In-class ESL	Native language instruction	Sheltered instruction	
A teacher trained and certified to work with ELLs pulls students out of the regular classroom for ESL instruction.	The classroom teacher is trained and certified to work with ELLs and provides ESL instruction within the classroom.	One or more content areas are taught in students' native languages.	One or more content areas are taught in English using sheltered instruction strategies and techniques.	The classroom teacher employs a variety of strategies and techniques involving the effective use of students' native languages to increase their comprehension of English during ESL and sheltered content instruction.

ground knowledge to understand cultural references in the text. These same issues can lead to difficulties for students when writing in English. ESL at the intermediate and advanced levels focuses on these areas.

ESL instruction is usually delivered in one of two ways—through a pull-out program or in class by the regular classroom teacher. These methods are discussed later under "English-Medium Program Models."

Content-Area Instruction

Comprehensible content-area instruction is the second essential component of every program for ELLs. The most effective way to make content comprehensible to ELLs is to teach it in the students' native languages. When native language instruction is not possible, teachers use sheltered instruction.

Native Language (L1) Content-Area Instruction

Learning new concepts and skills can be difficult, and it's even harder in a language you don't know or don't know very well. Students learn best in the language they understand best. Thus, providing ELLs with content-area instruction in their native or first language (L1) while they are learning English (their second language or L2) helps to ensure that they will learn complex academic content and master grade-level content standards. It also ensures that they won't fall farther behind their English proficient peers in those academic subjects (Wiley, 2005a).

The same principle applies to native language literacy instruction. It is much easier for students to learn to read and write in the language they know best. Students need to learn how to read only once. Many of the skills students develop when they are learning how to read and write in their native language easily transfer to English. This ease of transfer is true for all written languages, even those that do not use the same script (letters, alphabet) as English (Pu, 2008). Native language (L1) instruction is the distinguishing feature of the bilingual education models described in this chapter.

Providing effective content-area instruction in ELL students' native language requires having a certified bilingual teacher who is fully proficient in English and that native language. It also requires having appropriate curricular materials in the students' native language. Native language content-area instruction follows the content standards established for native English speakers, with the exception that some states, such as Texas and the 19 states (plus the District of Columbia) in the WIDA (World-class Instructional Design and Assessment) consortium, have adopted separate Spanish language arts standards aligned with the English language arts standards. Spanish language arts standards reflect unique aspects of reading and writing instruction in Spanish.

As we see in our discussion of bilingual education program models, the amount of native language instruction is reduced gradually as students learn more English.

Sheltered Instruction

Sheltered instruction refers to grade-level content-area instruction that is provided in English but in a manner that makes it comprehensible to ELL students while promoting their English language development (Echevarria, 2007). The word *sheltered* is a metaphor for simplifying the language without watering down the content, while protecting ELLs from the language demands of mainstream instruction that may be beyond their comprehension. In California, sheltered instruction is called specially designed academic instruction in English (SDAIE), and this term is now commonly used in other states.

I prefer the term *SDAIE* because it emphasizes that the instruction is different from regular instruction in English but it is on grade level and appropriately challenging. *SDAIE* has a positive connotation, suggesting that ELLs can and will learn academic content in English if the instruction is designed especially for them. But because the term *sheltered instruction* is widely used and recognized, I use this term from here on.

The Sheltered Instruction Observation Protocol (SIOP) model offers guidance to teachers who use sheltered instruction by helping them systematically plan, teach, observe, and evaluate effective instruction for ELLs. The model was developed by Jana Echevarria, MaryEllen Vogt, and Deborah J. Short (2007), who recognized the importance of sheltered English instruction but were concerned that teachers lacked a clear understanding of how to provide it consistently and effectively. The SIOP model identifies eight key components of effective sheltered instruction: *preparation, building background, comprehensible input, strategies, interaction, practice and application, lesson delivery,* and *review and assessment.* Thirty items are organized into these eight components. The SIOP model is field-tested, and experimental research demonstrates its validity and reliability as an observation protocol, as well as its effectiveness as a pedagogical approach (Guarino, Echevarria, Short, Schick, Forbes, & Rueda, 2001).

The items under *preparation* include having clear language and content-area objectives, appropriate content concepts, and plans for introducing meaningful activities and using supplementary materials. *Building background* items include building on students' prior knowledge and teaching key vocabulary. *Comprehensible input* items include providing clear explanations of academic tasks and teachers' adjusting their speech (vocabulary, pace, sentence complexity, etc.) to an appropriate level for their students. *Strategies* include using scaffolding, promoting higher order thinking skills, and teaching learning strategies. *Interaction* items include using wait time effectively, grouping students, and using primary language support to maximize students' ability to interact with the teacher and each other. *Practice and application* items include hands-on, cooperative learning activities that integrate the four language skills (listening, speaking, reading, and writing) and allow students to apply their content and language knowledge. *Lesson delivery* items include meeting stated language and content-area objectives, pacing the lesson appropriately, and ensuring that students are engaged in the lesson. The *review and assessment* items include reviewing vocabulary and key concepts, providing feedback, and conducting assessments of students' learning.

The SIOP model has become very popular, and school districts and schools are encouraging their teachers and administrators to receive SIOP training through professional development workshops.[2] Many of these districts and schools, however, have the false impression that SIOP training alone is sufficient to prepare teachers to work effectively with ELL students. SIOP training in isolation is not enough. Professional development in second language acquisition and ESL teaching methods, as well as an understanding of the sociocultural, historical, economic, and political factors that can affect students' English language acquisition and academic content learning, provides the foundation for effective sheltered instruction in the classroom. Educators also need to understand how sheltered instruction fits into their overall instructional program for ELLs, whether bilingual or English-medium.

A key feature of the SIOP model is its inclusion of language objectives within the context of content-area instruction in English. For example, the content objectives of a SIOP math lesson plan for teaching long division would include the math standards for long division, as well as language objectives for learning the vocabulary associated with long division and the language needed for talking about and completing long division problems. Note, however, that this combination of language objectives with content objectives does not eliminate the need for separate ESL instruction. Echevarria, one of the creators of the SIOP model, emphasizes that ELLs need ESL instruction in addition to sheltered instruction (Echevarria & Graves, 2007). Sheltered instruction was originally designed for English learners with at least intermediate proficiency and basic literacy skills; however, due to a nationwide shortage of bilingual teachers, the scarcity of bilingual programs in languages other than Spanish, and policies in some states that discourage bilingual education, many teachers are forced to provide sheltered content instruction to ELLs before they are really ready for it.

Echevarria and Graves (2007) list the subject areas where sheltered content-area instruction would be appropriate for ELLs at each of the five levels of English language proficiency (preproduction, early production, speech emergence, intermediate, and advanced) (see Table 4.2). At the preproduction (non-English-speaking) level, they suggest that ELL students are not ready for sheltered content-area instruction in any subject other than, perhaps, art, music, and physical education. The best teachers can do is to provide ESL instruction that "focuses on developing English while providing a link between the content areas and their associated English vocabulary, oral and written language functions, and structures" (p. 18). This suggestion is more consistent with the original concept of content-based ESL than with sheltered instruction, because the focus at this level is on teaching English rather than the content. If ELLs received sheltered instruction in art, music, and physical education, activities would be limited to those that students could complete by watching and imitating their teacher and peers. Music at this level would really be more like ESL and would provide a good way to help students learn new vocabulary. But the deeper levels of these important content areas, such as the fundamentals of art and music and the principles of health and fitness, would not be accessible to ELLs at the preproduction level.

2: See www.cal.org/siop for more information.

Table 4.2	Appropriate Subjects for Sheltered Instruction/SDAIE for ELL Students at Different Levels of English Language Proficiency
Language proficiency level	**Appropriate subjects and instruction**
Preproduction (non-English-speaking)	"Students are not ready for sheltered instruction" • May be possible to include students in art, music, and physical education using sheltered English strategies • At this stage, content-based ESL is more appropriate (i.e., content areas are used as topics of instruction, but the focus is on English language development)
Early production	"Subjects where context clues facilitate understanding" • Math computation and problem solving • Science labs
Speech emergence	Subjects that have a "contextual nature" and that are "more visual and hands-on" • Science • Math
Intermediate	• English language arts • Social studies • All other content areas
Advanced	• Instruction focused on "refining and developing advanced uses of academic English" • Explicit instruction in learning strategies

Source: Based on Echevarria and Graves, 2007, pp. 18–19.

At the next level of English proficiency, early production, Echevarria and Graves note, "sheltered instruction is used in subjects where context clues facilitate understanding," such as math computation and problem solving and science labs. At the third level of English proficiency, speech emergence, they suggest that ELLs are ready for sheltered instruction in science and math, because these subjects are more visual and hands-on than English language arts and social studies, which are more abstract. Only at the intermediate level of English language proficiency do Echevarria and Graves suggest that ELLs be introduced to sheltered language arts programs, that is, grade-level reading and writing instruction in English and sheltered social studies instruction.

Once ELLs reach the advanced level of English language proficiency, they may be able to handle some mainstream content-area instruction. But as Echevarria and Graves (2007) note, "it is not uncommon for students to be at the intermediate or advanced fluency levels while having significant gaps in their academic ability" (p. 19). Thus, sheltered instruction should continue for ELLs at the advanced level, with a specific focus on "refining and developing advanced uses of Academic English" and providing explicit instruction in learning strategies (p. 19).

The Difference between ESL and Sheltered Instruction

There is much confusion among educators about the difference between ESL and sheltered instruction. Many believe they are the same thing. They are not, and it is imperative that educators understand the difference. The focus of ESL is teaching English; the focus of sheltered instruction is teaching academic content. (See Table 4.3.)

Table 4.3	**Difference between ESL and Sheltered Instruction**	
	ESL Instruction	**Sheltered Instruction**
Definition	Teaching English to students who are not yet proficient in the language.	Making content area instruction comprehensible to ELLs in English while supporting their English language development.
Concepts or areas of focus	Listening, speaking, reading, writing vocabulary, communicative competence.	Language arts, math, science, social studies, art, music, physical education, and other content areas.
Standards	State English language proficiency standards.	State content-area standards.
Goal	Communicative competence for social and academic purposes.	Content-area knowledge and skills.
Assessment	State English language proficiency tests.	State academic achievement tests.
	Classroom-based formative and summative English language proficiency assessments.	Classroom-based formative and and summative content-area assessments.

To illustrate the difference between sheltered instruction and ESL, let us return to the earlier example of teaching long division. Both the sheltered instruction lesson and the ESL lesson include content and language objectives, as the SIOP requires, but the two objectives are weighted differently. The primary instructional and assessment goals of the sheltered instruction lesson involve content. The instructional goal is for ELLs to understand the concept of long division and to be able to solve long division problems on their own. While addressing the same math standards for all students, the math instruction and assessments are differentiated for ELLs based on their English language proficiency level. The teacher teaches the language of math (vocabulary, listening, speaking, reading, writing) so that ELLs can participate and achieve in the content-area instruction, but content learning is the major concern. In contrast, during the ESL lesson, math may be the topic, but the primary instructional and assessment goals are language. The ESL instruction would focus on helping ELLs learn and use specific math vocabulary correctly and appropriately, verbally explain in English the steps and procedures involved in solving a long division problem, and read and comprehend long division problems. The ESL teacher uses the math lesson as a vehicle to teach language, and language learning is the primary concern. If students are struggling with math concepts and skills, they can learn the language they need in ESL to be able to explain to their math teachers what they don't understand.

The overlap in content and language suggests points of collaboration for sheltered instruction and ESL teachers. For example, the sheltered instruction teacher can identify the ways that reading, writing, listening, and speaking are used for academic purposes in the specific content area, and the ESL teacher can provide more focused ESL instruction in these academic language functions across content areas. If the classroom teacher is responsible for teaching both ESL and the content areas, he or she is in an excellent position to ensure that ESL instruction provides the support needed for the ELLs to be successful in sheltered content lessons.

Again, the inclusion of language objectives alongside content objectives in sheltered instruction is an important and effective way to help students develop proficiency in English while they are learning content. These language objectives are not, however, a substitute for ESL instruction. Language learned in ESL lessons supports student learning in sheltered content instruction and lays the foundation for further language acquisition to take place through the language objectives of the sheltered content lessons. Simply stated, sheltered content instruction *supplements* but does not *supplant* effective, systematic, and direct ESL instruction for ELL students. Effective programs for ELLs include both ESL and sheltered instruction.

A Note on ESL and Language Arts

There is often some confusion about the relationship between ESL and English language arts. Providing language arts instruction to ELLs in English is not the same as teaching ESL. Even if the language arts instruction is provided using sheltered instruction strategies, it cannot substitute for ESL instruction. Recall from Chapter 3 that NCLB requires states to have English language proficiency standards as well as language arts standards. These content standards are to be aligned but nonetheless are separate. As Rosa Castro Feinberg (2002) points out, ELLs are learning English language skills that their English-speaking peers have already developed and these skills are prerequisite to learning in other areas of the curriculum. Native speakers, in contrast, are refining skills in a language they already know. English language arts instruction is designed for students who are native speakers of English. Few high school English teachers would describe themselves as language specialists. To them, English is a subject to be mastered, not a language to be learned. ESL teachers are more like foreign language teachers, who teach a language and culture that is not native to their students.

Language arts instruction in the United States focuses on teaching reading and writing. Regular classroom teachers spend little time, if any, on oral language skills because native English speakers are already proficient listeners and speakers of the language. Indeed, native English-speaking students who have trouble with listening or speaking in English are usually referred to special education. While native English speakers will expand their vocabulary through language arts instruction, ELLs need assistance to develop basic vocabulary, in addition to the new vocabulary their English proficient peers are learning.

Unfortunately, efforts are being made in some states to combine English language arts instruction and ESL instruction. Some textbook companies are producing language arts series that include peripheral suggestions in the teachers' guides for meeting the needs of ELLs during the language arts lessons. They sometimes also include additional materials for ELLs to use during the lessons or to supplement the lessons. These materials are welcome additions insofar as they may help teachers shelter their language arts instruction for ELLs. But they must not replace direct ESL instruction. A better approach, which other textbook companies have taken, is to provide a comprehensive ESL program combined with a separate but correlated sheltered language arts programs.

Program Models for ELLs

The many different program models currently in use for ELL students can be classified as either bilingual or English-medium. A bilingual program is defined here as any program in which there is some content-area instruction in the students' native languages. An English-medium program—which may (and should) provide primary language support—provides all content-area instruction in English.

One major problem we face in the field of language education is inconsistency in how programs for ELLs are labeled, in the literature and in practice. This brief review of prototypical program models for ELLs uses the following guiding questions to clarify terms here:

1. Who are the target populations?
2. What are the goals of the program?
3. How is the program structured?
4. What does the research say about the effectiveness of the program?

Using consistent terms allows us to compare different program types to determine which are the most effective for ELLs and which are the most appropriate for a particular school and community.

Bilingual Models

The following sections examine five bilingual models found in the field today: transitional bilingual education programs, developmental bilingual education programs, dual language programs, bilingual immersion programs, and heritage language programs.

Transitional Bilingual Education Programs

Transitional bilingual education (TBE) programs, also called early-exit programs, are the most common type of bilingual program in the United States. TBE programs target ELLs who speak the same L1, and they are usually found in the primary grades of elementary school. The goal of TBE programs is to transition ELLs to a mainstream English-only classroom as quickly as possible. By providing content-area instruction in the students' native languages, schools can ensure that students do not fall behind academically while they are learning English.

Most TBE programs begin in kindergarten. Through these programs ELLs learn about 90% of their language arts and other content areas in their native language and about 10% through sheltered instruction. Students also receive daily ESL instruction. Each year the amount of native language instruction is decreased and the amount of sheltered instruction is increased. Students first learn to read and write in their L1, which ensures that they do not fall behind academically while learning English. After 2 to 3 years, the students are transitioned to English language arts instruction, and the following year they are placed in mainstream English-only classrooms (see Figure 4.1). Some weaker versions of this model at-

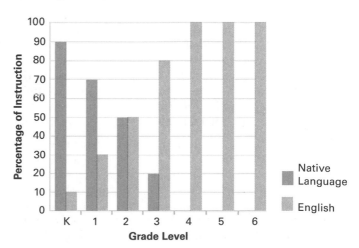

Figure 4.1
Transitional bilingual education model

Table 4.4	Content-area and ESL Instruction in Transitional Bilingual Education Programs			
	Kindergarten	**1st grade**	**2nd grade**	**3rd grade**
Native language instruction	Language arts, social studies, science, math	Language arts, social studies, science	Language arts, social studies	Language arts
Sheltered instruction	Art, music, PE	Math, art, music, PE	Science, math, art, music, PE	Language arts, social studies, science, math, art, music, PE
ESL (daily)	30–60 minutes	30–60 minutes	30–60 minutes	30–60 minutes

tempt to transition students to all-English instruction much sooner. Table 4.4 presents a sample of the subjects that a school might offer in kindergarten through 3rd grade, gradually transitioning from mostly native-language instruction to mostly sheltered instruction.

Longitudinal research on the effectiveness of different types of bilingual and English-medium programs demonstrates that TBE programs are more effective than English-medium programs, but they are less effective than other bilingual education models in ensuring that ELLs reach parity with their English-speaking peers by the time they complete the program (Ramirez, Yuen, Ramey, & Pasta, 1991; Thomas & Collier, 2002).

Researchers and practitioners have identified the following challenges associated with TBE:

- TBE programs tend to have a "language-as-problem" orientation and thus take a deficit view of ELL students. Also, because the goal of TBE programs is quick transition to English, these programs tend to lead to subtractive bilingualism. Many researchers and practitioners see the TBE model as essentially a remedial program (see, e.g., Crawford, 2004; Gonzalez, Yawkey, & Minaya-Rowe, 2006).
- TBE programs reflect an assumption that ELLs can become proficient in English in 2 to 3 years and thus be ready for all-English instruction in a mainstream classroom. However, as we saw in Chapter 1, few students learn a second language fluently that quickly. Thus, many ELLs are pushed into mainstream classrooms before they are ready.
- ELLs in TBE programs may be segregated from the academic mainstream for most or all of their instructional day, making it difficult for them to find opportunities to interact with and learn alongside English proficient peers.
- Many ELLs do not begin school in the United States in kindergarten. They start in the grade level that matches their age at their time of arrival. Since most TBE programs are in the elementary grades, there may not be a TBE program available for many ELLs who need it.

Despite these concerns, TBE programs have been the most common form of bilingual program mainly because this model has received the greatest amount of governmental support and encouragement since the passage of the Bilingual Education Act of 1968. Also, the TBE approach is still much preferred over English-only models. Offering students, particularly young children, an opportunity to develop literacy skills and academic content in their native language while they are learning and developing proficiency in English is much more humane than simply

Box 4.1

ELL Program Profile

Transitional Bilingual Education (TBE)

Other name . . . . Early-exit bilingual education.

Target population . . . . ELLs who speak the same L1.

Typical grade span . . . . K–3.

Language goals . . . . Learn English as quickly as possible to transition to academic mainstream.

Academic goals . . . . Meet the same grade-level content-area standards as English-fluent peers and enter an English-only mainstream classroom as soon as possible.

Culture goals. . . . . Acculturation to mainstream school and community; assimilation common.

ESL instruction . . . . 30–60 minutes a day.

Content-area instruction . . . . . . Initially about 90% in L1 and 10% through sheltered English instruction. L1 instruction decreases rapidly as students are quickly transitioned to sheltered instruction as they move up in grade level. (See Figure 4.1.)

Primary language support . . . . Provided during sheltered instruction and ESL instruction as needed.

Effectiveness research . . . . TBE programs are more effective than English-only programs but are less effective than other models of bilingual education in ensuring that ELLs achieve parity with their English-speaking peers.

throwing them into an English-only classroom where they may become frustrated and discouraged. Schools that have established effective TBE programs are often able to evolve to one of the stronger models of bilingual education described in the following sections. Box 4.1 provides an overview of the TBE model.

Developmental Bilingual Education Programs

Developmental bilingual education (DBE), is also sometimes called maintenance or late-exit bilingual education. DBE programs are much less common than TBE programs in the United States in large part because of the lack of federal support over the years for this model. Like TBE programs, DBE programs target ELL students who speak the same L1, they are most often found in elementary schools, and they are taught by qualified bilingual teachers. However, the goals of DBE programs are different. DBE programs aim to help the students develop both English and their native language, so that they become fully bilingual and biliterate, achieving academically through both languages and developing a positive sense of their cultural heritage and ethnolinguistic identities.

Most DBE programs begin in kindergarten and continue through the highest grade level in the school, which might be 5th or 6th grade. Some DBE programs in K–8 schools last through the middle-school grades. As in TBE programs, ELLs initially receive about 90% of their content-area instruction, including initial literacy instruction, in their native language. Sheltered instruction increases with each grade level until students receive an equal balance of instruction in both languages. Figure 4.2 shows the relationship between the native language and English instruction in DBE programs.

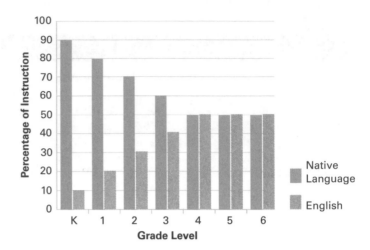

Figure 4.2
Developmental bilingual education model

Because of its emphasis on bilingualism and biliteracy, DBE is a much stronger model for ELL students. In this model the native language of the ELLs is viewed as a resource, used for instructional purposes, and further developed even after ELL students have attained sufficient proficiency in English to handle mainstream instruction. Because a DBE program could constitute half or more of a child's education and in such a program students have the opportunity to develop their native language skills to a higher level than in a TBE program, they are much more likely to be proficient bilinguals by the time they graduate from high school. Wayne Thomas and Virginia Collier's (2002) longitudinal research shows that ELLs who graduate from well-implemented DBE programs eventually achieve educational parity with their English-speaking counterparts. DBE programs are empowering to the parents who lack proficiency in English, because they are able to be much more involved in their child's education, including being able to help their children with their reading and other homework.

Currently, many schools with DBE programs are facing political pressure to push English literacy earlier and faster, particularly in states where high-stakes tests are administered only in English (Wright, 2007). Many school and district administrators worry that if extensive English literacy and content instruction in English is delayed to the later elementary grades, students will not have the English skills necessary to pass the test. This is not a flaw in the DBE models but a flaw in the testing and accountability systems that do not value and fail to accommodate high quality education programs for ELLs. Box 4.2 provides an overview of the DBE model.

Dual Language Programs

Dual language programs, sometimes called two-way immersion or dual language immersion, are designed for even numbers of English speakers and ELLs from the same language background. These programs aim to develop the following for both groups of students: bilingualism and biliteracy, academic achievement in two languages, and cross-cultural understanding. Dual language programs typically begin in kindergarten (or pre-K) and continue through the elementary school grades, though a growing number of these programs can also be found in middle schools and high schools.

English speakers and ELLs in dual language programs spend most of the day together in the same classroom, where they receive content-area instruction in both languages from qualified bilingual teachers. Content-area instruction is taught in sheltered English and in a sheltered version of the other language, such as

Box 4.2

ELL Program Profile

Developmental Bilingual Education (DBE)

Other names	Maintenance bilingual education; late-exit bilingual education.
Target population	ELLs who speak the same L1.
Typical grade span	K-6
Language goals	Bilingualism and biliteracy.
Academic goals	Meet the same grade-level content-area standards as English-fluent peers. Be prepared to fulfill societal needs requiring citizens with bilingual skills.
Culture goals	Biculturalism.
ESL instruction	30–60 minutes a day.
Content-area instruction	Initially about 90% in L1 and 10% though sheltered instruction. L1 instruction decreases slowly as sheltered instruction increases as students move up in grade level. Instruction continues in both languages until the end of program, even after students attain proficiency in English. (See Figure 4.2.)
Primary language support	Provided during sheltered instruction and ESL instruction as needed.
Effectiveness research	ELLs achieve parity with English-speaking peers and become bilingual, biliterate, and bicultural.

Spanish, to make instruction comprehensible for the non-native speakers of those languages. Students learn to read and write in both languages, either simultaneously or first in one language and later in the other. Teachers also provide daily ESL instruction for their ELLs, and instruction in the other language for the native English-speaking students (e.g., Spanish as a second language).

The two prototypical dual language models are the 50/50 model and the 90/10 model, referring to the percentage of time allocated to each language for instructional purposes. Thus, in the 50/50 model, 50% of the instruction is in the native language of the ELLs and 50% is in English (see Figure 4.3). In the 90/10 model, 90% of instruction is in the native language of the ELL students for the first few years and 10% is in English. As students move up in grade level, the amount of instruction in each language balances out to 50/50 (see Figure 4.4). Some schools prefer an 80/20 or 70/30 model, which operate on the same principles but include more English at the beginning. For ELLs, the program functions as a developmental bilingual model and for the English speakers, the program functions as a bilingual immersion model (discussed in the next section). The researchers and practitioners who developed the idea of dual language programs advocated a rigid separation of the two languages for instructional purposes. This practice has received more and more criticism, however, because it does not reflect how languages are used in real life, it does not take advantage of the two linguistic systems for social or academic purposes, and it does not affirm students' identities (Sayer, 2008).

Dual language programs vary considerably in the amount of time spent for instruction in each language, which language is used for initial literacy instruction, and which subjects are taught in which languages. Most dual language programs in the United States are for Spanish and English speakers, but there are also pro-

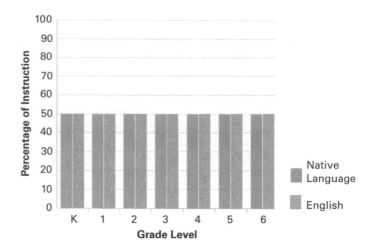

Figure 4.3
Traditional 50/50 dual language model (or two-way immersion)

grams for speakers of Vietnamese, Russian, French, Mandarin Chinese, Korean, Navajo, Arabic, Japanese, and Portuguese. The Center for Applied Linguistics maintains a searchable directory of two-way immersion programs in the United States (www.cal.org/twi/directory) that provides details of the programs it lists.

What is exciting about the dual language model is that theoretically it puts the ELL students on an equal footing with the English-only students. When instruction is in the non-English language, the English-speaking students must rely on their ELL peers, just as the ELLs must rely on the English-speaking students when instruction is in English. The ELLs' native language is viewed as a resource to help them learn English and academic content; it is also a resource for the native English speakers learning the native language of their ELL peers. Dual language programs have successfully moved bilingual education from the realm of remedial education into the realm of enrichment education (Perez, 2004). Comparative longitudinal research demonstrates that dual language programs are the most effective programs for ELLs and English speakers.[3]

Dual language models have grown in popularity with increases in federal support and the growing demand of ELLs parents and parents of monolingual English speakers who want their children to be bilingual. As of January 2010, the CAL directory listed 356 programs in 28 states and the District of Columbia.

Student and community demographics have led to innovative variations in dual language programs. Whereas the original dual language model seeks classroom compositions of equal numbers of ELL and native English speakers, Bertha Perez (2004) notes, for example, that in more and more communities the English speakers are heritage language speakers who have some proficiency in their home language. In other words, a dual language classroom may comprise all Latino students, half of whom are ELLs and half of whom are proficient English speakers with varying levels of proficiency in Spanish.[4] Leo Gómez, David E. Freeman, and Yvonne S. Freeman (2005) describe a dual language model designed for schools in regions where the majority of the students are Latino (e.g., South Texas), which follows a unique 50–50 model that divides language of instruction by content area as well as by time. In this model there does not need to be an equal distribution of

---

3: For examples of this research, see Collier, 1995; Freeman, 1996, 1998; Lindholm-Leary, 2001; Lindholm-Leary & Fairchild, 1990; Perez, 2004; Ramirez, 1992; Ramirez et al., 1991; Thomas & Collier, 2002.

4: For English-dominant Latino students in dual language programs, the program functions more like a heritage language program.

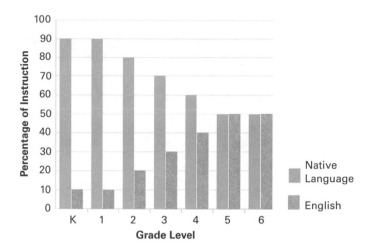

Figure 4.4
90/10 dual language model
(or two-way immersion)

ELLs and English dominant students. Educators who want to develop dual language programs in their school and community contexts need to begin with a clear understanding of their target populations and design their program accordingly.

Scholars have identified several issues and challenges related to dual language programs.[5] Whereas Spanish programs are relatively easy to develop because of the large number of Latino ELLs and the availability of Spanish bilingual teachers and materials, it can be quite difficult to develop programs in other languages where there are fewer students, and teachers and materials are in short supply. Also, while native English speakers may be interested in learning high-demand languages such as Spanish, Chinese, Japanese, and Arabic, there may be little interest for languages such as Vietnamese, Khmer, or Haitian Creole.[6] Another major issue is the fact that English is the dominant language of the United States. This makes it very difficult to value both languages equally within a dual language program and school. English, and proficient speakers of English, will always be more privileged. Research by Ester de Jong and Elizabeth Howard (2009) shows that dual language educators must carefully address this issue to ensure that ELL students attain the linguistic, academic, and cross-cultural benefits that dual language programs claim to offer. Guadalupe Valdés (1997) notes that dual language educators need to be careful not to address the interests of more vocal middle-class English-speaking constituents over less vocal minority constituents in placement or instruction. Valdés also warns that if dual language educators fail to consider language and power relations among target populations (e.g., English speakers and Spanish speakers) at school and in the community, ELLs may be exploited for the language resource that they provide for White English speakers without actually gaining access to equal educational opportunities at school or job opportunities in society.

Despite these challenges, scholars have acknowledged the potential of dual language programs to encourage friendships and cross-cultural understanding between the English-speaking students and the minority-language students, as well as among their families.[7] Perhaps these graduates of dual language programs will be at the forefront of resolving many of the social inequities our past genera-

---

5: See C. Baker, 2006; Diaz-Rico & Weed, 2006; Freeman, 1998; Oller & Eilers, 2002; Palmer & Lynch, 2008; Valdés, 1997.

6: This problem can be overcome in programs that follow the model in which all students are from the same language background, but half are ELLs and half are English dominant.

7: See Genesee & Gandara, 1999; Gómez, Freeman, & Freeman, 2005; Lindholm-Leary, 1994.

Box 4.3

ELL Program Profile

Dual Language Programs

Other names	Two-way immersion; dual language immersion.
Target population	ELLs who speak the same L1 and English speakers who want to learn the L1 of the ELLs.
Typical grade span	K-6
Language goals	Bilingualism and biliteracy.
Academic goals	Meet grade-level content-area standards. Be prepared to fulfill societal needs requiring citizens with bilingual skills.
Culture goals	Biculturalism, cross-cultural understanding, cultural pluralism.
Content-area instruction	50/50 model: 50% in L1 of ELLs and 50% in English. (See Figure 4.3) 90/10 model: initially 90% in L1 of ELLs and 10% in English. Instruction evens out gradually to 50/50 as students move up in grade level. (See Figure 4.4.)
Primary language support	May be provided for ELLs during English instruction or English-speakers during instruction in the L1 of the ELLs, though dual language programs make efforts to separate the languages of instruction as much as possible.
Effectiveness research	English speakers and ELLs reach or exceed grade-level expectations and become bilingual and biliterate with strong cross-cultural communication skills.

tions have failed to solve. Box 4.3 provides an overview of the dual language program model.

Bilingual Immersion Programs

Bilingual immersion programs in the United States (not to be confused with English immersion), target English-speaking students exclusively. The goals are for English speakers to become bilingual and biliterate, to achieve academically in both languages, and to develop cross-cultural understanding. This model was developed in Canada, where native English speakers are immersed for content-area instruction in French, and extensive research demonstrates the effectiveness of these programs (Genesee, 1995). In the United States, the bilingual immersion model is commonly implemented with Hawaiian and Native American students to help them learn their "native" language, which they may or may not have learned at home (see Figure 4.5). Because indigenous languages in the United States are threatened with extinction, educators working with students from these language groups view bilingual immersion programs as a key component for helping to preserve these indigenous languages by passing them down to the next generation.

Bilingual immersion instruction begins in the non-English language, which is typically the language in which the students have the least amount of proficiency. Some programs provide up to 100% of instruction in the non-English language for the first year or two of the program. As the students increase their proficiency in the non-English language, English is slowly introduced and eventually both languages

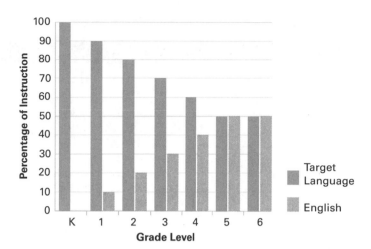

Figure 4.5
Bilingual immersion model

are given an equal amount of instructional time. Bilingual immersion programs are most commonly found in elementary schools and last for several years, usually up to 5th or 6th grade. (See Figure 4.5.) Box 4.4 provides an overview of the bilingual immersion model.

Heritage Language Programs

The term heritage language programs is fairly new in the United States and refers to a wide range of programs (including the bilingual models described earlier), such as in-school and after-school or weekend programs, in which language minority students have an opportunity to learn their "native" or "heritage" language. A heritage language student can be either an ELL or a student who is proficient in English and may have little or no proficiency in his or her heritage language, as is common for second and third generation immigrant students (Valdés, 2001). The term is also being applied to university-level foreign language classes geared to heritage speakers of the language being taught.

In-school heritage language programs are those that offer foreign language classes at the secondary school level geared to native speakers. These courses are called Spanish-for-Spanish speakers, Korean-for-Korean speakers, Arabic-for-Arabic speakers, and so forth. Educators have found that courses like these are particularly effective because ELLs typically need foreign language credit to graduate from high school or to get into colleges and universities with foreign language study requirements. Students who take these courses tend to be highly motivated by opportunities to develop greater proficiency and literacy abilities in their native languages, particularly because the vast majority have lost some proficiency in their own language because of English-only education programs.

These foreign language courses for heritage language speakers are much more appropriate and effective than the regular foreign language classes. The foreign language classes that target native English speakers teach, in Spanish classes for example, the standard Spanish dialect, which may differ substantially from the variety of Spanish spoken by the native Spanish-speaking ELL students. A good heritage language class recognizes and builds on the strengths of heritage language speakers by recognizing that these students may already have some vocabulary as well as listening, speaking, and perhaps literacy skills in the language. The courses can also be designed to recognize and value the variety of the native language spo-

Box 4.4

ELL Program Profile

Bilingual Immersion

Other name.................	Immersion program
Target population............	Language minority students (ELL and/or non-ELL) who have little to no proficiency in their L1 (e.g., Native American students, Hawaiian students); native-English speakers who want to learn a world language.
Typical grade span..........	K–6 (some programs may extend up to 8th grade).
Academic goals	Meet grade-level expectations. Be prepared to fulfill societal needs requiring citizens with bilingual skills.
Culture goals................	Biculturalism, cross-cultural understanding and communication skills.
ESL instruction	30–60 minutes a day (only if program includes ELL students).
Content-area instruction	Initially 90% to 100% in the non-English language for the first year or two of the program. Instruction evens out gradually to 50% instruction in English and 50% in the non-English language as students move up in grade level. (See Figure 4.5.)
Primary language support	May be provided as needed, though bilingual immersion programs make strong efforts to separate the languages of instruction as much as possible.
Effectiveness research	Language minority students and language majority students reach or exceed grade-level expectations and become bilingual, biliterate, and cross-culturally competent.

ken by the students, while helping them to develop proficiency in a standard dialect of the language.

Schools that have transitional bilingual programs are well-positioned to offer heritage language programs for former ELLs who have exited the bilingual program. Learning in a heritage language program (e.g., Spanish for Spanish speakers) gives these students opportunities to maintain and develop their L1 after they enter mainstream English instruction and helps counter the trend toward subtractive bilingualism we see in most TBE programs.

Many after-school and weekend heritage language programs are operated by community-based organizations within language minority communities, such as Chinese and Korean schools run on the weekends by Chinese American and Korean American organizations, temples, and churches. However, some public schools provide heritage language classes after school. This trend has been particularly important in California and Arizona because of legislated restrictions on bilingual programs during the school day. In Fresno, California, for example, the school district, in cooperation with local community organizations, offers the Khmer Emerging Education Program (Project KEEP), 2 days a week at one of its elementary schools (Olsen, 2001). The district has collected data showing that Khmer American students who participate in the program do better academically in their regular classes than their peers who do not participate (Multilingual/Multicultural Office, 2001). Because of this success, the district has expanded its after-

Box 4.5

ELL Program Profile

Heritage Language Programs

Other names . . . . Community language programs; foreign language programs for native speakers (e.g., Spanish-for-Spanish
speakers).

Target population . . . . Heritage language speakers (ELL or non-ELL) who have
varying levels of proficiency in their heritage language.

Typical grade span . . . . Any grade levels, pre-K–12, and college/university.

Language goals. . . . . Broaden linguistic repertoire in heritage language, with
attention to the standard variety and literacy in that lan-
guage.

Academic goals. . . . . Meet the grade-level content-area standards related to
foreign language learning or native language arts stan-
dards. Be prepared to fulfill societal needs requiring citizens with bilingual skills.

Culture goals . . . . Biculturalism, cross-cultural communication skills.

Program features . . . . The heritage language is taught as a separate subject in
school, for between 1 and 5 or more hours a week. Out-of-
school programs and foreign language courses designed
for native speakers at the college/university level are also
offered.

Effectiveness research. . . . . . Little research to date on these relatively new programs,
but heritage language students typically make much
faster progress and attain higher levels of proficiency in
the target language than traditional (non-heritage language) foreign language students.

school program to offer heritage language classes in Spanish, Lao, and Hmong. Box 4.5 provides an overview of the heritage language program model.

English-Medium Models

Although bilingual education programs are more effective than English-medium programs, they are not always feasible. In a few states anti-bilingual education legislation mandates English-only approaches; in some communities educators, parents, or community members may be opposed to bilingual education because of their ideologies or misunderstandings of the program; and in many other communities, there are simply too many language groups in a single school without sufficient numbers of speakers of the same L1 to make offering a bilingual education program practicable. In these instances, English-medium programs are the next best option. In English-medium program models all subjects are taught in English. Effective programs provide a combination of sheltered content instruction, ESL instruction, and primary language support. The following are English-medium programs commonly found in schools today.

Pull-out ESL Instruction

The goal of ESL instruction is to enable ELLs to increase their English language proficiency each year and ultimately to be redesignated as "fluent English proficient" (FEP) and no longer in need of ESL instruction. Pull-out ESL is a commonly used model, particularly in elementary schools where ELLs make up a small portion of the total school population. In these schools ELLs are typically spread out across several classrooms (usually mainstream classrooms taught by teachers who are not trained in sheltered instruction strategies but ideally from classrooms taught by certified sheltered instruction teachers). A certified ESL teacher pulls small groups of ELL students out of their regular classrooms to provide ESL instruction, typically for 30 to 60 minutes or more a day. While students are entitled to daily ESL instruction, some schools are able to offer it only 2 or 3 days a week due to shortages of ESL teachers.

The pull-out ESL model has been highly criticized as the least effective model.[8] The problems are many. First, and perhaps most important, students miss out on instruction in their regular classrooms when they are pulled out. Second, pull-out ESL may lead some mainstream classroom teachers to the view that the ELL students are exclusively the responsibility of the ESL teacher. Third, many students feel stigmatized about being pulled out day after day in front of their English-only peers. In a study of former ELL students I conducted in California, one of the students described her feelings about being pulled out: "The other kids wouldn't say anything, but I would feel lost. Here I go again. Why do I have to do this? I felt so dumb. I felt like I'm dumb" (Wright, 1998).

And finally, ESL instruction provided by the pull-out teacher typically is not coordinated with what the students are learning in their regular classrooms, largely because ESL teachers generally pull students from several different classrooms, making it very difficult to coordinate with every teacher. Furthermore, pull-out ESL teachers sometimes find that mainstream teachers are unwilling to collaborate.

Pull-out ESL may be more expensive than other models because it requires that one or more teachers be hired in addition to the regular teaching staff. Another difficulty is finding space for the pull-out ESL class, because many schools are already overcrowded. In some instances ESL classes are held in portable classrooms far away from the main buildings where "real" learning is taking place. In other instances ESL teachers do not have their own classrooms, and they conduct class wherever they can, including in the cafeteria, the auditorium lobby or on the stage, and in teacher lounges, converted broom closets, basements, storage rooms in the back of other teachers' classrooms, and hallways. These poor accommodations may send the signal to the ELL students, and to the teachers, that ESL instruction is a low priority and that ELLs are second-class citizens within the school.

Despite these drawbacks, there are some benefits of pull-out ESL. For example, in my research with former ELLs in California (Wright, 1998, 2004a), I found a number of students who did not receive any pull-out ESL instruction but were simply placed in mainstream English-only classrooms. These students described feeling frustrated and lost during the first few years of their education. One student commented, "I just sat there." Another mentioned that occasionally his teacher would try to call on him but he would simply sit quietly until she called on someone else because he could not understand the questions. Many of the students sought help outside of school. Pull-out ESL would have been a much better alternative for these students who received no help at all. In a study I conducted in Texas of newly arrived Khmer students in the 5th grade who received pull-out ESL instruction (Wright & Li, 2006), I found that although their regular classroom teacher did an excellent job trying to accommodate their needs in her classroom, these students were much more active, engaged, and vocal during their ESL time. The ESL teacher created a safe environment that effectively lowered the affective filter of her ELL

8: See, e.g., Ovando, Combs, & Collier, 2006; Thomas & Collier, 2002.

students. The students enjoyed their time in the ESL classroom and developed a wonderful relationship with their ESL teacher. They made much greater progress in both language and academic development than they would have without pull-out ESL instruction, and their experiences in the positive, supportive environment of the pull-out ESL class made their school experience much more enjoyable. Box 4.6 provides an overview of the pull-out ESL model.

In-Class ESL Instruction

In-class ESL instruction is provided by the regular classroom teacher. This is preferred over the pull-out ESL model for several reasons: (1) the students do not miss anything in class by being pulled out, (2) classroom teachers can coordinate their ESL instruction to prepare ELL students for specific sheltered content lessons, (3) the classroom teachers take full responsibility for the education of all their students, (4) what the classroom teachers learn about the ELLs through ESL instruction can help them tailor their content-area instruction to appropriate levels, and (5) the classroom teachers can coordinate interactions between ELLs and English proficient students in the classroom that will further assist ELLs in acquiring English. Furthermore, the school saves money by not having to hire additional teachers.

To provide effective ESL instruction, classroom teachers must complete certification in their state (if available) that authorizes them to provide this instruction in their classrooms. But they must also be provided with an ESL curriculum and instructional materials. There are many frustrated ESL teachers who find they need to create their own curriculum and make or buy their own materials because their schools and districts fail to provide them.

Once classroom teachers have been trained to provide ESL instruction, they must do so. It is not enough for a teacher to claim, because there are ELLs in the classroom, "I teach ESL all day." ESL is a separate content area, with its own content standards, curriculum, and teaching materials (see Table 4.3). Thus, when there is no ESL-pull out program in place, the classroom teacher must provide the same type of instruction that a pull-out ESL teacher would provide.

Box 4.6

ELL Program Profile

Pull-out ESL

Other name . . . . ESL withdrawal classes.
Target population . . . . ELLs.
Typical grade span . . . . K–6. (In secondary schools ESL is provided as a separate class period.)
Language goals . . . . Help students attain proficiency in English.
Academic goals . . . . Help students gain the English proficiency needed to understand content-area instruction.
Culture goals . . . . Acculturation to mainstream school and society; assimilation common.
ESL instruction . . . . 30–60 minutes a day.
Primary language support . . . . May be provided as needed.
Effectiveness research . . . . Pull-out ESL in isolation does not enable ELLs to achieve parity with English-speaking peers. It is, however, an integral part of effective sheltered English programs when ESL is not provided in the classroom. (See Box 4.7)

Some pull-out ESL teachers are now doing "pull-ins" or "push-in ESL," meaning that the ESL teacher goes into the regular classroom to work with the ELL students. In the least effective model, the ESL teacher works in the back of the room and provides support to the classroom teacher, functioning as little more than a paraprofessional rather than as a fellow teacher. In the most effective model, the ESL teacher and content-area teacher team teach, working together to address the content and language objectives. However pull-in or pull-in ESL is handled, the ESL teacher must find ways within the context of the mainstream classroom to provide focused ESL instruction for ELLs.

In secondary grades, ELL students are typically provided with one or two course periods of ESL. These courses, too, must be taught by a certified ESL teacher who has a curriculum to follow and materials to use. This instruction can be made more effective if the ESL teacher coordinates with the ELLs' general education teachers, though just as in the elementary school, coordination can be particularly challenging because of the large number of teachers in a typical middle or high school.

Sheltered (Structured) English Immersion

Sheltered English immersion (SEI), sometimes called structured English immersion, typically refers to self-contained grade-level classrooms for ELLs with teachers who are trained and certified to provide language and content instruction for ELL students. In SEI classrooms, the classroom teacher provides daily ESL instruction and sheltered content-area instruction. In addition, even though all instruction is in English, teachers should use ample primary language support to help make English instruction more comprehensible. SEI is the model mandated by the English for the Children initiatives in California, Arizona, and Massachusetts, and even these laws acknowledge the role of primary language support, stating that teachers "may use a minimal amount of the child's language when necessary."

When a bilingual program is not viable for policy, ideological, or practical reasons, an SEI program is the next best option. It is helpful to think of effective SEI instruction according to the following formula, where PLS stands for primary language support:

$$SEI = ESL + sheltered\ instruction + PLS.$$

In other words, a high quality SEI program includes daily direct, systematic ESL instruction, sheltered content-area instruction, and ample primary language support. The three English for the Children initiatives say that ELL students should be in SEI classrooms only for a period not normally intended to exceed 1 year. But, as we saw in Chapter 2, there is no research that suggests that most ELLs can learn enough English in 1 year to be placed in a mainstream English-only classroom. Furthermore, federal law makes it clear that ELL students are to receive ESL and sheltered instruction until they are redesignated as fluent English proficient and thus no longer in need of special services.

One area of concern is that many SEI classrooms are SEI in name only. If the classroom teacher is not certified to work with ELLs or fails to provide ESL and sheltered instruction, then the classroom is not an SEI classroom at all. It's a mainstream, sink-or-swim, English-only classroom. Box 4.7 provides an overview of the SEI model.

Newcomer Programs

Newcomer programs recognize that newly arrived ELLs with little to no proficiency in English will have a very difficult time learning in a classroom where English is the language of instruction (including SEI classrooms). Newcomers are best served

Box 4.7

ELL Program Profile

Sheltered English Immersion (SEI)

Other names	Structured English immersion; sheltered classrooms; self-contained ESL classrooms. (At the secondary level: sheltered math, ESL science, SDAIE social studies, etc.)
Target population	ELLs (but class may also contain non-ELLs).
Typical grade span	K–12. (In secondary schools sheltered subject areas are provided as separate class periods.)
Language goals	Help students attain proficiency in English.
Academic goals	Meet the same grade-level academic standards required for all students.
Culture goals	Assimilation or acculturation.
ESL instruction	30–60 minutes a day, provided in class by the classroom teacher.
Content-area instruction	All subjects taught in English through sheltered instruction.
Primary language support	Provided as needed during ESL and sheltered instruction.
Effectiveness research	More effective than pull-out ESL in isolation but not as effective as bilingual program models.

by bilingual programs, but when these are not available, a newcomer program may be the best approach. Newcomer program classrooms are taught by trained and certified ELL teachers who provide intensive ESL instruction focused on helping students develop listening, speaking, reading, and writing skills in English. Such instruction is more effective if teachers can speak the languages of their ELLs and thus can provide primary language support to the students and effectively communicate with their parents.[9]

Newcomer programs also attempt to provide sheltered instruction, especially to address literacy and numeracy development when the newcomers have had limited former schooling. The greatest focus, however, is on providing intensive ESL instruction so the students can acquire enough English to participate in an SEI classroom 1 or 2 years later. Some school districts establish separate newcomer schools where district resources and personnel can be concentrated to best meet the students' needs. Students are sometimes bussed to the newcomer center from their neighborhood schools and stay there all day or stay for part of the day and then return to their home school. Other newcomer programs are centers within existing schools where newly arrived ELLs may spend anywhere from a couple of hours to the whole day. Many newcomer centers also help ease newly arrived students into the American culture and school system, and many provide counselors and outreach programs to assist students and their families with social, medical, and health services (Crawford, 2004).

Newcomer programs have been criticized for segregating ELLs into separate classrooms or schools, for lacking a focus on content-area instruction, and for

---

9: See Short & Boyson, 2004, for discussion of these programs across the United States.

being expensive to operate. For newcomer programs to be effective, there must be a real commitment on the part of the district to provide the school with the best teachers, adequate resources, a clear curriculum, and small class sizes. High stakes testing and school accountability have posed serious challenges to these programs, however, because newcomer students are rarely ready to take and pass state tests in English. Box 4.8 provides an overview of the newcomer program model.

Submersion (Sink or Swim)

One final approach to teaching ELLs is to do nothing at all for them. Submersion means placing an ELL student in a mainstream classroom where there is no ESL instruction, no sheltered instruction, and no primary language support. Furthermore, the teachers are not certified to teach ELL students. Thus, as the alternative name implies, these students are left to sink or swim. Unfortunately, submersion is very common, even though it is in violation of federal law.

There are many excellent and experienced mainstream teachers with no training in ESL who regularly have ELL students placed in their classrooms. These teachers should take the initiative to complete ESL certification and other trainings to better meet the needs of their students. With such training they can transform their

---

Box 4.8

ELL Program Profile

Newcomer Programs

Other name	Newcomer centers.
Target population	ELLs who have recently arrived to the United States and have little to no English proficiency (and sometimes limited former schooling).
Typical grade span	Any grade levels, pre-K–12.
Number of years	1–2 years.
Language goals	Help newcomer ELLs learn enough English to be able to participate in a sheltered English immersion classroom the following year or two.
Academic goals	Help newcomer ELLs learn basic reading and writing skills in English and expose them to the content areas with a focus on developing the vocabulary and language skills needed to learn these subjects through sheltered instruction once they exit the newcomer program.
Culture goals	Acculturation to mainstream school and society; assimilation common.
ESL instruction	Intensive, for 1 hour or more a day.
Content-area instruction	Sheltered instruction uses the content areas for vocabulary and other English language skills development, with a focus on beginning skills in English reading and writing. Some programs may also include L1 content-area instruction.
Primary language support	Ample primary language support throughout the day.
Effectiveness research	Little research on these innovative programs.

mainstream classrooms into sheltered English classrooms fairly quickly. In addition they should advocate for the creation of one or more of the models described in this chapter and insist their schools and districts provide the materials and support necessary to do so. (Advocacy, document)

Teachers should be aware that many SEI classrooms are SEI in name only. Box 4.9 provides a helpful checklist to determine whether an SEI classroom is really a

---

Box 4.9

Is It SEI or Submersion (Sink-or-Swim)?

Use this checklist to spot submersion (sink-or-swim) classrooms disguised as SEI classrooms.

❏ All textbooks and materials used are identical to those used in mainstream classrooms.

❏ All in-class assignments and homework are identical to those used in mainstream classrooms.

❏ The teacher does not possess state certification for teaching ELL students, or the state's certification requires only a minimal amount of training for such certification.

❏ The teacher cannot immediately identify the ELL students in the classroom or cannot describe their level of English language proficiency.

❏ The teacher is unable to identify or describe each ELL student's home country, ethnicity, home language, prior schooling, literacy in L1, or length of time in the United States.

❏ The teacher makes ignorant comments about the ELL students' language background, such as, "She speaks Mexican" or "I think he speaks Asian."

❏ The teacher knows little about the ELL students' cultures.

❏ The teacher makes little to no effort to modify his or her speech to make it more comprehensible for the ELLs.

❏ There is no regularly scheduled time for daily ESL instruction.

❏ The teacher claims, "I teach ESL all day."

❏ The teacher cannot articulate specific sheltering strategies or techniques used to make instruction comprehensible for the ELL students.

❏ The teacher makes comments about the strategy for teaching the ELL students, such as, "I just try to simplify everything," or "I don't give them as much work."

❏ The teacher claims that the strategies used are "just good teaching."

❏ Content-area lessons do not contain both language and content objectives.

❏ ELL students do not actively participate or are excluded from classroom discussions and other activities.

❏ The teacher makes little to no use, or allowance for, the ELLs' primary language in the classroom.

❏ Much of the teaching of the ELLs has been delegated to a paraprofessional.

❏ The teacher uses one-size-fits-all or scripted curricular programs.

❏ There is a heavy focus on test-preparation using test-prep materials and frequent benchmark testing with materials designed for English-proficient students.

❏ When you ask the teacher about sheltered instruction, he or she responds, "What's that?"

❏ The teacher can tell you the number of hours of ELL training he or she has received but little about the content of the training.

❏ The teacher has a negative attitude toward the ELL students and would prefer that they were not in his or her classroom.

❏ The teacher admits to feeling ill-prepared to work with the ELL students.

Source: Based on findings from Wright & Choi, 2005.

submersion (sink-or-swim) mainstream classroom in disguise. If any of the items on the checklist applies to a program designated SEI, major changes need to be implemented if ELLs are to make progress in learning English and academic content.

Collaboration among ESL, Bilingual, Sheltered Instruction, and Mainstream Teachers

Often several of the programs described in this chapter are found in a single school. An elementary school may have an ESL specialist who pulls students out of bilingual, sheltered, or mainstream classrooms for daily ESL instruction or who pushes into those classes to work with ELL students. At the secondary level, ELLs typically have one or two periods of ESL in addition to some combination of sheltered, bilingual, and mainstream classes. To provide the most effective instruction possible, the ESL teacher needs to work collaboratively with these classroom teachers to identify the language learning needs students are facing in their classrooms and support their English language development. While challenging, this collaboration can be accomplished formally through regular meetings with teachers before or after school in grade-level or content-area faculty meetings. The ESL teacher could also spend time during planning periods observing regular instruction in different classrooms with ELLs. Chatting informally in the hallways, finding excuses to drop by classrooms even for just for a few minutes, or eating lunch with the classroom teachers can also help. The purpose is to find out what is being taught in the classrooms so that relevant lessons can be provided in ESL.

In schools that have a variety of programs but no ESL specialist, the bilingual and sheltered classroom teachers can help each other and the mainstream teachers by sharing ideas and resources with members of the same grade-level teams and help look over ELL students' work. I recall a sheltered-English teacher at my former elementary school who was puzzling over the writing of one of her Spanish-speaking beginning ELLs. The writing appeared to be in Spanish but the student insisted it was in English. When the teacher showed the writing sample to one of her bilingual teacher colleagues, the bilingual teacher laughed and said, "This is a perfect example of a student with Spanish writing skills using Spanish phonics to write in English. Here, let me read it to you." As she read, it became clear the student had indeed written the paper in English. The bilingual teacher provided suggestions for helping the student transfer her Spanish literacy skills to English. For successful collaboration such as this to work, teachers in a school need to move beyond the view of "my students/your students" to "our students" and make a shared commitment to ensuring that all students in the school succeed.

Baker's Typology of Program Models for ELLs

Colin Baker (2006) has created a typology of programs for ELLs in which he classifies program models as (a) monolingual forms of education, (b) weak forms of bilingual education, or (c) strong forms of bilingual education. These classifications relate to the societal aims and language outcomes of different program models. In Table 4.5 I have adapted Baker's typology to classify the programs discussed in this chapter. The strongest forms are those that help ELL students—and in some instances, native English speakers—become fully bilingual, biliterate, and bicultural. Monolingual forms of education, in contrast, are the weakest of all as these programs. They make little to no use of ELLs' native languages, they aim for social and cultural assimilation of students, and they frequently result in the loss of students' ability to speak their first language, that is, they result in subtractive bilin-

Table 4.5   Typology of Program Models for ELLs

Program model	Students	Language of instruction	Societal aim	Aim in language outcome
Monolingual forms of education for ELLs				
Mainstream (submersion)	ELLs	English	Assimilation	English monolingualism
Pull-out ESL	ELLs	English	Assimilation	English monolingualism
Sheltered/ structured English-immersion (SEI)	ELLs	English	Assimilation	English monolingualism
Newcomer centers	ELLs	English	Assimilation	English monolingualism
Weak forms of bilingual education				
Transitional bilingual education (TBE)	ELLs	Moves quickly from L1 to English	Assimilation	Relative English mono-lingualism
Heritage language programs (provide a few hours each week of heritage language instruction, e.g., after school)	Heritage language speakers with varying degrees of proficiency in the heritage language	Heritage language	Biculturalism	Broaden linguistic repertoire of heritage language speaker
Strong forms of bilingual education				
Developmental bilingual education (DBE)	ELLs	Bilingual with initial emphasis on L1	Biculturalism	Bilingualism and biliteracy
Dual language	ELLs and English-proficient students	English and the L1 of ELLs	Biculturalism	Bilingualism and biliteracy
Bilingual immersion	Language minority students with little proficiency in L1; native-English speakers	Bilingual with initial emphasis on the non-English language	Biculturalism	Bilingualism and biliteracy
Heritage language programs (provide 1 hour or more a day of heritage language instruction, e.g., Spanish-for-Spanish speakers)	Heritage language speakers with varying degrees of proficiency in the heritage language	Heritage language	Biculturalism	Bilingualism and biliteracy

Source: Adapted from Baker, 2006.

gualism. As Baker's classification illustrates, not all bilingual education programs are strong. The societal aim of TBE programs is the same as the monolingual forms—assimilation.

The accuracy of any system of categorization like this is limited because of variations in programs. For example, I categorize heritage language programs in two places. Those that provide only a few hours of instruction each week fall under weak forms of bilingual education and those that provide a hour or more a day are under strong forms. Strong forms include classes on the model of Spanish for Spanish speakers. The value of such a topology, however, is that it reveals that programs for ELLs are multidimensional. As Baker (2006) observes, "Bilingual education is not just about language, [for] there are sociocultural, political, and economic issues ever present in the debate over the provision of bilingual education" (p. 214). This statement applies to English-medium programs as well.

SUMMARY

All program models for ELLs must, at a minimum, ensure that ELLs (1) learn English, and (2) learn academic content. Thus, each program model must include ESL instruction and content-area instruction. The teaching of content areas may be provided through native language instruction or sheltered instruction or a combination of the two. Schools should also provide as much primary language support as possible, especially in nonbilingual programs. Although dual language and DBE are considered the strongest program models for ELLs, no single approach is appropriate for all contexts. The appropriate model for a school will depend on the characteristics and needs of the ELL students, the desires of their parents and community, and the resources of the school. Regardless of the program models selected, schools and teachers must fully commit to implementing them to the best of their ability. Failure to do so means ELLs will be left behind.

Discussion Questions

1. **On-line Discussion Board**   Which programs does your school offer for ELLs? Do you feel these programs are appropriate and effective? Why or why not?
2. What minimally should be included in any program model for ELLs? Why are these components critical? What can result if one or more of these components are left out of a program for ELLs?
3. Some districts and states attempt to mandate a single program model for all ELL students. Why is this one-size-fits-all approach problematic?
4. What factors should a school take into consideration when deciding which program models to offer?
5. One of the major issues involved in meeting the unique language and academic needs of ELL students is whether or not they should be taught in separate classrooms or programs. This consideration raises the sensitive issue of segregation. When might separate classrooms or programs be needed? What are some possible solutions to the segregation problem that still address the needs of the ELLs?

6. **On-line Discussion Board**   How can a submersion program be transformed into, at least, an effective SEI classroom?

Research Activities

1. Conduct an evaluation of your own school if you are currently a teacher or working in a school, or of a school you are familiar with. Interview the administrators and classroom teachers and conduct observations in the classroom to answer the following questions:
   a. What program models are being used in the school?
   b. How long do ELL students typically stay in these programs?
   c. What are the linguistic goals of these programs?
   d. What are the academic goals of these programs?
   e. What are the cultural goals of these programs?
   f. What curriculum has been adopted or created for these programs?
   g. Are the teachers properly trained and certified to work with ELLs?
   h. How is each program evaluated to determine whether it is meeting the needs of ELLs?
   i. How effective are these programs in the opinions of the administrators and teachers?
   j. Do you believe that, considering the school's population, the programs being offered are the most effective and appropriate? If not, what program models do you believe would be the most effective for these students and why?
2. **Wiki This**   SEI or submersion? Observe an elementary school classroom that is officially designated as a sheltered English instruction (SEI) classroom. Complete the checklist in Box 4.9 to determine whether it is truly an SEI classroom or if it is really just a mainstream sink-or-swim classroom. If it is not a real SEI classroom, what changes would be needed to transform it to one?
3. Collect clippings from your local newspaper related to programs for ELL students. What types of programs are discussed, and how are they portrayed?

Recommended Reading

Echevarria, J., Vogt, M., & Short, D. J. (2010a). *Making content comprehensible for elementary English learners: The SIOP Model.* Boston: Allyn & Bacon.

The authors introduce their SIOP model. The chapters provides the theoretical and research background of the 30 items on the SIOP and include vignettes of elementary school sheltered instruction for readers to evaluate and discuss using the SIOP.

Echevarria, J., Vogt, M., & Short, D. J. (2010b). *Making content comprehensible for secondary English learners: The SIOP Model.* Boston: Allyn & Bacon.

Follows the same format as the preceding volume but with examples and vignettes drawn from junior high and high school classrooms.

Freeman, R. D. (2004). *Building on community bilingualism* Philadelphia: Caslon.

The author makes a strong case for bilingual and heritage language programs and presents compelling evidence of their benefit to students. She offers guidelines for schools to create their own language policies and programs, with examples from different language groups based on her extensive experience working with schools.

García, O., & Baker, C. (Eds.). (2007). *Bilingual education: An introductory reader.* Clevedon, UK: Multilingual Matters.

These 19 previously published articles by leading experts who have been influential in the field provide an outstanding comprehensive overview of bilingual education in the United States and abroad.

Lindholm-Leary, K. J. (2001). *Dual language education*. Clevedon, UK: Multilingual Matters.

A thorough overview of the dual language program model, drawing on data and examples from 20 programs from across the United States.

Perez, B. (2004). Becoming biliterate: A study of two-way bilingual immersion education. Mahwah, NJ: Lawrence Erlbaum.

An in-depth look at the process two schools went through to create successful dual language programs. The author's findings provide a rich resource for any school hoping to establish or improve dual language programs.

5

Assessment

Everything that has to do with the test has been given such a high priority, that there is no priority any more but that. The bottom line question comes down to, "Well, what's going to help them do better on the test?" And if it's not going to help them do better on the test, well, we don't have time for that right now.

—Nicole Soto, sheltered English immersion elementary school teacher

KEY TERMS

- testing
- assessment
- evaluation
- summative assessment
- formative assessment
- norm-referenced test
- criterion-referenced test
- reliability
- standard error of measurement (SEM)
- validity
- bias
- accommodations
- performance assessment
- self-assessment
- peer assessment
- portfolio assessment
- multiple measures

GUIDING QUESTIONS

1. What are the differences between testing, assessment, and evaluation?
2. Why should ELL educators be wary of overreliance on standardized tests of ELLs' academic achievement and English language proficiency?
3. Why is there a need for multiple measures?
4. How can ELL educators provide valid and reliable evidence of ELLs' growth and achievement?
5. How can ELL educators use evidence of ELL growth and achievement to inform their decision making?

ELLs are probably the most tested students in our educational system. In addition to taking the same federal and state tests required for all students, ELLs take language proficiency tests every year. ELLs also participate in district-level and school-level tests, and they take classroom-based tests developed by classroom teachers. In one Texas school district, between March and the end of a recent school year, 5th grade bilingual students were required to take nine different state and district tests.

Educators need to be aware of the heavy testing burden placed on ELL students and the impact test results can have on students' and teachers' lives. Test results are often used to determine whether students are placed in or exited from special programs, allowed to progress to the next grade level, required to attend summer school, or awarded a high school diploma. Test scores are also often used to judge the adequacy and skills of teachers, to determine, for example, which teachers receive monetary rewards, which teachers must obtain additional training, and which teachers may be required to find another job. Elena Shohamy has outlined specific features of the power inherent in tests (see Box 5.1).

Box 5.1

The Power of Tests

Tests are administered by powerful institutions
- Taken by individuals with little power
- Institution has non-negotiable control over knowledge

Tests use the language of science
- Statistical, objective, empirical
- Grants authority, status, and power

Tests use the language of numbers
- Symbol of objectivity, scientism, rationality

Tests use written forms of communication
- The written exam is a one-way act of communication
- No consideration of test-taker's views, interpretations

Tests rely on documentation
- Test takers redefined as describable, analyzable objects
- Measurement of overall phenomenon and individual groups

Tests use objective formats
- Objective items (true/false; multiple-choice)
- Calls for 1 correct answer, one truth, one interpretation

Source: Shohamy, 2001, pp. 20–24.

This chapter provides a foundation for fair assessment of ELLs. First we explore basic principles of assessment and then look critically at current testing requirements for ELLs. Finally, we explore alternative and authentic forms of assessment and highlight the need for multiple measures of ELLs' learning.

Assessment Basics

Testing refers to the administration of tests. A test is a single instrument designed to systematically measure a sample of a student's ability at one particular time. A test is like a photographic snapshot. A snapshot can be misleading because it cannot show what took place before or after it was taken, or the context in which it was taken. Likewise, a single test does not provide any information about what a student could do before or after taking the test. Nor can a test possibly measure everything a student knows and can do. A test can collect only a "sample" of a student's knowledge and ability. In mathematics, for example, only a small sample of problems can be tested, and from this sample we attempt to make an inference about the test taker's math ability in general.

Assessment is much broader than testing. Margo Gottlieb (2006) defines assessment as "the systematic, iterative process of planning, collecting, analyzing, reporting, and using student data from a variety of sources over time" (p. 185). Assessment involves (1) planning what, how, and when to assess, with attention to the varied purposes of different constituents or stakeholders, including students, parents, teachers, and local and state administrators; (2) collecting appropriate data from a variety of sources, ranging from informal observations of students in class to more formal scoring of student performances on specific tasks using common rubrics; (3) analyzing student performance data, looking for strengths to build on, and identifying areas in need of further instruction and assistance; (4) reporting student strengths and needs in ways that are beneficial to students, teachers, and the school; and (5) using student performance data to identify what a student must learn in order to progress to the next level. Thus, assessment offers a much more comprehensive picture of student growth and achievement than a test allows.

Evaluation refers to the use of the evidence gathered through assessment to make a judgment about the effectiveness of students' learning, of the teacher's teaching, or of the educational programs provided to the students. Final grades are one example of student evaluation. Teachers use assessment data to evaluate the effectiveness of their teaching, and they make adjustments accordingly. Assessment data can help educational leaders evaluate programs to determine whether they are meeting the needs of their students. Assessment data can also help educational leaders identify ways that they can improve their programs and practices to better serve those students.

Summative and Formative Assessments

A summative assessment provides a summary of what a student knows and can do. Summative assessments typically are given at the end of a unit or perhaps at the end of a school year. A formative assessment, in contrast, provides information to a teacher about how a student is doing and what modifications may be needed in instruction. Think of *form*ative assessments as helping in*form* teachers what to do next instructionally. A formative assessment may be a formal assessment, or it may be as informal as a teacher walking around and observing students' progress while they are working independently at their desks or in small groups. Effective teachers of ELL students make use of both formative and summative assessments.

Norm-Referenced and Criterion-Referenced Tests

A norm-referenced test is used to compare a student's score to those of other students. Test results are usually reported as percentile rankings. These represent how a student's score compares with the scores of students in the test's norming population, that is, a group of students—the "norming group"—who have already taken the same test. For example, a score at the 71st percentile means that the student scored higher than 71% of the students in the norming population. Norm-referenced tests are also used to compare the performances of classrooms, schools, districts, and even states. Commonly used norm-referenced tests include the Stanford Achievement Test, 10th edition (SAT-10), the TerraNova, the Iowa Test of Basic Skills (ITBS), the Metropolitan Achievement Test (MAT), and the Comprehensive Test of Basic Skills (CTBS). IQ tests, such as the Stanford-Binet and the Wechsler Intelligence Scale for Children, and college-entrance tests, such as the SAT, ACT, and the GRE, are also norm-referenced tests.

A criterion-referenced test, in contrast, determines how much a student has learned by tallying how many questions are answered correctly. These tests are designed to determine whether a student meets specific criteria, such as course objectives or state standards. Scores are usually reported as raw scores or converted to percentages. For example, a student who answered 45 out of 50 questions correctly on a math test would receive a score of 90%, indicating the percentage of correct answers. Most of the tests designed by teachers for classroom use are criterion-referenced tests. Many school districts also develop their own criterion-reference

Norm-Referenced Test Score Inflation

The Lake Wobegon Effect

Fans of Garrison Keillor's National Public Radio program *A Prairie Home Companion* are familiar with his stories about his fictional hometown, Lake Wobegon, where "all the women are strong, all the men are good looking, and all the children are above average." The humor of this famous line, of course, is that it is mathematically impossible for all children to be above average.

Despite this impossibility, the results of norm-reference test scores have revealed a national pattern that puts most children at a rating of above average (Sacks, 1999). Some refer to this phenomenon as the "Lake Wobegon Effect." How is this possible? Recall that these tests are first normed on a sample of students to establish what the "average" score is—the point at which half the students score above and half the students score below. The tests are then administered to students throughout the country, and typically several years go by before the test is revised and new norms are established.

In the meantime teachers become familiar with what is on the tests. With the pressure to raise test scores, they teach to the tests. The result is test score inflation—test scores go up "without an underlying gain in real achievement" (p. 136). The public thinks the students are getting smarter because of the rise in test scores, while in fact students are learning less because their instruction has been narrowed to only what is on the test.

tests to monitor student and school progress. Creators of criterion-referenced tests establish minimum passing scores (called cut-scores).[1]

The standards-based tests required by NCLB are criterion-referenced tests. Cut scores are established by states and are often reported at three or four levels. For example, students who do not meet or exceed the passing score may be deemed "below the standard"; those who score at or just above the passing score may be deemed "basic"; and those who score well above the passing score may be deemed "proficient" or "excelling."

Note the tremendous differences between norm-referenced and criterion-referenced tests. Norm-referenced tests do not actually tell us how well students did in answering the questions or mastering the content; they tell only how a student performed in comparison with other students. Theoretically, if all students answered every question correctly, all students would be at the 50th percentile, that is, they would all be average. Likewise, if all students got every answer wrong, all students would be at the 50th percentile, because zero would be the average score. Of course, these extremes do not occur because norm-referenced tests are designed to sort and rank students along a bell-curve distribution, and test developers tinker with their tests until they achieve this distribution in the norming population. Thus, tests are also designed so that it is highly unlikely that all students at a given grade level will be able to answer all the questions correctly.

Both norm-referenced and criterion-referenced tests are problematic for ELLs. With norm-referenced tests, ELLs are unlikely ever to be deemed "above average," because ELLs typically are underrepresented, if included at all, in the norming population and the purpose of these tests is to rank students along a bell curve. Criterion-referenced tests may be considered fairer for ELLs, because their scores on these tests supposedly reflect their knowledge of the content, rather than how they

---

1: See www.fairtest.org (home page for the National Center for Fair and Open Testing) for more information on different types of tests, as well as information about uses and abuses of high-stakes testing.

compare with their native English-speaking peers. However, both norm-referenced and criterion-referenced tests in English are problematic for ELLs because they lack proficiency in the language of the test. Also, both types of test are subject to test score inflation, particularly when they are part of high-stakes accountability systems and teachers feel pressured to teach to them. The pressure on schools to have high average passing rates to meet the criteria of state and federal accountability programs may lead to the temptation to use questionable strategies that minimize or eliminate the impact of ELL student test scores. Thus, many ELLs are made invisible in the very system that claims to be making them visible and addressing their needs. (Norm-referenced vs. Criterion-referenced Tests, document)

Efforts to minimize the impact of ELL test scores on district and school averages could also be seen as acknowledgment that there are unresolved issues related to the reliability and validity of test scores for ELL students, and thus it is unfair to schools to include ELL scores for accountability purposes. Let's now look at these issues of reliability and validity.

Reliability

The concept of reliability recognizes that no test (or testing situation) is free from error, and that these errors result in misrepresenting students' knowledge and ability. Reliability, according to W. James Popham (2004), "refers to the consistency with which a test measures whatever it's measuring," or "the extent to which students' scores on tests are free from errors of measurement" (pp. 29–30). Think of reliability as consistency, which can be illustrated by the following three types of reliability evidence:

1. *Internal reliability.* How consistently do the test items function?
   You have likely encountered poorly written or simply bad questions on a test, questions that even the most prepared students may not be able to answer correctly. These items lack consistency with other test items. If there are many poorly written or unfair questions, the test will lack internal reliability. It will not be able to properly distinguish between higher-level and lower-level students, or between students who are well prepared and those who are not.

2. *Stability.* How consistent are the results of a test across different testing occasions?
   Theoretically, if a teacher gives a test on Monday and gives the same test on Tuesday and does not provide any additional teaching on the topic between the two tests, the results should be the same. However, many factors can affect test results, as any teacher can attest. Did the students eat breakfast? Is a student feeling ill or concerned about a problem at home? Did the students see something on television covering the same topics on the test after school on Monday? These and other factors can introduce errors of measurement.

3. *Alternative forms.* How consistent are two or more different forms of a test?
   Teachers, or testing companies, may want more than one form of their test available to prevent cheating, or, if a test is reused in the future, to prevent teachers and students from remembering the questions or the answers. Of course, alternative forms are not identical, and thus the possibility of measurement error is introduced.

In instances of more holistic assessment, such as scoring a student essay, reliability refers to the consistency of those who are doing the scoring. If one teacher grades all the essays, how consistent is she in how she grades the papers at the top of the pile compared with how she grades those near the bottom? Or if two or more people are grading the essays, how consistent are they in applying the same scoring criteria? If they read the same essay, would they give it the same score? This issue is referred to as inter-rater reliability. It is nearly impossible to have 100% inter-rater reliability, because people are different and the grading of essays is highly subjective.

Procedures for determining the reliability of testing instruments are often based on mathematical formulas, resulting in numbers proclaiming just how reliable an instrument is internally, or how consistent it is at different times or in different forms. For large-scale assessments, such as state tests, a standard error of measurement (SEM) should be reported. The SEM indicates a range of trustworthiness of an individual student's score. For example, if a test has an SEM of 3, and the student scores 49, then the student's actual score is 49 +/− 3, that is, somewhere between 46 and 52.

The implications of the SEM are enormous. Consider, for example, if the cut score for passing a test is 50 but an ELL student scored 49, he would be deemed as failing the test. But if the SEM for the test is 3, his score may have actually been 50, 51, or 52, which are passing scores.[2] Imagine if the student were held back a grade or denied a high school diploma because of his "failing" score. It is possible the student was unfairly penalized, with major social consequences, all because of errors inherent in the test, not in the students' actual performance.

Also problematic related to the SEM is the tendency for schools to focus all of their instructional attention on students who "just barely" missed passing the test by a few points. Linda McNeil (2000) observes that in many schools these students are referred to as the "bubble kids." Again, the SEM reveals that if these students are given the exact same test again, they may pass it without any instructional interventions, simply because their "failing" score was due to measurement error. Thus, these schools may be wasting tremendous amounts of instructional time that could be put to much better use, such as providing ESL instruction rather than test preparation. (Bubble Kids, document)

Validity

Validity refers to the accuracy with which a test or assessment measures what it purports to measure. Although people talk about a test being valid, tests themselves do not possess (or lack), validity. Popham (2004) explains that it is the *validity of a score-based inference* that is at issue. Thomas Haladyna (2002) explains further that validity refers to how test scores are interpreted and used. So, for example, if a teacher wants to measure students' English spelling ability, scores from a subtraction test would not allow for any valid inferences about their spelling ability.

Essential to understanding validity is the notion of assessment domains—the broad range of concepts, knowledge, and skills that a teacher wants to assess in a given subject or area. For example, consider the assessment domain of whole number 2-digit multiplication. To make valid score-based inferences, the test obviously must ask students to solve 2-digit multiplication problems. Could the teacher give a test with every possible 2-digit multiplication problem? Technically it's possible, but a test with thousands of problems would be a bit too much. A more reasonable test would include just a sample of 2-digit multiplication problems. Students' performance on this sample would allow the teacher to make an inference about their ability to solve this type of problem, including similar problems not on the test.

Samples, however, must be carefully selected to ensure that they are representative of the entire domain. If, for example, the multiplication test had just three

2: Likewise, a student who passes with a score of 50 may actually have obtained a failing score of 47 to 49.

problems, or if it consisted solely of numbers multiplied by 10, or did not include problems that require regrouping, the teacher could not make valid score-based inferences about the students' ability to multiply 2-digit numbers. Determining an appropriate number of test items and identifying items that are truly representative of the entire domain is a serious challenge in developing tests from which valid score-based inferences may be drawn.

Unlike reliability, validity cannot be established though mathematical formulas. Rather, just as a lawyer gathers evidence to make a legal case, a variety of evidence must be gathered to make the case for validity. That evidence can be one of the following three types, as described by Popham (2004, p. 55):

1. *Content-related evidence* refers to "the extent to which an assessment procedure adequately represents the content of the assessment domain being sampled." The earlier examples of the subtraction test used to measure spelling and the multiplication test that includes only numbers multiplied by 10 are examples of tests that lack content validity.
2. *Criterion-related evidence* refers to "the degree to which performance on an assessment procedure accurately predicts a students' performance on an external criterion." Language proficiency tests are supposed to predict how well a student would perform in a mainstream classroom. Criterion-related evidence for these tests should be gathered with data showing that students who score low on the test struggle with the language demands of a mainstream classroom, while those who score high on the test are better able to cope. However, such data are rarely, if ever, collected.
3. *Construct-related evidence* refers to "the extent to which empirical evidence confirms that an inferred construct exists and that a given assessment procedure is measuring the inferred construct accurately." This is similar to content-validity, but constructs are much more abstract, broad and complex.

Let's consider reading comprehension as an example of an inferred construct. First, how do we define reading comprehension and how do we measure it? Would ability to follow directions on a medicine bottle be sufficient? Does a student lack reading comprehension skills if he is unable to explain the multiple layers of meaning of the John Keats poem "Ode on a Grecian Urn"? Since there are multiple skills involved in reading comprehension that cannot possibly all be measured, which skills are selected? Most reading comprehension tests involve reading passages that are followed by questions, but how are the reading passages selected? How representative are the selected passages of the entire domain of possible texts students may come in contact with? How representative are the types of questions (e.g., factual recall, main idea, supporting details, inferences, author's purpose) that are selected? Reading comprehension is a complex construct, and measuring it is not easy.

Haladyna (2002) describes tests as flawed measuring instruments and points out that test scores can be affected by factors that are unrelated to what the test is supposed to measure. These factors are sources of what testing experts call "construct-irrelevant variance." Haladyna offers a more practical term: *test score pollution*. Any factor that interferes with an accurate interpretation can be viewed as polluting the valid interpretation of the test score. Test score pollution that results in threats to validity include "mismatched tests, cheating on the test, inappropriate test preparation, inappropriate or unfair test administration, and failing to consider the context for a student's or a group of students' performance" (p. 57). Haladyna notes that ELLs' limited English proficiency is a major source of "test-score pollution" that can seriously affect a student's score.

Consider the example of a math test in English that is full of word problems. An ELL student may have been a top math student in her home country but would have

Box 5.2

Threats to Valid Interpretations of ELL Test Scores

1. If the test is timed, the student may not have enough time to finish the test, because the thought process for translation requires extra time.
2. The English reading comprehension level of the test may be too difficult, so the test becomes a measure of English reading comprehension instead of a measure of achievement.
3. The education program of a transplanted student is not likely to be very strong, resulting in lower achievement and lower test scores
4. The teaching quality may be inferior, especially if a bilingual teacher is needed [but not available]
5. If teaching is done in English and the student's English language proficiency is not good, not only is the child failing to learn English but he or she also is not keeping up in other areas of study.
6. If these students attend schools in school districts with limited services (e.g., poverty-stricken areas), they are less likely to receive the special attention that more affluent school districts provide. Underfunded schools tend to have underfunded programs for the neediest students.
7. If these students live in social or cultural isolation, they are likely to underachieve.

Source: Haladyna, 2002, pp. 186–187.

great difficulty passing this test because she has trouble reading or understanding the questions in English. The math test becomes instead a test of English reading comprehension—not the construct the math test was designed to measure. Hence, lack of English proficiency is a source of construct irrelevance, the test score is polluted, and we cannot make any valid interpretations about the student's math ability. Haladyna outlines several threats to the valid interpretation of ELL test scores (see Box 5.2).

Bias

Bias in testing and assessment refers to the qualities of an assessment instrument that penalize a group of students because of their gender, religion, ethnicity, socioeconomic status, or any other characteristic that defines them as a group. The issue of bias is really an issue of validity, because bias is one of the threats to valid test score use and interpretation; or as Haladyna would say, bias is a source of test-score pollution.

Concerned educators have long pointed out examples of questions on standardized tests that focus heavily on sports and thus may be biased against girls and in favor of boys or that use names common only among White Americans. Bias is harder to find these days because test developers have become more sensitive and many now strive to eliminate potential bias in their testing instruments. Most companies have developed bias elimination handbooks and guidelines for their internal use that go beyond the superficial sprinkling of ethnic names throughout test questions. Despite these efforts, problems still occur and educators continue to find examples of subtle forms of bias in test questions, for example, items that require familiarity with the cultural norms and practices of White middle-class Americans.

Reducing bias is more complex than using diverse names and avoiding certain topics. The biggest source of bias for ELLs is the language of the test. Simply put, a test written in English is biased in favor of students who are native or fluent speakers of English and biased against those who are not.

In an effort to understand the extent to which linguistic bias may be present on a state high-stakes test, my colleague Xiaoshi Li and I analyzed the 5th grade math Texas Assessment of Knowledge and Skills (TAKS) and compared it with math worksheets that had been completed over the school year by newcomer ELLs students from Cambodia (Wright & Li, 2006, 2008). The students, Nitha and Bora, spoke no English when they arrived 2 months into the school year, yet they were expected to pass the math TAKS test—in English—less than 6 months later. Both students were very bright and made great progress in learning English, math, and other subjects during the school year. They had done well in math in Cambodia, but the academic standards in Texas were much higher than those of the Cambodian education system, where impoverished schools do not have enough textbooks and most teachers never attended or graduated from high school. Their school in Texas worked hard to provide as much math instruction as possible in an effort to help them catch up to their grade-level peers. With assistance—including assistance in their native language—the girls were able to complete dozens of worksheets as part of their math instruction throughout the year, most of which contained simple word problems written for students below the 5th grade level.

When comparing vocabulary, we found that the number of unique words on both the worksheets and the math TAKS were around 300 words. The math TAKS, however, contained nearly twice as many academic and math-specific vocabulary words than Nitha and Bora had encountered on their math worksheets. Many math-specific academic words, such as *digit, diagram, parallel, congruent, rectangular,* and *transformation,* to name just a few, did not appear a single time in their worksheets, yet understanding these key words was necessary to solve the problems on the TAKS. These newcomer ELL students simply did not have the English math-specific vocabulary necessary to read and understand the test questions. We then did a comparison of syntactic complexity and found that the TAKS had a greater variety of syntactic features, and over twice as many of the more complex syntactic features (see Figure 5.1). This means that when the girls attempted to take the TAKS test, they encountered long sentences that were much more complex than anything they had ever encountered during their regular math instruction.

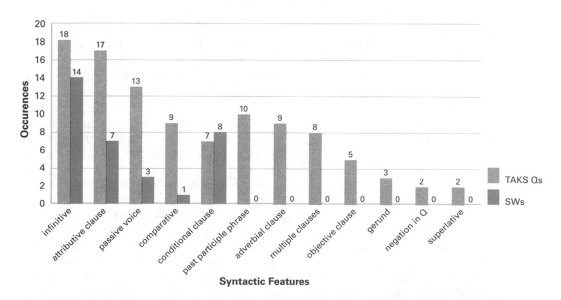

Figure 5.1 Linguistic complexity of students' math worksheets (SWs) compared with that of the 5th grade math Texas Assessment of Knowledge and Skills (TAKS Qs). (Source: Wright & Li, 2008.)

The following concluding sentences from word problems illustrate the difference between the syntactic complexity of the worksheets and that of the TAKS:

- *Student worksheet:* How many does he have left?
- *TAKS:* What information is needed to find the approximate number of sheets of paper Juan had left after the school year was over?

Note how the student worksheet question is a single clause, whereas the TAKS question contains multiple clauses of different types. The TAKS question is much more linguistically complex and would pose a significant challenge to newly arrived ELLs—even for those who are really good at math. For native and fluent speakers of English, however, the linguistic complexity of this sentence would not pose a significant challenge. Thus, this test question exemplifies the type of the linguistic bias that is inherent in tests administered to students who are not yet proficient in the language of the test.

A Critical Look at Testing Requirements for ELLs

Equipped with an understanding of assessment basics, we now review specific problems with testing requirements for ELLs. We begin with a look at professional standards for test development and use related to the testing of ELLs. Then we take a critical look at the content and language testing requirements for ELLs as mandated by NCLB. Finally, we explore alternative and more authentic assessments and procedures with the potential to provide more accurate measures of what ELLs know and can do.

Joint Standards

Three major national professional organizations—the American Education Research Association, the American Psychological Association, and the National Council on Measurement in Education—have developed a set of standards for educational and psychological testing. These are commonly referred to as the Joint Standards. The latest version, published in 1999, contains an entire chapter (chapter 9) that outlines 11 standards related to the issue of testing students with limited English proficiency. (Joint Standards, document)

The Joint Standards recognize that lack of English proficiency is a source of construct irrelevance. That is, any test given to ELLs in English becomes, in effect, a language test, with results that may not accurately reflect the students' competencies in the construct intended to be measured. The Joint Standards declare that test norms based on native speakers of English should not be used with students whose first language is not English. The standards acknowledge the problems of translation, noting that we cannot assume that a translation of a test is equivalent in content, difficulty level, reliability, and validity to the original English version. The standards also recognize that simply testing a student in his or her native language alone is problematic because a bilingual student may not test well in either language

Key to proper test use, the Joint Standards declare, is an understanding of an individual student's bilingualism. Also addressed are issues related to the use of interpreters, modifications of tests (accommodations) for ELLs, the need for validity evidence, and guidance in interpreting test scores. When a test is used to make high-stakes decisions, for example, the standards suggest that the test user review the test itself and consider using additional tests, observational information, or modified forms of the chosen test to ensure that the enough adequate information is obtained before making a high-stakes decision. The attention the Joint Standards brings to issues of testing ELLs is greatly needed. Unfortunately, there are no enforcement mechanisms for the Joint Standards. In other words, there is no accountability system in place by which to hold accountable those whose develop, use, and interpret tests for accountability purposes!

The political push with federal mandates for high-stakes state tests that include ELLs has revealed many examples of how the Joint Standards are being ignored and violated, with unfair consequences for ELL students and their schools based on test score interpretations of questionable validity.

Content-Area Testing

The main purpose of content-area testing is to determine how well students are performing in a particular subject area. Teachers often create their own content-area tests throughout the year (e.g., spelling tests, math tests) or use the end-of chapter or unit tests that come with their curricular programs, for both formative and summative assessment purposes. States also create their own large-scale content-area assessments that are aligned with their state content standards and use the standardized assessment data for summative purposes.

The most commonly tested subject areas on large-scale content-area assessments are reading/language arts, math, and science, because NCLB mandates that each state test students in these areas. However, many states also test students in writing, and some also test students in social studies/history and other content areas.

Large-scale standardized content-area tests are used for purposes of accountability for teachers and schools, as well as students. In addition to the federal school accountability system through NCLB, states have their own school accountability programs. State programs usually differ substantially from the federal system, so much so that it is not uncommon for a school to be labeled as "failing" under NCLB, but "excelling" under the state's system. Most states argue that their accountability system is more fair and accurate than NCLB's. To date, however, both state and federal accountability programs rely heavily on the results of high-stakes standardized content-area tests.

Accommodations for ELLs

In partial recognition of the problems involved in testing ELLs, NCLB simply mandates that ELLs be assessed in a "valid and reliable manner" through the use of "reasonable accommodations." These accommodations could include, "to the extent practicable, assessments in the language and form most likely to yield accurate data on what such students know and can do in academic content areas, until such students have achieved English language proficiency."[3]

Providing tests in the ELLs' native language or using other accommodations is not as easy as it might seem. Charlene Rivera and her colleagues conducted extensive reviews of the research on testing accommodations for ELLs and on state-level accommodation policies. They found only 15 relevant studies, most of which were inconclusive and unable to document whether the accommodations actually worked. So far, research can suggest that there are only two kinds of accommodation with the potential to support ELL's access to test content: testing students in their native language (L1) and simplifying the language used in the test (Rivera & Collum, 2006).

3: NCLB §1111(b)(3)(C)(ix)(II).

L1 tests appear to be the best accommodation. Indeed, if students are tested in the language they know best, they should have a better chance of demonstrating what they know and what they can do. It is not possible, however, to simply translate a test from English to another language. Creating L1 tests that are truly equivalent to the English versions is difficult, expensive, and time consuming. Only a small number of states have L1 versions of their state tests, and nearly all of them are in Spanish. Thus, the vast majority of ELLs, especially those who speak a language other than Spanish, have no access to this accommodation. Even states that have L1 tests may have them for only certain grade levels and typically place restrictions on how many years students can take them.

Furthermore, L1 tests are not beneficial to all ELLs. Many ELLs are illiterate in their native language because they have received literacy instruction only in English. Even if they are literate in the L1, they may not be familiar with L1 academic vocabulary if most of their instruction has been in English. Thus, L1 tests are appropriate only for ELLs who (1) are literate in their L1, and (2) have received L1 content instruction in the subjects being tested (e.g., students enrolled in bilingual education programs or newcomers with schooling from their home country).

The other accommodation that appears to have potential is to simplify the language so that ELLs have a better chance of understanding the questions. This accommodation, referred to as linguistic simplification, may not be appropriate for a reading test, since comprehending grade-level text is the targeted construct. Therefore most efforts are currently focused on math tests. A few states are beginning to experiment with linguistically simplified (or "plain English") tests. But it is difficult to create such tests that still cover the same construct as the original versions. More research is needed to determine whether linguistic simplification is beneficial to ELLs, and whether with its use validity can be maintained.

Given the demands of NCLB, Rivera and her colleagues have called on the federal government to provide funding for research on testing accommodations (Rivera & Collum, 2006). The fact that they have had to do so reveals, however, that NCLB requires something we really do not know how to do yet—test ELLs in a valid and reliable manner through the use of accommodations.

Despite the virtual lack of a research base to guide practice, states are piecing together accommodation policies for districts to follow when testing ELLs. These practices vary widely and most states are using accommodation frameworks that were developed for special education students, many of which are not appropriate for ELLs. More important, they do not address the unique linguistic needs of ELLs.

Rivera and colleagues also call on states to create an ELL-responsive framework to organize and categorize accommodations according to whether they provide direct or indirect linguistic support. Not all accommodations are appropriate for all students. For example, an accommodation allowing students to use a bilingual dictionary is of little benefit to Laotian American students who cannot read Lao. An ELL-responsive accommodation framework would require schools to make individualized accommodation decisions based on each student's specific background and needs. Having such a framework in place, however, would still not resolve the fact that we know little about how to provide accommodations that are actually beneficial to the ELL students while maintaining the validity of the test. There are problems associated with all of the commonly used testing accommodations for ELL students (see Table 5.1).

Flaws in Determining AYP for the LEP Subgroup

Two major flaws in NCLB impact schools with large numbers of ELL students. The first is related to the annual measurable achievement objectives (AMAOs) set by

Table 5.1   **Rationale and Problems Associated with Testing Accommodations for ELLs**

Accommodation	Rationale	Problems
Tests administered in the native language	Results will be more accurate if students are tested in the more proficient language.	• Practical only if there are large concentrations of ELLs who speak the same L1. • Effective only if students are literate in their L1, and have received L1 content instruction in the subject being tested. • Direct translations of English tests may change the tested constructs or difficulty level. • Development of parallel tests in other languages is expensive and time consuming.
Linguistic simplification	Removing difficult vocabulary/syntax may help ELLs comprehend questions.	• Requires the creation of a separate test, which can be expensive. • Difficult to create linguistically simplified test items covering same constructs as the original test • May not be appropriate for reading tests where comprehension of grade-level text in English is part of the construct being assessed.
Bilingual dictionaries or glossaries	Allowing ELLs to look up words they do not know can help them comprehend the questions.	• Feasible only if students can read in their L1 and know how to use a (bilingual) dictionary. • Dictionary may provide definitions, explanations, or examples that give away answers. • Students who learn content in English may not be familiar with content words in their L1. • Using dictionary takes up a lot of time. • Referring to dictionary may be embarrassing to ELLs in front of their peers.
Oral translation	Oral translation by a bilingual interpreter can make the questions more comprehensible for ELLs.	• Translating test directions does little to help with understanding the actual test items. • Translation of long or complex problems can be difficult to follow and comprehend orally. • Students taught in English may not know equivalent key content words in their L1. • Translation of reading comprehension tests changes test construct to L1 oral listening. • Difficult to find qualified interpreters who can fully comprehend and translate questions. • Difficult to provide accurate translation without providing additional information or explanations that may unfairly give away the answer.

(continued)

Table 5.1 *Continued*

Accommodation	Rationale	Problems
Tests read aloud in English	Hearing the questions can help ELLs who have difficulty reading in English.	• Of little use to ELLs who also have low levels of English speaking and listening ability. • Long complex problems are difficult to follow and comprehend orally. • ELLs may be embarrassed to request or receive this assistance in front of their peers. • Reading aloud on reading comprehension tests changes construct to listening comprehension.
Extra time	ELLs may read more slowly and may be translating in their head, thus they need extra time to finish the test.	• Not an accommodation for ELLS because most state tests are not timed. • Of little benefit to ELLs at the lowest levels of English proficiency.
Individual or small group administration	ELLs may feel more comfortable away from their English-proficient peers; Can take test with trained teacher who can provide other accommodations	• Unless done to facilitate the provision of direct linguistic accommodations, does nothing to address linguistic needs of students.

the states. Recall from Chapter 3 that AMAOs are the percentage of students in each subgroup (including the LEP subgroup) that must pass the state test each school year in order for the school to be deemed as making adequate yearly progress (AYP) toward the goal in 2014 when NCLB mandates that all students (100%) will pass the test. Schools with large numbers of ELL students will likely be well below the AMAOs for any given school year and thus have farther to go to catch up than other schools. For example, among 3rd graders tested for reading in Arizona in 2006, at least 53.3% (or slightly over half) of the students in each subgroup were required to pass the reading test for the school to be deemed as making AYP, according to the state's AMAO requirements. (see Figure 5.2). A school in Arizona where only 12% of 3rd grade ELL students had passed the reading test the year before would have to make much more improvement than would a school where 50% had passed the test the year before.

Many states (including Arizona) set their AMAOs in tiers so that they initially stayed constant for 3 years before moving to the next, intermediate goal, giving schools extra time to get more and more ELLs (and other low-scoring students) to pass the test before the AMAO increased. This strategy, however, does not account for the fact that newcomer ELLs can arrive at any time in any grade level. No matter how much a school improves its instruction for students in the prior grades, newly arrived ELLs never received that instruction. Under this system, schools are punished for the performance of students they may have just begun teaching.

To illustrate this problem, let's say in 2012 a school has 30 ELLs in 3rd grade. According to Figure 5.2, the expectation for that year is that over 80% of a school's 3rd grade ELLs will pass Arizona's reading test in English. To meet the 2012 AMAO, at least 24 of the school's 30 ELL students would have to pass the reading test. Even if all 30 had been in the school since kindergarten, this goal would be challenging enough, because most would not yet have attained the level of proficiency in English required to read and fully comprehend the test. But what if 10 of those 30 students had arrived in the United States only the year before? How reasonable would it be then to expect at least 24 of the students pass the test? The following year, let's say there are 35 ELLs in 3rd grade, only half of whom have been in the United States since kindergarten. Now the expectation is that 95% of these stu-

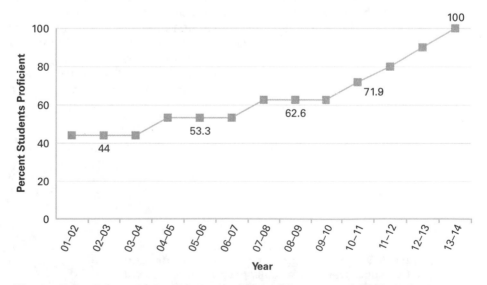

Figure 5.2 **Arizona's annual measurable achievement objectives for grade 3 reading.** (Source: Arizona Department of Education, 2004, p. 7.)

dents—all but 1—will pass the 3rd grade reading test in order to meet the AMAO. You can see that as schools receive new ELL students, and as the AMAOs increase, it becomes increasingly impossible to meet the expectation.

The second flaw is more problematic and could eventually cause every school with ELL students to be deemed as failing and subject to state takeover. Title I treats the LEP subgroup as it does all other subgroups. But unlike the membership of other subgroups (e.g., ethnicity), that of the LEP subgroup does not stay the same. Few students who enter school LEP are still LEP by the end of 12th grade; they eventually learn English and are no longer classified as LEP. Thus, each year, the top students in the LEP subgroup are redesignated as fluent English proficient (FEP). They are no longer members of the subgroup and are replaced by newly arrived ELLs with the lowest levels of English proficiency. In other words, the ELLs with the highest levels of English proficiency, those most likely to pass the test, are replaced by those with the least amount of English proficiency, those least likely to pass the test (see Figure 5.3). This movement into and out of the group makes it difficult and ultimately impossible for the LEP subgroup to meet the AMAOs set by the state. As a result, the LEP subgroup will continually appear as though no progress is being made. The LEP subgroup will fail to make AYP, and thus the entire school will be labeled as failing and ultimately subject to state or private takeover.

In partial recognition of this flaw, the U.S. Department of Education (2004) announced two changes to the way the LEP subgroup is treated for AYP purposes. First, LEP students could be excluded from the reading test in English for the first year and instead take the English language proficiency test, though results would not be included in school AYP calculations. Second, scores of redesignated LEP students would be counted in the LEP subgroup for 2 years after their redesignation. Newly arrived ELL students, however, were still expected to take—and pass—the state's math test, and their scores did count in the school's AYP calculations. Two years later, in 2006, however, the Department of Education (2006a) made a slight change to this requirement as well. ELLs who had been in the country for less than 12 months would still be required to take the state math test, but their scores could be excluded from the school's AYP calculations.

Unfortunately, these changes are insufficient and, at best, delay the problem rather than solve it. What is the sense in requiring newly arrived ELLs to take the state's math test when their scores will just be excluded? It is not reasonable to expect newly arrived ELL students to learn enough English in 1 school year (around 180 school days) to pass the same reading and math tests as their English-fluent peers.

While the allowance for counting ELLs for 2 years after redesignation may help a little, it does not solve the basic problem of the highest students' being replaced by the lowest students in terms of English language proficiency. Thus, this is mainly a cosmetic fix and is insufficient to ensure that the LEP subgroup will be able to make AYP.

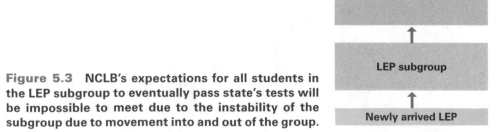

Figure 5.3   NCLB's expectations for all students in the LEP subgroup to eventually pass state's tests will be impossible to meet due to the instability of the subgroup due to movement into and out of the group.

By NCLB's own definition, an LEP student's difficulties with the English language "may be sufficient to deny the individual the ability to meet the State's proficient level of achievement on State assessments."[4] Nonetheless, the law mandates that they do just that. To identify a group of students who, by definition, cannot meet the standards, treat that group as static, and then require that 100% of students in that group attain proficiency in those standards is not reasonable.

Language Proficiency Testing

As noted in Chapter 3, when parents enroll their children in school, a home language survey is given to determine whether a language other than English is used in the home, and if so, the extent to which this language is used with and by the children. Different states use different home language surveys, but the purpose is to identify students with a primary home language other than English (PHLOTE). Each PHLOTE student is then flagged for language proficiency testing to determine whether he or she is an ELL, and if so, at what level of English language proficiency. Many school districts also assess PHLOTE students' proficiency in the standard variety of their native language.[5] This practice sometimes results in falsely labeling some young Latino students as both non-English and non-Spanish speaking (see Box 5.3).

Once students have been identified and placed in appropriate ELL programs (if available), their language proficiency should be assessed regularly to determine their progress in learning the language. Ideally, students should receive formative assessments that provide information that can drive effective ESL instruction. Language-testing experts call the influence language tests and assessments have on teaching the "washback effect." Washback can be positive, meaning it provides useful feedback and drives beneficial instruction. Or washback can be negative, perhaps better referred to as "backwash," such as in the cases where high-stakes tests force instructional attention to just a narrow set of discrete skills.

At the end of each school year, a summative language proficiency test or assessment is administered to determine the students' progress in learning English over the school year. The results are used to determine or help inform decisions about when each student has reached a high enough level of proficiency to be redesignated as FEP and thus no longer in need of specialized ELL programs and services. Results of English language proficiency assessments must be reported to the state and the federal government for accountability purposes. Thus, language tests serve several purposes: identification, program placement, monitoring of progress, reporting for accountability purposes, redesignation, and program evaluation.

Complexity of the Language Proficiency Construct

Mandates for language proficiency testing are pushing practices that are on shaky research ground. As noted in Chapter 2, language proficiency is an extremely complex construct for which there is no simple measure. How one uses language varies according to time, place, interlocutors, setting, purpose, topic, and so on, and thus demonstrating one's competence in a language is very different from demonstrating competence in other kinds of knowledge (Valdés & Figueroa, 1994, p. 66). No test can ever fully capture a student's true ability in English, or any other language.

The situation is still more complex for ELLs because they are emergent bilinguals with varying degrees of proficiency in their native language or languages and

---

4: NCLB, Title IX, Part A, §901(25)(D)(i).

5: See MacSwan, Rolstad, & Glass, 2002, for a critique of this practice.

Box 5.3

Non-Nons

Are There Students with No Language?

Non-nons is a term used in some schools to refer to Latino ELL students officially designated as non-English-speaking and non-Spanish-speaking. This designation results from language proficiency tests administered to students in both Spanish and English. Students who perform poorly on both tests are deemed as not having proficiency in any language. Teachers often buy into this construct, complaining about students who "don't know English or Spanish." Linguistically, this is an absurd notion. All normal children (i.e., those without cognitive or speech-related disabilities) naturally acquire and master the language or languages of their speech community, typically by the age of five.

Jeff MacSwan, Kellie Rolstad, and Gene Glass (2002) investigated the non-non issue and determined that the problem is not children with no language but rather invalid language tests. They found that the tests gave heavy weight to literacy skills and standard Spanish. Students who spoke vernacular varieties of Spanish daily at home were deemed as non-Spanish-speaking simply because they never had the opportunity to learn standard Spanish or to read and write in Spanish.

They concluded that language proficiency tests, and the resultant non-non labels, create a false and potentially harmful description of many ELL students. The non-non label draws attention away from the real issues, such as the need to help ELLs further develop their native language at school in order to build a foundation on which to build their new language, and the need to help ELLs learn a standard variety of Spanish without devaluing the variety they speak at home.

English. Language tests, however, are based on the norms of monolingual speakers and therefore treat bilingual students as if they were two monolingual speakers of two different languages in one person. But bilingual individuals' brains are not simply divided in half with L1 on one side and L2 on the other. Rather, the two languages interact in ways that linguists and cognitive scientists are just beginning to explore. As Guadalupe Valdés and Richard A. Figueroa (1994) point out:

> When a bilingual individual confronts a monolingual test, developed by monolingual individuals, and standardized and normed on a monolingual population, both the test taker and the test are asked to do something they cannot. The bilingual test taker cannot perform like a monolingual. The monolingual test cannot "measure" in the other language. (p. 87)

Lisa Pray (2003) documented another problem with language proficiency tests—when they are given to "native" speakers of English, the test results classify many as limited English proficient. Thus, on one hand, these tests appear to hold ELLs to a higher standard of proficiency than their native English-speaking peers. On the other hand, some language proficiency tests may falsely indicate that students have attained proficiency in English when in fact there are many gaps in their language skills. The danger here is that students may be exited from ELL programs before they are ready for mainstream instruction. With NCLB's pressure on school districts to demonstrate progress and redesignate ELLs as quickly as possible, some states may be tempted to make less demanding language proficiency tests that push students into mainstream classrooms before they are ready.

In the past, language proficiency tests attempted to measure discrete, isolated skills. Since the late 1960s, the notion of communicative competence developed by

Dell Hymes has led to attempts to measure students' abilities to actually use language to accomplish authentic and specific communicative tasks. But as Bernard Spolsky argues, language testing does not assess *authentic* language behavior, and there is no such thing as a test of authentic or natural language use (Cohen, 1994). Thus, all language tests are indirect measures of the complex construct of language proficiency, and results of these tests can provide only weak inferences about students' language abilities.

Problems with NCLB Requirements for Language Proficiency

The mandates and expectations of Title III of NCLB that hold schools accountable for ensuring that ELLs make progress in learning English and ultimately attain proficiency in the language create many problems for schools, the first of which is that there has to be some reasonable limit on the percentage of ELLs expected to be redesignated as FEP each year. States may consider the length of time ELLs have been in school, but the law is unclear about how this information can be used in determining AYP. Also, although few would disagree with the expectation that students make progress every year toward the goal of proficiency, there is a disconnect between current research, which suggests that it takes between 4 and 7 years to obtain fluency in a second language (Crawford & Krashen, 2007), and the structure of state assessments, which typically define only 4 or 5 levels of English proficiency. Thus, if a state has only 4 levels of proficiency but it takes a student 6 years to become fluent and the student is expected to move up one proficiency level each year, he or she will run out of levels. In California, for example, state reports have documented that ELL students move quickly from one level to the next at the lower levels but get stuck in the higher levels for several years (Hill, 2006). The biggest problem with Title III's AYP expectations, however, is that making AYP under Title III requires that ELLs make AYP under Title I, which calls for their passing state content-area tests. As discussed earlier, it is highly unlikely that most ELLs will do well on a content-area test written in English, because they have not yet attained full proficiency in the language of the test.

In short, as expectations increase each year, it becomes increasingly difficult and ultimately impossible for school districts to make AYP under Title III. This failure to make AYP will have nothing to do with how well students are progressing in learning and attaining English fluency, but rather will be due to illogical reasoning and technical flaws within NCLB. It comes as no surprise that in a 2008 report from the U.S. Department of Education to Congress on Title III, not one single state met all of the grade-level performance targets for AYP.[6]

Another issue related to Title III's requirement is inconsistency in how states assess ELLs' English language proficiency (Abedi, 2004) and inconsistency in how states (and school districts) use the results of language proficiency assessments to make decisions about when to exit students from ELL programs. The inconsistency is due in large part to confusion over the AYP requirements of Title III. Many states have failed to comply with even some of the most basic requirements. Recognizing that the ambiguities and technical flaws in Title III were partially responsible for this failure, and in an effort to provide clarifications and guidance to help states and districts comply with it, in late 2008 the U.S. Department of Education issued 10 "Final Interpretations" of Title III (Spellings, 2008). It remains to be seen whether these clarifications will result in more reasonable expectations for ELLs in learning English, and greater state and district compliance with the federal law.

6: This biennial report used data for the 2005–2006 school year. Only one state reached all Title I ELL performance targets in math. No state met all performance targets in reading or math.

Consequential Validity

Samuel Messick (1995) has raised the issue that validity should also be concerned with the consequences associated with the interpretation and use of test scores. He argues, "Any negative impact on individuals or groups should not derive from any source of test invalidity such as construct underrepresentation or construct-irrelevant variance. . . . Moreover, low scores should not occur because the measurement contains something irrelevant that interferes with the affected students' demonstration of competence" (p. 7). Messick's concerns are often described as consequential validity. Chief among the many threats to the valid interpretation of test scores for ELL students is that the students' lack of proficiency in the language of the test—English—introduces a major source of construct irrelevance (e.g., a math test becomes an English proficiency test). Yet, despite the validity issues, test scores of ELLs are used to make high-stakes decisions.

Many bad decisions are based on invalid interpretations of test scores, and these decisions can have harmful effects on ELL students, teachers, classrooms, and schools. Research has documented the following:

- Narrowing of the curriculum to only those content areas covered on the test; little instruction in social studies, art, music, physical education, health, or other nontested subjects; the elimination of recess to make more time for instruction and test preparation
- Adoption of curricular programs designed to raise test scores; one-size-fits-all scripted phonics and reading programs; literacy interventions that are inappropriate for ELLs; frequent benchmark testing using tests similar in format and content to the state test that take important time away from instruction; funds used to purchase test-preparation materials rather than appropriate ESL materials
- Elimination of bilingual and heritage language programs so that the language of instruction is exclusively in the language of the test (English); replacement of much-needed ESL instruction with test preparation
- Reduction in the use of sheltered instruction strategies that make complex content-area instruction comprehensible to ELLs; reduction in the amount of time to engage students in conversations and other interactive activities that promote English language development; restrictions placed on certain activities or strategies such as drawing, use of video, or field trips that benefit ELLs' language and academic development but yet are deemed as wasting instructional time
- Purposeful underidentification of ELLs so the school can avoid being held accountable for an LEP subgroup; encouraging secondary ELLs students to drop out; using high school exit exams that often deny ELLs a high school diploma upon completion of school and thus restrict their future opportunities
- Creation of stressful school environment focused on testing leading to test anxiety for students; elimination of recess; less fun; high turnover of teachers and administrators, with ELLs taught by least experienced teachers
- Poor performance of ELLs on high-stakes tests, leading to lowered self-confidence; inappropriate placement or retention of students; frustrated and demoralized teachers who become reluctant to work with ELLs; parents who complain about presence of ELLs at school[7]

7: For research documenting these and other harmful effects of bad decisions based on the invalid interpretations of ELL test scores, see Amrein & Berliner, 2002a, 2002b; Haney, 2000, 2002; Kohn, 2000; Kozol, 2005; McNeil, 2000; Nichols & Berliner, 2007; Sacks, 1999; M. L. Smith, 2004; Smith, Heinecke, & Noble, 1999; Valenzuela, 2004; Wright, 2002, 2003b, 2004b, 2005a, 2006a, 2007.

Consequential validity dictates that these harmful effects must be taken into consideration and changes made. Although to date these harmful effects have been discounted or ignored by proponents of NCLB and its mandates for high-stakes testing, mounting concerns over the harmful effects of high-stakes testing and NCLB have led a large number of professional organizations to issue statements or position papers related to these issues. The National Education Association (2008) issued a joint statement on NCLB with 144 national organizations representing a broad range of educational, ethnic, religious, and professional groups. TESOL, a signatory on the joint statement, has issued several of its own position papers and written testimonies to the federal government on different aspects of NCLB, several of which discuss the impact of NCLB on ELL students and call for changes to be made to the law. (NEA's Position on NCLB, related links)

Arne Duncan, appointed by President Barack Obama as the U.S. Secretary of Education in January 2009, should understand these problems. He was the superintendent of Chicago Public Schools from 2001 to 2008, and many of the schools in his district, and his district as a whole, was designated as failing to make AYP over the last 4 years of his administration. Contributing to this failing status was the low test scores of LEP students. At the time of this writing, Duncan has made a few public comments about the need to change the mandates of NCLB with regard to LEP students, but to date the Obama administration has only outlined a few generic proposals to change the law. The administration has, however, set the stage to make the situation worse by insisting that states receiving stimulus funding and states contending for Race to the Top grants tie student test scores—including ELL test scores—to teacher evaluations. Without changes to NCLB, teachers will be held accountable for ELL test scores of questionable validity. Opposition to this new requirement is growing, and it remains to be seen whether the administration will listen and provide the change educators have been hoping for.

Alternative Authentic Assessments for ELLs

Because of the difficulties involved in assessing the learning and progress of ELL students using standardized tests, particularly the high-stakes tests mandated by NCLB, effective teachers of ELL students use alternative authentic assessments throughout the school year. These assessments are alternative because they are unlike the standardized tests and traditional pencil-and-paper classroom-based tests created by teachers or pulled from textbooks. And they are authentic because they more closely match instructional practices in the classroom and they reflect the knowledge and skills ELLs need outside of the classroom.

According to Socorro G. Herrera, Kevin G. Murry, and Robin M. Cabral (2007), authentic assessments:

- Are generally developed directly from classroom instruction, group work, and related classroom activities and provide an alternative to traditional assessments
- Can be considered valid and reliable in that they genuinely and consistently assess a student's classroom performance
- Facilitate the student's participation in the evaluation process
- Include measurements and evaluations relevant to both teacher and student
- Emphasize *real-world* problems, tasks, or applications that are relevant to the student and his or her community (p. 23)

The authors also note that authentic assessments "identify and build on student strengths such as language, prior experiences, interest, and funds of knowledge to facilitate learning" (p. 24).

Some common alternative authentic assessments include observations, performance assessments, self-assessments and peer assessments, and portfolio assessment. We now look briefly at each of these.

Observations

The easiest way to assess ELL students is simply to watch them. Want to know how they are progressing in listening and speaking English? Talk with them. Observe their interactions in the classroom during group and pair work, during informal transition periods in class, and out on the playground or in the hallway. Want to know how well they are reading? Listen to them read. Want to know how well they are writing? Watch them while they are writing and read what they write. Want to know how well they understood the math lesson? Observe them completing independent math work at their desk or in cooperative groups. Informal observations can be facilitated through the use of anecdotal records. This means jotting down quick notes on things you observe the student doing. I used to carry around a clipboard on which I had an index card for each student. The index cards were taped onto the clipboard in a flip-file fashion to make it easy to quickly find and flip to a student's card (large sticky notes work just as well). I would make notes about the students' linguistic and academic performances during lessons as I observed them working collaboratively and independently, including the date of the observation. Once a student's card was full, I would review it and then drop it in his or her portfolio. The clipboard also enabled to me to quickly figure out which students I had been ignoring and needed to spend more time observing. The anecdotal records helped me focus on the students and their progress and alerted me to students in need of extra assistance. I also shared the records with parents during parent conferences.

Observations can be conducted more systematically with a checklist. Teachers can create their own checklists or use those provided in a given curriculum program. A checklist to track students' progress during silent reading time, for example, might include some of the following items:

☐ Read at least 90% of the time
☐ Selected books appropriate to reading level
☐ Held the book properly
☐ Tracked text with finger while reading
☐ Read aloud
   ☐ with great difficulty
   ☐ with moderate difficulty
   ☐ with good fluency

Checklists should be reviewed by the teacher, placed in the students' portfolio, and shared with parents and students themselves. When students know the teacher is watching—and, more important, what the teacher is watching for—they are more likely to live up to the teacher's high expectations.

Performance Assessments

A performance assessment is also a form of observation but more structured. Students are asked to perform a specific task or create a specific product, and the teacher evaluates the process, the final product, or both, according to a preestablished set of criteria. For example, suppose a teacher wanted to observe students' ability to retell a story they had read or that had been read to them. A checklist for this task could look something like this:

☐ Identified the main characters
☐ Identified the setting
☐ Told what happened at the beginning of the story
☐ Told what happened in the middle of the story
☐ Told what happened at the end of the story
☐ Identified the problem
☐ Identified the solution

Such a checklist could be customized for a specific book, listing characters and key plot sequences.

Most performance and other forms of authentic assessments are evaluated according to a rubric, which is a more sophisticated form of observation checklist. Rubrics contain several categories, with the performance for each category scored on a scale (typically between 1 and 4)—the higher the number, the better the student did in meeting the teacher's expectation for the given category. Figure 5.4 is an example of a rubric a teacher could use for a performance assessment of students given the task to create a bar graph showing their favorite (or what they consider the least disgusting) cafeteria food.

Rubrics are an effective tool for assessing performance because they allow the teacher to establish up-front the expectations for a particular assignment or activity. Unlike a single score or grade, the rubric allows students to see precisely where they met the expectations and where more work was needed. The most effective use of rubrics entails going over the rubric with students before they start working on the task. If students are to meet high expectations, they need to know what those expectations are. Some teachers involve students in the creation of the rubrics.

Self-Assessments and Peer Assessments

Authentic assessments can be made even more effective if students are involved in assessing their own work and performance and that of their classmates. Self-assessment and peer assessment can be facilitated though the use of a checklist or a rubric. A student might use the following checklist to score a report about a field trip:

Field Trip Report Checklist

Content
☐ My report has a title.
☐ I wrote at least 3 paragraphs.
☐ My report tells where we went.
☐ My report tells when we went.
☐ My report tells what we did.
☐ My report tells what I liked and didn't like.
☐ My report tells what I learned.

Format and Mechanics
☐ I started each sentence with a capital letter.
☐ I ended each sentence with a "." "?" or "!"
☐ I indented each paragraph.
☐ I proofread my story and corrected spelling and grammar errors.

A similar checklist could be used for students to assess a report written by another student.

Rubrics can be used in the same manner for self- or peer assessments. For younger students, however, rubrics may need to be simpler than those used by the teacher. For example, Figure 5.5 is a rubric that could be used by kindergarten or 1st

Bar Graph Evaluation

Student Name:

Category	4	3	2	1
Title	The title is creative and clearly relates to the problem being graphed. It is printed at the top of the graph.	The title clearly relates to the problem being graphed and is printed at the top of the graph.	A title is present at the top of the graph.	A title is not present.
Labeling of X axis	The X axis has a clear neat label that describes the units used for the independent variable.	The X axis has a clear label that describes the units used for the independent variable.	The X axis has a label.	The X axis is not labeled.
Labeling of Y axis	The Y axis has a clear neat label that describes the units and the dependent variable.	The Y axis has a clear label that describes the units and the dependent variable.	The Y axis has a label.	The Y axis is not labeled.
Units	All units are described in a key and are appropriately sized for the data set.	Most units are described in a key and are appropriately sized for the data set.	All units are described in a key but are not appropriately sized for the data set.	Units are neither described nor appropriately sized for the data set.
Accuracy of plot	All values are depicted correctly and are easy to see. A ruler was used to make the bars neatly.	All values are depicted correctly and are easy to see.	Some values are depicted incorrectly.	All values are depicted incorrectly.
Neatness and attractiveness	Exceptionally well designed, neat, and attractive. Colors that go well together are used to make the graph more readable.	Neat and relatively attractive.	Lines are neatly drawn but the graph appears quite plain.	Appears messy and "thrown together" in a hurry. Lines are visibly crooked.

Figure 5.4 Example of a rubric for performance assessment (Note: Created with Rubistar at rubistar.4teachers.org)

Figure 5.5 Example of a self-assessment rubric

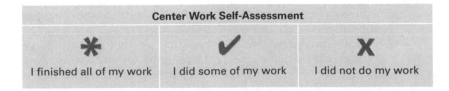

Center Work Self-Assessment		
✳	✔	✗
I finished all of my work	I did some of my work	I did not do my work

grade students to self-assess their work at learning centers. Self-assessments can also take the form of prompts students complete to reflect on their learning and work. These reflections can be done through discussions, teacher-student conferences, or daily or weekly reflection logs, with prompts such as these:

- Today I learned . . .
- I am going to use what I learned to . . .
- Today I did a good job in . . .
- Today I had trouble with . . .
- Tomorrow I am going to try harder to . . .
- I need more help with . . .
- I want to learn more about . . .

Reflective self-assessments can be very effective in making students aware of what they have learned and how they are progressing and can prepare them for further learning that can advance them to the next level.

Peer assessment can be very effective, but teachers should keep in mind that students need to be well trained in how to assess their peers. Proper training in peer assessment can help students do higher quality work themselves because they know exactly what the evaluation criteria are. Training can also help avoid conflicts over fairness and whether one student is evaluating another's work too harshly or incorrectly. Care also must be taken in determining which students assess which students. A newly arrived ELL with little to no English proficiency, for example, should not be expected to assess the writing of a more advanced ELL student. Peer assessment, however, does not replace teacher assessment. The purpose of peer assessment is for students to internalize the high expectations and provide assistance to each other in meeting these expectations. It is not a strategy to save the teacher time by having students grade each other's work. In fact, this practice is forbidden in many schools because student privacy laws forbid teachers from making a student's grades known to other students in the class. But even in schools where such rules are strictly enforced, as long as the peer assessments do not result in final scores or grades that get entered into a teacher's grade book, the types described here should be allowed because of the valuable feedback peers can provide to each other.

Portfolio Assessment

Portfolio assessment is one of the most effective ways to measure a student's progress. The teacher collects samples of the student's work throughout the year and organizes it systematically in a portfolio. Much like an artist's portfolio, a student portfolio is a collection of work that demonstrates the student's progress and achievement in meeting grade-level standards. That collection, however, should not be just a hodgepodge resembling the overloaded backpack of a student whose parents never bother to check it and clear it out each day.

Effective student portfolios are well organized and provide evidence of student learning. Most include samples of student work along with some indication of how the student rated himself or herself on the work, and evidence of how it met grade-level curricular standards (Herrera et al., 2007). Some teachers use working portfolios, which hold samples of students' work in progress. Others use showcase portfolios, which hold samples of the students' best work. With showcase portfolios, many teachers prefer to decide what goes in, but others argue that the students should be allowed to pick their best work for inclusion. I prefer a mixed approach, with some pieces chosen by the teacher and others by the student and teacher together.

A portfolio should be organized by content area (or separate portfolios should be set up for each content area) and should include representative work samples from the beginning, middle, and end of the school year. Students' progress in writing, for example, could be easily observed by comparing writing samples completed by students during the first few weeks of school, those completed just before winter break, and those completed near the end of the school year. If these are accompanied by completed rubrics and student self-assessments, the portfolio will present a clear record of the students' learning and mastery of the writing process and proper use of writing conventions and style.

Teachers will want to ensure that there are samples of different genres of writing in the portfolio. However, to allow for useful comparisons of each student's work throughout the year, there should be at least three samples from the same genre. For example, the writing portfolio could include a first-person narrative written at the beginning of the year, another in the middle of the year, and a third at the end of the year. A math portfolio might include a timed test of addition facts given at the beginning of the year and repeated at the middle and end to document the students' improvement in speed and accuracy.

In many schools, grade-level teams decide what to include in student portfolios to ensure consistency in portfolio assessment for each grade level. In my former school district, we had districtwide standards for math portfolios. Some teachers felt that this rigidity defeated the purpose of a portfolio as an alternative and authentic assessment; others were grateful for the guidance. All agreed, however, that the variety of samples in the portfolio provided a much better indication of their students' progress in learning math than did the state math test given at the end of the school year.

Some schools also use a pivotal portfolio, which follows the student year to year throughout the program. Teams of teachers decide what kinds of summative and formative student data to include in the pivotal portfolio, when to collect it, and what rubrics to use. The use of common assessments ensures that teachers share a language and a practice that is focused on improved student performance. Teachers use this balanced assessment and accountability system to counter the overreliance on high-stakes standardized tests that NCLB has created (Gottlieb & Nguyen, 2006).

The Need for Multiple Measures

Among the many other problems with state high-stakes tests is that they provide just one piece of evidence about what students know and can do. As we have seen, this evidence is relatively weak and of questionable validity, especially for ELL students. The reality is that despite the inadequacies of standardized high-stakes tests, they are not likely to go away any time soon. Therefore, it is imperative that teachers use several alternative and authentic assessments throughout the year. In other words, teachers need to use multiple measures of a student's progress. Multiple measures of ELL students are particularly important because, as the school year progresses, ELLs learn more and more English. At any point, they probably know more English than they did the last time they took a test or completed an assessment. Thus, along with providing strong evidence of student's knowledge and skills, multiple measures enable teachers to track the student's progress and growth during the school year.

When I was an elementary school teacher, I was required to administer the state's high-stakes test (SAT-9) in English to my 2nd grade students, all of whom were ELLs. Their scores were not very high. At the end of the school year, when I was required to sit down with my principal to go over my students' test scores, I brought along samples from their portfolios. The portfolios provided evidence that when many of my students came to me at the beginning of the school year they were reading at the kindergarten or beginning of 1st grade level but most had made over a year's growth in their reading ability. I showed him writing samples from the beginning of year, which revealed that many students had struggled just to write a full sentence, and then I showed him how these same students by the end of the year were writing full paragraphs and stories. I showed evidence that students who began the year unable to add or subtract were now able to do grade-level math work. In short, the multiple measures of my students gathered in their portfolios throughout the year demonstrated that most of them had made tremendous progress. The state's test made my students—and me as their teacher—look like failures. The authentic assessments, in contrast, provided substantial evidence that my students worked hard and made more progress than most students make in a single school year. They were anything but failures. My principal agreed that these alternative assessments painted a more fair and accurate measure of the progress of our students than did the state test.

One of the major weaknesses of high-stakes tests is that success is defined as students' meeting or exceeding a predetermined bar—the cut score that students must meet or exceed to be deemed as passing. Such tests cannot show students' growth during the school year. Consider Figure 5.6. Student A, a typical native English-speaking student, began 4th grade at about grade level and learned enough during the school year to pass the state test for his grade level. Student B, a very bright ELL student from a poor country who had been in the United States for less than a year before entering the 4th grade, began the school year at just above the kindergarten level. She made over 2 years' worth of growth in the 4th grade. Nonetheless, student B is deemed a "failure" (along with her teacher) because she did not meet or exceed the passing standard for the 4th grade test, whereas her classmate, who had significantly less growth in the same period, is deemed a "success."

What is needed are assessment systems that can measure growth. There is work under way in several states to create tests that can be used for accountability purposes that are based on growth models. The education stimulus funding from the Obama administration is also encouraging states to use growth models and better track student progress. This new emphasis on growth models is a positive and welcome development. But unfortunately, these models are still in the experimental stage and continue to rely on standardized tests. I suspect there will continue to be many problems with the standardized tests used with ELLs and that it will take several years to determine how we can get valid and reliable measures of

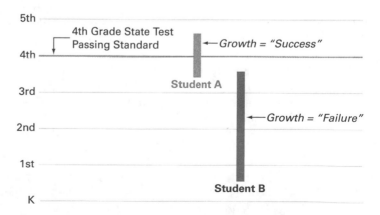

Figure 5.6   Illustration of how state high-stakes test cannot account for students' growth

ELL students' academic growth. Multiple measures of ELL students using a wide variety of alternative and authentic assessments given throughout the school year currently provide the most accurate (valid) and fair assessment of student's knowledge, abilities, and growth.

SUMMARY

Providing ELLs with effective instruction requires the appropriate use of assessment. Assessment involves systemic planning and collection of student data from a variety of sources throughout the school year. Periodic summative assessments can provide a summary of what students have learned, but on-going formative assessments are essential to provide information that drives instruction appropriate to the students' strengths and needs. Norm-referenced tests may be inherently unfair to ELLs because their performance is compared to mainly (or exclusively) English-proficient students. Criterion-referenced tests may be more fair for ELLs, since these tests report the extent to which students learned the tested content. Both types of test, however, are problematic for ELLs because of unresolved issues about how to test ELLs in a valid and reliable manner. ELLs' lack of proficiency in English means that academic tests given in English cannot provide a fair and accurate measure of the students' true academic ability. Language tests, while important for tracking the progress of ELLs, can likewise never fully measure a student's proficiency because of the complexity of the construct of language proficiency and the multifaceted nature of bilingualism. Given these unresolved issues, the mandates of NCLB to use ELLs' high-stakes test results for school accountability purposes are problematic. Recent requirements to tie these scores to teacher evaluations are even more problematic. Furthermore, flaws in the logic and requirements of NCLB set up unreasonable expectations for ELL students. Thus, the frequent use of alternative authentic assessments, such as observations, performance assessments, self- and peer assessments, and portfolio assessment, is crucial for obtaining an accurate picture of ELL students' progress. When used consistently over the course of the school year, these assessments provide multiple measures of student performance that document students' growth and thus provide a clearer and more accurate picture of ELL students' language learning and academic progress.

Discussion Questions

1. Why are norm-referenced achievement tests in English inherently unfair for ELL students? What would be the likely reaction of testing companies and policymakers if most ELLs students scored above the 50th percentile on a norm-referenced test in English?

2. Miguel, an advanced-level ELL, obtained a raw score of 56 on the state reading test but needed a score of 57 to pass. Because he "failed" the test, he and several other students who missed passing by a few points are pulled out of class over the next few months to be drilled by hired tutors on reading exercises similar to those on the test, in preparation for retesting. Is this a good use of instructional time? Why or why not? Did Miguel really "fail" the test? (Hint: standard error of measurement.)

3. Most people believe the higher the test scores, the better the school. However, Alfie Kohn (2000), author of the book *The Case Against High Stakes Testing: Raising the Scores, Ruining the Schools*, argues that a rise in a school's test scores

should not be a cause for celebration but rather a cause for mourning. How can rising test scores be an indication of declining quality of instruction and education in a school?

4. **On-line Discussion Board** This chapter lists many of the potentially harmful effects high-stakes testing may have on ELLs. Have you observed any of these effects? Have you experienced any of them first-hand as a student or as a teacher? How can these harmful effects be minimalized?

5. **On-line Discussion Board** Early in its educational reform efforts, the Obama administration insisted that teachers' evaluations be tied to their students' test scores. Based on what you read in this chapter, why might this policy be unfair for teachers of ELL students? What changes in federal assessment requirements for ELLs do you feel should be made before ELLs' assessment performances are used to evaluate teacher effectiveness?

6. The current paradox of testing and ELLs is that if ELLs are not included in statewide high-stakes testing and accountability programs, schools will likely ignore their needs, but when ELLs are included, their test scores are invalid but used in harmful ways. Are there other ways that schools could be held accountable for addressing the needs of their ELL students without having to rely on problematic high-stakes tests?

7. Why are multiple measures crucial for valid assessment of ELLs? What are some examples of the measures that should be collected over time and how should these assessment data be evaluated?

Research Activities

1. **Wiki This** What is your state's policy for the inclusion of ELLs in the state's testing and accountability program? What is the minimum group size established by your state for the LEP subgroup? Based on this number, how many of the schools you are familiar with would be required to have an LEP subgroup for NCLB accountability purposes?

2. Talk to teachers in a school you are familiar with. Ask them to describe any curricular changes that have taken place in response to state or federal testing and accountability mandates. Ask them how these changes have impacted their ELL students.

3. **Wiki This** Interview a teacher of ELL students. Ask what alternative authentic assessments he or she uses with the students. Ask whether he or she feels these assessments provide more accurate information about the students' knowledge and skills than the state's test.

4. What testing accommodations are allowed for ELLs on your state's test? How many of these accommodations are responsive to the ELLs' linguistic needs? Do you feel these accommodations are sufficient to assess an ELL student in a valid and reliable manner?

5. Conduct an analysis of your state's English language proficiency test (or language proficiency assessment system). What types of questions are asked? What kinds of tasks are students asked to complete, and how are these scored? Overall, how effective do you feel this test is in measuring students' ability to listen, speak, read, and write English?

Recommended Reading

Gottlieb, M. H. (2006). *Assessing English language learners: Bridges from language proficiency to academic achievement.* Thousand Oaks, CA: Corwin Press.
  Viewing valid assessment of ELLs as crucial to their academic success, the au-

thor provides an excellent framework for authentic language and content-area assessment of ELLs students.

Menken, K. (2008). *English learners left behind: Standardized testing as language policy.* Clevedon, UK: Multilingual Matters.

Drawing on data collected from New York high schools, the author describes how testing policy functions as language policy and documents the harmful effects of high-stakes testing on the teaching and learning of secondary ELL students.

Nichols, S., & Berliner, D. C. (2007). *Collateral damage: How high-stakes testing corrupts America's schools.* Cambridge, MA: Harvard Education Press.

A principle from the social sciences states that when a single measure is used to measure a social phenomenon, that measure tends to corrupt the very thing it is trying to measure. Drawing on this principle, the authors document how NCLB and state policies that rely on high-stakes tests as the sole measure of a school's quality are actually corrupting our nation's schools.

Popham, W. J. (2004). *Classroom assessment: What teachers need to know* (4th ed.). Boston: Allyn and Bacon.

A teacher-friendly overview of assessment basics and issues and a helpful guide teachers can use to create their own classroom assessments.

Valenzuela, A. (2004). *Leaving children behind: How "Texas-style" accountability fails Latino youth.* New York: State University of New York Press.

NCLB was modeled after education reform efforts in Texas while former President George W. Bush was governor. The author provides evidence of the harm these policies have had on Latino students in Texas, and how NCLB is extending this same harm to students nationwide.

6

Listening and Speaking

It's like our saying to the students, "Sorry, I can't listen to your story about your puppy because I have to read you this book about a dog."

—Linda Veal, sheltered English immersion kindergarten teacher

KEY TERMS

- silent period
- wait time
- total physical response (TPR)
- minimal pairs
- cooperative learning
- SOLOM (Student Oral Language Observation Matrix)

GUIDING QUESTIONS

1. What does the research tell us about the relationships between ELLs' oral language development, literacy development, and educational achievement?
2. How can an understanding of ELLs' listening and speaking strengths and needs inform a teacher's choices of instructional approaches, methods, and strategies?
3. How can the TESOL standards guide instruction and assessment for ELLs?
4. How can teachers promote oral language use in the classroom as a foundation for ELLs' literacy development and academic achievement in English?
5. How can teachers promote the development of higher levels of oral language proficiency for ELLs?

Of the four traditional language skills, listening is by far the one we use most frequently. Think about how much time you spent listening today. Then think about how much time you spent speaking, which typically is second to listening. Right now you are reading, and you might even write a few notes as you read. What you read here could later become the topic for oral discussions. Oral language dominates our day, and even reading and writing tasks provide the impetus for oral conversation.

In the past, language educators considered listening and reading to be passive skills, with students simply receiving oral or written input. Speaking and writing, in contrast, were considered active skills, with students actively involved in producing oral and written language. This view no longer holds. Today, as Elaine Horwitz (2008) explains:

> Language scholars recognize that listening and reading are by no means passive processes and that both listeners and readers must actively construct the meaning of any language they encounter. Of course, whenever we listen, the words themselves are not the only source of meaning. Gestures, facial expressions, tone of voice, and the setting and context of the conversation all contribute to our understanding of what another person is saying. (p. 69)

Evidence that listening is an active skill of constructing meaning can be found in the fact that, as political debates and personal arguments attest, even native speakers of English may hear the same thing but interpret it differently.

What do ELLs need to do to be able to actively construct meaning through oral English? Consider some of the following challenges:

- English speakers do not pronounce individual words separately and distinctly with space in between them as for the written words on this page. At the most basic level, ELLs have to attend to each phoneme in each word, because the change of one phoneme can change the meaning of an utterance (e.g., *bit/pit*). In normal, everyday speech, however, all the words run together. One friend might ask another, "Did you eat?" using a phrase that sounds more like "Dijaeat?" or "Djeet?"

- English speakers do not always speak in complete sentences. Much of my own research involves audio recording interviews with participants and then making a full transcription of every word the participants say. English speakers often start a sentence but then get off on a tangent and start talking about something else without finishing their earlier thought. Oral language is full of sentence fragments, run-on sentences, false starts, hesitations, and embedded clauses, which make it challenging for ELLs to fully comprehend (Flowerdew & Miller, 2005).

- Oral language is invisible (unless someone transcribes it verbatim). Once spoken, an utterance is gone forever (unless someone audio or video records it). ELLs cannot rewind real life conversations to hear an utterance they missed. They cannot pause and look up a word they hear in the dictionary. If they make a mistake when talking, there is no way to go back, erase it, and try it again. They have to either let it go or try to say it again, if there is still an opportunity to do so.

- Speaking is much more complicated than simply selecting the correct vocabulary words and stringing them together with proper syntax to make sentences. To be comprehensible, an ELL must have adequate pronunciation, a smooth rate and flow of speech, and sufficient vocabulary and grammar, as well as a working understanding of the sociocultural context of the speech event.

- Different types of speech activities are structured by unwritten norms that are known by native speakers but may be elusive to ELLs (e.g., having a friendly conversation, giving a formal presentation, asking the teacher a question, giving opinions in class about a reading, agreeing and disagreeing with another student during a small group activity). Even in everyday conversations, there are norms governing turn-taking, adding a point, changing the subject, and ending the conversation. There are also norms governing the use of nonverbal communication, for example, to demonstrate that you are listening and paying attention (e.g., making eye contact, nodding your head, saying "uh-huh"). Many cross-cultural misunderstandings in oral communication can be explained by differences in pragmatics.

One of the ironies of oral language is that we know it is important and the most often used mode of communication, but we tend to spend the least amount of classroom instruction time helping ELLs develop it. This chapter is intended to address that gap. First, we look at what we know about oral language development from two recent and thorough reviews of the scientific literature. Next we discuss basic issues related to oral language in the classroom. Then we consider how the TESOL standards for listening and speaking can help sheltered instruction and ESL teachers plan instruction and establish reasonable expectations for ELLs at different levels of English proficiency. With this foundation, we look at a range of practices, strategies, techniques, and activities for promoting oral language development in the classroom. We conclude with a discussion of assessments that teachers can use to plan instruction that helps ELLs advance to higher levels of English proficiency and that teachers can use to provide evidence of English language development.

What We Know from Research about Oral Language and ELLs

Major reviews of the scientific research literature on language and literacy instruction for English language learners were conducted recently by the Center for Research on Education, Diversity, and Excellence (CREDE), whose report is titled *Educating English Language Learners: A Synthesis of Research Evidence* (Genesee, Lindholm-Leary, Saunders, & Christian, 2006), and the National Literacy Panel (NLP) on Language Minority Children and Youth, whose report is titled *Developing Literacy in Second Language Learners* (August & Shanahan, 2006a). Both studies received support from the U.S. Department of Education's Institute for Education Science, and both involved experts in language, literacy, and other academic fields who identified, read, and synthesized relevant academic research. The findings outlined in the CREDE and NLP reports highlight what we currently know—and what we don't—about how to help ELL students in language and literacy learning. The CREDE review focused on oral language development; the NLP review focused on the relationship of oral language to literacy.

CREDE Report

William M. Saunders and Gisela O'Brien (2006) were the lead scholars for the CREDE report who reviewed and synthesized the research on oral language development (hereafter referred to as the "CREDE reviewers"). Their review resulted in the following major findings:

The empirical literature on oral language development in ELLs is small.

The CREDE reviewers found that "there is virtually no U.S. research on how classroom instruction might best promote more academic aspects of oral language development, and there is very little research on oral language proficiency beyond the elementary grades" (p. 19). Our limited understanding of L2 oral language development means that we have little empirical basis for planning educational interventions that would promote language development. Although educators everywhere recognize the importance of oral language, the report speculates that oral language remains in the shadows of research because researchers tend to focus on English reading and writing outcomes and general measures of academic achievement. Also, as the CREDE reviewers point out, because oral language is hard to assess using paper and pencil tests, it rarely gets included on high-stakes tests. And if it is not on the test, it does not get emphasized in the curriculum or garner much research attention.

It takes time for ELLs to develop oral English proficiency.

The CREDE reviewers found that ELLs, on average, require several years to develop oral English proficiency and tend to make more rapid progress from lower to middle levels of proficiency (i.e., from Level 1 to Level 3) and slower progress as they move beyond Level 3. They found that by grade 5, "ELLs are performing 3.5 years below native-English speaker norms." They suspect this slowdown is due to the lack of instructional attention to oral language development once students reach the middle levels of English proficiency. Also, the reviewers found, on average, ELLs' L2 oral language development proceeds at a fairly constant rate that is unrelated to the program they are in. Thus, these findings from the CREDE Report (1) challenge claims that English-only programs will help ELLs learn English faster than bilingual programs, (2) provide evidence that native language instruction in bilingual classrooms does not delay or impede students' acquisition of English, (3) contradict policies based on the assumption that ELLs can learn English in 1 year, and (4) provide strong evidence that direct, systematic ESL instruction is imperative—especially at higher levels—so students can avoid a slowdown at the middle levels and continue to make progress toward becoming fluent English proficient.

ELLs need some English proficiency before interaction with native speakers is beneficial.

The CREDE report challenges the notion that ELLs must interact with native or fluent English speakers in order to learn English—a notion that has been used in some cases to justify closing bilingual and ESL programs and placing ELLs in mainstream classrooms. The CREDE reviewers found that interaction in and of itself is not sufficient and that ELLs cannot really begin to associate with English speakers until they attain at least some level of English proficiency. The reviewers describe a study in which a newcomer non-English-speaking ELL failed to benefit from work with English-speaking peers because the class assignments were well beyond her proficiency level, and her peers had no idea how to help her. Nevertheless, the report concludes, interactive activities can be beneficial if they pair ELLs with native or fluent English speakers and careful consideration is given to the design of the task, the training of the non-ELLs, and the language proficiency of the ELLs.

Use of English outside of school enhances ELLs' oral English development.

The CREDE reviewers caution that this finding comes with three qualifiers: (1) simultaneous development of students' L1 does not slow down their development of English oral proficiency, (2) for students at higher levels of English proficiency, their use of English outside of school may not be as critical as their use of English in the school, and (3) the ways in which students use their L1 and English at home are interrelated, and their L1 and English language development are mediated by a wide range of sociocultural factors. Although using English outside of school seems important, the reviewers are forced to conclude that "it seems quite clear that the relationship among L2 development, L1 maintenance, and language use is quite complex" (p. 34).

Use of L1 for beginning-level ELLs contributes to academic development.

The CREDE reviewers describe a study that found that the newcomer elementary school ELLs who received ample primary language support and who spoke little English in class during the first half of the year scored higher on an achievement assessment in English than newcomer ELLs who spoke mostly English in class and received little primary language support. Like other CREDE report findings, this finding challenges those who advocate for English-only classroom policies and highlights the importance of primary language support.

English oral language proficiency tests fail to capture the full oral language proficiency of bilingual students.

This finding reiterates a point made in Chapter 5, where we saw that this problem with language proficiency tests is due to the complexity of bilingualism and oral language proficiency and to the fact that tests can measure only a very small sample of oral proficiency skills. The CREDE reviewers also found that the notion of "academic language proficiency" is problematic because it is often confounded with literacy. They note that more research is needed to clarify what academic oral language proficiency is, independent of literacy and in relation to traditional constructs of literacy. Finally, they note that because of the limitations of these language proficiency tests, decisions about when to place ELLs in mainstream classes should be based on a combination of informed teacher judgments and oral language assessments that are academically oriented and broad in scope.

National Literacy Panel Report

The NLP report found a close relationship between L2 oral proficiency and reading. Nonie Lesaux and Esther Geva (Lesaux & Geva, 2006; Geva, 2006) were the lead scholars for the NLP report reviewing and synthesizing the scientific research in this area (hereafter referred to as the "NLP reviewers"). Their review resulted in the following major findings:

Oral language skills are more important for reading larger chunks of text for comprehension than for reading at the word level.

The NLP report makes an important distinction between reading larger chunks of text for comprehension and reading at the word level. The reviewers found that students can learn to decode words, including nonsense or "pseudowords," even if they do not know what those words mean.

Oral language skills in English are strongly associated with English reading comprehension.

The NLP reviewers found that these oral language skills needed for reading comprehension include vocabulary knowledge, listening comprehension, syntactic skills, and the ability to handle metalinguistic aspects of language, such as the ability to define words. The more English ELLs can speak and understand, the more they are able to comprehend what they read in English. The reviewers note, however, that the relationship between English oral language proficiency and English reading comprehension is also mediated by several contextual factors, including language use and literacy practices at home, socioeconomic status, and the students' prior education experiences and the types of instruction they have received. Simply being able to speak English well, however, is not sufficient for students to become strong readers in English. ELLs need to have relevant prior knowledge about a particular concept and have the oral language skills necessary to talk about it, in order to be able to read with comprehension about it in English. The reviewers found that other sociocultural and instructional factors must also be taken into consideration.

Oral language skills in English are associated with better English writing.

The NLP reviewers found the oral language skills that are related to writing include listening comprehension and vocabulary knowledge. Other aspects of oral language proficiency found to be important for English writing include decontextualized language skills, grammatical skills, and knowledge of cohesion devices (e.g., anaphora, relativization, temporal reference, and conjunctions). These skills are necessary for writers to express ideas that are not limited to the here and now.

English oral language proficiency is not strongly related to English spelling skills.

The NLP reviewers found that students' ability to spell individual words correctly is not related to vocabulary and syntactic knowledge. In other words, students can memorize the spellings of words without knowing their meaning or how to use them in a sentence. They warn, however, that this conclusion is tentative, because only a small number of studies have addressed this relationship.

L1 language literacy skills plus good English oral language skills are strongly associated with good English reading comprehension skills.

The NLP reviewers found that students who can read in their L1 and who have developed good oral English proficiency also have an advantage in learning to read in English. In contrast, they found that students with lower levels of oral English proficiency are less able to apply their L1 reading skills to reading in English.

ELLs need consistent ESL instruction.

The findings of the NLP report make it clear that "just good teaching" of reading and writing is not sufficient for ELLs to develop English literacy skills. For this "good teaching" to be effective, the research shows, it must be combined with ESL instruction that has a strong focus on helping students develop their English language oral proficiency skills. When such ESL instruction is neglected, ELLs may develop word recognition, spelling, and decoding skills but continue to lag behind their peers in reading comprehension and vocabulary. The NLP report calls for an early, ongoing, and intensive effort to develop English-language proficiency, suggesting, as does the CREDE report, that ESL instruction is imperative for ELL students at all levels of proficiency, not just those at the beginning levels.

Basic Issues for Oral Language Development in the Classroom

Our understanding of necessary conditions for second language acquisition helps us with some basic issues related to ELLs' oral language development. Recall from Chapter 2 that the goal is to help ELLs develop communicative competence and for that development to occur, students must receive comprehensible input and have opportunities to produce comprehensible output. Recall also that meaningful interaction with other speakers of the language is a necessary condition for second language acquisition. From a cognitive psychological perspective, this interaction provides the means for learners to receive and process comprehensible input and to produce comprehensible output. From a sociocultural perspective, learning, including language learning, takes place through interaction in the students' zone of proximal development (ZPD) with the teacher and more competent peers (Lantolf, 2000).

These principles of second language acquisition can help teachers determine how much oral language to expect from students at different levels of English proficiency. In this section we apply these principles to the following issues: the silent period, wait time, teacher talk in the classroom, and correcting student speech errors.

The Silent Period

Non-English-speaking students who are just beginning to learn the language (i.e., those starting at Level 1) may not be ready to start speaking when they first enter the classroom. Most second language learners therefore go through a silent period before they begin to speak. Teachers should not assume that because students do not talk, they are not learning. During the silent period, learners are developing their receptive listening skills as they acquire bits and pieces of the language and process the input for meaning. They are also beginning to figure out how their new language works. Thus, teachers should not force students to talk before they are ready.

For some ELL students, the silent period might be just a few hours. For others, it could be several weeks. ELLs born in the United States may not need any silent period because they have likely had a great deal of exposure to English before entering school and do not need to adjust to living in a new country. Non-English-speaking newcomer ELLs, in contrast, may need a long silent period. However, the more teachers are able to lower students' affective filters by creating supportive classrooms and the more opportunities teachers scaffold and provide for oral language development, the shorter the silent period will likely be. Also, students may feel comfortable speaking in some tasks, such as a familiar chant with the whole class, but do not yet feel ready to contribute to a classroom discussion where they have to speak alone in front of all the other students.

Wait Time

When ELLs do feel ready to speak, they may need time to process the input and time to draw from their developing linguistic system to formulate their thoughts in English before speaking. If a teacher asks them a question, they may need first to mentally translate the question, figure out the answer, and then translate that answer before they can respond to the teacher. Giving students time for this process after asking them a question or requiring them to respond is called wait time. Some students may be able to formulate most of what they want to say in English but need a bit of extra time to recall new vocabulary or appropriate forms before speaking. Cultures differ in what is considered an appropriate pause before responding to a question, and so what seems like a very long pause for one cultural group may be very short to another cultural group. Many teachers mistakenly interpret silence as an indication that the student does not understand the question or does not know the answer. This misunderstanding has potentially negative consequences for the ELL who may be denied opportunities to participate effectively in the classroom interaction.

Teachers must be patient after asking a question. One strategy is simply to wait. Another is to find creative ways to build in wait time. For example, the teacher might ask the class a question for which multiple answers are possible, such as, "Can you tell me a food that is good for our bodies?" then go down the line of students and have each give an answer in succession. The ELL students know their turn is coming up and will have to time to process the question and prepare an answer. Also, hearing the preceding students' answers can help the ELLs confirm their understanding of the question. Another simple strategy is to respond to an ELL student who appears unready to answer a question by saying, "Keep thinking, and I'll come back to you in a second." Chances are, when the teacher comes back, the student will have an answer ready.

Teacher Talk in the Classroom

Teachers typically do most of the speaking in the classroom; thus, two important issues need to be addressed. First, teachers should talk less and plan classroom activities that give students regular opportunities to speak. Gallagher, an American comedian, has poignantly observed, "They send us to school to learn to communicate, but all day long the teachers tell us to shut up!" I once took a group of university students to observe a middle school classroom where the teacher had his students sitting at their desks, which were arranged in a large circle, discussing the classic book *Animal Farm* by George Orwell. The teacher stood in the middle and directed the discussion. Initially, my students were very impressed with the inter-

Box 6.1

Adjusting Speech to Make It Comprehensible

■ Slow down! Use a slower rate of speech when talking to beginning-level ELLs than you would in normal conversation with native speakers, but maintain a steady pace.

■ Speak clearly, but do not overenunciate to the point where the words sound unnatural.

■ Speak at a normal volume. Shouting does not make English more comprehensible.

■ Use simple sentence structure with beginning-level ELLs (e.g., subject-verb-object). Avoid long, complex sentences with embedded clauses.

■ As students make progress, increase the complexity of the vocabulary and syntax appropriate to their English-language proficiency.

■ Emphasize key vocabulary through frequent repetition of these new words throughout the week and across subject areas.

■ Avoid idioms, unless they are explained or were previously taught.

■ Avoid cultural references that may be unfamiliar to ELL students, unless they are explained.

■ Use gestures, facial expressions, realia, and other visuals.

■ Repeat, paraphrase, or use other recast techniques when students do not understand.

active discussion. Later, however, when they analyzed their video transcript of the lesson, they discovered that the teacher did over 95% of the talking! Only a few of the children spoke and those who did gave only very short answers to the teacher's narrow questions. Thus, there was actually very little discussion going on in this "classroom discussion."

One effective approach for encouraging more student talk is to use open-ended and higher-order questions and short probes that require students to elaborate, such as, "What else did you notice?" "Why do you think that was?" "What do you think is going to happen next?" "Val, do you agree with Mai? Why not?" In this way the teacher can scaffold a discussion within the students' ZPD by guiding them to think more deeply with opportunities to express and elaborate their ideas orally.

Second, and equally important, teachers need to adjust the way they talk with their ELL students to ensure that their speech provides comprehensible input (see Box 6.1). Any modifications should take into account the students' level of English proficiency. For ELLs at the beginning levels of English proficiency, teachers should slow down their rate of speech, enunciate clearly, and use a simple sentence structure, avoiding long sentences with complicated syntax. Teachers should also be careful when using idioms and explain the meaning of any that are unfamiliar to ELL students. However, as students make gains in their English language proficiency, they need more complex input in order to make continued progress.

Correcting Student Speech Errors

Teacher talk also entails how teachers respond to their students when interacting with them in conversations. A major issue is when and how to correct ELL students' speech errors. Errors are a normal part of language acquisition, but, on one hand, if students are corrected by their teachers every time they open their mouths, they are likely to get frustrated; their affective filters may be raised so high they will never want to talk again in class. On the other hand, if students are never corrected, their development of oral English skills may be impeded.

Teachers should correct only those errors students are ready to learn how to correct. We know from Krashen's natural order hypothesis that learners acquire some grammatical forms earlier than others, and those that are acquired later may be impervious to direct correction. Thus, it may be a waste of time, for example, to correct errors related to the proper use of *-s* for third-person verbs (e.g., He jump*s*) before a student has a basic vocabulary of verbs and pronouns and an understanding of simple verb conjugation.

A key issue is how corrections should be provided. To keep the affective filter low, students' errors should be corrected in a manner that avoids embarrassment, particularly in front of their peers. But should the correction be explicit or implicit?

According to one aspect of Michael Long's (1983, 1996) interaction hypothesis, discussed in Chapter 2, native speakers should provide corrective feedback when they interact with ELLs. Consider the following two examples of the response Jin receives when he tells his teacher about his trip to the mall:

Example 1

> JIN: Teacher! Yesterday I goed to mall with my friend.
> TEACHER: No, Jin, don't say *goed*. It's *went*. Remember, *go* is an irregular verb. And it's *the* mall, you're forgetting the definite article. Now, try again.

Example 2

> JIN: Teacher! Yesterday I goed to mall with my friend.
> TEACHER: You went to the mall with your friend? Cool! I went to the mall last week with my son to buy clothes. What did you buy?

Example 1 is a direct correction, or what Long refers to as negative feedback. Example 2 is an example of positive feedback. Here the teacher does not correct the student but instead models the correct usage through a positive and reinforcing response, using the correct forms *went* and *the mall*, twice in her response. Such a response in authentic conversations is a form of scaffolding. These indirect forms of corrections are referred to as recasts. According to Schmidt's (1990, 2001) noticing hypothesis, learners need to notice specific language features in the input in order to acquire them. Of course, there is no guarantee that Jin will notice this modeling, but if teachers consistently engage their students in conversations and respond to student errors in this manner, they will be providing comprehensible input, and students will likely eventually notice and acquire the correct form unconsciously.

Other error correction issues are related to the students' level of English proficiency, the context of the conversation in which the error occurs, and whether or not the error leads to misunderstanding or potential embarrassment for the student (see Box 6.2).

Promoting Oral Language Development in the Classroom

In this section we discuss classroom activities, strategies, and techniques teachers can use during ESL and sheltered instruction to enhance oral language use and development by promoting listening and speaking through engaging students in meaningful interactions. Effective teachers use a principled approach to select strategies based on an understanding of second language acquisition. Teachers identify the strengths and needs of ELLs in their classes, with attention to their

> ### Box 6.2
>
> ## When and How to Correct Student Speech Errors
>
> ### When to Correct
>
> ■ Correct errors of form when students are ready to learn the correct form (e.g., beginning-level ELLs who say "da" for "the" should not be corrected).
> ■ Correct errors when they impede comprehension (e.g., "The stove is in our chicken" [kitchen]).
> ■ Correct errors when they impede communication (e.g., correcting verb tense errors may not be appropriate during a lesson on the metric system).
> ■ Correct errors during ESL or other language-focused instruction when a particular language form has been taught and is being practiced (e.g., to practice the use of the future tense, students are talking about their plans for the weekend; the teacher listens and helps students having difficulty using the correct future tense form).
> ■ Correct errors in the use of a target language form during content-area instruction (e.g., a language objective about using the past tense in combination with a lesson about historical events).
> ■ Correct errors that are unintentionally offensive or that could be embarrassing if the student made the error in front of fluent English speakers (e.g., "I saw a whore [horse] at the farm.").
>
> ### How to Correct
>
> ■ Provide implicit corrections through recasts by responding naturally but in a manner that models the correct form (e.g., Student: "My mom, she buy me shirt red." Teacher: "Your mom bought you a red shirt? Very nice! My wife bought me a blue jacket.").
> ■ Provide explicit corrections in a manner that does not embarrass or ridicule the student (e.g., "I think you mean your stove is in your *kitchen.* Is that what you meant?").
> ■ Provide corrections with gentle reminders of past instruction (e.g., Student: "At my house we have four pet." Teacher: "Remember how we practiced making plural words? So how would you say you have more than one pet?" Student: "Pets." Teacher: "You got it. Great job!")

English language proficiency level, L1 literacy, background content-area knowledge, and cultural considerations. They also identify the knowledge and skills (content, language, literacy, cultural) students need to participate and achieve in the activities, lessons, and units that they develop. This information about students and goals enables teachers to (1) select strategies that will enhance the oral language use and development of specific ELLs and (2) differentiate instruction for the range of learners in their classes.

This section begins with a brief review of the TESOL standards for listening and speaking, followed by descriptions of strategies and activities that focus on listening, those that focus on speaking, and those that facilitate meaningful interaction in the classroom. Although our attention in this chapter is on listening and speaking, effective language instruction does not isolate listening, speaking, reading, and writing, but rather integrates these four traditional domains.

TESOL Standards for Listening and Speaking

The five TESOL standards focus on (1) communicating for social, intercultural, and instructional purposes, (2) the language of language arts, (3) the language of mathematics, (4) the language of science, and (5) the language of social studies. For each of these areas, TESOL provides sample performance indicators organized by grade level and proficiency level in English (for a review, see Table 3.1). These indicators provide examples of observable language behaviors that ELLs at different levels of proficiency can be expected to demonstrate when completing various classroom tasks.

Each performance indicator contains three parts: content, language function, and support or strategy. For example, consider the following sample performance indicator for the 4th/5th grade *language of science* standard in the domain of *speaking*, on the topic of *Earth's* materials and natural resources at the *Expanding* level (Level 4) of English proficiency: "Discuss and give examples of uses of natural phenomena from collections or pictures" (TESOL, 2006a, p. 43). Here the language function is, "Discuss and give examples," the content is "uses of natural phenomena," and the support or strategy is "from collections or pictures." TESOL stresses that the sample performance indicators are not the standards themselves but examples of how to put the English language proficiency standards into operation; they are meant to be flexible and dynamic and adaptable to different contexts of instruction.

Consider the examples in Figure 6.1 for Standard 1, Communicating for social, intercultural, and instructional purposes, in the domains of listening and speaking. For listening, with students at Level 1 of English proficiency, the teacher might say, "Clap your hands," then clap his or her hands to model the desired response. With students at Level 2, this one-step direction can be increased to multistep directions with visual support. At Levels 3 and 4, students can be expected to role-play

Standard 1: Communicating for Social, Intercultural, and Instructional Purposes
Grade level cluster: 6–8

Domain: Listening
Topic: School behaviors or activities

Level 1	Level 2	Level 3	Level 4	Level 5
Follow one-step oral commands supported by visuals or gestures.	Follow multistep oral directions supported by visuals or gestures.	Role-play situations in small groups based on dialogues, video clips, or field trips.	Simulate scenarios in small groups based on broadcasts or multimedia presentations.	Create or enact skits or short plays based on videos, assemblies, or multimedia presentations.

Domain: Speaking
Topic: School life; social interactions

Level 1	Level 2	Level 3	Level 4	Level 5
Respond to and offer formulaic greetings, introductions, compliments, and farewells with peers or family members	Ask and answer questions to exchange information with peers or family members.	Initiate or engage in conversations with peers or in small groups (e.g., "Please tell me tonight's homework.").	Respond or engage in conversations involving nuances, idiomatic expressions, or slang.	Express or respond to humor or sarcasm in conversations (e.g., "Sure I plan to study all weekend.").

Figure 6.1   TESOL ELP Standards, sample performance indicators for listening and speaking. (Source: TESOL, 2006a, p. 78.)

situations or simulate scenarios based on some kind of visual stimulus, with the support of doing so in a small group. At Level 5, students can be expected to create their own skits or short plays based on something they have seen and heard. In the domain of speaking, at Level 1 ELLs can be expected to produce basic greetings and at Level 2 they can be expected to ask and answer basic questions in the supportive context of speaking with peers or family members. At Level 3, ELLs can be expected to initiate a conversation with peers. By Level 5, they can be expected to participate in conversations with more nuanced expressions, such as idioms and slang, or they might employ humor and sarcasm.

For both listening and speaking, note how the difficulty increases with each level as the amount of support decreases. Using the TESOL sample performance indicators as a guide, teachers can establish appropriate expectations for their ELL students at different levels of English proficiency in ESL and sheltered content-area lessons and in other classroom activities. The performance indicators also provide a guide for determining the type of instruction needed to help ELL students move to the next level of English proficiency. The sections that follow offer suggestions for activities that successful teachers of ELL students have found to be effective. The recommended readings at the end of the chapter provide more ideas for oral language development. (Examples of strategies, video links)

Listening

We know from second language acquisition theory that to learn English, students must receive comprehensible input and much of that input comes from listening in the context of meaningful interaction. Interactive strategies and activities, such as those described in the following sections, can take place within the students' ZPD, and thus with proper scaffolding from the teacher or English proficient peers, students can improve their listening skills and reach higher levels of English proficiency.

Total Physical Response

Total physical response (TPR) was developed in the 1970s by James Asher (1977). While rarely used today as a stand-alone method, it remains a popular strategy in language learning classrooms throughout the world.[1] Teachers using TPR provide a set of commands in the target language to which students have to respond by taking a specific action. At the initial stages, the teacher models the action as he or she gives the command and thus helps students understand the language in a stress-free manner. For example, a simple TPR lesson for beginning students might entail commands such as, "Stand up," "Sit down," "Pick up your book," "Put the book on the table," and "Put the pencil next to the book." Once students are able to comprehend the teacher's commands, they can take the role of the teacher and give the commands and thus develop their speaking ability.

Many believe TPR is appropriate only for beginning-level ELLs. Note, for example, in Figure 6.1, TPR activities are used for Levels 1 and 2 in the listening sample performance indicator of the TESOL ELP standard. Asher (1995), however, provides examples of how TPR can be used with intermediate and advanced ELLs to pre-teach new vocabulary words students will encounter in their reading:

1: Asher's classic TPR book, *Learning Another Language through Actions*, is now in its 6th edition (Asher, 2000), along with many other current books that promote TPR strategies. Information and commercial products are available from TPR World at www.tpr-world.com

Let's take the vocabulary item "crooked." You can TPR the item with directions in the target language such as, "Luke, make a crooked arm." "Elena, make a straight arm." "Jaime, go to the board and draw a crooked tree." "Maria, run to the board and draw a straight tree." (pp. 2–3)

Today TPR is used by many teachers in its broadest sense to describe any strategy or technique that requires students to physically respond when listening to the target language. Thus, rather than lessons in which teachers merely bark commands at students to follow, students can demonstrate their comprehension by responding with their whole bodies within the context of a variety of academic lessons or tasks. For example:

- Students do a thumbs-up or thumbs-down to respond to a true-false question related to a unit of study (e.g., "Pigs are reptiles. Thumbs up if this is true; thumbs down if this is false").
- Students use personal chalkboards or white boards to draw or write a response to an oral question and then hold it up when they are finished (e.g., "Draw and write the name of your favorite food." "What color is my shirt?" "What is five times eight?").
- Students point to an illustration or word (or part of a word) in a book that is being read aloud (e.g., "Stacey, show me where the library is in this picture." "Hong, point to the word that means the same as "hop." "Josue, point to the part of the word *unhappy* that means 'not.'").
- Students perform a skit or act out a story.

Other language learning activities, strategies, and techniques that could fall under the umbrella of TPR are described elsewhere in this book.

Listening Comprehension Tasks

Listening comprehension tasks require students to listen to a source of spoken language and then complete a task that demonstrates their comprehension. In traditional ESL classrooms, students listen to an audio recording, for example, of a folktale or a conversation between two friends and then answer a series of comprehension questions about it. Listening tasks can also focus on particular vocabulary or forms that teachers notice have been problematic for students. Elaine Horwitz (2008) points out, however, that commercially produced listening materials do not simulate authentic speech, and therefore they may actually be more difficult to understand. She explains:

Natural listening experiences almost always include a context. People rarely have to understand speech without knowing in advance who is speaking, why the conversation is taking place, and what kind of information is likely to be communicated. Thus, language students are at a distinct disadvantage when their teacher abruptly announces, "I am going to play a tape for you" and they have to listen without any background information. (p. 70)

Horwitz notes that in real life conversations the speaker conveys the same information in several different ways, creating communicative redundancies. Thus, if listeners did not catch the meaning the first time around, these redundancies can clue them in to what the speaker is talking about.

Video recordings of authentic speech samples may be a better source for listening comprehension tasks. The video enables students to see the additional visual clues conveying meaning together with the oral language. This combination of seeing and hearing is more authentic, since, other than speaking on the telephone or listening to the radio, most real life listening tasks are in face-to-face interactions. For the most authentic speech samples, teachers can also use video clips from popular media, which are now readily available from network television Web sites, from social networking video-sharing sites such as YouTube (www.youtube. org), and from other on-line sources.

The difficulty of the listening comprehension tasks should be determined by the students' level of English proficiency. For example, for lower-level ELLs, teachers might offer shorter, simpler recordings with speech at a slightly reduced rate than what they provide for advanced ELLs, who should be working with recordings featuring native-speaker interaction. Or teachers might ask lower-level ELLs basic questions about recordings that feature native speakers interacting (e.g., "What are these two friends talking about?"), whereas they might ask advanced ELLs more detailed questions (e.g., "What reasons did Fred give for wanting to join the Marines?"). For longer or more complex tasks, teachers can provide a listening guide, perhaps with places for students to make notes, to support their completion of the task.

Listening Centers

A listening center is a designated spot in the classroom with a tape, CD, or MP3 player with multiple headphones, where students typically listen to recordings of books and follow along in hard copies. Recordings of books, from children's literature to best-selling novels and nonfiction titles, are readily available from publishing companies and school and community libraries. Public libraries throughout the country now even make it possible for patrons to check out audio books through the Internet from home. Many language arts curricular programs provide recordings of some of the books in the program. Teachers can make their own audio recordings of books, songs, poems, chants, and articles in newspapers and popular magazines or have strong readers in the class create them for their peers. Teachers can create their own listening comprehension exercises and tasks for students to complete at the centers.

The listening center provides a space in the classroom where students can receive comprehensible input in a low-stress environment. Materials placed in the listening center should reinforce classroom instruction. For example, a teacher might leave a recording of a book or article he or she has read aloud so that students can hear it again. This type of repetition is particularly beneficial for ELLs, because they are likely to understand more of the story after each repeated listening.

Many listening centers have replaced the old tape recorders and large bulky headphones with audio CDs and smaller headphones. Some teachers have introduced iPods or other MP3 players that students can use in class or take home for extra practice. And some teachers have posted audio and video recordings on classroom Web sites that students and their families can access at home.

A popular and effective resource I used in my classroom was a take-home listening kit. Soon after I began teaching, I realized that few of my ELL students had parents at home who could read aloud to them in English and many parents were also unable to read in their native language. To address this challenge, I took five old tape recorders, long discarded, that I found in a cabinet in our custodian's office and placed each one in a canvas bag along with a picture book and an audio cassette with a recording of the book. Each day, five students would take them home overnight, and with their families listen to the tape and follow along in the book. The next day another five students would check them out. The students loved the kits, which gave them opportunities for listening practice at home with the support of their families. Inexpensive CD or MP3 players can also be used for this purpose.

Speaking

Although some theorists who take an innatist perspective have downplayed the importance of speaking in second language acquisition, speaking plays a prominent role in interactionist and sociocultural perspectives. When students are in situations where they must communicate with others and create comprehensible output, they may become aware of gaps in their developing language and may be pushed to pay more attention to input containing what they need to successfully communicate with others. Students also need to practice speaking in order to learn to speak in a manner that other speakers can understand. The strategies and activities described in the following sections can be used to provide ELL students with opportunities to practice speaking in English within the context of meaningful classroom interactions with their teacher and peers.

Oral Retellings

Commonly used with reading as a comprehension check, oral retellings are simply explanations students give in their own words of something they have heard or read. In oral retellings, students might retell a story they read or that was read to them. In a content-area lesson, they might summarize a section of the textbook they read, describe their work on a small group math activity or science experiment, or explain a concept the teacher presented orally. Oral retellings allow teachers to make a quick assessment of an ELL student's comprehension and provide opportunities for ELLs to practice using target words and language structures they have acquired through listening or reading. Oral retellings can be presented in front of the whole class or in pairs or a small group. The more opportunities the students have to use their new language for the authentic purpose of retelling something they know in a variety of contexts across the curriculum, the more progress they will make in their English language development.

Songs and Chants

Add a rhythm or a tune to a piece of text and it becomes more memorable. Because learning to sing songs in English can be an enjoyable way to learn the language, music is a big part of many classrooms for ELL students of all ages and proficiency levels. Songs can also help students master the proper intonation of words and phrases, and chants (also called jazz chants) or raps can help make learning new vocabulary and language structures easier. YouTube has a plethora of examples of ESL teachers from around the world using music with their students (Songs and Chants for Oral Language Development, video links).[2]

To be most effective, the song should be sung at a moderate pace, and the lyrics should be clearly audible. For added support, the lyrics of the song could be projected on a screen or presented on a poster or student handout; graphics can be used to illustrate key vocabulary. Many ESL curricular programs include recordings of songs with accompanying posters with the lyrics and graphics that provide visual support. Teachers and students can easily create their own posters to go along with popular songs. Adding gestures to the songs also provides support for learning vocabulary (Songs and Chants for Oral Language Development, video links). Re-

---

2: Some scholarly critiques, based on the notion that singing and speaking use different parts of the brain, have questioned the value of using music to learn a new language. This problem can be mitigated, however, by working with the lyrics as a written text before and after singing them. Also, songs can be referenced for information. (Have you ever sung "30 Days Hath September" to remember how many days are in a particular month?)

search has shown that adding gestures, movements, or signs does more to increase receptive vocabulary than singing without gestures (Madsen, 1991; Schunk, 1999). Adding gestures also allows ELL students at low levels to participate even before they are ready to sing the words, providing visual evidence to the teacher that the students are actively participating. Singing with gestures is also another form of TPR.

Oral Presentations

A simple but effective oral presentation is the traditional show-and-tell. Students show something cool they have brought from home, tell their classmates all about it, and answer their questions about it. This activity promotes meaningful interactions. The student showing and telling is highly motivated to speak, and the other students are highly motivated to listen. For ELL students it is also an opportunity to show things from home that can help other students learn about their culture. Although show-and-tell is usually associated with younger students, variations can be used with older ELLs. For example, students could be asked to bring objects and photographs from home to create a personal time capsule and then engage in conversations with their teacher and peers to explain what these items mean to them and why they selected them for the capsule.

Other types of oral presentation provide opportunities for ELLs to use their language skills to create a project individually or in a small group and then to describe it to the class. The completed projects help support the ELL students' presentations. For example, a poster will contain images and words the students can use to help organize their thoughts and remind them of the needed vocabulary. Students can point to the appropriate parts of the poster as they talk, also facilitating understanding for the ELLs and other students who are listening. PowerPoint and other multimedia presentations provide excellent support for ELLs in making oral presentations. Each students' level of English language proficiency must be taken into account to ensure that the expectation for the presentation is reasonable. It is also important for teachers to create a supportive environment where students feel safe speaking English in front of the class without fear of being laughed at.

Minimal Pairs

Minimal pairs are words or phrases that differ by only one phoneme, for example, "pen"/"pan," or "he *b*it the boy"/"He *h*it the boy." Working with minimal pairs can help ELLs discriminate between words that initially may sound the same to them. They can also help with pronunciation, particularly when students may be having difficulty with phonemes that are not a part of their native language and their errors make it hard for others to understand what they are saying. Lynn T. Diaz-Rico and Kathryn Weed (2006) note that although minimal pair work comes from drill-and-kill exercises associated with the audiolingual approach, minimal pairs can still be used within a communicative language teaching approach. Supporting this view, the veteran ESL teacher Jerry Jesness (2004) suggests that teachers can make minimal pair practice more interactive and meaningful through the use of pictures. For example, a teacher might show a picture of a person making a bed and person bidding at an auction and ask, "Who is making a bed?" and "Who is making a bid?" or a picture of a child riding a sheep and another of a sailor on the deck of a ship and ask, "Who is on a sheep?" and "Who is on a ship?" Jesness adds, however that many students, especially younger students, learn to differentiate English sounds without drills. Drilling these students, then, would be a waste of valuable instruction time. Thus, minimal-pair work should be used only on particularly problematic and persistent pronunciation errors, especially those that have the potential to impede meaning in a real conversation.

Strategies for Classroom Interaction

The most important and beneficial listening and speaking that students will do is through interaction with the teacher, their fellow ELLs, and proficient English speakers within the sociocultural contexts of their classroom, school, and neighborhood. Interaction is crucial for second language acquisition. The following strategies and activities create opportunities for meaningful interaction in ESL and sheltered instruction contexts as students use their developing oral English skills to accomplish authentic tasks.

Cooperative Learning

Cooperative learning refers to student collaboration in pairs or in small groups to solve a problem, complete a specific task, or complete a project. It is most effective when the task is made clear and each student is given a clearly defined role. Although cooperative learning was not created specifically for ELLs, language educators have fully embraced it as an effective strategy for helping ELLs learn both language and academic content. To be effective the tasks given must be appropriate in terms of the knowledge and language proficiency of the ELL students. Also, the English proficient students in the group need guidance about how to interact with their ELL group members appropriately.

Cooperative learning is a form of scaffolding provided by classroom peers that contributes to the oral language development of ELLs in several ways. The students have to talk and listen to each other to get the job done. ELLs may feel more comfortable (i.e., have a lower affective filter) speaking with their peers in the small group than they are being called on to speak in front of the whole class. The hands-on learning that is typical of cooperative group work provides context and visual support to make the language used more comprehensible. And during the group work, ELL students can practice using key vocabulary previously taught in the lesson. For example, if students are working with scales and other materials related to a math unit on weight, they will be able to practice using such new vocabulary words as *scale, weights, pounds, balanced, heavier, lighter, more, less, fewer, weight, ounces, grams,* and *pounds.* Finally, cooperative learning makes it possible for ELLs to participate in and complete projects that they might have had great difficulty doing on their own.

Spencer Kagan (1997) has outlined structures for organizing cooperative learning groups that can be used for practically any content area at any grade level. Julie High (1993) has shown how these structures can be used effectively with ELL students. I have used many of these structures in my own classrooms, from kindergarten all the way to my courses for graduate students. I describe four of these structures here and explain how they support oral language development.[3]

Think-Pair-Share.   The teacher assigns each student a partner and asks a question related to whatever topic the students are studying. Students are given time to think of their answer (and maybe jot down a few notes). Then, at the teacher's signal, they turn and discuss their answers with their partners. The teacher can wander around and eavesdrop on the conversations, providing support as needed. After a few minutes, the teacher may call on pairs of students to report what they talked about. Think-Pair-Share provides built-in wait time in a low-risk environment. Everyone is talking at once, and the ELLs are talking with only one peer. If

---

3: Further detail on these cooperative learning structures and others can be obtained from the Division of Instructional Innovation and Assessment at the University of Texas (Austin) at www.utexas.edu/academic/diia/research/projects/hewlett/cooperative.php

their answers are not quite right, their partners may be able to help them clarify misunderstandings. If they are asked to report their answer to the class, they have already had a chance to practice answering with their partners and thus can answer with greater confidence.

Roundtable.   The teacher assigns students to small groups of three to six students. Each group is given a single sheet of blank paper (or chart paper) and a task that involves brainstorming ideas related to whatever they are currently learning in class. For example, students might be asked to brainstorm ideas about why a character acted a particular way in a story or ideas for alternative endings. Or, as a simple ESL lesson for lower-level ELLs, students could be asked to brainstorm a list of items they might find in a kitchen. Each student in the group is given the opportunity to add something to the list and a recorder writes down their response on the paper.

Roundtable works well with ELLs because they are working collaboratively with a small group of their peers on a fairly narrow task. They must listen to their peers to make sure they do not repeat something that is already on the list. Their contributions are given equal status by being added to the list along with those of all other group members. Misunderstandings can be clarified by other students in the group. Finally, ELLs are likely to pick up new vocabulary and ideas based on the contributions of others in the group.

Concentric Circles.   The teacher divides the class into two equal groups. One group makes a circle, with each student facing out. The other group makes a circle around the first circle, with each student paired off with and facing a student in the inner circle. The teacher asks a question or announces a particular topic to discuss or task to complete (e.g., "What is your favorite holiday and why?"). On the teacher's signal, the students in the inner circle give their answers and then the students in the outer circle give theirs. After each student has spoken, the teacher instructs one of the circles to rotate until each student is facing a new partner (e.g., "Outside circle, rotate two students to your left"). The students will then discuss the same question or topic with their new partner. The process repeats until students have rotated to new partners several times.

What makes Concentric Circles so effective for ELLs is the practice they get listening and speaking in English. In the typical classroom lesson, the teacher talks and calls on one student at a time. Thus, in a 30 to 45 minute lesson, only a small number of students may be given the opportunity to speak, and each student has time to say only a little. With Concentric Circles, in a fraction of the time, each student can talk about ten times more. Even better, the repetition of the task with new partners provides beneficial practice—each time the ELL student will feel more comfortable and confident, and the conversations will feel more natural. During ESL instruction, Concentric Circles works particularly well for practicing target language forms over and over in a stress-free way. It also works well for sheltered content instruction, such as reviewing material learned and providing repeated opportunities for students to use new vocabulary (e.g., "Tell your partner the three states of matter and give an example of each").

Concentric Circles can be used for students at any level of English proficiency. For example, using the example of the TESOL sample performance indicator for speaking in Figure 6.1 as a guide, Concentric Circles could be used with students at Level 1 to practice formulaic greetings, introductions, and compliments, or with students at Level 4 to practice using idiomatic expressions in conversations.

A variation of Concentric Circles is *Shifting Lines,* which works well in a classroom where it may be difficult to make a circle. The same principle and procedure applies, only students are in two straight lines facing each other. When it is time to change partners, one line shifts to the left, and the student at the front moves to the end of the line.

Numbered Heads Together. Students are assigned to groups of four. Each group is given a number (Group 1, Group 2, . . .) and each student within the group is given a number (Student 1, Student 2, . . .). The teacher asks a question or gives each group a task to complete. When students are finished, the teacher randomly calls out a group number and then a student number (using spinners, dice, slips of paper in a sack, etc.) and asks a question related to the task (e.g., "Group 3, Student 2, What is the third planet from the sun?"). Because any member could be called on to answer the question for the group, each group must make sure that each member is ready to respond. Thus, a great deal of interaction takes place between group members as they prepare. Numbered Heads Together can be combined with Roundtable for groups to report the ideas from their brainstorming. The level of complexity of the tasks and the questions should be based on the proficiency level of the students. In a class with a variety of levels, the teacher can decide the level of difficulty according to which student stands up to answer.

Role Play

Traditional ESL textbooks are full of uninspiring and remarkably unnatural dialogues that are designed to highlight specific language forms for students to learn. Rather than reading these dialogues right out of the book, a better strategy is to put students into role-playing situations where they will need to use the target form. For example, if students are practicing forming and asking questions, they could role play a situation where a student is buying shoes at a shoe store. One could be the salesperson and the other the customer. The customer could make comments and ask questions such as, "I am looking for some running shoes," "Do you have any on sale?" "Do you have size 8?" "These are too tight," and "How much do they cost?" The salesperson would have to respond appropriately. Sometimes the sillier the role plays, the more fun they are and the more likely students are to acquire language unconsciously. Teachers can put different situations on slips of paper and put them in a bag or a hat, and students have to role play whatever they get: "An alien lands in your backyard and wants to know about your planet," or "You are Oprah Winfrey and you are interviewing Tom Cruise."

Other role plays should try to mirror real life situations the students are likely to find themselves in, such as visiting a school counselor, looking for a book at a bookstore, talking to landlord, or doing a job interview. For students at Levels 1 and 2, the role plays may need to be kept fairly simple and focus on using previously taught vocabulary and language forms (e.g., role play giving directions). The role plays can be more elaborate and open-ended for ELLs at higher levels of English proficiency. Each student could be given a list of information about the person they are playing that the other person does not know about. In the bookstore example, the customer might have a list of book topics he or she is interested in, and the bookstore employee has a list of books matching those topics. In sheltered instruction, role plays can be used to practice and understand key concepts along with key vocabulary and new language structures. In math, for example, students could set up a shop and practice making purchases and making change, while in social studies students could role play a political debate between two candidates or participate in a mock trial.

Barrier Games

Students are put into pairs. One student in each pair is the designated artist and is given paper and a pencil. The partner is given a pattern or picture, which he or she places behind some type of barrier where the artist cannot see it. The partner looks at the pattern or picture and then, using English and with hands behind his or her back (to prevent pointing), tells the artist how to draw it. For barrier games to be successful, particularly with ELLs at lower levels of English proficiency, teachers should pre-teach necessary vocabulary and language structures that can then be practiced through this activity. For more advanced ELLs, the games could involve higher-level content-area vocabulary (e.g., "Draw a cylinder adjacent to a cube in the top right quadrant").

Obstacle Course

In this activity, which is well suited for beginning-level ELLs, the teacher sets up an obstacle course in the classroom or outside on the playground. Students are put into pairs or small groups. One student in each pair or group is blindfolded and must make it through the obstacle course guided only by instructions from his or her partner or team mates, who must speak in English and may not touch the blindfolded student. To be successful, students would need to first learn basic vocabulary and simple phrases related to directions (turn left, go forward, walk backwards, step sideways to the right, stop, etc.).

What Am I?

Students wear a headband with a card on the front that they cannot see but others can. Alternatively, a card could be taped to each student's back. The card has a picture or the name of some object, animal, or person. Each student has to figure out what is on his or her card by asking questions of other students, such as, "Am I an animal?" "What color am I?" "Do I have wings?" For the game to be successful, the teacher should first make sure the students have learned the vocabulary and language forms necessary to play. For lower-level ELLs, this game could be used to practice basic vocabulary, such as the names of household items, animals, or food. More advanced ELLs can be encouraged to use vocabulary that is associated with a particular unit of content area study, asking, for example, "Am I surrounded on all sides by water?" ("No.") "Am I surrounded on three sides by water? ("Yes.") "Am I a peninsula?" ("Yes!").

Acting Out Stories

While oral language development is important for helping students learn to read, reading is also a means for developing oral language. Students learn many new words, grammatical forms, and language structures from reading. Acting out stories is a great way for students to internalize new language learned from reading by incorporating it into the oral performance. Student must also communicate with their peers to collaborate in planning, creating props and scenery, and preparing for the performance. Acting out stories, however, need not involve the use of elaborate costumes, scenery, and props. Beginning-level ELLs can act out simple stories or play the characters with the least amount of dialogue, and more advanced ELLs can act out more elaborate stories or take on roles with the most dialogue. Alternatively, the students could create and act out a variation or extension of a story. For example, students could act out what would happen if the characters were interacting with each other and the host of a TV talk show as they discuss and debate the central problem of the story.

Class Discussions

The quotation at the beginning of this chapter denotes the frustration some teachers of ELLs feel. With increasing pressure to focus on tested subject areas, there is often little time left to simply engage their students in meaningful extended conversations. Nonetheless, class discussions are critically important for ELL students' oral language and academic development. These discussions enable students to demonstrate their knowledge and communicate their thoughts and ideas with their classmates and teachers. The teacher facilitates the discussion and ensures that it takes place within the students' ZPD, providing scaffolding as necessary so students can comprehend and learn. Class discussion should take place in connection with reading a book together or viewing a film, or as part of a content area lesson. Within these discussions, students are given opportunities to hear and use key vocabulary, and new language structures and forms, and reinforce content-area concepts learned.

Even outside of formal learning tasks, it is important for the class to engage in meaningful discussions other about things of interest or concern to the students, many of which are not covered in the official curriculum. I recall having excellent discussions with my students about gangs and crime in their neighborhood that grew out of questions they asked. My primary purpose in having these discussions with my students was not to develop their oral language. However, the students were deeply engaged in the discussion, probably much more so than in the more "academically" oriented discussions we had had. Even my squirmy students sat still, listened attentively, and participated in the discussion. The topic was of great relevance to them, and they were learning to see things in whole new ways. Much of a new language is acquired subconsciously through meaningful interaction; thus class discussions such as these play a key role in students' oral language development.

Assessing Listening and Speaking

The only way to effectively assess ELL students' oral English language proficiency is to talk with them and listen to them talk. The strategies, techniques, and activities described in this chapter provide avenues for observing students' oral language use. In addition, teachers should become skilled at eavesdropping, listening to the students when they are not necessarily engaged in structured academic tasks—when they are coming into the classroom, when they are lined up to go to lunch, when they are eating lunch, when they are out on the playground or in the halls, when they chat with their friends before an assembly starts. Teachers should also talk with their students in these less structured situations.

In Texas, teachers of ELL students are trained to observe their students' English language use in the classroom in order to make holistic assessments of the students' proficiency. The Texas Education Agency (2005) lists activities during which teachers can assess students' listening and speaking ability (for a partial list, see Table 6.1).

Any time students are listening and speaking teachers have an opportunity for assessment. But teachers will likely find it necessary to also sit down one-on-one with each student and give him or her a task that requires oral language use. One easy and commonly used technique is to show the student an illustration of a scene depicting a lot of activity, such as at a park or a grocery store, and ask the student, for example, "What do you do see?" or "What is going on in this picture?" If the student just points to and names objects, the teacher should use more specific and open-ended prompts, for example, "Why do you think these two children are running to the playground?" or "What do think will happen here?"

Another easy way to elicit oral language in a one-on-one situation is to read a book together and have the student retell the story. Wordless picture books also

Table 6.1	Activities That Provide Opportunities to Assess ELLs' Oral Language Proficiency		
Listening	**Listening and speaking**		**Speaking**
• Reacting to oral presentations • Responding to text read aloud • Following directions	• Cooperative group work • Informal, social discourse with peers • Large-group and small-group interactions in academic settings • One-on-one interviews • Individual student conferences		• Oral presentations • Classroom discussions • Articulation of problem-solving strategies

Source: Texas Education Agency, 2005.

provide excellent stimuli for students to talk as they use the illustrations to tell a story. Also important is to just chat with students. Ask them to name their favorite television show and then tell you about it. Ask them what they like to do after school. When students talk about their interests, teachers will likely get a good sample of their oral language ability in English.

Teacher observations can be guided by rubrics. It is tempting to focus on just one aspect of a student's speech, but rubrics make it easy to keep track of the many aspects of oral language. One commonly used rubric is the SOLOM (Student Oral Language Observation Matrix) developed by bilingual educators in California (see Figure 6.2).[3a] The SOLOM helps the teacher focus on five different aspects of a student's oral language proficiency. (1) *comprehension:* How much does the student understand when he is spoken too? How well does he follow classroom discussions? (2) *fluency:* Does the student have a hard time speaking? Is it difficult to have a conversation with him? Does the student's speech flow well but occasionally gets stuck as he searches for the correct word? (3) *vocabulary:* Is the student able to say everything he wants, or does he struggle because he lacks the vocabulary to fully describe what he is thinking? Does he ever use the wrong words? (4) *pronunciation:* Do others have to struggle to understand what he is saying because he has a strong foreign accent? Do accent or intonation patterns sometimes lead to miscommunication? (5) *grammar:* Are grammar errors so frequent it is hard to understand the student? Or do they only occasional obscure the meaning he is trying to convey?

For each of these five areas, students are given a score of 1 to 5, with 1 the lowest and 5 the highest. A student who receives all 1s (total score = 5) would effectively be a non-English speaker, and a student with all 5s (total score = 25) would be considered a proficient English speaker. The SOLOM provides a description of each level. When assessing a student with the SOLOM, the teacher scores each aspect and adds them together to determine the students' overall oral language proficiency (Cindy's Presentation, video).

Now, let's practice using the SOLOM to assess a student's oral language proficiency. The following transcript is from an oral presentation by a Taiwanese middle-school-aged student named Cindy of a poster she created to tell about her favorite show, *Pudding Dog and Kitty*.[4] A video of her presentation is available on

---

3a: Some educators have criticized the wording in the SOLOM which tends to focus more on what students can't do rather than on what they can do in their new language. Nonetheless, the SOLOM can be used to identify both strengths and areas in need of improvement.

4: Cindy was a student in Kenneth Dickson's ESL school in Taiwan. Kenneth was kind enough to grant permission to create this transcript of Cindy's presentation and to post his video of Cindy's presentation on the Companion Web site.

Figure 6.2 SOLOM Teacher Observation: Student Oral Language Observation Matrix. (Source: SOLOM, n.d.)

Levels	1	2	3	4	5
Comprehension	Cannot be said to understand even a simple conversation.	Has great difficulty following what is said. Can comprehend only "social conversation" spoken slowly and with frequent repetitions.	Understands most of what is said at slower-than-normal speed with repetitions.	Understands nearly everything at normal speed, although occasional repetition may be necessary.	Understands everyday conversation and normal classroom discussions without difficulty.
Fluency	Speech is so halting and fragmentary as to make conversation virtually impossible.	Usually hesitant; often forced into silence by language limitations.	Speech in everyday conversation and classroom discussion frequently disrupted by the student's search for the correct manner of expression.	Speech in everyday conversation and classroom discussions generally fluent, with occasional lapses while the student searches for the correct manner of expression.	Speech in everyday conversation and classroom discussions fluent and effortless, approximating that of a native speaker.
Vocabulary	Vocabulary limitations so extreme as to make conversation virtually impossible.	Misuse of words and very limited vocabulary; comprehension quite difficult.	Student frequently uses the wrong words; conversation somewhat limited because of inadequate vocabulary.	Student occasionally uses inappropriate terms and/or must rephrase ideas because of lexical inadequacies.	Use of vocabulary and idioms approximates that of a native speaker.
Pronunciation	Pronunciation problems so severe as to make speech virtually unintelligible.	Very hard to understand because of pronunciation problems. Must frequently repeat in order to make himself or herself understood.	Pronunciation problems necessitate concentration on the part of the listener and occasionally lead to misunderstanding.	Always intelligible though one is conscious of a definite accent and occasional inappropriate intonation patterns.	Pronunciation and intonation approximate that of a native speaker.
Grammar	Errors in grammar and word order so severe as to make speech virtually unintelligible.	Grammar and word-order errors make comprehension difficult. Must often rephrase and/or restrict himself or herself to basic patterns.	Makes frequent errors of grammar and word order that occasionally obscure meaning.	Occasionally makes grammatical and/or word-order errors that do not obscure meaning.	Grammatical usage and word order approximate that of a native speaker.

Based on your observation of the student, circle the block in each category that best describes the student's abilities. Add the scores to determine the student's level.

SOLOM Levels: Level 1, Score 5–11 = non-English proficient
Level 2, Score 12–18 = limited English proficient
Level 3, Score 19–24 = limited English proficient
Level 4, Score 25 = fully English proficient

the companion web site. As you watch the video and read the transcript, score her performance with the SOLOM.

Pudding Dog and Kitty

Hello everybody. My name is Cindy. I like Pudding Dog show because I like to eat pudding. Pudding Dog was friend and, and he have two mice friend. One day Pudding Dog went to his friend home. He took a very many pudding and choose them, for give friend. Uh, Pudding Dog open them, she see Kitty because Kitty is Pudding Dog, guh friend, good friend. In the afternoon, everyday, they went to park to play base, basketball, baseball, soccer and dodge ball. But Kitty was angry because she, T-shirt was dirty, so she run home. Pudding Dog said we can make the cake for Kitty. So everybody went to Kitty's home. Two mice, say, two mice say, say [giggles], this cake, cake is for you. Please don not cry. Pudding, er, [giggles] uh, Kitty was, was happy. She said "thank you very much."

Here is how I scored Cindy's oral performance. For *comprehension,* I gave her a 3. It's really hard to judge Cindy's comprehension because we do not hear her answer any question, and so we can only infer. But considering her overall performance, I suspect that she would understand most of what her teacher says to her, as long as the teacher slowed down his speech and repeated when necessary. For *fluency,* I gave Cindy a 3. Although the words flow at a good and even rapid rate, there are a few spots where the flow is interrupted when Cindy struggles a little figuring out what to say next. For *vocabulary,* I gave Cindy a 4. She appears to have adequate vocabulary to describe the story, though there are spots where she seems to have trouble finding the words to express what she wants to say and has to rephrase her ideas. Particularly at the end, she has trouble describing what the mice said to Kitty and finding the right words to describe Kitty's reaction, and thus she resorts to the simple feeling word "happy." For *pronunciation,* I gave Cindy a 3. I found that I really had to concentrate to understand what she was saying. And there are still some spots that are unclear to me, such as the part where Pudding dog seems to have given some pudding to Kitty. For this same reason, I gave Cindy a 3 for *grammar.* Her errors are frequent, but for the most part they do not obscure the meaning. Her story is easy to follow, except for the part about giving pudding to Kitty.

Based on my ratings, Cindy's total score is 16, placing her in Level II, the lower of the two limited English proficient levels. How did my scores compare with yours? Perhaps you were harsher on Cindy than I was and may have given her a 2 in some areas where I gave her a 3. This does not mean you are wrong. Perhaps I am too easy on her. In cases where two raters disagree by 1 point, just award the number in between. Thus, in Cindy's case, we would give her a score of 2.5.

The exact scores are not as important as how teachers use this information. Figure 6.3 is an evaluation form that can be used along with the SOLOM. The most important part is the three questions. For question 1, *What are this student's strengths?* I would say Cindy has several strengths. Her vocabulary is pretty good. She is able to describe nearly everything she wants. Her rapid speech shows she is comfortable speaking the language and does not struggle to find each word she wants to say. Her pronunciation is good enough that native speakers can understand her if they concentrate. And her grammar is sufficiently developed to make her speech comprehensible.

For question 2, *In what areas is this student in need of improvement?* I would say Cindy's pronunciation needs to become clearer so that it is easier for native speakers to understand her. She needs to improve her grammar so that errors do not prevent listeners from understanding her intended meaning. Because her vocabulary is still limited, she had problems with fluency, causing her rapid speech at times to be halted.

For question 3, *What oral language development strategies, techniques, and activities would be beneficial for this student?* I would say, if I were Cindy's teacher, that

Evaluation of the SOLOM

Student name _____

Grade level _____

Scores

Comprehension _____

Fluency _____

Vocabulary _____

Pronunciation _____

Grammar _____

Total SOLOM score _____ **English proficiency level** _____

1. What are this student's strengths?

2. In what areas is this student in need of improvement?

3. What oral language development strategies, techniques, and activities would be beneficial for this student?

Figure 6.3   SOLOM evaluation form.

I would continue to provide her with lots of opportunities in class to use her oral language in authentic ways. I would not give her direct pronunciation drills, but I would expose her to more models of fluent English through audio recordings and videos. For grammar I might focus on practicing the use of past tense. In her presentation, Cindy was able to use the past tense appropriately in some sentences but not in others. This level of achievement suggests to me that she is ready to learn more and practice using the past tense more consistently. I also think Cindy is ready for vocabulary lessons focusing on words to describe feelings (e.g., *excited, grateful, touched*) that she could have used to describe how Kitty felt when she got the cake from Pudding Dog and the mice. What other activities or lessons do you believe would be beneficial to Cindy?

The listening and speaking sample performance indicators for the TESOL standards (see Figure 6.1) can also be used as a rubric for assessing students' oral language development. The level of difficulty and the extent to which students needed some form of support to accomplish a particular listening or speaking task can help teachers identify the level at which the student performed. Teachers can also create their own performance indicators for particular academic tasks. In addition, or alternatively, teachers can create their own rubrics tailored to special oral language tasks.

Oral language assessments not only provide important information about where students are at in their oral language proficiency development but, more important, they can be used as formative assessments to help the teacher determine what to do next to help the student continue to make improvements in his or her listening and speaking ability.

SUMMARY

The reviews of the scientific literature by the CREDE and the NLP found strong evidence of the need for ongoing ESL instruction focused on oral language development. According to the CREDE review, it usually takes several years for ELLs to attain proficiency in English. ELLs tend to get stuck at the higher proficiency levels, most likely because of the lack of focus on oral language development at those levels. Interaction with native speakers is important but not essential, especially at the beginning levels. And though interaction with proficient speakers is important beyond the beginning levels, for the interaction to be effective, non-ELLs need to be trained in how to interact effectively to provide scaffolding for their ELL peers. Students can learn English without having to sacrifice their first language. Primary language support can be an effective means of helping students develop English oral proficiency. Oral language proficiency tests are limited and mostly fail to capture the true abilities of ELL students, thus highlighting the need for multiple, authentic, formative, on-going assessment measures.

The NLP found strong evidence that oral language proficiency is essential for reading comprehension. They found that ELLs can learn word-level skills, such as spelling and decoding, without any comprehension of the words. They also found that good literacy instruction or "just good teaching" alone is not sufficient for ELLs; this instruction must be combined with substantial oral language development instruction. Thus, teachers who focus only on spelling, phonics, and decoding skills are failing to meet the oral language development needs of their ELLs, and as a result, ELLs will struggle in reading because they will not be able to understand what they read. Both the CREDE and the NLP report demonstrate the need for ESL instruction that has a strong focus on oral language development.

In oral language development, non-English-speaking ELLs typically go through a silent period where they listen and absorb oral English before they are ready to speak it. Wait time allows ELLs to think, and translate in their heads if necessary, before being required to respond to a teacher's or peer's question. Teacher talk should be adjusted to make it more comprehensible for ELLs. Adjustments include slowing down for beginning-level students and controlling for vocabulary use and sentence structure appropriate to the level of their ELL students. Teachers must decide when and how to correct student speech errors, keeping in mind whether or not the error impedes comprehension, what the relationship is between the error and the task at hand, whether or not the student is ready to learn to correct the error, and whether the error can be corrected by itself with indirect correction through modeling or recasts, or if more direct correction methods are appropriate.

The sample performance indicators of the TESOL English Language Proficiency Standards help teachers plan appropriate instruction for ELLs and establish reasonable expectations for ELLs at different levels of English proficiency. The indicators can also be used for assessment, helping teachers determine students' current level and the type of instruction and support they need to advance to the next level.

Teachers can create opportunities for students to use their developing English oral language skills in the classroom through meaningful practice and authentic interactions by using TPR, listening centers, listening comprehension tasks minimal pair practice, cooperative learning structures, oral presentations, songs and chants, interactive games, acting out stories, role playing, and class discussions.

The SOLOM is an excellent tool for helping teachers focus on different aspects of their student's oral language ability. Information obtained from the SOLOM or other language proficiency assessments should be used to identify students' strengths and needs and thus inform instruction needed to help students progress to higher levels of oral language proficiency.

As the CREDE and NLP reports point out, oral language development is typically neglected in the classroom. My own research, and that of many others, has shown that the heavy focus on high-stakes testing and accountability may be largely to blame. The pressure to raise scores on high-stakes tests means many teachers—often pressured by their administrators—are forgoing ESL instruction in favor of test-preparation-driven instruction. For ELLs, this is huge mistake. If ELLs are to succeed, teachers must provide explicit and on-going ESL instruction, and sheltered instruction that includes a strong focus on oral language development for ELLs at all levels of English language proficiency.

Discussion Questions

1. **On-line Discussion Board** If you have learned (or tried to learn) a second language, what struggles did you have with oral language development? What did you find helpful in improving your listening and speaking abilities?
2. Why is oral language development so important for ELLs? How is oral language related to literacy? What happens to ELLs in classrooms that neglect oral language development and focus on teaching word-level decoding skills?
3. **On-line Discussion Board** Which activities described in this chapter have you observed or used in the classroom? How effective were they? What ideas did you gain from this chapter that you would like to implement in your current or future classroom? What other strategies or techniques have you used or observed that you believe have been effective for ELLs' oral language development?
4. Because of the heavy emphasis schools put on high-stakes testing and accountability, many teachers have reported that it is becoming increasingly difficult to take the time to have conversations and classroom discussions with their students. What effect might this trend have on ELL students' oral English language development, on teachers' ability to accurately assess their students' oral language proficiency? What are some ways teachers (and schools) can resolve the tension between the need to prepare for high-stakes testing and the need to take time for conversations and class discussions?
5. Politicians and opponents of bilingual education, and even some educators, have claimed that ELLs can and should be able to learn English in 1 to 3 years. How do these claims compare with the findings of the CREDE and NLP reports? Why do you think it takes so long for ELLs to attain fluent English proficiency?
6. Some researchers and educators have raised concerns about using cooperative learning for groups of ELL students. One concern is that students will model poor English for each other, which will confuse them and also take time away from the teacher as a model of proper English. Do you agree or disagree that this is a problem? Explain your response.

Research Activities

1. Using the SOLOM (Figure 6.2), assess the oral language proficiency of an ELL student. Use the evaluation form in Figure 6.3 to identify the student's strengths and areas in need of improvement. Describe appropriate strategies, activities, and techniques from this chapter and other resources that you feel would be effective for improving the student's oral language proficiency. Discuss the findings with the student's teacher, or, if you are a teacher, implement them in your classroom. (SOLOM, form; Post-SOLOM Evaluation, form)

2. **Wiki This**   Observe a classroom, and keep track of how much time is spent by the teacher talking and how much time is available for the students to talk. If you are a classroom teacher, keep track in your own classroom. Determine whether there is an appropriate balance between the two, or whether changes are needed to allow more time for ELLs to talk. What strategies from this chapter or from other sources might you use to increase the ELL students' opportunities to speak in the classroom?

3. Do another classroom observation, but this time focus on a single ELL student. Keep detailed notes on how much time the student spends listening, speaking, reading, and writing. Determine whether this is an appropriate balance, and discuss ways changes could be made to better meet the needs of this student.

 4. **Wiki This**   Interview a former or advanced ELL student about the difficulties he or she faced in developing oral proficiency skills in English. Ask for a description of particular problems he or she had with idioms or cultural references that left him or her confused. What did you learn from this interview that can help inform your work with ELL students in your current or future classroom?

Recommended Readings

Asher, J. J. (2000). *Learning another language through actions* (6th ed.). Los Gatos, CA: Sky Oaks Productions.

The author, the creator of Total Physical Response (TPR), provides an overview of the method and guidelines for using it in the classroom.

Flowerdew, J., & Miller, L. (2005). *Second language listening: Theory and practice.* New York: Cambridge University Press.

An excellent overview of theories and research related to second language listening, with useful guidelines and suggestions for putting these into classroom practice.

Folse, K. S. (2006). *The art of teaching speaking: Research and pedagogy for the ESL/EFL classroom.* Ann Arbor: University of Michigan Press.

This teacher-friendly book provides an overview of the theory and research related to teaching speaking in a second language, with a wide range of suggested activities for classroom instruction.

High, J. (1993). *Second language learning through cooperative learning.* San Clemente, CA: Kagan Cooperative Learning.

Cooperative learning is popular strategy used with all students, but the author demonstrates how it can be an especially beneficial with ELL student. Includes many great ideas for use in the classroom.

7

Reading

The only way to help students improve their reading is to read with them and talk to them about their reading.

-Juli Kendall, author and middle school ESL teacher

KEY TERMS

- reading wars
- whole language
- phonics
- emergent, early, early fluency, and fluency levels of literacy development
- before, during, after (BDA)
- read-alouds
- shared reading
- guided reading
- language experience approach
- independent reading
- narrow reading
- Reader's Workshop
- word study
- concepts of print
- running record
- reading self-assessments

GUIDING QUESTIONS

1. How have the "reading wars" influenced literacy instruction in schools?
2. How does reading promote second language acquisition?
3. How can teachers balance their attention to meaning and skills within the context of reading instruction for ELLs?
4. What does the research tell us about effective reading instruction for ELLs?
5. How can an understanding of ELLs' reading strengths and needs inform a teacher's choices of instructional approaches, methods, and strategies?

Reading is one of the most important skills students learn at school. ELL students face the tremendous challenge of learning to read in a language they are not yet proficient in. They are also expected to learn academic content through reading. The NLP report *Developing Literacy in Second Language Learners* (August & Shanahan, 2006b) declares:

> Language-minority students who cannot read and write proficiently in English cannot participate fully in American schools, workplaces, or society. They face limited job opportunities and earning power. Nor are the consequences of low literacy attainment in English limited to individual impoverishment. U.S. economic competitiveness depends on workforce quality. Inadequate reading and writing proficiency in English relegates rapidly increasing language-minority populations to the sidelines, limiting the nation's potential for economic competitiveness, innovation, productivity growth, and quality of life. (pp. 1–2)

Everyone agrees that reading is crucial, and yet it is one of the most contested areas of the school curriculum.

Literacy instruction for ELLs, like language instruction, is highly controversial and political. We begin this chapter with the "reading wars." Then we discuss how reading promotes second language acquisition and review what we know from re-search about reading and reading instruction for ELLs. Next we explore a variety of strategies and techniques that sheltered instruction and ESL teachers can use to pro-mote reading development, along with ideas about how to encourage more reading at home by ELLs. The chapter concludes with a discussion of reading assessment.

The Reading Wars

Since the 1980s, what has become known as the reading wars has raged between proponents of the whole-language philosophy of literacy instruction and those who argue for a skills-based approach.[1] The media often depict the conflict as "phonics vs. whole language," whereas researchers are more likely to describe it as a conflict between those who support bottom-up and those who support top-down text processing reading theories and approaches (Carrell, Devine, & Eskey, 1998).

Whole language educators view reading as a holistic (top-down) process that is highly complex and multifaceted, and thus they favor instructional programs that begin by immersing students in whole, authentic texts. Once students become fa-miliar with a text as a whole, it becomes meaningful and thus can be used for more direct reading instruction. Skills-based advocates take a more linear (bottom-up) approach to literacy, arguing that students must first learn sounds and letters and use them to decode words and then sentences before they can go on to read the extended text of paragraphs and books. This approach has led to a growing trend that uses scripted reading programs to teach phonemic awareness, phonics, and other discrete reading skills (see Box 7.1). Whole language educators argue that reading is much more than the sum of individual skills. Reading cannot be broken up into a set of isolated skills that have to be mastered in a fixed order. Whole lan-guage proponents use a cake metaphor—one cannot learn what a cake is or what it tastes like by eating each ingredient (flour, sugar, baking powder, raw eggs, butter, etc.) separately and in isolation. Skills-based advocates claim, however, that whole language is too fuzzy, that it lacks a clear instructional focus and provide a few guidelines for teachers. They falsely depict whole language as being in opposition to the teaching of phonics and other skills students need in order to learn to read.

The division between whole language and phonics is a false dichotomy. The two really cannot be compared. Whole language is a philosophy of how children learn to read, whereas phonics is just one component in a set of many reading skills. Further, despite claims to the contrary, whole language is not opposed to the teach-ing of phonics. As the author and whole language expert Regie Routman (1996) de-clares, "It would be irresponsible and inexcusable not to teach phonics" (p. 91). Rather, the issue is how and when phonics should be taught, and which specific phonics skills require explicit instruction.

Many phonics rules do not need to be taught, because students will acquire them subconsciously the more they read (Freeman & Freeman, 2004; Krashen, 1993; F. Smith, 1999). Frank Smith (1994) explains that students "do not learn to sound out words on the basis of individual letters or letter clusters whose sounds have been learned in isolation, but rather by recognizing sequences of letters that occur in words that are already known." He further explains, "A single [known] word can provide the basis for remembering different rules of phonics, as well as the exceptions, since not only do words provide a meaningful way to organize dif-ferent phonics rules in memory, they also illustrate the phonic rules at work" (p. 145).

1: For studies by proponents of the whole-language philosophy, see Edelsky, 2006; Freemen & Freeman, 1992; K. S. Goodman, 1986; Krashen, 1996; McQuillan, 1998; Routman, 1996; F. Smith, 1999, 2006. For proponents of a skills-based approach, see Adams, 1995; California Reading Task Force, 1995; Foorman, 1998; National Read-ing Panel, 2000.

Box 7.1

Phonemic Awareness Training and Phonics Instruction for ELLs

Skills-based advocates favor scripted programs that begin with phonemic awareness and phonics drills, and reading materials controlled for students to practice recently learned phonics rules.

■ Proponents of phonemic awareness training claim that students need to be able to hear and distinguish between phonemes before they can learn to read (e.g., between the /t/ and /n/ that distinguish the words *cat* and *can*). Phonemic awareness training includes rhyming, initial sound recognition, blending, segmentation, and substitution drills, generally for 15 to 30 minutes a day using a scripted program that follows a rigid scope and sequence.

■ As students become "phonemically aware," they receive phonics instruction to learn how to match phonemes to graphemes (letters) in order to decode (sound out) words. Direct, systematic phonics programs include drills on one or two new letter-sound relationships each day, with reading materials that use a limited set of words exemplifying new and previously learned letter-sound relationships.

Criticisms of Scripted Phonemic Awareness Training for ELLs

■ ELLs may not get much out of the drills because they are manipulating the sounds of words they don't know.

■ ELLs may have great difficulty with drills using phonemes that do not exist in their native language.

■ These drills can be very frustrating for ELLs.

■ Instructional time could be much better spent on more meaningful literacy activities.

Criticisms of Scripted Phonics Programs for All Students

■ There are too many phonics rules.

■ There are too many exceptions to phonics rules.

■ Phonics instruction isolated from authentic texts is not beneficial.

■ Phonics lessons are a waste of time for students who have already acquired the target letter-sound correspondence naturally.

■ Phonics lessons are a waste of time for students who may need to learn more basic letter-sound relationships.

■ For students who may be ready to learn the target letter-sound relationship, phonics lessons are typically much longer than needed, and other activities could help them acquire the target sound more naturally.

■ Texts or "books" created for phonics decoding practice are too contrived to focus on particular letters and sounds; they feel unnatural and lack the appeal of real children's books that motivate reading.

■ Instructional time would be much better spent teaching phonics and other reading skills within the meaningful context of authentic literature.

Criticisms of using Scripted Phonics Programs with ELLs

■ They take a one-size-fits-all approach to literacy instruction.

■ Most of these programs were not developed with ELL students in mind and thus fail to address their unique linguistic and academic needs.

■ Because ELLs are not yet proficient in English and thus lack vocabulary knowledge, students are often forced to decode words they do not know yet.

■ They often result in students who can decode (word-level skills) but cannot comprehend what they read (text-level skills).

■ Takes time away from the type of ESL and literacy instruction ELLs need to develop literacy skills in English.

Phonics instruction may need to focus only on learning the alphabet and sound-spelling correspondences that help facilitate making meaning from text (Krashen, 1996; F. Smith, 2004, 2006). Furthermore, for phonics instruction to work, it must be taught within a meaningful context created by reading simple books, songs, poems, and chants. Once students are familiar with the text, that is, they know the meanings of all the words and can sing it or read along with the class and teacher (perhaps from memory), it can be used for phonics instruction. Phonics lessons need not be long. Most skills can be taught as mini-lessons, brief but explicit (Fountas & Pinnell, 2006b).

Teaching phonics in this manner is efficient and effective. Students are given multiple opportunities to learn many of the letter-sound relationships on their own. Direct instruction is needed only for those letter-sound relationships that students do not pick up on their own and is provided only when students are ready to learn them. These relationships are taught within the context of meaningful texts, which make them easier to learn and remember.

Many effective ELL educators have found top-down approaches to be beneficial for ELLs because of the emphasis on meaning and authenticity. These teachers often use teaching and learning strategies associated with whole language in combination with skills-based strategies, taking an "interactive approach" that views top-down and bottom-up processing as in constant interaction with each other (Eskey, 1998). In many schools, teachers call this a balanced literacy approach.

The reading wars continue to be fought in research and in curriculum and assessment programs. Although "reading wars" is a strong metaphor, it reflects the atmosphere surrounding the recent Reading First scandal (see Box 7.2). Reading First is a federal grant program created by Title I of NCLB and administered by the U.S. Department of Education. The advisers to President George W. Bush who created the Reading First program favored skills-based approaches and were staunch opponents of the whole language approach. Reading First is designed to improve students' reading ability, particularly in schools that have had low reading test scores. Although Reading First has been adopted by many school districts across the country, there is little evidence that its mandate for skill-based instruction has been effective.

Today phonics is often represented by the media as the "winner" in the reading wars, and whole language is often described as a "failed" approach. But a review of California students' reading test scores found little evidence that whole language is to blame for lower reading achievement (see Box 7.3). This winner/loser rhetoric masks the political forces at work to push the skills-based approach to reading held by powerful policymakers and creates the illusion that scientific research ultimately determined the "winner." Caught in the middle of the reading wars are ELL students, on whose unique needs little of the debate has focused. The emphasis on the skills-based approach has resulted in instruction ill-suited to help ELLs develop strong English literacy skills. In this chapter, we move beyond reading wars to discuss the type of instruction ELLs need to become successful readers in English.[2]

How Reading Promotes Second Language Acquisition

Reading is an excellent source of comprehensible input that enhances second language acquisition (Krashen, 2004c). Unlike oral English, to which some ELLs may

---

2: For discussions of the politics of reading instruction that illustrate the problems with this "research" and how it has been politicized, see Coles, 2000; Edelsky, 2006; McQuillan, 1998; Routman, 1996; Taylor, 1998.

Box 7.2

Reading First Scandal

Schools that receive Reading First grants are subject to federal mandates regarding their reading curriculum and instruction. Supporters claimed that Reading First's mandates to provide "scientifically based reading instruction" were working. But in September 2006, the Office of Inspector General of the U.S. Department of Education (2006b) released its final investigation report on the Reading First program's grant application process, exposing a scandal.

The inspector general found that the panel of reviewers that approved grant applications included only individuals who shared the directors' views about what constitutes scientifically based reading instruction (i.e., direct skills-based instruction), and that several of the panel members were in positions to pressure school districts to purchase curricular programs to which the panel members had commercial ties. The inspector general also found that the review panel did not follow proper procedures for awarding grants, and the criteria the panel used were not specifically addressed by NCLB.

Chris Doherty, director of Reading First, resigned soon after the report was issued. No one else resigned or was fired despite the wide-scale misuse and abuse of $4.8 billion in taxpayer money for education. The scandal quickly dropped off the media's radar, but many Reading First schools remained stuck with the programs they were coerced into adopting. Panel members continue to profit. There are many ELLs in Reading First schools, as well as many frustrated teachers who are rightfully questioning whether their mandated curriculum is appropriate for meeting the needs of their students.

A recent internal U.S. Department of Education impact study (Institute of Education Sciences, 2008) found that, In comparison with schools that did not adopt Reading First, Reading First schools failed to show improvements in students' reading comprehension test scores.

Box 7.3

Did Whole Language Fail?

In the reading wars, whole language has been blasted and accused by those favoring a skills-based approach as responsible for lower reading achievement. Specific claims were made in California, where the state's 1987 English Language Arts Framework was viewed as promoting a whole language philosophy. Critics pointed to low reading-test scores and blamed whole language and the 1987 framework and thus gave leverage to a new emphasis on skills-based approaches.

Jeff McQuillan (1998) found, however, that in the years preceding and following 1987, test scores in California were mixed, with declining scores in some grades but steady or increasing scores in others. Furthermore, he reviewed an analysis of 1992 data from the National Assessment of Educational Progress that includes teacher self-reports of their methodological approach to reading. McQuillan found that "those children in classrooms with heavy emphasis on phonics clearly did the worse" in comparisons with classrooms that used whole language or literature-based approaches (p. 14). He argues that there is little evidence that whole language failed in California.

have limited access, students have a virtually unlimited number of opportunities to encounter written English through books, magazines, newspapers, the Internet, and other written sources. Furthermore, ELLs have much greater control over what they read than over what they hear. They can choose the topic and the level of difficulty of the text they read. If they do not understand something, they can go back and read it again. They can take time to figure out the meaning of new words and structures by looking up words in a dictionary, asking a teacher or friend, or figuring out the meaning from the context. Also, they will probably encounter words, phrases, and structures that are unlikely to occur in spoken English. Correlation studies show that students who read more are faster and better readers, as well as better writers, and also that students who read more have more practical knowledge (Krashen, 2004b, n.d.).

My own research with ELL students (Wright, 2004a) supports these findings. One former ELL student I interviewed, Chanty, who started school in the United States in 2nd grade, had not attended school previously. She was in an ESL program for the first 8 years of her schooling, and much of her ESL instruction focused on grammar, drills, and worksheets. She complained:

> The grammar stuff, it confuses me more. It didn't help me at all. The only time I started to realize what works and what doesn't was in high school, when I started to be interested in books. During the summer, all I did was read books. I read almost half the books in the library. I realized that you have to read so many books to understand how grammar is used. To me, it's wrong when a teacher tries to explain grammar to students. I mean, yeah, you can pick up some points. But the most important thing is reading, because, after reading, you know how to use it, and you just remember it. (p. 11)

What We Know from Research about Reading Instruction for ELLs

The two extensive reviews of the scientific literature on language and literacy development of ELL students that were supported by U.S. Department of Education's Institute of Education Sciences, the NLP report (August & Shanahan, 2006a, 2006b) and the CREDE report (Genesee, Lindholm-Leary, Saunders, & Christian, 2005, 2006), discussed in Chapter 6, included the following findings on reading instruction:

Literacy instruction approaches for mainstream students are not sufficient for ELLs.

The CREDE report found that despite similarities between English literacy development for native speakers and ELLs, for ELLs the process is much more complicated. The NLP report declares that for ELLs to receive the maximum benefit from instruction in phonemic awareness, phonics, fluency, vocabulary, and text comprehension, the instruction should be adapted to their unique needs. The report adds that for ELLs to read and write proficiently in English, instruction in these areas is necessary but not sufficient.

English oral language development is critical for English literacy development beyond word-level skills.

Recall from Chapter 6 the important distinction the NLP report makes between word-level (i.e., decoding) skills and text-level (i.e., reading comprehension) skills. The CREDE report notes that whereas phonological awareness skills in English are directly related to word-level skills, they are not directly related to reading comprehension. The NLP found that word-level skills in literacy are often taught well enough to allow language-minority students to attain levels of performance equal to those of native English speakers but text-level skills are not, and therefore language-minority students rarely approach the same levels of proficiency in text-level skills achieved by native English speakers. The reason ELLs often learn how to decode words but have trouble comprehending what they read is the lack of attention to the ELL students' oral English language development. Both reports conclude that students with well-developed oral skills in English achieve greater success in English reading than students with less well-developed skills.

Literacy instruction must be combined with high quality ESL instruction.

The NLP report found that teaching reading skills alone to ELL students is not enough. In order for ELLs to develop strong English literacy skills, high quality literacy instruction must be combined with early, ongoing, and extensive oral English development.

Oral proficiency and literacy in the first language is an advantage for literacy development in English.

This finding has major implications for bilingual programs and challenges those who claim English-only instruction is superior. Indeed, according to the NLP report, effective instructional programs provide opportunities for students to develop proficiency in their first language. The review of research revealed that at both the elementary and secondary levels students instructed in their native language as well as in English performed better, on average, than students instructed only in English on measures of English reading proficiency. Similarly, the CREDE report found that L1 language and literacy skills can be transferred to support English literacy development. Diane August, the principal investigator for the NLP report, has outlined what we know from research about transfer between the first and second language (see Box 7.4).

Box 7.4

Transfer between the First and Second Language

- Word recognition skills acquired in a first language transfer to the second language.
- There is positive transfer of vocabulary knowledge for words that are cognates.
- Children use spelling knowledge in the first language when they spell in their second language, and errors associated with first language spelling disappear as students become more proficient in their second language.
- There is evidence of cross-language transfer of reading comprehension in bilinguals of all ages, even when the languages have different types of alphabets.
- For comprehension, there is also transfer from students' second language to their first; bilingual students who read strategically in one language also read strategically in their other language. Moreover, the more students use strategies in reading, the higher their reading performance.
- For writing, the studies suggest there are cross-language relationships for writing, but levels of first language and second language proficiency may mediate these relationships.

Source: August, 2006, pp. 71–72.

Individual differences contribute significantly to English literacy development.

No two ELL students are the same, and the NLP found that individual differences, such as general language proficiency, age, English oral proficiency, cognitive abilities, previous learning, and the similarities and differences between the first language and English will have an impact on each student's literacy development. This finding underlines the importance of the point made in Chapter 1 that teachers must know each of their students individually so they can adequately address their unique linguistic and academic needs during literacy instruction.

Most literacy assessments do a poor job of gauging ELL strengths and weaknesses.

The NLP calls into question claims that tests of letter naming and phonological awareness in English are good predictors of English reading performance. The NLP found that in studies related to these tests, researchers did not control for such critical factors as English oral proficiency and native language literacy. Noting that more research is needed, the panel found some limited evidence of the effectiveness of teacher judgment guided by thoughtful reflection on specific criteria to make program placement decisions or select students in need of intensive reading instruction.

Home language experiences can have a positive impact on literacy achievement.

Although empirical research is limited in this area, the NLP found some evidence that students perform better when they read or use material in the language they know better. The NLP also found that reading materials reflective of the students' cultures appears to facilitate comprehension. This evidence provides further support for bilingual approaches that build on the linguistic and cultural funds of knowledge that students bring to school from their homes, and it provides support for the use of multicultural literature. The NLP also found research evidence that the parents of ELLs are often able and willing to help their children achieve academic success but concluded that schools typically underestimate and underutilize parents' interest potential contributions. The panel concludes, however, that there is insufficient evidence to make policy and practice recommendations about home language use. This finding is important because it runs counter to the advice some teachers give to parents to speak and read to their children only in English.

Effective literacy instruction for ELLs provides direct instruction in interactive learning environments.

The CREDE report refers to the direct approach, which emphasizes explicit instruction in skills and strategies, and the interactive approach, which emphasizes learning mediated through interaction with other learners or more competent readers and writers, such as the teacher and other classmates. The NLP recommends direct instruction because it ensures that students have the opportunity to master skills that are often embedded and even obscured in complex literacy or academic tasks. But the NLP also recommends interaction because it provides a context in which teachers can provide modifications to literacy instruction to accommodate for students' individual differences and preferences. In short, this finding supports the practice of teaching literacy skills in interactive, meaningful contexts.

Complementing these findings are recommendations from the Institute of Education Sciences (IES), published in a practice guide titled *Effective Literacy and English Language Instruction for English Learners in the Elementary Grades* (Gersten et al., 2007). Based on a review of a small number of scientific quantitative research studies that met the rigorous standards to be included in the federal government's

What Works Clearinghouse (see www.whatworks.ed.gov), the guide offers the following five recommendations:

> Recommendation 1. Screen for reading problems and monitor progress.
> Recommendation 2. Provide intensive small-group reading interventions.
> Recommendation 3. Provide extensive and varied vocabulary instruction.
> Recommendation 4. Develop academic English.
> Recommendation 5. Schedule regular peer-assisted learning opportunities.
> (pp. 3–4)

Although only a small number of studies met their stringent inclusion criteria, the authors of the guide declared the level of evidence "strong" for all but Recommendation 4 (academic language). Their discussion of Recommendation 4, for which the level of evidence was deemed to be "low," reflects the problematic construct of "academic English." Specifically, the authors of the IES guide were unable to identify research or existing curricular programs with a solid empirical base that provide a scope and sequence aimed a building academic English. Recall our earlier discussions that the construct of "academic English" is problematic because it is too generic to account for the complexity of language proficiency and the variety of language and literacy skills ELLs may need to accomplish different academic tasks in different content areas.

Despite the limitations of the quantitative research base of the IES guide's recommendations, its findings and recommendations are essentially consistent with the findings of qualitative research and with the experiences of ELL educators in terms of practices that have been found to be effective in meeting the needs of the ELL students.[3] These practices include using on-going authentic literacy assessments, working with ELLs in small reading groups with work appropriate to their levels and needs, focusing on vocabulary development through effective ESL instruction, and providing ample opportunities for peer interaction. The reading instructional strategies and techniques outlined in this chapter are consistent with the panel's recommendations.

Promoting Reading Development for ELLs in the Classroom

The research is clear and it is consistent with the finding of the federal court in *Lau vs. Nichols* in 1974: we cannot teach ELLs to read the same way we teach native English speakers to read. The instructional strategies and techniques described in this chapter include those commonly used with mainstream elementary school students but with suggestions for ways they need to be adjusted (i.e., sheltered or specially designed) to make them appropriate for and effective with ELLs across grade levels and content areas.

ELLs need a balanced approach to literacy instruction that integrates reading, writing, listening, and speaking, that teaches reading skills and strategies within the context of meaningful, authentic communication, and that is differentiated to meet the diverse language and literacy needs of students in the class. Teachers need to understand their ELL students' reading strengths and challenges, and they need to be clear about what they want their students to know and be able to do with reading as a result of their instruction.

3: See, e.g., Calkins, 2000; Carrell, Devine, & Eskey, 1998; Diaz-Rico & Weed, 2006; Fountas & Pinnell, 2006b; Hadaway, Vardell, & Young, 2002; Jessness, 2004; Kendall & Khuon, 2006; Krashen, 2004c; Peregoy & Boyle, 2008; Routman, 1996.

Reading and learning to read does not take place just during the language arts time or in ESL and English classes. Students read all day in all content areas. Reading from textbooks and other supplementary materials is required for success in most content-area assignments and projects. Thus, for ELLs, all content-area reading is part of their English reading development and all teachers have a responsibility to help ELLs learn to read text associated with the content areas they teach.

This section begins with a brief discussion of how teachers can identify ELLs' reading levels, with attention to the complex relationship between English literacy development and English as a second language development. The majority of this section is about strategies and techniques that sheltered content instruction teachers and ESL teachers can use in their classes to facilitate ELLs' development of academic literacies across content areas.

Identifying ELLs' Reading Levels

Identifying ELLs' reading levels can be challenging because ELLs enter U.S. schools at different ages with different levels of literacy in their native language and different levels of English language proficiency, whereas the frameworks used to identify reading levels in schools are designed mainly for students who already speak English and who are learning to read in the early elementary grades. One commonly used framework identifies four levels of literacy development: emergent, early, early fluency, and fluency (see Table 7.1). Native English-speaking students typically begin at the emergent level in kindergarten and reach the fluency level by 2nd or 3rd grade.

Table 7.1 Levels of English Literacy Development

Emergent

- Understands that print carries meaningful messages.
- Begins to learn basic concepts about books, print, letters, sounds, writing.
- Reads books that are highly supportive, short, simple, and with direct picture-text match.
- Begins to realize that she can be an author who writes texts other can read.

Early

- Understands that books have exact and unchanging meanings.
- Understands that print is governed by conventions.
- Reads and writes simple stories and informational passages.
- Knows reading is a meaning-making process that uses problem-solving skills
- Reads word by word and often uses a finger to point as well.

Early fluency

- Begins to use multiple clues to make meaning.
- Relies less on illustrations as a clue to text meaning.
- Uses an array of problem solving skills in reading.
- Grasps books' main ideas and their emotional impact.
- Knows and uses a variety of strategies for unlocking unknown words.

Fluency

- Exhibits the behaviors of mature readers.
- Makes sense of books that are longer and more complex.
- Adopts strategies flexibly to fulfill a range of reading purposes.
- Orchestrates all the clues available to them to make meaning.
- Self-corrects flexibly and efficiently in order to maintain meaning.

Source: Rigby, n.d., p. 25.

For ELLs, these grade levels may not be relevant, because newcomer ELLs arrive in U.S. schools at all grade levels. Older newcomer ELLs who are literate in their native language will already have the basic understandings of print and books of the emergent and early levels but nonetheless will need time to transfer this knowledge to English reading. In addition, print conventions may vary between their L1 and English, and students need time to learn the differences.

Further complicating these levels of English literacy development are the varying levels of English proficiency among ELLs. ELLs at the preproduction and early production stages of second language acquisition are unlikely to surpass the emergent and early levels of English literacy development, regardless of their grade level, because their lack of proficiency in English will make it difficult for them to understand what they read, even if they are able to correctly decode each word in the text.

TESOL's English Language Proficiency Standards are useful for considering the language demands of specific reading tasks at different levels of English proficiency. Recall from Chapter 3 that these standards provide proficiency descriptors for five levels (Starting, Emerging, Developing, Expanding, and Bridging), across five grade-level bands (pre-K–K, 1–3, 4–5, 6–8, and 9–12), and across five standards (social, intercultural, and instructional language, language arts, mathematics, science, and social studies). The TESOL standards and performance indicators can give teachers at specific grade levels an understanding of what can be expected of students in the area of reading for social and instructional purposes, and across different content areas, and also what instruction and guidance will be needed to help students move up to the next level. This information is critical for lesson planning and for selecting appropriate books for reading instruction and practice, particularly for guided reading. Consider the sample performance indicator in Figure 7.1 for reading for grades 1–3 in the area of language arts under the topic of story grammar. Note that the level of difficulty of the reading task increases as the level of support decreases for each subsequent proficiency level.

Selecting Texts

Reading is a great source of comprehensible input that promotes second language acquisition and an important vehicle for content-area learning. Also, it provides a strong foundation for writing development. Students should have access to a wide range of texts across content areas about different topics in different genres at different reading levels, including authentic children's and youth literature—the type

Standard 2: Language of Language Arts
Grade level cluster: 1–3

Domain: Reading Topic: Story grammar				
Level 1	**Level 2**	**Level 3**	**Level 4**	**Level 5**
Identify story elements with visual support by names (characters) or places (settings).	Categorize story elements with visual support using graphic organizers by description of characters, settings, or events.	Sequence story events with visually supported text by beginning, middle, and end.	Match transition words (e.g., "finally") or phrases with sequence, main ideas, or details in visually supported stories.	Identify and order main ideas and details, using modified grade-level stories.

Figure 7.1   **TESOL ELP Standards, sample performance indicators for reading.** (Source: TESOL, 2006a, p. 61.)

of books you find in the children's and youth sections of public libraries and book-stores. Teachers should select texts for students to read that support specific instructional purposes, but student choice is also very important.

Reading is also an important entry point for addressing goals of multicultural education, such as recognizing and valuing students' home cultures, helping students learn about other cultures, and preparing them to live and work in a diverse society. As Irene C. Fountas and Gay Su Pinnell (2006b) argue, "they should see illustrations with people like themselves in books, and have their cultures reflected in the food, celebrations, customs, dress, holidays, and events they encounter in the stories" (p. 506). Books beyond this surface level of culture, however, are also needed. Some books lend themselves to discussion of critical issues and social problems that students and their families deal with in their communities and in the nation as a whole and can become an important part of multicultural education and critical pedagogy. Even younger children can be drawn into a discussion of such powerful issues as racism, discrimination, and civil rights by reading books such as *White Socks Only* by Evelyn Coleman, about a young African American girl in the segregated south who runs into trouble when she drinks from a water fountain labeled "White Only"; *The Story of Ruby Bridges* by Robert Coles, about the first African American student to attend a New Orleans elementary school after the Supreme Court's desegregation order; and *The Story of Latino Civil Rights: Fighting for Justice* by Miranda Hunter. Students are much more likely to engage in reading when books are reflective of themselves and the worlds they live in.

Structuring Activities

Teachers can use the before, during, after (BDA) structure (or into-through-and beyond) to create activities around the reading of any text in any content area. *Before* reading a text, effective teachers help their students activate their prior knowledge and survey or preview the text before reading it. *During* reading, effective teachers model reading strategies and help readers make connections between the text at hand and other texts they have read or experiences they have had. *After* reading, effective teachers help readers consolidate, elaborate, and deepen their understanding of the text and the connections they have made. The use of BDA is included in the following discussion of frameworks and strategies that teachers can use to help their ELLs become proficient readers of English.

Reading *to, with,* and *by* ELLs

One helpful way of conceptualizing reading instruction in the ELL classroom is to look at reading in three forms: reading *to,* reading *with,* and reading *by* ELL students. All three are essential. Although this framework was originally developed for use in mainstream elementary school classrooms, it can be modified to support ELLs' English literacy development at any grade level.

Read-Alouds

Read-alouds refer to teachers reading a book or other text aloud to their students. Reading aloud is one of the most important things teachers can do to help ELLs learn to read. Fountas and Pinnell (2006b) note that if students hear 1 book read aloud every day from kindergarten through 8th grade, they will experience over 1,600 books—3,200 if the teacher reads 2 books a day and 4,800 at 3 a day! In the upper elementary grades and middle school, the authors suggest, the "book" might be a section of a longer text or chapter book.

Read-alouds give students access to text beyond their current level of ability. When parents or teachers read aloud, they are demonstrating the connection between oral and written language while modeling fluent reading and oral production of English. Through read-alouds, students are exposed to new content and concepts, a variety of language patterns, and interesting vocabulary—including concepts they may not have been exposed to in their everyday lives and patterns and words they may never hear in ordinary oral interaction. Students are also exposed to a variety of genres and different writing styles. Finally, research has shown that the more students are read to, the more they read on their own (Krashen, 2005/2006).

Although reading aloud is important for all students, it is even more important for ELLs. Many come from homes where parents are unable to read aloud in English to their children; some parents may be unable to read in their native language because of limited educational opportunities in their home countries. Also, many ELLs come from low-income families that have little disposable income for books. The lack of books in the home may also mean ELLs rarely see adults or others reading and thus they do not have models of fluent readers who read for enjoyment and information. In addition, as research has revealed, students in lower-income neighborhoods have less access to public libraries, and schools in these neighborhoods tend to have the worst school libraries (Krashen, 1995). Nancy Hornberger (1996) made similar observations in her visits to the homes of young ELL students in inner-city Philadelphia, noting a scarcity of printed material but a relative abundance of audiovisual material.

Cultural differences may also influence how much parents read aloud to their children at home. As Shirley Brice Heath (1982) reveals in her classic research article "What No Bedtime Story Means," mainstream U.S. schools operate on the cultural assumption that children are read to at home (see also Heath, 1983), and thus literacy instruction in schools often privileges students who come from mainstream middle-class homes where reading bedtime stories and other literacy practices closely match the practices of the school. Students whose home literacy practices differ from those practiced by their schools typically face greater challenges in learning to read at school. To make up for this mismatch between school and home literacy practices, it is imperative that teachers read aloud to their ELL students as much as possible.

Teachers should have a clear purpose in mind when selecting a book to read aloud, and they should ensure that it is appropriate for the grade and English proficiency level of the students. The book may be selected because it goes along with a current theme, topic, or genre being studied in the classroom, because it addresses a particular topic of concern or interest of the students, or because it contains useful vocabulary and language patterns. Perhaps the teacher selects a high interest narrative that builds important background for subsequent reading of a more challenging grade-level expository text in a content-area class. Maybe the book is selected just because it is a great book the teacher knows the students will enjoy.

The length of time and type of text selected for a read-aloud will depend on the grade and English proficiency of the students. Younger and lower-level ELLs need simple and short books with vivid illustrations and only a few lines of text on each page. For older and more advanced students, grade-level chapter books, novels, and articles from magazines, newspapers, or the Internet are more appropriate.

Read-alouds in the classroom should involve the whole group. For a picture book, students should sit on the floor close to the teacher where they can see the pictures and point to words and pictures in the book when appropriate. Also, sitting close together on the floor creates a more informal atmosphere conducive to listening to and enjoying a book as a community of readers. Older students may prefer to sit at their desks, which is fine when there are few illustrations in the book or text. Regardless of the seating arrangement, students should be encouraged to chime in, using gestures, asking questions about the text, and making predictions about what they think is going to happen next. To engage students, teachers can exaggerate the dialogue and use gestures and different voices for different characters. The more interactive and fun it is, the more comprehensible the book or text will be for ELL students. And the more comprehensible it is, the more English they learn from the reading.

A good read-aloud is interactive and focuses on the meaning of the text and follows the BDA structure. For example, before reading *The Day Jimmy's Boa Ate the Wash* by Trinka Hakes Noble—a humorous picture book about a class field trip to a farm that ends up in chaos because Jimmy brought his pet boa constrictor along—the teacher could have a class discussion about field trips the students have been on and ask whether any of them has ever been to a farm. He could show the students the book, read the title, and discuss the cover illustration, which is sure to elicit conversations about snakes and farm animals. To engage students with the story before reading, the teacher can then do a picture walk with the students by looking at a few pages and talking with them about the illustrations. He might then ask the students to make predictions about what they think is going to happen in the story (e.g., "What do you think Jimmy's boa constrictor is going to do at the farm?"). This process establishes the context of the story and sets a purpose for reading. In addition, particularly for ELLs, this "before" discussion is an opportunity to pre-teach unknown vocabulary in a meaningful context. ELL students are likely to know the words *snake* and *clothes* but may not know *boa constrictor* or *the wash*.

Similar procedures can be followed when reading from chapter books with older students or more advanced ELL students. In addition, before reading each chapter, the teacher should lead a brief discussion to review what has happened in the book so far, make predictions about what might come next, pre-teach any key vocabulary, or build background knowledge for any difficult concepts that may be covered in the chapter. Likewise, when teachers read expository texts aloud, for example, from content-area textbooks, they can preview headings, photographs, captions, key words, summaries, and guiding questions.

During the read-aloud, the teacher can make the text more comprehensible and engaging for ELLs by using gestures, pointing to parts of the illustrations that provide hints for the meaning (i.e., pointing to the snake when reading "boa constrictor"), and rephrasing or explaining difficult words or phrases (e.g., "'The wash' means the clothes the farmer's wife just washed and is hanging up to dry"). Decisions about when to use gestures and what words or phrases require rephrasing or explanation are based on the proficiency level of the students. The lower the proficiency level, the greater the amount of gesturing, explaining, and rephrasing required. In a class with a wide range of levels, the teacher should provide the amount needed for the students at the lowest levels.

During the reading, the teacher can think aloud to model how proficient readers make sense of the text as they are reading, saying, for example, "I wonder why she did that? I'm going to read more to find out," or "It looks as though Sylvia has a problem. Let's read more to see how she solves it." The teacher can make the reading interactive by pausing to allow students to confirm their predictions and to make new ones (e.g., "Were you right that Jimmy's boa would chase the chickens?" "What do you think is going to happen next?"). Care must be taken, however, to ensure that these strategies fit naturally into the flow of the read-aloud and do not distract or take too much time away from the actual reading of the text. The teacher could also pause and allow students to fill in the words, indicating their comprehension.

"After" reading strategies and activities build and check students' comprehension of the book or text and help them extend and deepen their understanding. Too often, many teachers finish the real-aloud and quickly move on to an unrelated activity. Effective teachers make use of the magic moments created by the completion of a good read-aloud. After finishing the book or text, teachers can ask students whether their predictions were correct. They can talk with the students about the parts they liked best and relate the text to others they have read in class, to other content areas, or to out-of-school experiences. For ELLs at lower English proficiency levels, teachers can ask questions that require only a few words to answer and for more advanced students, open-ended questions that encourage greater elaboration.

Fountas and Pinnell (2006b) offer some additional suggestions for interactive read-alouds and literature discussions with ELLs:

- Increase the amount of time you read aloud and engage in extended discussion of the texts. This will help all students expand language knowledge.
- Stick to simple texts that your students will be able to understand. You can explain concepts, but there should not be too much to learn within any one text. Otherwise, a read-aloud will turn into one long vocabulary lesson and children will lose the meaning of the text.
- Choose texts with illustrations that your students will enjoy and that will expand their understanding.
- When you read aloud, be sure that English language learners are not seated in the peripheral positions (to the side or in the back). They especially need to see, hear and participate.
- Give English language learners a "preview" of the text by holding a brief small-group discussion with them before reading the text to the entire group. You can show pictures, talk about the content, and even read the whole book or sections of it. In this way, English language learners will hear the text twice, understand it better, and be able to participate more actively in the discussion. (pp. 505–506)

One final but very important tip: After a book has been read aloud, don't put it aside never to be seen again. Younger students especially love to hear the same books read over and over again. Repeated readings are especially beneficial for ELLs. The teacher can also make the book available to students to read during independent reading time, put the book and a recording of it at the listening center, or let the student take the book home to read with their family.

Shared Reading

Shared reading is an example of reading with students and has many of the same features as read-alouds. Here, however, the focus is on using texts closer to the students' reading ability and getting them to read along. Shared reading provides teachers with opportunities to teach important concepts of print, demonstrate strategies that good readers use, and involve students as a community of readers.

In the early elementary grades, teachers often have big books, which are oversized versions of books they can use to engage students with the text and illustrations. For students in the upper grades, any source of enlarged text can be used for shared reading, such as charts (commercial or teacher-made) with poems, chants, and song lyrics, a pocket chart with sentence strips, or text projected on a screen. Secondary school students could be given their own copies of the text.

Shared readings should be done with the whole group. Many texts are appropriate for shared reading. What is important is that the level of the reading be slightly higher than the students' current instructional level. For ELLs at the beginning or emergent levels of reading, the text should contain rhyme, rhythm, and repetition of words, phrases, and language patterns; the illustrations should provide maximum support for understanding the text. For more advanced ELLs, the text should more closely resemble grade-level reading materials but contain illustrations or other features to facilitate ELLs' comprehension of the text. Ideally, the text matches the current theme or topic of study. Also, like read-alouds, shared readings expose students to different genres. In classes with a wide range of reading and language levels, the teacher can vary the difficulty of the text read on different days. Even books at higher reading levels can be made accessible to lower-level ELLs through the scaffolding provided by the teacher during shared reading.

Shared reading follows the same BDA structure as read-alouds. One big book or enlarged text source can be used for shared reading lessons for a week or more. The first few sessions focus on getting students familiar enough with the text that they can read along; subsequent sessions focus on comprehension and the direct instruction of reading skills and strategies.

For students who are just learning to read, the teacher tracks the text by pointing to each word as she reads, using her finger or a pointer stick. As students become familiar with the text, they join in and share in the reading. This is easy for them to do, particularly when the text has rhyme, rhythm, and repetitions. Once students become familiar with the text, teachers can use echo reading, where the teacher reads a line and then students repeat. As the students become more competent with the reading, the teacher can invite them to come up individually and use their finger or pointer to track the text and lead the class in the reading of the book. Fountas and Pinnell (2006b) describe a shared reading text as a language resource for ELLs to learn new vocabulary and syntactic structures. They note that repeated readings maximizes ELLs' exposure to the English syntax in the text, which helps them subconsciously develop understandings of noun-verb agreement, plurals, and other concepts.

For older students with higher levels of English proficiency who can process several lines of print and follow it with their eyes, shared reading takes on the form of choral reading, where the emphasis is on the interpretation of text through the voice (Fountas & Pinnell, 2006b). All students read the text aloud in unison, though there can be variations with different students taking on different parts of the text, which they read alone or with a partner or small group. For example, in reading a poem such as "I Have a Story to Tell You" by Forever Krysia, which is a dialogue between a fish and the ocean, half the class could read the lines spoken by the fish and the other half the lines spoken by the ocean.[4] Fountas and Pinnell note that choral reading provides opportunities for students to practice expressive reading, develop new vocabulary and language structures, become aware of complex literary texts, and develop awareness of the ways particular words and phrases are stressed.

Echo reading and choral reading provide scaffolding for ELL readers and create a low-risk environment. Students can participate as they feel ready, and they will not be singled out, because their voices blend in with the other students. Subsequent readings can build comprehensible input though gestures, props, rephrasings, explanations, and so forth. Once students are familiar with the text (perhaps they are simply "reading" it by memory) teachers use the text to teach and model a wide variety of reading skills and strategies.

For example, for lower-level students who are still learning letters and sounds, the shared reading text can be used to teach phonics within a meaningful context.

4: I am grateful to Mayra Salinas, a San Antonio elementary school teacher, who introduced me to this poem and technique when she demonstrated it in one of my courses. The poem is available at www.poemhunter.com/poem/i-have-a-story-to-tell-you/

The teacher could call on individual students to come point to or mark (using sticky notes, highlighting tape, or other means) certain letters or sounds (e.g., "Phitsamay, can you find the letter *t?*" "Boravy, show me a word that starts with the /d/ sound."). Or specific reading strategies can be taught and modeled. For example, the teacher could cover parts of words and guide students to use picture, phonetic, semantic, or syntactic clues to figure out the words. The words could be revealed and checked to see whether students are correct. Teachers can also use think-alouds or other strategies to model effective reading strategies, such as visualizing, questioning, predicting, checking comprehension, rereading, and making connections.

"After" activities can also be extensive and varied. For example, if the teacher's purpose is to focus on vocabulary and syntax, an immediate "after" activity could be to copy selected sentences from the text onto sentence strips and then cut them up so each word is on its own card. Teachers could mix up the words and put them in a pocket chart for the students to put back in the right order. The students would be required to use a range of strategies to put the sentence back together again, demonstrating their knowledge of vocabulary and syntax. The possibilities for shared reading activities are far-ranging, with the ultimate purpose to help students learn the strategies and skills they need to become independent readers.

Teachers can make the big books and charts available for students to read during independent reading time. Books read in shared reading often become the most popular books students choose during independent reading. The regular-size versions of the books can be placed on students' desks, put in the classroom library, or even sent home for reading practice. Text from charts can also be reduced to a single page for students to take home and read with their families.

Guided Reading

Guided reading is conducted with small groups of students (three to six) who read at about the same level. Students have their own copies of the same text at their particular instructional level (defined as a text they can read with 90–94% accuracy). Guided reading fulfills the call from the Institute of Education Sciences for intensive small-group reading interventions for ELL students.

The purpose of guided reading is for students to practice reading and using the skills and strategies they have learned through read-alouds and shared readings. The teacher does not read the book to or with the students but instead prepares them to read it on their own. The teacher serves as a coach, providing scaffolding as needed to help students apply their skills to read and make sense of the text. The ultimate goal of guided reading is to help students move up to higher reading levels and become independent readers of increasingly difficult texts.

The source for guided reading is typically leveled books that come with reading curricular programs but can also include children's literature or even basal readers if the texts are at the students' instructional level. For beginning-level ELLs at the emergent reading level, the texts should be simple with lots of rhyme, rhythm, and repetition and illustrations that provide support for the meaning of the text. For higher-level ELLs beyond the emergent and early reading levels, the books should contain fewer of these supports and should increasingly resemble grade-level reading material. The text gradient created by Fountas and Pinnell (2006a) or the book leveling system used in Rigby's (n.d.) *On Our Way to English* program (Rigby Book Levels for ELLs, related links) offer guides for matching ELL readers to appropriate leveled texts.

In guided reading, the teacher follows the BDA structure used in read-alouds and shared readings, beginning with a discussion of the topic to activate prior knowledge and build background knowledge, followed by a discussion of the book cover, a picture walk, student predictions, pre-teaching of unknown vocabulary, and so on. The teacher reads the title of the book with the students but does not read any of the text. Next, the teacher directs the students to read the book aloud on their own. While the students are reading, the teacher listens in and provides help where needed, suggesting strategies they can use to figure out and make sense of words and phrases they do not know. Particular care should be taken that the reading does not become a choral reading, with all the students following the lead of the strongest reader in the group. Each student should be reading aloud on his or her own. To prevent choral reading, some teachers have found it useful to stagger when students start reading, directing the first student to read past the first page before inviting the next student to begin.

If the book the students are reading is relatively simple and short, they will likely have time for multiple readings. Once each student has read the book, the teacher can partner up the students to read to each other, and then they can trade partners when they finish. One student, also, could be selected to read with the teacher, who could do a running record of the students' reading. After the readings, the teacher leads the students through a postreading activity, such as a discussion of the book that includes comprehension questions.

While the students read, teachers identify words, phrases, and structures the students appear to struggle with, and use this information to create mini-lessons. For example, suppose students struggled with the word *chew* because they do not know the meaning of the word or the sound made by the consonant cluster *ch*. The teacher could first teach a mini-vocabulary lesson on the word *chew*, explaining and demonstrating its meaning, encouraging a discussion about things one should or should not chew (food, gum, pencils, fingernails, broken glass, etc.), and then return to the book to look at the context of the word *chew*. Next, the teacher could teach a mini-lesson on the /ch/ sound. The students could brainstorm other words that start with *ch* and write these words on paper, white boards, or chalk boards or make the words with magnetic letters or other alphabet manipulatives. They could then go back through the story looking for and reading all *ch* words.

Each guided reading session informs the next in terms of the level of books to be read and mini-lessons that need to be provided. Teachers must pay careful attention to the progress of individual students, moving them around and reformulating groups as needed to ensure that students are always engaging with texts at their instructional levels.

Fountas and Pinnell (2006b) offer the following suggestions for guided reading with ELLs:

- Select texts that have language structures, concepts, or vocabulary that will be within the readers' control with your support. Try not to include too many new things to learn in any one text.
- In the introduction, include as much "practice" as needed to help students become familiar with the new language structures. Identify language structures that will be challenging and repeat them yourself in conversation, but also have students repeat them several times and talk about their meaning.
- During the introduction, use pictures, concrete objects, or demonstrations that will help students understand the concepts and ideas in the text. Don't ask students to read any text they will not understand.
- As a regular routine, ask students to identify any words or phrases in the text that they cannot understand. This will help students learn to monitor their own understanding, provide feedback to you on the appropriateness of the text, and give you an opportunity to clarify concepts.
- Include word work. One or two minutes of preplanned emphasis on particu-

lar words will help students become familiar with how English works, learn many new high-frequency words, and make connections among other words. (pp. 507–508)

Language Experience Approach

One challenge in helping ELLs learn to read in English, particularly those at the lowest levels of English proficiency and older newcomers who lack L1 literacy skills, is finding texts without an abundance of unknown vocabulary and unfamiliar language structures. Another challenge is finding texts that are personally or culturally relevant to the student. The language experience approach can help resolve some of these problems.

The language experience approach is inspired by Paulo Freire's critical pedagogy (discussed in Chapter 2). The student identifies a problem in his or her life, tells a story about that problem, and explores solutions. Alternatively, the student can simply tell a story from his or her personal experience. The teacher writes down the story, and the resulting text is used for reading instruction with the student. This text is easier for the student to read because it consists of his or her own natural language, experiences, and knowledge. The language experience approach supports students' literacy development by helping them understand "What I say I can write" and "What I write I can read." As students make progress, this concept can be expanded to "What others write I can read." The problem-posing approach also encourages students to see literacy as a vehicle for taking action to improve their lives.

The language experience approach can be varied to accommodate students at different English proficiency and literacy levels, and it can be used for different purposes. For example, students at beginning levels of English speaking proficiency might bring a picture to scaffold their description of an experience or storytelling, working with a partner or the teacher to learn the vocabulary and language structures they need. Students with more advanced oral English proficiency but limited reading and writing skills are likely to provide more oral language, which may be difficult for the teacher to write down as they speak. One solution is to make an audio recording that can be transcribed by the teacher or another student. This approach can also be used with shared experiences in content-area classes. For example, a science experiment can be the basis for first talking and then reading and writing about science.

One challenge of using the language experience approach with ELLs is how to handle errors in students' oral language before writing it down. Although there is some debate about the best approach, teachers have found that if they offer corrective feedback, the resulting texts that students read help reinforce correct forms while maintaining the authenticity of the students' own words.

Independent Reading

The purpose of reading *to* and *with* students is to get them to the point where they do independent reading. Students need to be provided time in class every day to read independently. Younger students need about 10 or 15 minutes, older students 20 minutes or more. Many schools use the term *sustained silent reading* (SSR), though for younger students, it is anything but silent, since most students read out loud. Some schools come up with cute alternative names for SSR, such as DEAR time (Drop everything and read), or USSR (uninterrupted sustained silent reading). Others refer to independent reading as *free voluntary reading*, stressing the fact that students should be free to choose what they read.

To be successful, SSR requires an extensive classroom library where students can find books they are genuinely interested in reading that are also appropriate to their language proficiency and reading level. Many teachers have found it helpful to organize their classroom libraries by theme or genre. Books and texts used for read-alouds, shared reading, and guided reading should also be made readily available. Even magazines and comic books are appropriate. One of the main reasons some students are reluctant readers is that they lack access to interesting books and other reading material; students who have greater access to interesting reading materials do more reading and are better readers (Krashen, 1993). Students should be free to choose any book they like and be allowed to stop reading any book that doesn't hold their interest. Forcing students to read material that does not interest them is a sure way to kill their enjoyment of reading.

Although students should be given open access to any reading materials in the classroom, they also need to be guided to make proper choices. Teachers should monitor the students to make sure they do not always choose books that are too easy or too hard and should also monitor to make sure the students are actually reading. Teachers should always be reading a book of their own choosing. In doing so, they offer the model of an adult who loves to read for enjoyment—something students may not see at home.

To make SSR enjoyable, some teachers allow students to sit anywhere they like in the classroom—at their desk, under the desk, on the desk, on the floor, on bean bag chairs, on a sofa, on mats, and so on. Some teachers play soft instrumental music in the background to enhance the reading environment. Lower-level ELLs not yet be capable of reading even simple books on their own could listen to a book read aloud by the teacher or another student, listen to a book at the listening center, or interact with an electronic book on the classroom computer.

Krashen (2004b), who cites overwhelming research evidence that the use of SSR in the classroom for students of all ages can transform them into lifelong readers, strongly recommends that SSR time be simply for enjoyment, with minimal accountability. Teachers should not feel the urge to follow up on SSR time with quizzes, reports, or contests in which students earn points and awards for reading. In many schools, however, independent and home reading programs are supplemented with computer-based comprehension quizzes. One of the most popular programs is Accelerated Reader, which some literacy experts have criticized (see Box 7.5).

Narrow Reading

Narrow reading is a form of independent recreational reading identified by Krashen (2004b) that entails reading several books on the same subject, by the same author, or in the same genre. Narrow reading can also include reading several books in a series, with recurring characters, themes, and plot lines that may or may not build on earlier books in the series (e.g., Sweet Valley High, Babysitters Club, Captain Underpants, Magic Tree House, Cam Jensen, Harry Potter, Twilight). Krashen argues that narrow reading is an efficient way to acquire a second language because it can maximize comprehensible input and be very motivating. Students who read several books on the same topic accumulate a great deal of background knowledge, which facilitates comprehension of each new text read on the topic. In a similar manner, reading books by the same author helps students improve their reading skills by increasing their familiarity with that author's style, favorite expressions, and overall use of language.

Reader's Workshop

In recent years, educators have begun to extend the balanced literacy framework that was originally developed for elementary school into secondary schools. While

Box 7.5

Accelerated Reader

Accelerated Reader (AR), according the publisher's Web site (www.renlearn.com/ar/), is in use in over half the schools in the United States. With AR, students take computer-based comprehension quizzes on books they have read. The program has a system for leveling books and includes quizzes for over 100,000 books in its latest database. Students earn points based on the number of books they read and quizzes they pass. Many schools use the points to award prizes.

Dozens of studies support the use of AR (see Renaissance Learning, n.d.). Many teachers and students appear to like it very much. It encourages students to read authentic literature, and teachers have reported that the amount of reading at home and at school has increased dramatically. Many literacy experts, however, are critical of the program's emphasis on extrinsic rewards, pointing out that students frequently appear more interested in the number of points and prizes they earn than in what they are actually reading. The quizzes are not difficult, and critics contend that the software promotes only basic recall rather than higher-order thinking.

If AR is used, teachers should ensure that it is only used as a supplement to their reading program. Teachers should conduct their own reading assessments and ask students their own comprehension questions and not rely on AR as the only source of information. The use of extrinsic rewards should be limited or eliminated. And teachers should constantly remind student that reading is its own reward and its purpose is not to get points and prizes.

the reading process itself does not change, what does change at the secondary level is the difficulty of the reading material, the range of genres, and the complexity of thinking needed to comprehend texts. Additionally, schools are structured differently at the secondary level, and the range of ELL students' reading levels is often greater. Reader's Workshop is one structure that many secondary schools have used to meet these challenges.

Nancy Atwell (1987) explains that in Reader's Workshop, the expectation is that all students will read, discover books they love, and, together with their teachers and peers enter the world of literature, become captivated, find satisfaction, and learn. According to Atwell, these expectations are demonstrated through the workshop's predictable structure and procedures. Reader's Workshop is offered at least two times a week for one class period and always begins with a 5 to 10 minute mini-lesson based on the teacher's assessment of student interest, strengths, and needs. The mini-lesson also enables teachers to demonstrate to students, for example, how to choose appropriate books, how to use strategies that effective readers use, and how to respond to literature.

Postreading Activities

The purpose of postreading activities—the *after* part of BDA—is to help deepen students' comprehension of the text they just heard or read and to extend their learning beyond the text. Suggestions for postreading activities follow.

Class Discussions

The simplest postreading activity is a discussion involving the whole class or within small groups. Teachers ask comprehension questions, invite students to describe their favorite parts of a story, and allow students to share their thoughts on the text.

Teachers help students connect the literature to their daily lives—making what literacy experts call "text-to-self" connections. Teachers also help students make "text-to-text" connections, that is, to relate the book or text to something they read previously. These interactive class discussions help students expand their comprehension and develop new perspectives.

Reader Response

Responding to reading goes beyond reading comprehension and encourages the reader to reflect on and extend understandings as they evolve. As readers think about what they read, they ask authentic questions, make comments and connections, and form opinions. Through reader response, students develop a sense of what is important in the text and are able to form judgments about what they are reading. As students share their responses orally (e.g., in literature circles, book clubs) or in writing (e.g., dialogue journals, reader response logs, readers notebooks) with their peers and the teacher, they interact with other readers and their responses to text, and develop new perspectives. Response to reading can include, for example, personal responses or reactions to characters, setting, plot and other aspects of a story, open-ended questions, summaries, and reviews.

Graphic Organizers

Graphic organizers help students break a text down into its essential components. For example, story maps highlight key developments of the story in sequence. The simplest form of story map is the beginning-middle-end chart, in which students indicate the key plot elements at these points in the story. A problem-solution chart can be used to represent the basic conflict and resolution in the story. Graphic organizers can also be used with expository text structures. For example, venn diagrams or comparison charts can be used with texts that feature contrast and comparison, webs or feature charts can be used with texts that feature description, tree diagrams or outlines can be used with texts that feature enumeration, and flow charts, sequence chains, and cycles can be used with texts that feature chronological or sequential structure, or cause and effect. (Graphic Organizers, video links)

Graphic organizers are beneficial for ELLs because they represent the main ideas and other content visually with just a few words. ELLs can demonstrate their comprehension of the text by completing their own graphic organizers. Graphic organizers also provide an important oral language scaffold for ELLs to talk about and retell stories or summarize expository texts.

Class Books

Students can draw pictures of their favorite parts of a story or of how they might extend the story. For example, after my class read *It Looked Like Spilt Milk* by Charles Shaw, a book about seeing familiar pictures in clouds, my ELL students made their own cloud drawings. They then wrote a sentence for their picture following the structure used in the book ("Sometimes it looked like a face, but it wasn't a face"). We put the drawings and sentences together to make our own class book. Making class books based on the content and language structure of a particular text helps students comprehend the text and gives them practice using new vocabulary and language structures featured in the story.

Alternative Endings

Another activity that is fun but also meaningful is to write alternative endings to stories read. With lower-level students, creating alternative endings to stories the whole class has read is best done with the class as a group. ELLs with more advanced levels of English proficiency can create alternative endings in small groups or individually. To write an alternative ending, students must understand the story well. Creating alternative endings gives students practice in using new vocabulary and language structures learned in the story, since these will likely be needed in the new endings the students create.

Performed Reading

One of the most enjoyable ways to help students comprehend stories they read is to have them act them out, using the ideas presented in Chapter 6 for promoting oral development. The easiest method is to use simple props representing the characters (e.g., pictures of characters glued to tongue depressors) or just have students hold up or wear signs with the characters' names on them. Or students could act out the story as a puppet show or put on a live play complete with costumes, scenery, and props or read from a script in an activity called "Reader's Theater."

For Reader's Theater, teachers can find many scripts available free on the Internet at Web sites such as Reader's Theater Scripts and Plays (www.teachingheart .net/readerstheater.htm). But it is most effective when the students help write the script. Through this process, ELLs engage in what Richard Kern (2000) describes as "transformed practice." By taking a piece of text and transforming it into a different form or genre (in this instance, a script), students must use a wide range of cognitive strategies and higher order thinking skills that facilitate comprehension. ELLs also benefit from Reader's Theater because it allows them to practice reading with expression and provides extensive practice in using the new vocabulary and language structures learned from the book (Fountas & Pinnell, 2006b). Detailed guidelines, suggestions, and examples can be found in Jo Worthy's (2005) book *Readers Theater for Building Fluency*.

Strategies for Reading across the Curriculum

Notemaking Guides

For secondary and more advanced ELLs, notemaking guides provide a powerful literacy scaffold as they work to make sense of complex academic texts. The word *notemaking* is used, rather than *notetaking*, to highlight the active process of meaning making involved in this activity. A very simple notemaking guide asks students to write down the purpose for their reading at the top of the form. The rest of the form is divided into two columns. Students make notes on the important facts, or what the author says, in the left-hand column, and their response in the form of questions or comments about what they think as they read and connections they have made in the right-hand column. Space may be provided at the bottom of the form for students to write a short summary statement, or a supplemental question may be added there that encourages students to extend their reading beyond the text. (Notemaking Guide, document)

Notemaking guides are easy to create, and they can be adapted for different text types. Teachers can review students' notemaking guides to assess how well they understand main ideas and to learn about the connections students are making. Students can use their notemaking guides to support their discussions of expository texts and to consider multiple perspectives on the same text. Notemaking guides also encourage ELLs to use the language associated with specific academic content areas.

Word Study and Interactive Vocabulary Mini-Lessons

Vocabulary is taught implicitly and explicitly through read-alouds, shared reading, guided reading, Reader's Workshop, and performed reading. **Word study** exercises can be integrated into these instructional modes or can be presented on their own as mini-lessons. The purpose is to help students learn the meaning of new words by talking about how they are used in a sentence, moving them around within a sentence, adding prefixes or suffixes, or manipulating them in graphic organizers so they can use them successfully in oral and literacy tasks. Fountas and Pinnell (2006b) identify the following graphic organizers that can be used for word study:

- **Word web.** A diagram with a single word in the middle (e.g., happy) from which branches extend, showing synonyms or closely related words (e.g., joyous, overjoyed, elated, pleased, stoked, jazzed, excited).
- **Semantic map.** A diagram in which words are organized by their relationship to each other. For example, for the word insect, the boxes could be synonyms (e.g., bug, pest), types of insects (e.g., fly, ladybug, mosquito, bee, cricket), characteristics (e.g., small, ugly), and places the students associate with insects (e.g., trash, garden, backyard, cafeteria).
- **Semantic feature analysis table.** A table in which the semantic features of a group of related words are analyzed in rows and columns. For example, the names of several animals could be listed in the rows (e.g., bear, sparrow, hornet, bass, frog, lizard) and the semantic features in the columns (e.g., can fly, can swim, has fur, has feathers, has scales, breathes air, lives on land, lives in water, has four legs).
- **Venn diagram.** A style of diagram that uses overlapping parts to compare and contrast. When used for word study, two related words, for example, *glass* and *cup* could be compared with the middle overlapping section of the diagram containing phrases that refer to both, such as "container to drink from" and "beverage holder," the section for *glass* could include "made of glass," "transparent," "easy to break," "expensive," or "windows," and the section for *cup* could include "made of plastic, wood, metal, or paper," "cheap," or "a measurement."
- **Hierarchies chart.** A list of related words ordered by their hierarchal relationship. For example, *homes* could be broken up in subcategories of single-unit homes (e.g., house, mansion, cabin, hut) and multiple-unit homes (e.g., apartment, condo, duplex, townhouse).
- **Linear relationships chart.** A string of words or phrases that have a linear relationship arranged along a continuum. For example, words having to do with wealth could be organized along a continuum that begins with broke: broke → poor → getting by → middle class → rich → millionaire → multi-millionaire → billionaire.

Fountas and Pinnell also suggest the following word-study exercises:

- **Word analogies.** Just like those questions you dreaded on the SAT exam: *clock* is to *wall*, as *watch* is to _____.
- **Word substitutions.** The teacher displays a sentence, then removes words and asks students, "What's another word we could use here?" When several suggestions have been made, the teacher discusses the substitutions and how they change the meaning of the sentences.
- **Words in context.** The teacher pulls words and their sentences from previously read books to explore how the context affects their meaning. For example, for the word *up*, the teacher might pull "Saveth walked *up* the stairs,"

"When she woke *up,* everyone was gone," and "'What's *up?*' Octavia asked when I walked into the gym."

- **Word sorting.** Students are given a group of words to sort. Words could be sorted by part of speech (noun, verb, adjective, etc.), semantic category (animals, plants, school objects, kitchen items, etc.), or by their prefixes, suffixes, or base words.

 Examples of some of these techniques can be found on the Companion Web site (Examples of Strategies, video links; related links). Additional ideas for incorporating word study into language arts and ESL instruction for ELLs may be found in the book *Words Their Way with English Learners: Word Study for Phonics, Spelling, and Vocabulary Instruction* (Bear, Helman, Invernizzi, Templeton, & Johnston, 2006).

Assessing Reading

To help ELLs improve their reading ability, teachers must use formative assessments to continually monitor their reading. To ensure that students are receiving the appropriate instruction, teachers cannot wait for the results of high-stakes reading tests or other summative assessments at the end of the year. Also, as discussed in Chapter 5, state-level high-stakes standardized tests are of questionable validity for ELLs.

Teachers need to be aware of slick, quick-and-easy skills-based commercial reading assessments that claim to give accurate measures of students' reading ability in a short time. For example, the DIBELS is now widely used in many schools, particularly those with Reading First grants. The DIBELS, however, was not developed for ELLs (even though Spanish versions of the test have been created). Its widespread use may be more political than pedagogical (see Box 7.6). The following sections describe alternative authentic assessments for ELL reading.

Concepts of Print Checklists

For ELLs of any age at the emergent level of literacy, it is important to assess their development of concepts of print, which include understanding the differences between letters and words and words and spaces, knowing where to start reading and how to do a return sweep to continue reading the next line, and understanding the basic features of a book, such as title and front and back cover, and even how to hold it properly. Although to literate adults these concepts may appear to be common sense, in fact they are concepts that must be learned. Children who have parents who read to them at home typically develop these concepts before entering kindergarten. Young ELLs from homes with few books, however, or even older ELLs who lacked opportunities for formal education in their home country may need to develop these concepts at school. ELLs who are literate in their native language will transfer most of these concepts, but they will need to learn about any differences between print conventions in their native language and English.[5] The Concepts of Print checklist (see Figure 7.2) can help teachers identify areas in need of instruc-

---

5: Some languages are read right to left or top to bottom, or both; the front and back covers of books in some languages are the opposite of what they are on English books, with reading proceeding from back to front; some languages are not alphabetic (e.g., Chinese); some alphabetic languages do not follow a strict left-to-right encoding sequence, with symbols written one or more levels above or below the main text line or surrounding another symbol on both sides; some languages do not use a space between words. These are just a few examples of differences that may exists between English and other writing systems.

Box 7.6

DIBELS (Dynamic Indicators of Basic Early Literacy Skills)

The DIBELS represent a skills-based (bottom-up) approach to reading. They are short (about 1 minute) tests that are widely used, particularly in Reading First schools, to monitor students at the beginning stages of reading development. The DIBELS are given frequently (sometimes monthly, sometimes weekly) to students who score low. The idea is that frequent monitoring will help the teacher pinpoint areas in need of intervention.

DIBELS is highly controversial, and its growing number of critics includes teachers who are forced to use it. Although its creators claim it is scientifically based and supported by validity studies, literacy experts argue that the research base is flawed and that the DIBELS fails to accurately capture even the discrete skills it claims to measure. For example, a retell fluency test score is based on the number of words the student says while retelling the story within 1 minute, with no analysis of the content, accuracy or quality of the retell.

Ken Goodman (2005), former president of the International Reading Association, refers to the DIBELS as a "bunch of silly little tests." He adds, "If it weren't causing so much grief to children and teachers it would be laughable" (p. 27). P. David Pearson (2006) calls the DIBELS "the worst thing to happen to the teaching of reading since the development of flash cards" (p. v). The DIBELS were at the heart of the Reading First scandal, in which individuals with commercial ties to the test personally profited by applying federal pressure on districts to purchase and use the program. Further information and examples of teachers' criticisms of the DIBELS are collected at (NOT the Official) DIBELS Clearinghouse (susanohanian.org/dibels/).

tional focus. The prompts can be used to elicit the responses needed to complete the checklist, although a simple observation of students during SSR could also suffice.

Running Records

A **running record** is an excellent tool for in-depth observation of a student's reading performance. A running record is essentially a visual recording of the student's reading word by word. It enables a teacher identify the reading strategies the student may or may not be using and the types of errors the student makes while reading. These errors reveal what is going on in the student's mind as he or she attempts to make meaning from the text. Running records allow a teacher to quickly assess the student's strengths and areas in need of improvement.

To administer a running record, the teacher provides the student with a book judged to be at his or her current reading level. As the student reads, the teacher makes a series of specialized marks on a running record recording sheet (see Figure 7.3). A check mark indicates each word read correctly, and other special markings are used to indicate words that have been omitted, inserted, or substituted with an incorrect word. Notes are made of inserted and substituted words. Other marks can be used to indicate when students self-correct their errors, when they repeat words or phrases, and when they have to ask the teacher for help. The lines of check marks and other markings correspond with the lines and pages of the book, so the teacher can easily go back and figure out which marks go with each word. Alternatively, a preprepared running record could have the text of the book already typed on the form, as in Figure 7.3. However, a blank piece of paper is also sufficient for conducting a running record.

Assessing Print Understanding

Student name:

Concepts of Print   ✔ where child answered correctly ⌐↓

1. Holds book correctly .... ☐
2. Recognizes front and back of book.. ☐
3. Identifies title or title page.. ☐
4. Knows where to begin reading.. ☐
5. Differentiates words and spaces.. ☐
6. Differentiates first and last letter .... ☐
7. Realizes that print contains meaning.. ☐
8. Is developing directionality and return sweep .... ☐
9. Recognizes difference between words and letters......................... ☐
10. Is developing one-to-one correspondence (word match)............ ☐
11. Knows some lowercase/capital letters .... ☐
12. Identifies some basic punctuation (period) .... ☐

Concepts of Print Prompts

Directions: Choose a simple storybook. Tell the child that you will read the story aloud, but that you need his or her help. Then ask these questions and record the word or actions the child uses to answer.

1. If someone were going to read this book, how would he or she hold it? Show me.
2. Show me the front of the book. The back. *(Give 1/2 point for each.)*
3. Where is the title? Show me with your finger.
4. If someone were to read this story, show me where he or she would begin reading.
5. How many words do you count on this page? *(Use a page with three or four words.)*
6. Look at these words. Find one word and tell me the first and last letter.
7. Show me the part that tells the story. *(Show a page with picture and print.)*
8. Show me where you would begin reading on this page. Then where would you go? *or* Where would someone look if he or she were reading this page? Then where? *(Make sure to cover the return sweep and possibly the page turn.)*
9. How many letters are on this page? *(Use a page with about three words.)* How many words?
10. This page says, "_____" *(Use a simple and repetitive page with only a few words on it, no more than three or four.)* Now you read it and point to each word.
11. Would you show me some capital letters on this page and tell me their names? Now show me some lowercase letters and tell me their name? *(Give 1/2 point for each.)*
12. *(Point to the period.)* Do you know what this is?

Figure 7.2   Concepts of print checklist. (Source: Adapted from Wisconsin Literacy Education and Reading Network Source, n.d.)

Running Record

Student name:

Grade level:

Book title:

Author:

Book level:

	Errors	Self-corrections

Words read correctly _____ ÷ _____ total words = _____ %.

    Self-corrections: _____

$$95\%^+ = \text{Easy}$$
$$90\% - 94\% = \text{Instructional}$$
$$\text{Less than } 90\% = \text{Frustration}$$

Evaluation

1. What are the student's strengths?

2. What types of errors did the student make? Why might the student have made these errors?

3. Describe specific mini-lessons, strategies, and activities that would be beneficial for this student?

Figure 7.3 **Running record and evaluation form**

After completing a running record, the teacher asks comprehension questions or asks the student to retell the story. This is a crucial component, because it reveals whether the student understood what he or she read or was merely "barking" at the print, that is, reading each word separately and distinctly with pauses in between as if they were a list of isolated words.

Once a running record has been completed, the number of words read correctly (total words minus the errors) is divided by the total number of words. This calculation provides a score that indicates the accuracy of the student's reading. More important, it provides an indication of how appropriate the level of the book is for reading instruction. Books read with 95% accuracy or higher may be too easy for use in guided reading. Books read with 90–94% accuracy are considered to be at the student's instructional level, or within the zone of proximal development (ZPD). That is, the book is sufficiently challenging that, through guidance, the student can gain new reading knowledge and skills by reading from this book or others at the same level. Books read with 89% accuracy or less are considered to be at the frustration level and generally are not appropriate for either guided or independent reading. A running record score is a key tool for matching a student to appropriate books. The student's performance and individual errors, however, provide even more valuable feedback.

Consider, for example, the completed running record in Figure 7.4 of an ELL student's reading of a passage from *Frog and Toad Are Friends* by Arnold Lobel. An untrained teacher only casually listening to this student, Ly, read might conclude that he just needs more phonics instruction. However, phonics lessons on initial consonant and basic vowel sounds would be a waste of time for Ly. The running record shows that he has strong phonics knowledge and is applying it in specific ways. Notice, for example, that in most instances substituted words all start with the same initial consonant as the correct word. Ly's self-corrections of *spring* and *corner* also illustrate his use of phonics knowledge to figure out unknown words. And *closet* for *closed* was actually very close phonetically, differing in spelling only by the final letter.

Some of the errors also show that Ly is reading for meaning. For example, he first read *horse* for *house* but likely made the change when he realized *horse* did not make sense. There is no horse in the story but there is an illustration above the text showing Toad's house. The substitution of *yelled* for *shouted* did not change the meaning of the text. Neither did errors such as *walking in* for *walked in* and *lie down* for *lying* (in bed). Although these words are not syntactically correct, the correct meaning is still conveyed. Even the omission of *inside* did not alter the meaning. The substitution of *kicked* for *knocked* (notice the similarity in the spelling of these words) was awkward but semantically it is a viable possibility. Thus, despite these errors, it is clear that Ly is reading for meaning.

Some of the errors may be attributed to Ly's lack of English proficiency. His knowledge of suffixes and verb tense is not yet fully developed, as revealed by the problems he had reading *melting, walked, lying,* and *closed* with full accuracy. There are also some gaps in his vocabulary. He did not know the words *blah* and *shutters*. Perhaps he was unable to self-correct *closet* with *closed* because when the teacher told him the word *shutters*, he did not know the meaning. If he had known what shutters are, he might have been able to make the semantic connection with *closed*.

Perhaps Ly does know the word *voice* but simply did not recognize it in print because it is a difficult word to decode. Note however, that he did make use of the letter sounds for *v, o,* and *c* and consistently read the word as *vock* all three times it appeared. Another strategy he used, as revealed by the running record, is repeti-

Running Record Practice

Frog and Toad Spring

		Errors	SC
Frog ran up the path	✓ ✓ ✓ ✓ ✓		
to Toad's house.	✓ ✓ horse | house (SC)		I
He knocked on the front door.	✓ kicked ✓ ✓ ✓ ✓	I	
There was no answer.	✓ ✓ ✓ anger? | an... | (T)	I	
"Toad, Toad," shouted Frog	✓ ✓ yelled ✓	I	
"wake up. It is spring!"	✓ ✓ ✓ ✓ ss | pp | ing | sing? spring (SC)		I
//"Blah," said a voice	(T) ✓ ✓ vock	II	
from inside the house.	✓ — ✓ ✓	I	
"Toad, Toad," cried Frog.	✓ ✓ ✓ ✓		
"The sun is shining!	✓ ✓ ✓ R" ✓		
The snow is melting. Wake up!"	✓ ✓ ✓ mmm | R | melt ✓ ✓	I	
"I am not here," said the voice.	✓ ✓ ✓ ✓ ✓ ✓ vock	I	
Frog walked into the house.	✓ walking in ✓ ✓	II	
It was dark.	✓ ✓ ✓		
All the//shutters were closed.	✓ ✓ (T) ✓ closet	II	
"Toad, where are you?" called Frog.	✓ ✓ ✓ ✓ ✓ ✓		
"Go away," said the voice	✓ ✓ ✓ ✓ vock	I	
from a corner of the room.	✓ ✓ R | corn | corner (SC) ✓ ✓ ✓		I
Toad was lying in bed.	✓ ✓ lie down ✓ ✓	II	

91
−15
76

76 / 91 = 83 % **Number of Self Corrections** 3

Figure 7.4 **Running record of an ELL student's reading of "Spring," from *Frog and Toad Are Friends***

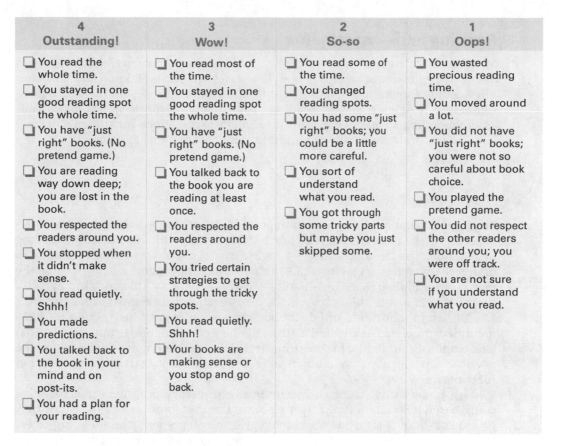

4 Outstanding!	3 Wow!	2 So-so	1 Oops!
☐ You read the whole time.	☐ You read most of the time.	☐ You read some of the time.	☐ You wasted precious reading time.
☐ You stayed in one good reading spot the whole time.	☐ You stayed in one good reading spot the whole time.	☐ You changed reading spots.	☐ You moved around a lot.
☐ You have "just right" books. (No pretend game.)	☐ You have "just right" books. (No pretend game.)	☐ You had some "just right" books; you could be a little more careful.	☐ You did not have "just right" books; you were not so careful about book choice.
☐ You are reading way down deep; you are lost in the book.	☐ You talked back to the book you are reading at least once.	☐ You sort of understand what you read.	☐ You played the pretend game.
☐ You respected the readers around you.	☐ You respected the readers around you.	☐ You got through some tricky parts but maybe you just skipped some.	☐ You did not respect the other readers around you; you were off track.
☐ You stopped when it didn't make sense.	☐ You tried certain strategies to get through the tricky spots.		☐ You are not sure if you understand what you read.
☐ You read quietly. Shhh!	☐ You read quietly. Shhh!		
☐ You made predictions.	☐ Your books are making sense or you stop and go back.		
☐ You talked back to the book in your mind and on post-its.			
☐ You had a plan for your reading.			

Figure 7.5   Student self-assessment for independent reading. (Source: Calkins, 2000, p. 78. Also available at www.middleweb.com/ReadWrkshp/RWdownld/IndReadRubric.pdf)

tion. He repeated "The sun is" three times before determining that the next word is *shining*. This repetition shows that he was reading for meaning, combining meaning and phonics clues to figure out the correct word. *Corn* was corrected to *corner* in a similar manner.

Ly made 15 errors (self-corrections and repetitions do not count as errors). Thus, he read 76 words correctly out of a total of 91 words, meaning he read this selection with 83% accuracy-well below the frustration level. An analysis of this running record will give the teacher several ideas for the next few reading lessons. First, she knows Ly should be asked to read a slightly less difficult book in the next guided reading session. Second, she may decide that Ly is ready for some word-study lessons on verb tenses and suffixes, particularly because he was able to read some of these correctly but not all of them. Finally, she may decide that Ly could benefit from some phonics mini-lessons on words starting with *kn* and words with *oi*. She might also start asking Ly to help open and close the shutters on the classroom windows for the next few days, just to help him learn and remember this new vocabulary word.

Running records take practice but once teachers get the hang of it, they can do them with ease. As a teacher, I conducted running records almost every day, usually when listening to one of my students read to me during guided reading groups. This exercise helped me plan guided reading sessions for the next day. Other times I would conduct very formal running records, particularly on district-identified benchmark books that officially determined students' reading levels. These records would be added to the students' reading portfolios as important indicators of their progress.

Reading Self-Assessments

Many teachers use reading self-assessments for students to keep track of their own use of strategies and to assess their ability to stay on task. Well-known ELL teacher Juli Kendall, for example, used the rubric shown in Figure 7.5 for her students to self-assess their independent reading.[6] Note that this rubric is not just a self-assessment. It also makes explicit the teacher's expectations for students' behaviors and use of strategies during this important part of the school day.

SUMMARY

Reading is arguably the single most important skill students develop in school. Perhaps this is the reason there is so much debate and politics surrounding reading instruction. The "reading wars" are raging over the best way to teach reading to mainstream students, leaving ELLs in the "struggling reader" category while the main source of their reading difficulty—their lack of oral proficiency in English—typically gets lost in the debate. Recent research review reports from the NLP, CREDE, and the Institute of Education Sciences on literacy instruction for ELLs identified problems associated with skills-based instructional approaches that lack emphasis on reading for meaning and have brought renewed attention to the need for oral language development and balanced literacy instruction in meaningful contexts.

ELL students who are placed in unbalanced literacy programs that focus on skills-based instruction typically are able to decode words successfully (i.e., they have word-level reading skills) but struggle to comprehend the meaning of extended texts (i.e., text-level skills). ELL students need balanced literacy instruction that provides greater emphasis on actual reading of authentic texts. Extensive reading of such texts allows students to naturally acquire knowledge and skills, such as new vocabulary and language skills, with scaffolding from their teacher. Teachers provide skills-based instruction as needed within the context of these meaningful texts.

English literacy development for native speakers progresses through four levels: emergent, early, early fluency, and fluency. For ELLs, however, progress through these levels is affected by age and level of English proficiency, as well as literacy skills in the native language. The reading *to, with,* and *by* framework helps teachers structure effective instruction for their ELLs students. Interactive read-alouds expose students to the joys of reading and provide models of fluent reading. Shared reading provides a meaningful context and scaffolding as students read a book or other text at an appropriate instructional level with the teacher, who uses the text to teach and model a wide range of reading skills and strategies. Guided reading removes some of this scaffolding as students, after being prepared by their teacher, set off on their own to read authentic texts appropriate to their level, with scaffolding as needed from the teacher. Through independent reading even more scaffolding is removed as students are provided with time in class each day to read for enjoyment any book of their choosing (with guidance from the teacher as needed to help them make appropriate choices), and to practice the strategies and skills modeled and learned through read-alouds, shared reading, and guided reading. Nar-

---

6: The late Juli Kendall is the co-author of two books on ELL literacy (Kendall & Khuon, 2005, 2006) and was an active contributor to the literacy and ESL sections of MiddleWeb (see www.middleweb.com), a Web site for middle school educators committed to reform and high quality instruction.

row reading is supportive of student's English language development because each new book builds on the background knowledge gained from previous readings. Reader's Workshop employs many of the same features as the reading *to, with,* and *by* framework but adapted to the structure of secondary school and the needs of older ELL students.

BDA provides a framework to support students' development of prereading (before), during reading, and postreading (after) strategies that maximize comprehensible input. Word study and interactive vocabulary mini-lessons are also effective ways to maximize students' learning of new vocabulary encountered while reading.

To assess students' reading skills and knowledge, teachers can use concepts of print with emergent readers and running records with students at all levels to determine their reading level and identify miscue (error) information. Self-assessments in reading enable students to monitor their own progress and internalize and meet their teacher's high expectations.

Discussion Questions

1. **On-line Discussion Board**   If you have learned (or tried to learn) a second language, what challenges did you face in learning to read in that language? What role do you feel your native language played in your development of your reading ability in that language? Relate your experience to the challenges ELLs face in learning to read English.

2. Why is English oral language development such an important factor in ELL students' reading development in English? And how does reading support English language acquisition for ELLs?

3. Current research reports from NLP and CREDE point out that ELLs who learn to decode may have trouble comprehending what they read. What are some of the sources of this problem? How can the framework of reading *to, with,* and *by* ELLs be used to place greater emphasis on meaning and comprehension?

4. **On-line Discussion Board**   In many basal-reading programs, all students are expected to read the same story at the same time and receive the same lessons based on the story. How can such an approach be problematic for ELLs? If you were (or are) in a school that used (or uses) such a program, what are some ways you could match ELLs to books more appropriate to their language and literacy levels?

5. **On-line Discussion Board**   Why are read-alouds, shared reading, guided reading, and independent reading important for ELLs? What experiences have you had with these approaches in schools you have worked in or observed?

6. In a growing number of schools, much of the reading instruction now focuses on reading short passages and then answering a series of multiple-choice questions on the passage, all in preparation for the big state tests (as mandated by NCLB). What are some of the problems of such an approach to reading instruction, particularly for ELL students? Even if it works to raise test scores, do you feel such an approach to reading instruction is truly beneficial in helping ELLs become proficient readers who enjoy reading and become life-long readers? Provide examples or details to justify your answer.

Research Activities

1. **Wiki This**   Observe one or more reading lessons for ELLs in a classroom. Record details on the name of the curricular program (if any), the materials used in the lesson, and ways in which the teacher and students interacted with each

other and the text. Pay particular attention to the students' actual reading of the text and to evidence of their comprehension (or lack thereof) of the text. Discuss your observations with your classmates, focusing on what you thought was effective and what could be improved.

2. Conduct a running record (see Figure 7.3; Running Record, form) with an ELL student, using a book that is on about the same level as books he or she is currently reading in class for reading instruction. Determine, according to the results of the running record, whether the book is at the student's instructional level. Complete the evaluation of the students' strengths, errors, and instructional needs.

3. **Wiki-This** Conduct an analysis of the reading curriculum and supplemental materials used by a school with which you are familiar. What methods or approaches do these materials appear to represent? How does this approach compare with the suggestions in this chapter? How appropriate do you feel these materials are, and the approaches they represent, for meeting the unique language, literacy, and other academic needs of ELLs? What modifications to these materials, or to the program or approach in general, do you feel might be needed to better address the needs of the ELL students?

Recommended Reading

August, D., & Shanahan, T. (Eds.). (2008). *Developing reading and writing in second-language learners: Lessons from the report of the National Literacy Panel on language-minority children and youth.* New York: Routledge, Center for Applied Linguistics, and International Reading Association.
A trimmed-down, more reader-friendly version of the bulky NLP report that reviewed the scientific research literature and drew conclusions about what we know about literacy development for second language learners.

Genesee, F., Lindholm-Leary, K., Saunders, W. M., & Christian, D. (2006). *Educating English language learners: A synthesis of research evidence.* New York: Cambridge University Press.
This book is the CREDE report referred to in this and other chapters. It presents the findings of second language and literacy experts who reviewed the scientific research on what we know about the language, literacy, and general academic development of ELL students.

Goodman, K. S. (Ed.). (2006). *The truth about DIBELS: What it is, what it does.* Portsmouth, NH: Heinemann.
The author, a literacy expert and former president of the International Reading Association, undertakes a critical review of the DIBELS, a set of literacy tests that have been adopted widely in U.S. schools.

Fountas, I. C., & Pinnell, G. S. (2006). *Teaching for comprehension and fluency: Thinking, talking, and writing about reading, K-8.* Portsmouth, NH: Heinemann.
An outstanding resource for balanced literacy instruction. Although not developed specifically for ELLs, the practices described work well with ELLs, and the authors discuss ELL needs throughout the book.

Kendall, J., & Khuon, O. (2005). *Making sense: Small-group comprehension lessons for English language learners.* Portland, ME: Stenhouse.
Written by veteran ELL teachers, this useful book provides sample reading lessons that can be used in small groups of ELL students focused on different reading comprehension strategies. Each chapter focuses on one of the five stages of English proficiency from preproduction to advanced and includes lessons for both younger and older students.

Krashen, S. D. (2004c). *The power of reading: Insights from the research* (2nd ed.). Portsmouth, NH: Heinemann.

A review of the research on reading and how it can be put into practice in the classroom. The author also uses the research to challenge common skills-based instructional approaches and practices.

Smith, F. (2006). *Reading without nonsense* (4th ed.). New York: Teachers College Press.

The author argues against many of the practices associated with skills-based approaches to literacy instruction, drawing on theory and research to support his claims. By detailing how reading should not be taught, he helps educators gain a better understanding of reading and literacy development.

8

Writing

The only way to help students improve their writing is to read what they write and talk to them about their writing.

—Juli Kendall, author and middle school ESL teacher

KEY TERMS

- invented spelling
- modeled writing
- shared writing
- guided writing
- interactive writing
- independent writing
- journals
- process writing
- Writer's Workshop
- word wall
- thematic word chart
- personal word book
- holistic scoring
- analytic scoring
- primary trait scoring
- multi-trait scoring

GUIDING QUESTIONS

1. What does the research tell us about effective writing instruction for ELLs?
2. What does a theory of second language writing include?
3. How is writing related to oral language and reading?
4. How can an understanding of ELLs' writing strengths and needs inform a teacher's choice of instructional approaches, methods, and strategies?

Writing is one of the most important skills students learn in school, and like reading, it is crucial to ELL students' academic success because it is one of the principal means by which they display their knowledge and competence in academic subjects. It also encourages self-reflection, allowing students to chronicle their personal reactions and journey (Hadaway, Vardell, & Young, 2002).

Although all students face the challenge of developing their writing to grade-level expectations, ELLs face the additional challenge of learning to write before they are proficient speakers of English. An additional challenge, particularly for newcomers, is that they are learning to adjust socially and culturally to a new country and a new school. Dana R. Ferris and John Hedgcock (2004) point out that ELL students learning to write may need more of everything in terms of procedures, heuristics, content, practice, and feedback than native English-speaking students. They note that, unlike native English speakers, ELL writers

- begin with an intact L1 and a *developing* knowledge of spoken and written English as a second language; are simultaneously acquiring *language* and *composing* skills;
- may or may not be familiar with the Roman alphabet and may thus still be learning English orthographic conventions;
- may produce sentence level errors influenced by their primary language(s);
- may not have the same topic/schematic knowledge as native English speaking writers due to home country educational experience;
- may have little or no experience with peer response; and

- may have little or no experience using outside sources, paraphrasing, and quoting. (p. 15)

These issues and others are addressed in this chapter. We first review what we know from current research on writing instruction for ELLs. Next we discuss writing instruction through the framework of writing to, with, and by ELLs students. We then consider additional supports teachers can provide as ELL students develop their English writing skills. Finally, we describe ways to assess students' writing.

What We Know from Research on Writing Instruction for ELLs

The following findings are from the NLP report and the CREDE report discussed in earlier chapters, and the work of other experts on second language writing (Hadaway et al., 2002; Hudelson, 1989; Peregoy & Boyle, 2008; Samway, 2006).

The writing development process for ELL students is similar to the process for native English speakers.

Both ELLs and native English speakers must learn the (English) alphabet, spelling, proper syntax for forming sentences and paragraphs, and the conventions for writing specific genres. Both engage in literacy tasks in a variety of social contexts, and use writing to interact and develop interpersonal relationships.

ELL students' ability to express themselves in written English is highly dependent on their level of oral English proficiency.

The NLP and the CREDE report both found a close relationship between ELL students' oral proficiency in English and their ability to express themselves in written English. This relationship is consistent with research findings on the importance of oral language. With the exception, for example, of older immigrant students who learned to write English in English-as-a-foreign-language classes in their home countries, most ELL students are unlikely to use words in writing they do not know orally, and the language forms they use in writing will typically be limited, at least initially, to the forms they are able to use in conversation. Simply put, ELL students' writing may be only as good as their English speaking ability. This does not mean, however, that teachers should delay writing instruction until students are able to speak English well. Beginning-level ELLs benefit from writing instruction that focuses on topics they can talk about. Such instruction supports their English language development.

Students with literacy skills in their native language can transfer many of these skills to English writing.

Both the NLP and the CREDE report also found a strong relationship between students' writing ability in their native language and their writing ability in English. This relationship is similar to the one found between reading ability in the native language and reading ability in English. As with reading, students' native writing skills are a major asset because much of their knowledge will transfer to English. For example, a 4th grade student who attended grades K–3 in Mexico will already know how to hold a pencil, how to form letters, how to write words, sentences, and paragraphs, and how writing is used for communication. This student may also be familiar with the conventions of different genres of writing and will simply need to develop enough proficiency in English to use these skills in his new language, while learning the conventions, styles, and other features specific to English writing.

This transfer of skills is one of the primary reasons bilingual education programs place emphasis on helping ELLs first develop literacy skills in their native language. Furthermore, as Sarah Hudelson (1989) observes in her classic book *Write on: Children Writing in ESL,* "native language writing allows second language learners to demonstrate some of what they know in a language they control. Second language learners are thus able to show their competence rather than their incompetence and to grow in their confidence in themselves as learners. This, in turn, may have positive effects on learners' willingness to risk writing in a new language" (p. 46).

Research suggests that letter formation and spelling skills may most easily transfer for those literate L1 students whose native language, such as Spanish, French, German, or Tagalog, uses the same alphabet as English. But even if a student has literacy skills in a language with a different alphabetic script, such as Russian, Khmer, Hindi, or Arabic, or a nonalphabetic language, such as Chinese, many other writing skills will still easily transfer to English.

Not all transfer from the first language, however, is positive transfer. The CREDE report found instances of negative cross-language influences that might show up, for example, when a Spanish-speaking ELL student erroneously applies Spanish phonological and orthographic rules to English spelling. Consider the following sentence a Spanish-speaking ELL student wrote in her journal, describing what she did over the weekend:

> Dend ay it a sanwich end hotchetoos.
> [Then I eat a sandwich and Hot Cheetos.]

This student is using her knowledge of Spanish phonics to write words in English, thus *ay* for *I, it* for *eat,* and *end* for *and.* Because the /th/ sound does not exist in Spanish, the student approximates the spelling for *then* by applying Spanish phonics to how she hears and pronounces it, *dend.* The CREDE report is quick to point out, however, that this "negative" transfer is actually a good sign because it shows that the student is using an effective strategy, applying her Spanish writing skills to writing in English. Most students quickly figure out what does and what does not transfer. Also, teachers can plan instruction to help students recognize instances of negative transfer to avoid.

English oral language skills have little impact on English word-level writing skills.

Word-level skills such as spelling are not strongly related to oral language skills in English. Thus, ELL students can memorize the spelling of words without knowing their meaning or how to use them in a sentence.

English oral language skills have a strong impact on English text-level writing skills.

English oral language skills have a strong impact on writing when large chunks of text are involved, such as sentences, paragraphs, and complete narratives. Students with well-developed oral language skills in English therefore tend to have better writing skills in English. The oral language skills of listening comprehension and vocabulary knowledge were found to be specifically related to better writing.

As evidence of this finding, consider the responses to the prompt, "What did you do this weekend?" written by two Spanish-speaking students with different levels of oral English proficiency that appear in Figure 8.1. Note that both students are still relying on their knowledge of Spanish writing and so we see examples of negative transfer in both responses. Student B, however, clearly has better oral English skills. The length and variety of her sentence structures reveal that she has a larger vocabulary and greater knowledge of English syntax to draw on for her writing.

Student A	Student B
I go tu the puga en i go tu mi stesto jos en i go tu mi gamo jos en i go tu mi fen jos en spn the nit en I go tu pore den i go tu mi jos.[1]	This Friday i do my homework and wend i finchis my mom need help to do the tortillas to send en Mexico. Then wend my fahtre get home wiht my sisteher Mariana my mom med riec with milk and same time my great gran mother she meke os my mom then niting i went to bed and i went to seelp. This saturday in tha mornig i se carates and is april fool day. Then late time my famaly and i went mall to Buy some. Then the nitgn i read the book and is great then went to seelp. And This sunday i was sike and my siste curde me and I was felen good and tehn i tro up. Then at leat my fatrer just came home. My motrer made pinchillo-wit rice. Then at niting y went to seelp.

1. I believe this says, "I go to the pulga [flea market] and I go to my sister house and I go to my grandma house and I go to my friend house and spend the night and I go to party then I go to my house."

Figure 8.1 **Responses by 2nd grade Spanish-speaking ELLs to the prompt, "What did you do this weekend?"**

Age and prior knowledge impact ELLs' writing ability in English.

The demands and expectations for writing increase substantially by grade level. Writing tasks must be appropriate to the age and grade level of students. Notice, however, that "grade-level appropriateness" assumes that students have already progressed through English writing instruction and development in previous grades. Such an assumption cannot be made for newcomer ELLs, who may not have had the opportunity to attend school or develop strong native language writing skills before coming to the United States. Thus, what is appropriate, for example, for a 5th grade student born in the United States may not be appropriate for a 10- or 11-year-old refugee ELL student from Somalia. Teachers need to differentiate writing instruction for these students, ensuring that it is appropriate to their English proficiency and writing development level. Writing also requires prior knowledge about topic and genre. Students cannot be expected to write about a topic they know little about in a genre they do not know.

Theoretical Frameworks for Writing Research and Instruction

One major challenge in teaching ELL students to write in English is that the field of second language writing is relatively new and we lack a comprehensive theory of second language writing. Before the 1960s, ESL instruction focused on oral language. The first textbooks on ESL writing did not appear until the 1990s; the first academic journal on the subject, the *Journal of Second Language Writing,* appeared in 1992. Ferris and Hedgcock (2004) describe how research, theory, and practice in ESL writing has evolved since 1966 in four different areas of focus (see Table 8.1; see also Raimes, 1991). Much of this work parallels developments in first language writing, and each focus is aligned with a particular school of thought, though there is considerable overlap among them. As Paul L. Matsuda (2003) asserts, no single theory from a single discipline can account for the wide variety of processes involved in second language writing. Teachers need to understand different theories for both L1 and L2 writing, and the broad range of instructional issues for classroom writing.

Acknowledging that incompatibilities between different theories and practices can cause confusion for teachers, Ferris and Hedgcock (2004) recommend that teachers consider the following components related to the writing process when reviewing research and theory and making decisions about their classroom writing instruction:

- *The ESL writer.* The writer as a person—that is, his or her personal knowledge, attitudes, learning styles, cultural orientation, language proficiency, and motivation, in addition to his or her composing strategies.
- *The native English speaker reader as the ESL writer's primary audience.* The

Table 8.1   Evolution of ESL Writing Research, Theory, and Practice

Focus	Description	Instructional Practices
Form and "current-traditional rhetoric," 1966–	• Form-focused orientation in L2 writing (influenced by the audiolingual approach) • Writing to reinforce patterns of language taught and to test students' application of grammar rules	• Writing well-formed sentences • Narrow paragraph or essay assignments to practice particular syntactic patterns
The writer: expressionism and cognitivism, 1976	• Focus on what writers actually do as they write; the process and stages writers go through from conceptualization to publication	• Process writing • Writer's Workshop
Content and the disciplines, 1986–	• Focus on the need of ESL writers to compose texts for academic readers • Focus on writing academic genres needed by ESL students for their majors or academic courses	• English for specific purposes (ESP) • English for academic purposes (EAP)
The reader: social constructionism, 1986–	• Focus on socializing and apprenticing the writer as a member of one or more academic discourse communities	• Instruction that prepares students to anticipate and satisfy the demands of academic readers. • Highly compatible with content-based approaches to ESL

Source: Adapted from Ferris and Hedgcock, 2004, pp. 7–8.

native English-speaking reader's needs and expectations as a respondent or evaluator of the ESL students' written products.

- *The writer's text.* The writer's product as represented by its purposes, characteristics, and constituent elements—genre, rhetorical form, discursive mode, features of coherence and cohesion, syntactic properties, lexicon, mechanics, print-code features, and so on.
- *The contexts for writing.* Cultural, political, social, economic, situational, and physical dimensions of the text.
- *The interaction of all of these components in authentic educational settings.* (p. 9)

Relationship between Reading and Writing

Researchers have found a strong relationship between ELL students' reading ability and their writing ability in English.[1] The more students read at appropriate levels, the more vocabulary and language structures they will acquire. This knowledge, in turn, can be used in their writing. Findings from research reveal that the more students read, the more they write, the better they write, and the less apprehensive they are about writing (Krashen, n.d.).

Hudelson (1989) observes that when young ELL students are exposed to environmental print, such as traffic signs, store names, product names, logos, and print in lists, letters, brochures, books, and magazines, they come to understand that people read different kinds of materials for different purposes, that print carries meaning and that it makes sense. This understanding enables young ELLs to write different kinds of texts for different purposes. Hudelson also notes the important role of storybook reading with young ELLs to support their writing development. The students learn how to handle books, learn about story elements, and begin to understand the concepts of letter, word, sentence, and directionality. They take this knowledge developed from their reading and apply it to their writing.

Reading becomes more and more important to students' writing development as they gain greater proficiency in English. Kroll (1993) asserts that teaching writing is teaching reading (and vice versa). She notes three ways in which reading can support ELL students' writing. First readings can be used as a springboard for a topic to write about. For example, a teacher might read to the class the book *A Chair for My Mother* by Vera B. Williams, which describes a family's effort to save money to buy a comfortable chair for their apartment after losing their furniture in a fire. The students might then be encouraged to write about their own experiences saving money to buy something special. Short newspaper or magazine articles on controversial topics can be effective in motivating older students to write a response and express their own opinions. Second, readings can provide background information and source material for students to write about a specific topic. For example, if students write reports about their home country (or the home country of their parents), they can read related books and articles to find facts and details to include in their writing. Finally, readings can be used as a model of a particular writing feature for students to imitate. For example, if a teacher wants his students to include more dialogue in their stories using quotation marks and using words other than just *said* before or after each quotation, he could read with students a book such as *Arthur and the Lost Diary* by Marc Brown and draw the students' attention to the skillful way in which the author uses dialogue in his stories. Students

---

1: See, e.g., Carson & Leki, 1993; Grabe, 2003; Hudelson, 1989; Krashen, 2004b; Kroll, 1990, 1993; Vandrick, 2003.

could then practice imitating Brown's style and then integrate it into their own writing to create dialogues.

Effective teachers understand this strong relationship between reading and writing. They find creative ways to integrate reading and writing instruction across content areas. They provide meaningful instruction, guidance, and activities for students to use reading to further develop their writing ability.

Stages in ELL Writing Development

Several researchers have attempted to identify the stages ELLs may go through in their early writing development, noting that these stages are similar to those native English speaker writers go through.[2] Katherine Davies Samway (2006) lists six stages (Table 8.2). But she urges caution, pointing out that ELL students' writing development is not necessarily linear and varies from student to student, even when they speak the same L1 and have had similar amounts of exposure to instruction in English. She notes that quality and quantity may vary from piece to piece and draft to draft for the same writer and that some students may skip stages.

Students' writing often reflects their confidence and engagement as writers. Some students may write only words they already know how to spell. But as they gain more confidence in their writing, they start to take risks by including words they cannot spell correctly yet. To include these words, they approximate the spelling, using their knowledge of sound-symbol correspondence—a process teachers call invented spelling, or developmental spelling. Some adults worry that such spelling is a regression in the students' writing ability. Some accuse that teachers who allow students to use invented spelling are lazy and are harming students by not demanding standardized spelling and correcting their spelling errors. For this reason, some teachers may be afraid to send student writing home or display it on classroom walls if it contains invented spelling. It is also assumed that spelling tests are needed to help students learn how to spell words correctly (see Box 8.1).

Opposition to invented spelling shows ignorance of the development of children's writing. As Samway notes, it actually reveals the students' growth as writers. Invented spelling reflects knowledge of phonics but also demonstrates the limitations of phonics to help students determine a word's standardized spelling (e.g., Why isn't *said* spelled *sed?*). Many educators prefer to call invented spelling *temporary* or *transitional spelling*, because it truly is temporary. As students read and write more, and as teachers provide supportive writing instruction and practice, their spelling becomes more standardized (as shown in Table 8.2). And at some stages in the writing process, correcting spelling errors is appropriate.

Promoting Writing Development for ELLs in the Classroom

To ensure that ELLs learn to write for social and academic purposes, sheltered instruction and ESL teachers need to know their ELL students' strengths and needs in second language writing and have a clear idea of what they want their students to know and be able to do with writing as a result of their instruction. Teachers draw on their understanding of writing development for ELLs and select appropriate strategies to scaffold students' learning, differentiate instruction based on the

---

2: See, e.g., Hadaway et al., 2002; Peregoy & Boyle, 2004; Samway, 2006.

Table 8.2	Developmental Stages in Early ELL Student Writing	
Scribble writing (and drawing)	• Scribbles often reflect the orthography of the native language. • Letters are often approximations of standardized letters. • Scribbles for writing and drawing are often differentiated.	
Strings of letters	• There is no sound-symbol correspondence. • Numbers and other symbols are often interspersed. • Spacing between letters is often absent.	
Letters representing whole words or thoughts	• There is some sound-symbol correspondence. • There are some correctly spelled words, which are usually sight words and high frequency words that may be displayed in the classroom. • Some spacing appears between words (and sometimes between letters). • There is a simple message, which is often in the form of a label. • Pictures are often as important as the writing. • As first, writers of English tend to capture beginning consonants, then ending consonants, then medial consonants, and finally vowels. • At this state, students may have difficulty reading their own texts.	
Stylized sentences	• Writing is often patterned (e.g., This is a . . . ; This is a . . .) • Writers may rely on familiar words, often those displayed in the classroom. • Texts become longer and include more conventional spelling. • Students can usually read their own writing.	I see a hat. I see a dog. I see a cat. I see a man. I see a car and a tree and a house.
Emerging standardized writing	• Messages are longer, often reflecting the writer's eagerness to focus on quantity (frequent use of *and then* . . .) • Punctuation may not be used conventionally. • Spelling may become more unconventional as the writer takes more risks in incorporating less familiar or frequently occurring words. • If L1 uses the same alphabet as English, and the student is literate in L1, some spelling may be based on the sound system of the L1.	Afther dad I wend to the truck so we can go to church. Den chur was ofer. So we go to the park ten we go to the house afther tha a went to sleep beacouse eat was geatheang dark.
Standardized writing	• Writing is better organized and more focused. • Word choice is more varied and voice is more apparent. • Spelling is more standardized, except when writers are using unfamiliar vocabulary. • Punctuation is more conventional and varied.	The gratest memory with my family is when me and my family had a vacation to Galveston. I was so excited to go and to swim in the water. We all packed our close snaks and some food to eat. While my dad was driving I couldn't stop thinking of the fun we are going to through. After we go their we went to a store full of swimig suits sandals water volley balls and a lot of more stuff. Each of us bot swiming suits.

Source: Adapted from Samway, 2006, pp. 38–43.

Box 8.1

An Alternative Approach to Traditional Spelling Tests

The fact that literate individuals can spell tens of thousands of words they have never had on a spelling test provides evidence that students do not learn how to spell through spelling tests, such as those offered in the traditional approach to spelling.

The traditional approach with spelling tests does not take into account individual students' spelling strengths and needs. All students are given the same list of words, with little attention to their meaning. Many effective teachers have found that they can forgo spelling tests altogether and help students develop their spelling skills in the context of meaningful writing instruction as outlined in this chapter.

If spelling tests must be used, here are some guidelines for alternatives to traditional spelling tests:

- Avoid using one list of words for all students.
- Use informal and formal formative assessments to identify the words, or types of words student want and need to spell.
- Use these findings to create different spelling lists for different groups of students.
- Provide word-study mini-lessons throughout the week with each group based on their word lists
- Test each group of students on their own list of words.

If required to use a school or district prescribed spelling curriculum or list of words:

- Ensure ELLs know the meaning of each word, and provide vocabulary instruction as needed.
- Give a pre-test to see which words each student already knows how to spell.
- Only require students to practice and do homework with the words they got wrong.
- Provide word-study mini-lessons to small groups based on the words the students got wrong

writing needs of the students in the class, and use classroom-based assessments of writing performance to guide instruction and provide evidence of writing growth.

This section begins with a brief discussion of how to identify ELLs' writing strengths and needs in English. We then review a wide range of instructional strategies teachers can use to promote their ELLs' writing development in any content area and at any grade level.

Identifying ELLs' Writing Levels

Recall that under NCLB, each state must identify different levels of English language proficiency. Thus, each state has had to specify features of ELL student writing at each of the proficiency levels the state uses for accountability purposes. The state of Texas, for example, identifies four proficiency levels: beginning, intermediate, advanced, and advanced high. The state's proficiency level indicators for grades 2 through 12 in writing include lists of the abilities associated with each level and the writing features typically exhibited at each level.

Texas also has developed writing proficiency level descriptors for grades K-1, focusing on students still at the developing stages of writing (Texas Education Agency, 2008). But note that Texas has only four proficiency levels for two grade-level bands (K–1 and 2–12) and that these standards are not specific to any language or content area (see Figure 8.2).

Contrast the Texas descriptors to the TESOL English Language Proficiency Standards, which, as we have seen in previous chapters, have a much more complex but thorough set of proficiency level descriptors across five proficiency levels

(Starting, Emerging, Developing, Expanding, and Bridging), across five grade-level bands (pre-K-K, 1–3, 4–5, 6–8, and 9–12), and across five standards (social, intercultural, and instructional language; language arts; mathematics; science; and social studies). Rather than provide generic descriptions, the TESOL standards offer sample performance indicators for different topics within the five standards. These standards give teachers at specific grade levels a clear understanding of what can be reasonably expected of students in the area of writing for social, intercultural, and instructional purposes and across four content areas, and also what instruction and guidance will be needed to help students move up to the next level. Consider for example, the sample performance indicator in Figure 8.3 for writing for grades 4–5 in the area of social studies under the topic of immigration. Note that the level of difficulty of the writing task increases as the level of support decreases for each subsequent proficiency level. As these examples illustrate, ELLs progress through different stages and levels within their English language writing development but this development is not necessarily linear. Furthermore, researchers and states have different ways of identifying and defining these stages and for determining when ELLs are at one stage or another.

As a teacher, it is important to understand how your state defines these stages or levels, because they are used for accountability purposes. But you should also be familiar with other ELL writing development frameworks outlined by researchers or by TESOL (2006a). Most important, teachers need to know how to use the frameworks to understand the writing development of their ELL students and help them develop the knowledge and skills they need. They also need to provide the students with ample opportunities for authentic writing. These frameworks can guide teachers' efforts to help ELLs progress to the next stage or level, with the ultimate goal of being designated as proficient writers in English.

Writing *to, with,* and *by* ELLs

Like reading *to, with,* and *by* ELLs, writing *to, with,* and *by* ELLs allows teachers to model and scaffold the writing process to help ELL students become confident and skilled independent writers. Writing *to* ELLs includes modeled writing, and writing *with* ELLs includes interactive, shared, and guided writing. Writing *by* ELLs includes independent writing, such as journals, and Writer's Workshop.

Modeled Writing

Teachers demonstrate the writing process through modeled writing, producing a text in enlarged print on a writing easel, white board, chalk board, overhead projector or on a computer projected on a screen so that all the students can see the text as it is being written. This process is particularly important for ELLs, because they may lack models of proficient English writing at home.

In modeled writing, the teacher controls the pen and composes and writes the text on her own. As she writes, she thinks aloud. Suppose the teacher wants to model how to write a letter to her friend. Some of her comments as she thinks aloud might include the following:

- When I write a letter, I know the first thing I need is the date. I know I need to write that in the middle. First I need to put the month, then the day, then a comma, and then the year. So here at the middle of the top I'm going to write . . .
- Next I need my greeting. I'll skip a line and start writing that here on the left. I'm writing to my friend Phuong, so I'll write "Dear Phuong." I know *Dear* needs to start with a capital *D,* and I also need a capital *P* because *Phuong* is a name. I also remember that I need to put a comma at the end of my greeting.

(*text continues on page 216*)

BEGINNING	INTERMEDIATE
Beginning English language learners lack the English vocabulary and grasp of English language structures necessary to address grade-appropriate writing tasks meaningfully.	**Intermediate English language learners have enough English vocabulary and enough grasp of English language structures to address grade-appropriate writing tasks in a limited way.**

BEGINNING

These students

- have little or no ability to use the English language to express ideas in writing and engage meaningfully in grade-appropriate writing assignments in content-area instruction
- lack the English necessary to develop or demonstrate elements of grade-appropriate writing (e.g., focus and coherence, conventions, organization, voice, and development of ideas) in English

Typical writing features at this level

- ability to label, list, and copy
- high-frequency words/phrases and short, simple sentences (or even short paragraphs) based primarily on recently practiced, memorized, or highly familiar material; this type of writing may be quite accurate
- present tense used primarily
- frequent primary language features (spelling patterns, word order, literal translations, and words from the student's primary language) and other errors associated with second language acquisition may significantly hinder or prevent understanding, even for individuals accustomed to the writing of English language learners (ELLs)

INTERMEDIATE

These students

- have a limited ability to use the English language to express ideas in writing and engage meaningfully in grade-appropriate writing assignments in content-area instruction
- are limited in their ability to develop or demonstrate elements of grade-appropriate writing in English; communicate best when topics are highly familiar and concrete, and require simple, high-frequency English

Typical writing features at this level

- simple, original messages consisting of short, simple sentences; frequent inaccuracies occur when creating or taking risks beyond familiar English
- high-frequency vocabulary; academic writing often has an oral tone
- loosely connected text with limited use of cohesive devices or repetitive use, which may cause gaps in meaning
- repetition of ideas due to lack of vocabulary and language structures
- present tense used most accurately; simple future and past tenses, if attempted, are used inconsistently or with frequent inaccuracies
- descriptions, explanations, and narrations lacking detail; difficulty expressing abstract ideas
- primary language features and errors associated with second language acquisition may be frequent
- some writing may be understood only by individuals accustomed to the writing of ELLs; parts of the writing may be hard to understand even for individuals accustomed to the writing of ELLs

Figure 8.2   Texas English Language Proficiency Assessment System (TELPAS) Proficiency Level Descriptors, Grades 2–12 Writing. (Source: Texas Education Agency, 2008, p. 4. Available at www .tea.state.tx.us/student.assessment/admin/rpte/telpasrater/spring2008pld.pdf)

ADVANCED	ADVANCED HIGH
Advanced English language learners have enough English vocabulary and command of English language structures to address grade-appropriate writing tasks, although second language acquisition support is needed.	**Advanced high English language learners have acquired the English vocabulary and command of English language structures necessary to address grade-appropriate writing tasks with minimal second language acquisition support.**

ADVANCED

These students

- are able to use the English language, with second language acquisition support, to express ideas in writing and engage meaningfully in grade-appropriate writing assignments in content-area instruction
- know enough English to be able to develop or demonstrate elements of grade-appropriate writing in English, although second language acquisition support is particularly needed when topics are abstract, academically challenging, or unfamiliar

Typical writing features at this level

- grasp of basic verbs, tenses, grammar features, and sentence patterns; partial grasp of more complex verbs, tenses, grammar features, and sentence patterns
- emerging grade-appropriate vocabulary; academic writing has a more academic tone
- use of a variety of common cohesive devices, although some redundancy may occur
- narrations, explanations, and descriptions developed in some detail with emerging clarity; quality or quantity declines when abstract ideas are expressed, academic demands are high, or low-frequency vocabulary is required
- occasional second language acquisition errors
- communications are usually understood by individuals not accustomed to the writing of ELLs

ADVANCED HIGH

These students

- are able to use the English language, with minimal second language acquisition support, to express ideas in writing and engage meaningfully in grade-appropriate writing assignments in content-area instruction
- know enough English to be able to develop or demonstrate, with minimal second language acquisition support, elements of grade-appropriate writing in English

Typical writing features at this level

- nearly comparable to writing of native English-speaking peers in clarity and precision with regards to English vocabulary and language structures, with occasional exceptions when writing about academically complex ideas, abstract ideas, or topics requiring low-frequency vocabulary
- occasional difficulty with naturalness of phrasing and expression
- errors associated with second language acquisition are minor and usually limited to low-frequency words and structures; errors rarely interfere with communication

Figure 8.2 (*continued*)

Standard 5 Language of Social Studies
Grade level cluster: 4–5

Domain: Writing Topic: Immigration				
Level 1	**Level 2**	**Level 3**	**Level 4**	**Level 5**
List family members or historical figures with countries of origin, using maps or charts.	Create personal or historical family trees using graphic organizers and photographs.	Produce illustrated family or group histories through albums, journals, diaries, or travelogues.	Research (e.g., by conducting interviews) and report family or historical journeys.	Discuss, in paragraph form, cause and effect, historical patterns, or impact of movement of peoples from nation to nation.

Figure 8.3   TESOL ELP Standards, sample performance indicators for writing. (Source: TESOL, 2006a, p. 77.)

> ■ Now I'm ready to start my letter. I need to indent so . . .

In addition to talking about conventions and style, the teacher also talks about content. For example:

> ■ I want to tell my friend about a great movie I saw yesterday, so I think first I'll tell her I saw a great movie, and then in the next sentence I'll tell her the name of it.

As she writes she can talk about grammar decisions:

> ■ This is a movie I watched yesterday, so I need to use the past tense. "I saw a great movie yesterday."

The teacher can also discuss decisions about vocabulary and can even model making changes while writing to make better choices:

> ■ I think I need a better word than *great* to describe the movie because I loved it so much. I think I'll use the word *awesome* instead [crosses out *great* and writes *awesome*]. Oh, and now I need to change *a* to *an* because *awesome* begins with a vowel. "I saw an awesome movie yesterday."

And she can also discuss her use of punctuation:

> ■ To make this sentence sound more like how I would say it in an excited way, I'm going to change this period to an explanation point: "I saw an awesome movie yesterday!"

Modeled writing, as shown here, is an effective tool for teaching new vocabulary to ELLs within this meaningful and authentic context. If necessary, the teacher could draw simple pictures next to some new vocabulary words in the text to remind students of the meanings.

The text in modeled writing should be kept brief. Teachers should ensure that the complexity and vocabulary of the text is appropriate to the proficiency of their ELL students. They should focus on genres and key skills they want their students to learn and use in their own writing. The topics for modeled writing could be tied into themes or topics being studied in class, or even extensions of read-alouds or shared readings. For example, through modeled writing, the teacher could demonstrate writing a summary of the story or a science report or a persuasive essay. Many elementary school teachers incorporate modeled writing into their daily opening routine by writing morning messages. These typically tell the students about what they are going to be doing in class that day and thus may include a sentence such as, "Today we are going to the library to check out books."

Once modeled writing texts are complete, they should be kept on display in the classroom. Students can refer to them as they write. They also make engaging texts that students will want to read during independent reading time.

Shared Writing

Shared writing is similar to modeled writing, except that in shared writing, the students write *with* the teacher to help compose the text. The teacher controls the pen and acts as the scribe, allowing the students to dictate the text and make decisions about the content, vocabulary, conventions, grammar, and style. Having students help compose the text ensures that it is comprehensible at their current level of English proficiency. The teacher, however, does not just write whatever students say and how they say it, errors and all. Rather, she serves as a guide, sharing ideas and strategies to ensure appropriate vocabulary and correct sentence structure as she writes. For example, suppose the class is composing a text describing their field trip to the zoo, and a student suggests adding to a story, "We see monkey play in they house." The teacher could accept this addition but before or during writing she could prompt the students to help fix up the sentence:

- "We went to the zoo last week." Do we need to use the present or the past tense? What's the past tense of *see?*
- Was there more than one monkey? OK, so what is the plural form of *monkey?*
- We need a word before "monkeys." We saw [pause to allow the students to say "the"] monkeys.

Like modeled writing, shared writing is an effective tool for teaching new vocabulary and grammar to ELLs within a meaningful context. Here, for example, the teacher can teach the word *cage* to replace the word *house*. The teacher could also contribute to the sentence by suggesting "playing around" to replace "play." With such guidance, the student's initial suggestion is further crafted and added to the story as, "We saw the monkeys playing around in their cage." By asking questions like these and providing guidance, the teacher enables students to engage in writing beyond their independent writing level, that is, the teacher is able to scaffold the class's composition of well-written text.

The topics for shared writing, like those for modeled writing, could include current themes and topics, extensions of books from read-alouds and shared readings, or descriptions of shared experiences, such as an assembly or field trip. Shared writing is also an excellent way to introduce and practice a genre students will be expected to write independently, and an effective way for a teacher to focus on strategies or skills she notices are lacking in the students' own writing. For example, if it becomes evident from student journals that many are struggling with the future tense, the teacher could guide students in the composition of a text describing an upcoming activity or holiday that requires the use of this tense (e.g., "During spring break, I am going camping. I will go fishing with my dad.").

Shared writing should also incorporate the use of graphic organizers to model the prewriting stage. Graphic organizers can help students see relationships between ideas before they write and also help them generate ideas and vocabulary they will need for the writing. For example, suppose the class wanted to write about their field trip to the park. Together the teacher and students could create a graphic organizer by talking about and listing the different things they did at the park (see Figure 8.4). More details could be added to each of the three main activities. For

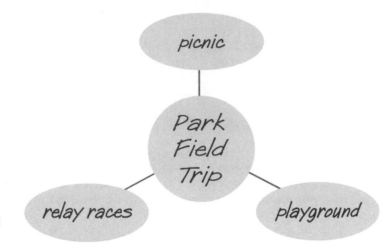

Figure 8.4 Prewriting graphic organizer created during shared writing

example, from picnic, the class could add circles for the different things they ate: sandwiches, chips, apples, and cookies. Then, the students could use this graphic organizer as they compose their shared writing text. Creating a graphic organizer also models for students the prewriting process they should use in their own writing.

Guided Writing

There are varying definitions and descriptions of guided writing, but all include the teacher guiding students through a particular writing activity designed to address an area of need within students' writing development. Typically guided writing starts with a mini-lesson on some aspect of writing. Students then practice the writing principle or strategy they were just taught, under the teacher's supervision, and then share their final written projects.

For example, when I noticed that many of my students were not using adjectives and that therefore their writing was very plain, I created a guided writing activity on adjectives. Our theme for the month was animals. I made a chart with the students, recreated in Figure 8.5. First I had students brainstorm a list of animals and then a list of words we could use to describe these animals (adjectives). Next we brainstormed a list of things these animals could do (verbs) and then the places where they might do these things. As we brainstormed these words, we talked about each one to make sure everyone understood them. Through this process, the students were learning vocabulary in a meaningful context.

Once our chart was completed, I called on a student to choose one animal and put a sticky note by its name (e.g., *monkey*). Next, students chose three adjectives from our list to describe the monkey (e.g., *hairy, playful,* and *wild),* and then a verb (e.g., *swings),* and finally the place (e.g., *jungle).* With all their choices marked, we read our full sentence: "The hairy, playful, wild monkey swings in the jungle." To liven it up, and as an additional support, we sang our new sentence to the tune of "The Farmer in the Dell."

> The hairy, playful monkey.
> The hairy, playful monkey.
> The hairy, playful, wild monkey swings in the jungle.

By now the students were anxious to create other sentences to read and sing, coming up with such jewels as "The yellow, dangerous, slimy snake crawls in the forest" and "The hairy, ugly, smelly dog sleeps in the house."

	Adjective	Animal	Verb	Preposition	Place
	hairy	bird	runs		house
	yellow	dog	swings		jungle
	beautiful	monkey	jumps		cage
	fluffy	cat	eats		zoo
	white	horse	crawls		water
The	dangerous	turtle	sings	in the	field
	ugly	cow	sleeps		farm
	slimy	scorpion	flies		park
	playful	spider	drives		barn
	smelly	snake	bites		forest
	wild	shark	plays		lake

Figure 8.5 Animal adjectives poster

Once we completed a few sentences together, the students were sent to their desks to write their own sentences from the chart. Everyone, including my reluctant writers, quickly filled up their papers with sentences. When they finished, they read them to each other or to the whole class. We kept our chart up for several weeks for students to read and refer to when doing their own writing. I knew this guided writing activity had been successful when I noticed students were using more adjectives in their journals and other writing.

Interactive Writing

Interactive writing is like shared writing because the students and teacher compose the text together. In interactive writing, however, the students share the pen. It is excellent technique for young ELL students who are at the beginning stage of writing and learning the alphabet, letter formation, and letter-sound correspondence. It can also be used with older newcomer ELLs, particularly those who lack L1 literacy skills. The teacher begins by guiding the class to form a sentence. It could be a sentence related to a current theme, an extension of a book read-aloud, a morning message, or the beginning of a story or other genre the class will compose together. Suppose, for example, the students are learning about animals that can fly. Using interactive writing, the students will write sentences demonstrating what they know about flying animals. The teacher could ask, "Who can tell me the name of an animal that can fly?" After listening to students' suggestions, the teacher could say, "OK, let's pick one of those animals. How about a bat? Let's make a sentence. *A bat* . . ." Then the students could join in " . . . *can fly*." The teacher could then ask, "Where does the bat fly?" The students would likely suggest, "in the sky." The teacher could then prompt students to put all the information together in a single sentence: "A bat can fly in the sky."

In preparation for writing this sentence, the teacher draws a line for each word, taking care to make the lines about the length of each word and adding the ending punctuation:

— _____ _____ _____ __ _____ _____.

The teacher then points to each blank line, prompting the students read the sentence as if the words were already written. Then, one word at a time, the teacher helps the students say the word slowly, listening for the letters they need. As the students figure out the letters, the teacher asks for volunteers to come up and write the next letter in the word. For example, the teacher might ask, "What letter does *bat* start with?" The teacher can then hand the pen to a student who suggests the letter *b*. If the student is unsure how to write the letter *b* the teacher can model it for him on a small white board or chalk board. Interactive writing is an effective way to teach phonics in a meaningful context because it allows teachers to teach the exact letter-sound correspondences students need to create their message.

When students are at this stage, the teacher should not worry about handwriting. If a student makes a mistake, the teacher can simply cover the error with a sticky note to mask it (some teachers call this a "band-aid"), and then the student can make the correction on top. As each word is completed, the students read it aloud and then go back to the beginning of the sentence and read up to the next word they need to add. This process continues until the sentence is complete, at which point they go back and read the entire sentence.

A sentence created this way could be the basis for a classroom book. The teacher could ask one or two students to illustrate the page. After a week or so of interactive writing on flying animals, with illustrations added, the students will have enough to put together into a book that can be used for shared reading, placed in the classroom library for students to read during silent reading time, or checked out by students to take home and read to their families. Interactive writing texts can also be displayed on the walls for students to read and refer to when writing on their own.

When I did interactive writing with my beginning-level writers, I found they got a little bored waiting for a turn to come up and write a letter or word. To solve this problem, I gave each student an individual white board and a marker and eraser. That way they were able to write along and get their own practice writing each letter and word.

As students progress in their writing, they can contribute entire words, and the texts can get longer and more complex.

Journals

Modeled writing, interactive writing, shared writing, and guided writing all provide scaffolding to help ELLs develop as writers and are forms of writing *to* and *with* ELLs. Independent writing is writing *by* ELLs. Teachers support independent writing by providing opportunities for students to write, to practice what they have learned, and to move up through the stages of writing development. Journals are an outstanding way to support this development. Each student is given an empty notebook and time to write in it every day; students include the date on each entry. Time allotted to journal writing can vary from 10 minutes to 30 minutes a day; older and more proficient writers may be given more time.

There are two general views about journal writing. One is that students should be free to write about anything they like, and the other is that teachers should assign a topic or use a prompt. A colleague of mine once showed me a journal entry from one of her 2nd-grade students, a girl who probably had been writing in her journal daily since kindergarten:

> I have nothing left to write about. I'm only 7 years old, and not that much stuff has happened to me yet.

As this young girl reminds us, students may need some guidance to generate topics they can write about. One technique is to do a shared writing activity during which students brainstorm a list of topics they could write about. The list of topics might include: my favorite TV show, my favorite cartoon or movie, foods I like or hate, my family, what I like or don't like about school, something funny that happened to me, a time I was really scared, what I want to be when I grow up, problems in our school or neighborhood, if I were President, and so on. A group of students can quickly fill up a large chart with their ideas. The chart can be posted on the wall so students can refer to it when looking for ideas.

Sometimes further guidance may be necessary. Once, in an effort to get my students to write more, I made a rule that they must write at least five sentences in order to go to recess. No problem, my students figured out:

> I like to play.
> I like to eat.
> I like to run.
> I like to jump.
> I like to sleep.

And off to recess they went! They seemed to be stuck at the *stylized sentence writing stage* demonstrated in Table 8.2, but I knew they were capable of doing more and, with a bit more motivation and guidance, could move into the *emerging standardized writing stage*. At our local teacher supply store, I found a little booklet of writing prompt ideas. It had goofy prompts, such as, "If an alien came to your house, what would you do?" and "If you had a million dollars, what would you buy?" I didn't want to stymie my students who were already producing good writing on their own topics, so I decided each day I would put up a prompt on the overhead projector and read it with the students but give them the option of responding to it or writing about something else of their own choosing. It was an instant success; students loved the prompts and were excited to respond to them. The new system helped to break them free from writing isolated lists of sentences. Even when they did not respond to the prompt, they began to write more in the prose style of the emerging standardized writing stage on their own topics.

As a general rule, journal writing should not be corrected. This does not mean, however, that teachers cannot provide corrective feedback. The most effective way to give this feedback is to make the journals interactive between the student and the teacher. These are also called dialogue journals. In this manner, writing becomes a means for authentic communication between the students and their teacher. The teacher reads the students' entries and then writes back to them in their journal, responding to their writing (see Figure 8.6).

Note that the student whose journal entry appears in Figure 8.6 appears to be at the emerging standardized writing stage and is relying on invented spelling. Note also that the teacher does not correct all of the errors directly but instead provides a form of corrective feedback. This process is similar to oral recasts, described in Chapter 6. Embedded in this response are the correct spellings for *Chuck-E-Cheese*, *with*, *played*, *some*, *video*, and *games*, as well as a model of the past tense of *go* (*went*), the plural form of *game* (*games*), and the need for the verb *was* before *fun*.

> i goed to chke chz wit my mom
> i ply sum vdo game
> it fun
>
> *I'm glad you went to Chuck-E-Cheese with your mom. I bet it was fun. I like to play video games too!*

Figure 8.6   **Interaction between the student and teacher in a dialogue journal**

Also modeled are proper capitalization and ending punctuation and running prose, with each sentence following the next rather than starting on a new line. Students may not be ready to learn all of these points at once. But the next time this student wants to write about Chuck-E-Cheese or video games, he is likely to flip back to this page to get the correct spelling from the teacher's response. He may also start capitalizing *I* and use ending punctuation. As he progresses, he will pick up more and more from the teacher's responses.

One exciting thing about journals is that they are a living record of students' writing development over the course of the school year. I gave students a new journal every month and then labeled their old journals with the name of the month and dropped them into their portfolios. The completed journals were very effective measures of the students' growth, and I showed them to students and parents during conferences: "Here's how Gabriela was writing at the beginning of the year, and here is what her writing looks like now! Notice how much she has improved in . . ."

Besides documenting students' progress in writing development, journals reveal their strengths and areas in need of improvement, allowing teachers when they read the daily entries to quickly ascertain the strategies and skills they need to focus on in shared and modeled writing, and the types of lessons needed in guided writing. Teachers can also pinpoint skills needed just by a small number of students and thus can develop mini-lessons just for these students. Journal writing can be used for formative assessment.

Process Writing and Writer's Workshop

Process writing involves guiding students through the writing process in stages, helping them to focus first on ideas and to take care of corrections related to grammar, spelling, and mechanics toward the end. Process writing generally has five stages: prewriting, drafting, revising, editing, and publishing. These stages were identified in the 1970s when writing research began to focus on how successful writers produce a text from its conceptualization to its final publication (see Table 8.1). One finding was that successful writers concentrate first on their ideas rather than worrying about having perfect spelling, grammar, and mechanics, otherwise their writing would suffer. Process writing works especially well for ELL students. "Correctness" is a challenge for them, but students are still capable of expressing their ideas in writing in less than fluent English (Samway, 2006). Once the students' ideas are down on paper, teachers can provide instruction and scaffolding to help them improve their writing as they go through the rest of the writing process. Teachers often teach process writing through a collaborative approach called Writer's Workshop, which involves the following activities at each stage:

Prewriting.   Students get their ideas together, determine the purpose of the writing, and identify who the audience will be (e.g., "My purpose is to tell about my sister's wedding, and my audience is my teacher and the students in the class."). They decide what the main idea will be and what supporting details they want to include. With or without the support of the teacher, they can use the following strategies to prepare to write:

- Talking over their ideas with peers or with the teacher
- Drawing pictures (works well for students at early stages of writing development)
- Brainstorming to create a list of things they can write about or a list of supporting details to include once the main idea has been identified
- Closing their eyes to visualize what they want to write about, concentrating on what they see, hear, smell, feel, and taste

- Using graphic organizers, such as the word web in Figure 8.4
- Creating an outline for organizing the text

The teacher can also provide some form of shared experience for students to write about, such as a book that is read aloud, a video watched in class, a science experiment, a field trip, or an assembly.

Drafting.   Students focus on getting their ideas down on paper as quickly as possible. The ideas and materials generated during prewriting are an important source at this stage. Those who are unsure where to begin should be encouraged to just start writing. Students should also be taught not to spend time worrying about spelling or grammar. This first draft is evaluated by how consistent the content is with its purpose and its appropriateness for the target audiences.

Revising.   After reading over their first draft, students may want to rewrite some sentences and move things around to better organize their arguments or supporting details. They may decide to add more details to support their main idea or feel the need to remove some sentences and details that they determine are off topic and that distract from their main idea and purpose for writing.

At this stage, students often need the help of their peers and the teacher. They meet in peer-response groups to read their drafts aloud and give feedback to each other, or meet individually with the teacher to read their drafts and talk about their writing. They ask questions and receive suggestions for improvement. For example, suppose a student wrote, "I went to the mall. It was fun." The teacher could prompt for more details. "What did you do at the mall? What did you do there that was fun?" After listening to the student's responses, the teacher can say, "Those are great details! Add those to your writing."

Editing.   When students have a strong draft in which the main idea and supporting details are present and well organized, one that meets its purpose and the needs of its intended audience, they focus on editing for correct spelling, mechanics, and grammar. The students first do their best to find errors and correct them on their own. If further help is needed, they can get corrections in peer-response groups and, finally, from the teacher in another teacher conference.

Correcting students' writing at this stage raises two issues: how to correct, and what and how much to correct. First, how to correct: the teacher could merely underline the errors and have the student figure out what's wrong and how to fix them. Or, the teacher could circle each error and give some type of clue by writing in the margin *sp.* for spelling errors, *ten.* for tense errors, or *pun.* for punctuation errors. Or, the teacher could make direct corrections for the student, indicating where the error is and writing in the correction.

In her research with adult ESL writers, Jean Chandler (2003) found that direct correction works best for producing accurate revisions. Students prefer this method because it is fast and easy for them, and it is fast and easy for teachers when there are several drafts. But Chandler also found that students felt they learned more when the teacher just underlined the errors and they had to correct them own their own. She concludes that both methods are viable and that the best choice depends on the goals of a particular assignment. These findings also hold for younger ELL writers. The teacher may want to use a mixture of the two, for example, underlining those errors he or she believes students are ready to self-correct and providing direct corrections for those errors students are not yet ready to deal with.

To determine what and how much to correct, the second issue, the teacher should focus on (1) errors students are ready to learn how to correct, and (2) errors that interfere with meaning. The teacher can also identify points of grammar and mechanics that students are ready to learn and provide instruction on these points through mini-lessons. Although the teacher's goal may be to help students move their writing to the publishing stage, the text does not need to be 100% free of errors.

Publishing. Once students have edited their work by making their own corrections and corrections from their peers and the teacher, they either rewrite their final draft in clear handwriting on high quality white paper or type it, using a computer with word processing software. Students can also add illustrations and a cover.

"Publishing" means making the final draft available to others. One common technique in Writer's Workshop is to read from the Author's Chair: the student sits in the teacher's chair (or another designated chair) to read his or her writing to the class. The class and the teacher can ask the author questions, pointing out the parts they liked and, if appropriate, giving constructive feedback to help the student in future writing projects. Published writing can be added to the classroom library or sent home for students to read to their families. Many teachers set up a special wall in the classroom to publish student writing, making it easily accessible for students and classroom visitors to read. Shorter pieces of writing published by students on the same topic can be compiled into a book that can be laminated and bound, then placed in the classroom library or checked out for students to take home and read to their families.

Shorter pieces of writing published by students on the same topic, such as a field trip, can be compiled into a book that can be laminated and bound, then placed in the classroom library or checked out for students to take home and read to their families. Student writing can also be published on the school's Web site or a class wiki or blog for the entire world to see. Making published writing available to a wide audience is an essential step. This is how ELLs develop a sense of audience and gain an understanding of the need for their writing to be well organized and correct so they can convey their intended meaning to their target audience. It also makes the writing much more authentic than it would be if they simply wrote something that the teacher grades and returns.

Support for Independent Writing

Teachers provide support for students' independent writing through resources such as word walls, thematic word charts, personal word books, dictionaries, and by facilitating peer assessment and by providing mini-lessons.

Word walls.   A word wall is a wall display of words arranged alphabetically under each letter in type large enough for students to read from their desks (see Figure 8.7). It should include the words students ask for or use most frequently when they are writing, including, at least initially, high frequency words. Notice, for example, that the word wall in Figure 8.7 includes "Austin," "Dallas," and "Fiesta Texas" (a local amusement park), all useful words for the students in this classroom who live in San Antonio, Texas.

The word wall should be built up throughout the year. As words are added students and the teacher discuss their meaning, and students help place the words in the proper location. If the words are affixed to the wall with Velcro or magnets, students can easily remove them and take them to their desk as needed to help with their writing. I used different colors for the word cards to make it easier for students to recognize and remember words they most frequently needed or for higher-level students to help lower-level students:

STEPHEN: How do you spell *said?*
VANNA: It's on the word wall, the blue card under *S.*
STEPHEN: I see it. Thanks!

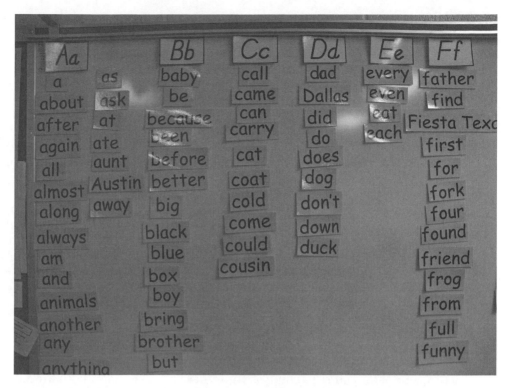

Figure 8.7 **Word wall from Mrs. Armstrong's 1st grade class, Scobee Elementary School, Northside Independent School District, San Antonio, Texas, 2007.** (Photo by author.)

Teachers can also develop a range of interactive activities, such as games where students must quickly find and remove a word from the wall, group words based on alphabetic or semantic properties, and put words back in their correct locations according to alphabetical order. Such activities help students develop their vocabulary skills and ensure that they know how to use the wall to support their writing. Many teachers have found that they can provide additional support by cutting the word wall cards out in the shape of the words or making an outline in a bold color around each word following its shape. (For more suggestions, see Lynch, 2005; Wagstaff, 1999.)

Thematic word charts. A thematic word chart displays words that relate to the theme being studied in class or to a special occasion, such as an upcoming holiday. Thematic word charts, like word walls, display words that students will likely want to use in their writing and help them learn new vocabulary. To make the word charts fun, students can design the chart in the shape of something representative of the theme. For example, during the month of October, many of my students were very excited about Halloween and wanted to write in their journals about their plans.[3] We made a large picture of a pumpkin out of chart paper. In a shared writing

---

3: Care must be taken when using holidays as a theme in your classroom. Some cultural or religious groups may not recognize or celebrate them and parents may prefer that their children not be included in any activities that resemble a celebration of the holiday. Most parents are comfortable with students' learning about the holiday, and teachers need to make sure any holiday theme activities have a clear curricular focus, such as teaching vocabulary and writing. The same words, for example, would be a resource for one student who wishes to write about the costume he will wear on Halloween and another who wishes to write in her journal, "I don't go trick-or-treating or carve jack-o-lanterns because in my religion we don't celebrate Halloween."

activity, we brainstormed Halloween-related words (*pumpkin, carve, jack-o-lantern, costume, trick-or-treating, candy, fall, autumn, monster, ghost*, etc.) and added them to the chart. During the month, when we read related books, we added new words to the chart. We also added new words when students discovered they needed them during writing. Teachers at the secondary level can create similar word walls for the academic subject they teach (e.g., math word wall, science word wall, history word wall).

Personal word books.   Word walls are great, but they take up a lot of classroom space, and it is just not possible to have all the words all the students need all the time. Thus, another great resource for each student is a personal word book. Typically the books are preprinted with high frequency words and other words students commonly ask for when they write. But the word books include space under each letter section for students to record their own words as they progress through the school year. They may record words that have been added to the word wall or to a temporary thematic word chart. They may come across words in their reading they want to remember and use in their own writing. They may also record words they learn in ESL or sheltered content-area lessons, and words they have asked a friend or a teacher how to spell. Personal word books are also a great place for students to record words for things they want to write about but that are likely not even in the dictionary, such as the names of TV shows, movies, video game systems and video games, the names of their favorite bands and singers, food products, the names of popular restaurants, and other places in the community and surrounding areas.

Personal word books are efficient because they include only words that remind students of the correct spelling of words they know. The definitions are not needed. Thus, the word books can contain a large number of words that students can quickly find when needed. As with word walls, however, students will need instruction, guidance, and practice using their personal word books before they can be an effective support for their independent writing.

Dictionaries.   Picture dictionaries (English monolingual and bilingual versions), which are organized by category, are useful for students at the lower and intermediate levels of English proficiency. If they want to write the word *bicycle*, for example, they can just flip to the transportation section, find the picture of the bicycle, and then look to see what it is called in English and how to spell it. The bilingual versions allow students who can read in their native language to make sure they have the word they are looking for. Regular bilingual dictionaries are also a great source for students who are literate in their L1, because they can quickly find the English equivalent of a word they want to write or confirm that a word in English is the word they were looking for. A regular English (monolingual) dictionary, appropriate to the grade-level of the student, is effective for students at higher levels of English proficiency who need to check on the precise meaning of a word or its spelling before they use it. Students can also use electronic handheld and on-line English, bilingual, and multilingual dictionaries, as well as translation tools embedded in programs such as Microsoft Word. Regardless of the type of dictionary used, for dictionaries to be effective, students will need to be taught how to use them as a resource to support their writing.

"Ask three, then me."   When students need help with the spelling or definition of a word, they can observe the rule "Ask three, then me." Before approaching the teacher, a student must ask three classmates. If none of them knows how to spell the word, the student may then ask the teacher. Encouraging students to use their peers as resources supports independent writing and frees up the teacher for one-to-one conferences with students and mini-lessons for small groups of students.

Mini-lessons.   Mini-lessons are an important source of scaffolding and instructional support for ELL student writers and a critical component of Writer's Workshops. The teacher becomes aware of issues that need special attention by reading journal entries and drafts during Writer's Workshop, by conferencing with students, and by conducting formal writing assessments. For example, if a teacher noticed four students who were having trouble following capitalization rules consistently, he could pull them together for a quick lesson. The best source for these lessons would be problematic sentences from the students' own writing (with their names removed). The small group can review the rules and then correct the sentences. The teacher then encourages the students to check their own writing for these issues. After a mini-lesson, the teacher monitors the students to see whether they are making improvements, and re-teach those who still need help.

Mini-lessons should also be used proactively to teach new concepts and techniques students can incorporate into their writing. For example, for older ELLs who are ready, a mini-lesson could focus on literary devices, such as flashbacks and foreshadowing, or on advanced punctuation, such as colons, semicolons, and dashes. The mini-lesson could involve finding incidents of these in texts with which students are familiar that they can use as models for their own writing.

Writing across the Curriculum

Students should be writing to learn, and therefore they should be writing all day, in all content areas, not just during the writing portion of language arts time. To encourage students to write to learn across the curriculum, many middle and high schools draw on the Collins Writing Program, developed by the literacy expert John Collins (n.d.). The program uses frequent, usually short, writing assignments to increase students' involvement in lessons, checks on their understanding of concepts, and promotes their thinking about academic content. The program suggests the following five types of writing:

Type 1: Capture ideas. Students write one draft to get a minimum number of ideas down on paper in a set amount of time. Writing is evaluated as complete or incomplete.

Type 2: Respond correctly. Students write one draft to demonstrate understanding. Writing is evaluated for correctness of ideas.

Type 3: Edit for focus correction areas (FCAs). Students write a draft with attention to up to three targeted writing skills (e.g., topic sentence, conclusion, supporting details, content-specific vocabulary, varied sentence structure, punctuation). Writing is evaluated for content and relative to FCAs.

Type 4: Peer edit for FCAs. Like Type 3 writing but critiqued by a peer.

Type 5: Publish. Students produce a publishable piece. Writing is evaluated for content and form.

Students can have journals for math, science, social studies, or even art, music, and physical education in which they record notes, describe new concepts they learn, and keep a record of activities they have completed, all examples of Type 1 or Type 2 writing. In math, students write word problems or respond to open-ended math problems. In science, students record observations, write answers to science questions, and write experiment reports. In social studies, students write responses to questions, notes while conducting research, and research reports. In music, students can write the lyrics to songs or even musical notation. Students can incorporate text into their art or write descriptions of their artistic creations. In PE, students can keep logs about issues related to exercise, nutrition, and health. They also write to keep track of their progress in meeting fitness goals. Each of these activities is an opportunity for students to focus on the language of the specific content area, with attention to content-area vocabulary and genres, and to develop their writing skills in English. When students write regularly for a wide range of purposes across the content areas, they become proficient writers.

Writing with Technology

Students today do much of their writing on computers and on hand-held communication devices. These technological developments are forcing teachers to rethink how writing is taught in the classroom (Richardson, 2006). On a computer, the writing process is less linear that it is on paper, because students can easily revise and edit as they write their first draft. When students write on the computer, they should be taught to take advantage of the ease of editing the computer offers along with the support of spelling and grammar checkers, dictionaries, thesauruses, and translation tools.

Students increasingly are using technology as an efficient means of written communication with others in their everyday lives. Students in the past may have occasionally written and mailed letters and postcards and perhaps written short notes in class to their friends. Students today, however, write hundreds of e-mail messages and postings on Internet social networking sites, blogs, and on-line discussion boards. They spend hours on-line in chat rooms and in instant messaging programs to "chat" live with others through text. They send dozens of text messages a week to friends from their cell phones and other hand-held devices. Instead of passing notes in class as in the good ol' days, students today may get busted for "texting" their friends in class. Teachers should not be afraid to embrace these new technologies in the classroom. They can be highly motivating because they reflect the type of writing students want to do and will do in real life.

With the increasing use of new technologies, teachers will need to find ways to address the writing in these contexts that differs from "standard" writing taught in our schools. sTuDeNts FoR eXaMpLe MaY wRiTe LiKe ThIs. Or dey myt Nd ^ ryTN a sentenC lk dis [or they might end up writing a sentence like this]. The first example shows how some young people write on-line when they want to look cool, in much the same way they might use a cool, youthful-sounding accent when they talk. The second example shows how some are creating a more efficient writing system with conventions for shorter spellings that are faster to write and send, particularly with hand-held texting devices, such as cell phones, which have fewer buttons than there are letters or buttons that are so small it is hard to press them quickly. You might see some new abbreviations in students' school writing, such as IMHO (in my humble opinion), LOL (laughing out loud), and IOW (in other words), or even emoticons, which are used in text environments the same way paralinguistic clues (e.g., facial expressions, gestures) are used in oral discourse to clarify the intended meanings of uttered words and phrases. As just a few examples, these include :-) for *happy,* :-(for *sad,* :-O for *surprised or shocked,* :-@ for *screaming,* and ;-) for *winking.* New abbreviations, emoticons, and other shortcuts are appearing all the time.

What should teachers do about this trend? First, although some consider what young people are doing to written standard English language an abomination (see, e.g., Kolesnikova, 2008), it is important to remember that languages are constantly changing. Consider, for example, the differences between Old, Middle, and Modern English or the deliberate changes Noah Webster and others made to British

English to help create standard American English. We may be seeing another phase in a natural progression of language, for language is changed by each generation to better fit into the ways they use it to communicate within their sociocultural contexts.

Nonetheless, teachers should not abandon efforts to teach students standard English. To do so would be irresponsible. Teachers do need to recognize and value nonstandard varieties of spoken and written English and help students recognize that these other forms of writing are appropriate in certain contexts but that standard English is essential for success in school and in the workplace. Native English speakers may have little difficulty "code switching" between these various forms of nonstandard and standard language, but ELL students may be less clear about appropriate boundaries and will need instruction to help them develop the correct forms to use in formal writing.

The Home-School Writing Connection

Writing can be a deeply personal form of reflection on the world and one's experiences in it. Teachers can open the way for students to engage in reflective writing by allowing them to write on topics of their own choosing in their journals, in Writer's Workshop, and in other writing projects. Students should be encouraged to draw on their funds of knowledge for their writing. They can also be encouraged to collect ideas by interviewing family members. For example, Joel E. Dworin (2006) describes the Family Stories Project he conducted with his 4th grade bilingual class. The students wrote stories using details they collected from family members in both English and Spanish. The transformative power of having students write about their own lives and experiences is highlighted in the 2006 feature film *Freedom Writers,* which tells the story of Erin Gruwell and her inner-city "at-risk" high school students, including many language-minority students, at Wilson High School in Long Beach, California. On the Freedom Writers Web site, the students explain:

> We began writing anonymous journal entries about the adversities that we faced in our everyday lives. We wrote about gangs, immigration, drugs, violence, abuse, death, anorexia, dyslexia, teenage love, weight issues, divorce, suicide, and all the other issues we never had the chance to express before. We discovered that writing is a powerful form of self expression that could help us deal with our past and move forward. (Freedom Writers Foundation, n.d.)

A collection of the students' work published in *The Freedom Writers Diary: How a Teacher and 150 Teens Used Writing to Change Themselves and the World Around Them* (Freedom Writers, 1999), provides a vivid example of power of critical pedagogy and the funds of knowledge orientation.

Assessing Writing

Standardized High-Stakes Writing Tests

Most high-stakes standardized tests use multiple-choice questions to assess students' writing ability. Although this technique saves time and money for the testing companies who score the tests, effective teachers know that the only real way to assess an ELL students' writing ability is to read something they have actually written. Fortunately, most states include writing prompts on their tests to which students must respond and that someone must evaluate. An important question to ask, however, is who actually reads and scores those essays on state high-stakes tests? (See Box 8.2.)

Another problem with high-stakes writing assessments is that they typically focus on a single genre (e.g., personal narrative, persuasive essay, expository text). And teachers, often under the mandates of their school and district administrators, may feel pressure to teach to the test and spend the majority of the year working on the genre required on the test. When writing instruction is narrowed to a single genre, students lose out. Rather than learning about the wide range of purposes and uses of writing, students learn that the main purpose of writing is to get a passing score on the writing test.

In real life, people rarely write five-paragraph essays or the types of writing assessed on state tests. Instead they write lists, letters, e-mail messages, text mes-

---

Box 8.2

Who Is Scoring Your Students' High-Stakes Writing Tests?

Most states have a writing portion of their high-stakes tests that someone must read to determine whether the student passes or fails. But who exactly is reading and scoring the students' writing?

Two journalists, David Glovin and David Evans (Glovin, 2000; Glovin & Evans, 2006), found that many states hired temporary "college-educated jobbers" to evaluate the writing. The readers were paid at rates just above minimum wage, though they could earn bonuses by working faster and scoring more exams. Many of those who were hired had questionable qualifications or even questionable degrees. Although some took the scoring of exams seriously, others were less careful and complained that the job was extremely boring. One scorer admitted: "There were times I'd be reading a paper every 10 seconds. . . . You could read them very fast. You could actually—I know this sounds very bizarre—but you could put a number on these things without actually reading the paper" (Glovin, 2000, p. 21).

Glovin and Evans documented many cases where students suffered adverse effects because of errors made by testing companies in scoring their tests and failing students who actually passed. Some of these students were forced to take remedial classes, others who were forced to repeat a grade, denied a high school diploma, or prevented from participating in graduation ceremonies. Others lost their admission to a college or university.

Glovin and Evans found that these errors are all too common because testing companies are under immense pressure to score and return tests as soon as possible. They predict that these errors and dire consequences for students are likely to continue because there is no oversight on the testing companies to hold them accountable for accurate scoring of tests.

When it comes to who scores student writing, Glovin (2000) asks, "Why not teachers?" Fortunately, some states do use their own teachers to score student writing, though teachers only scores students from schools outside their own. This practice does not ensure perfect scoring, but it is certainly better to use the professionals who actually teach writing to score student writing. Scoring is also an excellent form of professional development for teachers. After reading hundreds of student writing samples, they get a clearer sense of how students are doing and what changes they might make in their writing instruction.

sages, short notes, directions, instructions, and song or rap lyrics. They fill out forms. They post brief updates of what they are doing or thinking about on social networking sites on the Internet, such as Facebook, or via Twitter and write brief responses to their friends' posts. They post comments on-line in reaction to news articles, blog postings, videos, and their friends' photos, or they give feedback to others about products purchased or about the merchants they purchased them from. These more common uses of writing for authentic communication purposes within the lives of students in their sociocultural context typically receive little attention in the classroom. Teachers therefore need to ensure that their students are exposed to a wide variety of writing styles and genres. More important, teachers must help students see writing as a form of personal expression with many uses in real life and provide opportunities for students to write in class for authentic communicative purposes.

Classroom-Based Writing Assessment

Formative writing assessments used throughout the year enable teachers to gauge their students' progress and plan appropriate instruction and opportunities for students to improve their writing. As the quotation that opens this chapter points out, the only way for teachers to help ELLs improve their writing is to read what they write and then talk with them about their strengths and areas in need of improvement. In particular, teachers identify those areas in which they believe the student is ready to learn and make improvements. In addition, teachers assess student progress throughout the year by using portfolio assessments, and encourage students to assess their own work.

Andrew C. Cohen (1994) describes several forms of scoring student assessments: holistic, analytical, and primary trait or multi-trait. In holistic scoring, the teacher makes a judgment about the piece of writing as a whole and assigns it a single integrated score or level. Holistic scoring is typical in state English language proficiency assessments of writing, where teachers must determine the level of their students' writing. Figure 8.2 provides an example of the criteria used for holistic assessment of ELL writing in Texas. Cohen notes that the advantage of holistic scoring is that students are not assessed solely on the basis of one lesser aspect (e.g., grammatical ability) and that holistic scoring puts more emphasis on what the student did well rather than on the student's deficiencies. But there are several disadvantages. The single score (or level) does not provide diagnostic information, making it difficult to interpret the meaning of the score. Because several different subskills, of which the ELL student may have varying abilities, are lumped into one score, Cohen warns that the rating scale may confound writing ability with language proficiency.

Analytic scoring with a rubric is more common and helps teachers focus on different aspects of a student's writing. The rubrics consist of separate scales (e.g., 1–4) for each aspect, for example, *composing, style, sentence formation, usage,* and *mechanics* (see Figure 8.8). Cohen notes that although analytic scales keep the different categories separated and they are easy for teachers to learn how to use, they too have disadvantages. The use of specific categories may inhibit creative writing, particularly if teachers are tempted to teach students a stilted, paint-by-number style of writing that focuses on checking off the various categories. Writing, Cohen reminds us, is much more than the sum of its parts. Also, these scales require teachers to make qualitative judgments, which are difficult to make, and there is no assurance that teachers will use the scales according to the given criteria.

Domain Score*	Composing	Style	Sentence formation	Usage	Mechanics
4	Central idea with relevant details in a well organized text	Well chosen vocabulary; excellent sentence variety; tone that appeals to readers	Standard word order; no run-on sentences; no sentence fragments; effective transitions	Correct use of inflection (e.g., verb conjugations, plurals, prefixes, suffixes, adverbs, etc.); consistent tense; consistent subject-verb agreement; standard word meaning	Correct use of mechanics (capitalization, punctuation, spelling), and formatting
3	Central idea but with fewer details and some digressions	Acceptable vocabulary choices; some sentence variety; consistent but less appealing tone	Mostly standard word order, some run-on sentences; some sentence fragments; occasional omission of words; errors do not detract from meaning	Mostly correct use of inflections; mostly consistent tense and subject-verb agreement; mostly standard word meaning; errors do not detract from meaning	Mostly correct use of mechanics and formatting; errors do not detract from meaning
2	Lack of a focused central idea, or more than one idea; limited details and many digressions	Basic vocabulary; limited to no sentence variety; inconsistent tone	Some nonstandard word order; several run-on sentences; several sentence fragments; omissions of several words; errors somewhat detract from meaning	Some correct use of inflections; some consistency in tense and subject-verb agreement; several errors in word meaning; errors somewhat detract from meaning	Some correct use of mechanics and formatting; errors somewhat detract from meaning
1	Lack of a central idea; no details, random digressions	Limited vocabulary; choppy sentences; flat tone	Frequent nonstandard word order; mostly run-on sentences or sentence fragments; omissions of many words; errors frequently detract from meaning	Little to no correct use of inflections; frequent tense shifts; little to no subject-verb agreement; many errors in word meaning; errors fully detract from meaning	Little to no correct use of mechanics or formatting; errors fully detract from meaning.

*4 = consistent control; 3 = nearly consistent control; 2 = inconsistent control; 1 = little or no control

Figure 8.8 Analytic scoring rubric for writing. (Adapted from OMalley & Pierce, 1996.)

Primary trait and multi-trait scoring are commonly used for assessing writing on a specific topic. In primary trait scoring, the focus is on a single trait, such as the main idea. In multi-trait scoring, several traits can be considered, such as, for an opinion essay, clear opinion (main idea), adequate details to support the opinion, and a strong conclusion. The advantage of primary trait and multi-trait scoring is that they allow the rater to give detailed attention to just one or a few issues at a time. One disadvantage, however, is it is difficult for raters to focus on a single trait (or set of traits). Also, if the assessment does not consider other factors or traits, it may be too narrow.

The 6+1 Trait Writing model, developed by the Northwest Regional Education Laboratory, is an assessment and instructional framework that combines analytic and multi-trait scoring. It is used in schools throughout the country and teachers of ELLs have found it useful in assessing student writing and identifying the aspects of certain traits on which to focus their instruction to help students improve their writing. (6 + 1 Writing Trait, related links)

For an example of how a teacher might use an analytical scoring rubric to assess a student's writing, let's look at how Mr. Moreno, a teacher in San Antonio, Texas, evaluated a personal narrative essay by Maria, one of his 5th grade Spanish-speaking ELL students. Maria's writing sample, describing what she did over the spring break, is shown in Figure 8.9. Before looking at Mr. Moreno's scores in the text that follows, read the essay in Figure 8.9 and decide what scores, according to the analytic scoring rubric in Figure 8.8, you would give Maria in each of the five areas. Also identify Maria's strengths, the areas in which she is in need of improvement, and instructional strategies that could be used to help her improve her writing.

Spring Break

I wish this day never fines. On Sunday 12 I went to a cinsiañera, on tusday 16 I went to walk about 9 milles from san patrisio to San Fernando. on Sunday 19 I went to chuch and I went to a mexican resturant.

On Sunday 12 I went to a cinsiañero. The party was on San lorenso it began at 10.00 the fud was so good I curent stop eatan they were aibin Sopa de aros, carde gisada and carne asada! I eat som chocalet cake buit candy on top.

On tusday I went to wallk for my dad. I now you are wondering way. my dad was learnig about jesos. wen I was walking my cosend was en front of my so I acsededtly step on hes sou so he fel and then tasde kiun my wo is that meal

On Sunday I went to church the preace is my pren so he awis tas my hu.

The chure that I go to is cald San lorenso I went to See the birgen de guadalupe. Then I went to eat in las palapas.

wen you go to Spring Break you cald do stuf bery fun Taik my gent to church, I went for a walk, I went to a cinsiañera. ¿So wat did you do on Spring Break?

Figure 8.9 **Writing sample by Maria (pseudonym), a Spanish-speaking ELL student in Lizardo Moreno's 5th grade class, spring 2006.**

Mr. Moreno gave Maria the following scores:

Composing	4
Style	3
Sentence formation	3
Usage	2
Mechanics	2

While reflecting on Maria's strengths, the areas in which she is in need of improvement, and instructional strategies that could be used to help her improve her writing, he wrote the following comments:

> Maria is able to express her thoughts. She understands sentence structure. She knows that letters should be capitalized at the beginning of the sentence and that they should end with correct punctuation. She understands the concept of the different parts of the essay which includes the introduction, the body with 3 details, and the conclusion.
>
> Maria needs improvement with her spelling. She applies her prior knowledge of phonics in Spanish as she sounds out words in English, for example *wer* for *were* or *preace* for *priest*. For some words, she is not able to hear all the sounds of the letters and makes up the letters that she thinks go in it, for example *awis* for *always*. Maria learned that for an expository essay you should list the different topics you will write about, but brought that over into a narrative essay, where the author really needs to engage the reader using a story-like style.
>
> Maria would probably best be helped by enlisting the use of a personal word book where she could write the correct spelling for words that she likes to use all the time. In addition, I need to review with Maria the writing strategies for the different types of essays (narrative, expository, persuasive).

How did your scores compare with Mr. Moreno's? Do you agree with his assessment of Maria's strengths, needs, and strategies to help her improve? What more would you add? Might Maria, for example, benefit from some mini-lessons on capitalization and punctuation? It is clear from this sample that she has some knowledge of the rules. With a little more instruction, she can learn about the need to capitalize words at the beginning of sentences and proper nouns (e.g., Mexican, Tuesday, San Lorenzo) and to be more consistent in her use of ending punctuation.

Portfolio Assessment

An assessment of a single piece of student writing will not give a valid and reliable assessment of a student's writing ability. Students' writing development is not linear, and there may appear to be regressions as students take risks and try new genres. Thus, multiple measures are needed, in particular, portfolio assessment, based on writing samples collected throughout the year. The portfolio can include journal entries, early drafts and published writing from Writer's Workshop, samples from directed writing lessons, and samples of students' writing in different genres and content areas. It should include samples of unedited writing from throughout the year, and samples that highlight the students' strengths and areas in need of improvement. Some teachers determine what to include in the portfolio, while others work collaboratively with the students to determine which pieces to include.

Each entry should be dated and each should have been assessed separately. The teacher can then undertake formative assessments by reviewing student portfolios often throughout the year and summative assessments by reviewing them at the end of the school year.

Peer Assessment and Self-Assessment

Students should be involved in assessing their own writing and that of their peers. They can use the same rubrics the teacher uses, or a more "student-friendly" ver-

Writing Checklist

Conventions

- ❏ My paragraphs are sound.
- ❏ Each of my paragraphs has one main idea.
- ❏ I have used correct grammar.
- ❏ I have used correct punctuation.
- ❏ Periods are at the end of my sentences.
- ❏ I have quotation marks around dialogue.
- ❏ My spelling is correct.
- ❏ My handwriting is legible.

Fluency

- ❏ My sentences begin in different ways.
- ❏ My sentences build upon the ones before.
- ❏ My sentences are different lengths.
- ❏ The meaning of each of my sentences is clear.
- ❏ My sentences flow and use correct grammar.
- ❏ There are no run-ons.
- ❏ My sentences are complete.

Organization

- ❏ My report is sequenced in order.
- ❏ My introduction is exciting and inviting.
- ❏ My ideas flow and are well connected.
- ❏ I have a satisfying conclusion.

Capitalization

- ❏ I have capitalized the first word in each sentence.
- ❏ I have capitalized people and pet names.
- ❏ I have capitalized months and days.
- ❏ I have capitalized cities, states, and places.
- ❏ I have capitalized titles of books, movies, et cetera.

Word Choice

- ❏ Every word seems just right.
- ❏ I used a lot of describing words.
- ❏ My words paint pictures in the reader's mind.
- ❏ I used strong verbs like darted and exclaimed.
- ❏ I used synonyms to add variety.

Ideas

- ❏ I used a graphic organizer to create and organize ideas.
- ❏ My ideas are written in my own words.
- ❏ My report is clear and focused.
- ❏ I understand my topic.
- ❏ My details give the reader important information.
- ❏ My ideas relate to one another.
- ❏ I have listened to suggestions from the teacher or peers.

Figure 8.10   Self-assessment writing checklist. (Source: Manning, 2001.)

sion. Simpler versions are especially appropriate for younger students. Checklists are another form of assessment students can use to evaluate their own writing, especially during the editing stage of Writer's Workshop. The checklist in Figure 8.10 was developed by a teacher in Chicago. For rubrics and checklists to be effective, however, students must receive instruction, modeling, and practice in using them.

SUMMARY

Writing is a crucial skill for academic success in school and for effective communication in the sociocultural contexts in which students live. With new technologies, writing is becoming one of the primary means through which individuals in our society interact and communicate with each other. Research has revealed a strong connection between oral language proficiency, reading proficiency, and writing ability. Thus, teachers can help students become better writers by helping them become better listeners, speakers, and readers, and by helping them use books and other texts as models for their own writing.

The field of second language writing is relatively new, and though we lack a comprehensive model of second language writing, research has led to important findings. Writing development appears to be similar for English fluent and ELL students, and most students will move through predictable stages, though this development may not be totally linear. ELL student writing, however, differs in two important ways: (1) students with literacy skills in their native language can transfer many of these skills to English writing, and (2) ELL students' ability to express themselves in written English is highly dependent on their level of oral English proficiency. Thus, teachers should build on the strength of students' writing skills in their L1 (or develop them first in the L1, as in bilingual programs), providing extensive oral language development through ESL and sheltered content-area instruction. Writing should not be delayed until students reach a certain level of English proficiency, because students can also learn new vocabulary and further develop their oral skills through writing.

The writing *to, with,* and *by* model is a way of framing effective writing instruction through modeling, scaffolding, and ample practice for students to write meaningful text for authentic purposes. Writing *to* ELLs includes modeled writing; writing *with* ELLs includes interactive, shared, and guided writing. Writing *by* ELLs includes journal writing and Writer's Workshop. Process writing, through the Writer's Workshop model, provides scaffolding to help ELL students move through the various stages of the writing process, from the prewriting stage, during which they plan what they will write, through the publishing stage, during which they produce a polished draft and share it with real audiences, beginning with their teacher and classmates.

Teachers can support students' writing development during Writer's Workshop with regular teacher conferences and mini-lessons, and they can support independent writing through the use of word walls, thematic word charts, personal word books, and dictionaries, including bilingual ones.

Effective formative assessment of ELL student writing enables teachers to monitor their students' writing development and plan appropriate instruction and opportunities for guided practice accordingly. They can use analytic or multi-trait scoring rubrics to focus attention on various aspects of writing and pinpoint strengths and areas in need of improvement. Students can use these rubrics, in addition to checklists, to assess their own writing or that of their peers. Portfolios are an important tool for assessing students' growth as writers throughout the school year.

Discussion Questions

 1. **On-line Discussion Board**   If you have learned, or failed to learn, another language, what challenges did you face in learning to write in the new language? What role did your native language play in the development of your writing ability in that language?

2. Why is English oral language development such an important factor in ELL students' writing development in English?

3. What is the relationship between reading and writing ability? How can reading be used to help ELLs improve their writing?

4. Why are modeled writing, interactive writing, shared writing, guided writing, journal writing, and Writer's Workshop so important for ELLs? How does the writing *to, with,* and *by* framework provide scaffolding for ELLs to help them become proficient writers of English?

5. In a growing number of schools, much of the writing instruction focuses on narrowly training students to produce the type of writing required by their state's high-stakes test (e.g., personal narrative). What are some of the problems with this type of instruction? What can and what should teachers do about it?

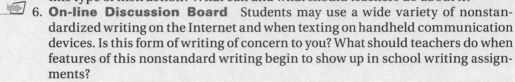 6. **On-line Discussion Board** Students may use a wide variety of nonstandardized writing on the Internet and when texting on handheld communication devices. Is this form of writing of concern to you? What should teachers do when features of this nonstandard writing begin to show up in school writing assignments?

Research Activities

1. **Wiki-This** Conduct a case study on the writing development of an ELL student. Collect several samples of the student's writing throughout the semester, including samples of different genres and from different stages of the writing process. Assess the writing using one or more of the following: (1) the rubric or criteria your state uses for its English language proficiency assessment of ELL student writing, (2) the rubrics provided in this chapter, (3) the 6+1 Writing Trait Scoring Guide (www.nwrel.org/assessment/pdfRubrics/6plus1traits.pdf). Using what you have learned in this chapter, discuss what you see as the growth and strengths in the student's writing and the areas in need of improvement. Determine instructional strategies to help the student improve his or her writing. In addition, compare your state's assessment rubric or criteria with the other rubrics you used. How appropriate or accurate do you feel the state version is? How did the results of the state version compare with the results of others? Which did you prefer, and why?

2. **Wiki This** Observe an ELL classroom, paying particular attention to the teacher's writing instruction. Describe the instructional techniques and strategies, and the skills he or she emphasizes. How many opportunities do students have to engage in independent writing? What scaffolding or other supports are available for students when writing? How much writing are students doing outside of their regular writing instruction? How effective do you feel the writing instruction for ELL is in this classroom? What strengths did you observe that you would like to include in your own classroom? What improvements could be made to the teacher's writing instruction?

3. Interview teachers about their writing instruction. What are their views about teaching writing to ELLs? What do they see as the role of writing in second language acquisition? How do they see the connections between reading and writing instruction? Do they view writing as an isolated academic subject, or do they view writing as an important communicative tool in sociocultural contexts? How do they balance providing effective writing instruction and helping students prepare for state high-stakes writing tests?

Recommended Reading

Ferris, D. R., & Hedgcock, J. (2004). *Teaching ESL composition: Purpose, process, practice.* Oxford: Routledge.
An overview of the theories and practices of the field of second language writ-

ing, with practical suggestions for effective writing instruction. Particularly appropriate for teachers of older ELL students.

Kendall, J., & Khuon, O. (2006). *Writing sense: Integrated reading and writing lessons for English language learners.* Portland, ME: Stenhouse.

A companion to *Making Sense,* also by veteran teachers Juli Kendall and Outey Khuon. Each chapter, as in the earlier book, focuses on one of the five stages of English proficiency, with examples for both younger and older ELL students.

Kroll, B. (Ed.). (1990). *Second language writing: Research insights for the classroom.* New York: Cambridge.

An in-depth and critical review of the research in the field of second language writing that includes discussion of the implications for classroom teachers.

Samway, K. D. (2006). *When English language learners write: Connecting research to practice, K-8.* Portsmouth, NH: Heinemann.

This teacher-friendly book focused on the elementary and middle school grades provides a review of research on the writing development of ELLs and shows teachers how to put this research into effective practice.

9

Content-Area Instruction for ELLs

Classrooms are, first and foremost, language environments. . . .
Language lies at the very heart of teaching and learning.

—Francis Bailey, Beverley Burkett, and Donald Freeman (2008)

KEY TERMS

- differentiated instruction
- sample performance indicators
- thematic teaching

GUIDING QUESTIONS

1. Why is it important for sheltered instruction to include both content and language objectives?
2. What are the benefits of an integrated, thematic approach to content-area instruction for ELLs?
3. What do the languages of math, science, and social studies include, and who is responsible for teaching them?
4. How can teachers integrate culture into their content-area instruction?
5. How can teachers differentiate their instruction for the ELLs in their classrooms?

ELL students face the challenge of learning to listen, speak, read, and write in English. At the same time they are also expected to meet the same grade-level academic content standards as their English-proficient peers. The school system is not set up to allow students to attain proficiency in English before learning academic content, nor should it be. ELL students are capable of learning academic content while developing proficiency in English if the instruction is specially designed.

The strongest program models for ELLs, as mentioned in Chapter 4, are bilingual programs in which some content areas are taught in the students' native language. Bilingual programs offer the best assurance that ELLs will not fall behind academically while they are learning English, and academic concepts learned in the native language can transfer to English once students have the language skills to talk about and use them. Even in bilingual program models, however, some content areas are taught through sheltered English instruction, the amount of which increases as students move up in grade level. In classrooms where native language instruction is not available or feasible, all content areas are taught using sheltered instruction.

In this chapter, we focus on ways in which teachers can provide effective sheltered instruction in the content areas of math, science, and social studies and also discuss the importance of art, music, and physical education instruction for ELLs. An overview of each content area is offered, followed by a brief discussion of the language demands that subject poses for ELLs and ideas for making instruction in these content areas comprehensible for ELLs. We look first at some of the principles of providing effective content-area instruction for ELLs.

A Principled Approach to Teaching Content to ELLs

The Sheltered Instruction Observation Protocol (SIOP) model provides a valuable tool for helping educators plan, deliver, and evaluate effective sheltered instruction (Echevarria, Vogt, & Short, 2007). The SIOP includes 30 observable items organized into eight key components of effective sheltered instruction (see Chapter 4 for details) and contains a rubric for evaluating each item on a scale of 0 to 4. The creators of the SIOP also provide lesson plan templates to help teachers design lessons based on these key components. Many of the principles, ideas, strategies, and techniques described in this chapter are also reflected in the SIOP.

Differentiated Instruction for ELLs in Content Classes

All students differ in terms of prior knowledge, academic proficiency, learning styles, sociocultural background, and so forth. Thus, one-size-fits-all instruction is extremely problematic, especially for the diverse group of students under the ELL label. When classrooms have a wide range of diversity in their students' language and academic proficiency, teachers should not provide all students with the exact same curricular materials, lessons, and instruction. Recall that the U.S. Supreme Court ruled in *Lau v. Nichols* that this sink-or-swim approach is unconstitutional because it fails to address the unique language and academic needs of ELL students.

Teachers need to tailor instruction to the unique language and academic needs of each student, that is, they need to provide differentiated instruction. This approach, of course, requires more work, but it is the hallmark of teachers who are true professionals. Anyone can give the same books, worksheets, homework, and tests to a group of students, praising those who do well and blaming those who fail. Effective teachers, however, know their students, and by using authentic formative assessments can continually determine their language and academic needs relative to the instructional goals. Teachers use this information to differentiate instruction so that their ELLs can achieve academically and continue to develop the English they need for academic success. This chapter illustrates ways that teachers can differentiate instruction for ELLs.

Language and Content-Area Objectives

Recall that sheltered instruction lessons include both language and content-area objectives, reflecting the fact that the content-area instruction is also language instruction for ELLs that supports but does not replace ESL instruction. When teaching content areas to ELLs, teachers must focus not only on helping students understand the concepts but also on helping ELLs learn the language necessary to communicate with others in accomplishing academic tasks related to the content-area concept.

For an example of how language and content-area objectives can be combined, consider a science lesson on the water cycle. Students will collaborate in small groups to create posters illustrating the water cycle and prepare an oral presentation to the class using their completed poster. The content and language objectives for this lesson might look something like this:

Content Objectives: *Students will . . .*

- Identify and describe the stages of the water cycle
- Create a poster illustrating the stages of the water cycle in sequence

Language Objectives: *Students will . . .*

■ Use key vocabulary to discuss and describe the water cycle
■ Use oral and written English with members of the group to *identify* the stages in the cycle, *describe* each stage, and *explain* the importance of these stages
■ Use oral and written English to collaborate with other students to *plan* and *develop* a water-cycle poster
■ Make an oral presentation to the class in which the group *identifies*, *describes*, and *explains* the stages of the water cycle *using sequencing language*

Note that the content objectives are the same for all students in the class. Note also that the language objectives direct attention to the language of the content area, that is, the key vocabulary, genres, and registers that all students need to learn. The language objectives, however, will need to be differentiated according to students' English language proficiency and literacy levels.

More specifically, in this lesson all students need to learn new academic vocabulary, such as *precipitation*, *condensation*, and *evaporation*. Key vocabulary about the water cycle also includes words such as *cloud, water, rain, storm, sun, sunshine, heat, rise, fall, puddle, lake, ocean*—common words already known by proficient English speakers that may be unknown by some of the ELLs. Further, all students need to be able to use the language of science to *identify, describe*, and *explain* the stages of the water cycle orally and in writing, and the formal language necessary for an oral presentation. English speakers will have the oral English they need to interact with others in their group, but ELLs may vary in their ability to use English to, for example, agree, disagree, give opinions, or make suggestions. ELLs also may vary in their ability to comprehend and use sequencing language in a discussion of the various stages.

Adding language objectives to a science lesson is one way to provide differentiated instruction, because it adds a focus beyond that provided for non-ELL students. However, the expected level of performance of each ELL related to the language objectives may not be the same. Each student's level of English proficiency must also be taken into consideration. A newly arrived ELL student, for example, would have great difficulty serving as the group's spokesperson to describe in detail the intricacies of the water cycle, even if he or she has the same knowledge and understanding as the non-ELLs. Students at this proficiency level could, however, label and read the names of the different stages on their group's poster, and then a student with higher language proficiency could provide detailed descriptions.

TESOL English Language Proficiency Standards for the Content Areas

The TESOL English Language Proficiency Standards for the content areas are a useful tool for differentiated instruction for ELLs based on their level of English proficiency. Recall that for each standard, TESOL provides sample performance indicators, which are examples of observable language behaviors ELLs can be expected to demonstrate as they engage in classroom tasks. As noted in Chapter 6, most of the performance indicators contain three parts: language function (e.g., *discuss and give examples*), content (e.g., *uses of natural phenomenon*), and support or strategy (e.g., *from collections or pictures*). These sample indicators can give teachers ideas for creating their own indicators in connection with each lesson or activity's language objectives.

The following discussion includes sample performance indicators for each of the grade-level clusters and each of the language domains for math, science and social studies. In each of these examples, pay attention to how the degree of linguistic complexity increases as the need for support decreases across the five levels of English proficiency while the content remains consistent.

Strategies for Modifying Textbooks and Instructional Materials

Grade-level content-area curricular materials were not developed with ELLs in mind, and therefore modifications are required to make grade-level content-area instructional materials accessible. Strategies for modifying text in textbooks include outlining, using graphic organizers, rewriting the text in simplified English, and reading it aloud with students, pausing to paraphrase, explain, or provide examples to help ELLs understand the meaning. Jodi Reiss (2005) suggests that teachers give instruction in and practice using textbook aides: the table of contents, the index, chapter titles and section headings, outlines and questions, chapter summaries and review sections, glossaries, text boxes and highlighted areas, text organizers, and graphics and other visuals. This exercise is an example of reading *with* students in the content-area classroom. Fortunately, there is a growing trend among publishers of content-area curricular programs to address the needs of ELL students. For example, some teacher's guides may include suggestions for modifying content and activities to make them more comprehensible for ELLs. Some publishers also provide separate supplemental materials in simplified English or in other languages.

Caution and professional judgment, however, must be exercised with these resources. Some ELL educators have found them to be superficial and forced. Fred Dobb (2004), for example, reviewed the ELL suggestions in science textbook teacher's guides and found many of these tacked-on strategies to be incomplete and of little use. He provides a list of questions teachers should ask when evaluating such teacher's guides (see Box 9.1). In most instances, more substantial modifications and adaptations may be needed to make the content accessible and comprehensible to ELLs.

Thematic Teaching and Lesson Planning

The number-one complaint among classroom teachers is that there is not enough time to teach everything. This problem has been exacerbated by pressure to raise test scores. More and more, teachers have been pressured to provide narrow teaching-to-the-test instruction, often using curricular programs and test-prep materials mandated by the school or district. To ensure coverage of all content areas, teachers can use thematic teaching. Teachers select a theme that can be explored through all content areas. For younger children the theme might be topics such as *Butterflies* or *Ocean Life*. For older students, themes can be more abstract and broad, such as *Change* or *Inequality.* Thematic teaching allows easy crossover among content areas. A science lesson on weather, for example, could incorporate elements of math, art, and writing by having students record the temperature every day for a week, draw pictures illustrating the weather for each day, and writing about which day they felt had best weather.

Thematic teaching, however, does more than save time. It provides and builds on students' background knowledge and thus facilitates comprehensible input. If students learn about the weather through science instruction, they will under-

Box 9.1

Evaluating ELL Suggestions in Mainstream Textbooks

A current trend among education textbook publishers is to make their curricular programs more marketable by including side-bar suggestions for adapting lessons to meet the needs of ELL students. Dobb (2004) suggests that teachers ask the following questions to evaluate "the overall seriousness and quality" of a teacher's guide ELL suggestions. Although his focus is on science textbooks, these questions can be modified to address any mainstream content-area textbook that includes ELL instruction suggestions.

1. Is there a means for checking ELL comprehension of the unit content? If students didn't get it, what do I do?
2. Do these strategies utilize and lead to the independent use of science process skills?
3. What correspondence exists between the strategies and the English language proficiency levels of my students?
4. Are strategies consistently placed throughout the teachers' guide?
5. Are the activities equal in rigor and challenges to those for all students?
6. Are strategies provided for scaffolding instruction in the introduction of new materials?
7. Are strategies provided which lead to an instructional conversation between ELLs and their teachers?
8. Do the activities capitalize on the visual and physical properties of science experiments and demonstrations? (p. 34)

stand more when they read about the weather in other content areas. Teachers can use a template to plan thematic lessons, filling in simple ideas for lessons in each content area (see Figure 9.1). For example, for the theme of Immigration, under Reading, we might put, "Read *How Many Days to America*"; under Writing, "Write stories about family's immigration"; under Math, "Make a bar graph showing from what countries students' families emigrated," and so forth. Once this form is complete, each idea can be developed into a full sheltered instruction content-area lesson or activity.

The Use of Literature across the Content Areas

Although grade-level textbooks are typically written at a level inaccessible to ELL students, teachers can find other books dealing with the same concepts at more accessible levels. They can read these books aloud to the class or use them for shared reading and guided reading to reinforce and further develop content-area knowledge. Works of both fiction and nonfiction with content-area themes are appropriate. For a social studies unit on the early settlement of America, for example, the teacher could supplement the material that appears in the textbook by reading aloud *Sarah Morton's Day*. The book contains vivid photographs and descriptions of life in Plymouth Plantation from the perspective of a young pilgrim girl. The California Department of Education provides an extensive and searchable database of literature that can be used to supplement math and science instruction (available at www.cde.ca.gov/CI/sc/ll/).

With older ELL students, teachers may be tempted to use content-area textbooks from lower grade levels. Although these books may be beneficial because they provide content similar to the more challenging grade-level textbooks but written at a more accessible level, teachers should be cautious about using them. As

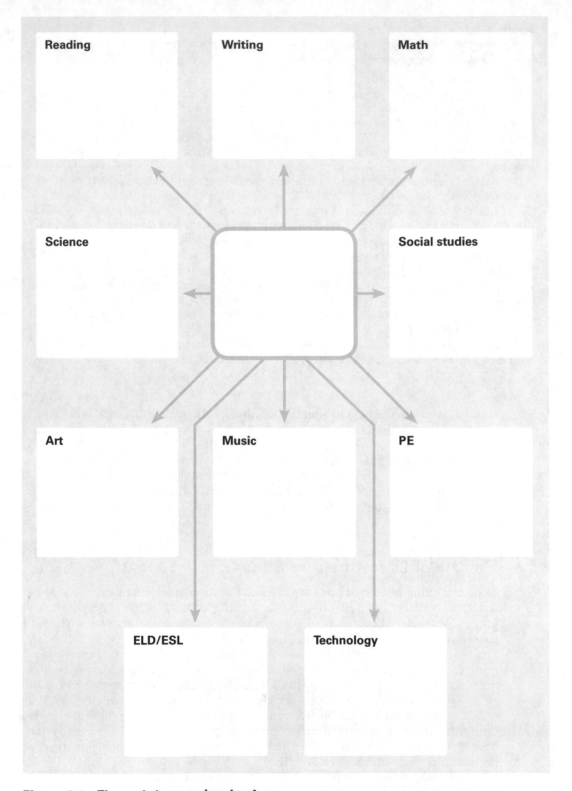

Reading

Writing

Math

Science

Social studies

Art

Music

PE

ELD/ESL

Technology

Figure 9.1 Thematic lesson planning form

Reiss (2005) notes, doing so may send a subtle, unintended message that the students using them are less capable than the other classmates.[1]

Some educational publishers, recognizing the need for supplemental textbooks, particularly for older ELL students, have begun publishing books that are designed to help ELLs learn academic vocabulary and key content-area concepts in English. These textbooks, which are aligned to specific content areas but not grade levels, feature simplified text, vivid graphics and illustrations labeled with new vocabulary, questions and exercises, and teacher's guides for providing lessons in the language of content areas. The series ACCESS: Building Literacy through Learning, by the Great Source Education Group, includes textbooks for ELLs in grades 5 through 12 in English, math, science, social studies, and other areas. Thomson/Heinle produces *Gateway to Science: Vocabulary and Concepts* for students in grades 6 through 12. It is important to note that these textbooks are not designed to replace grade-level textbooks but rather to provide a scaffold to prepare students to use grade-level texts.

Multicultural Perspectives

Integrating ELL students' cultures into instruction is easily achieved in language arts by reading relevant books. Instruction in math, science, social studies, physical education, and the arts can also incorporate multicultural perspectives and contributions and should go beyond the surface level of culture (e.g., food, clothing, and holidays). Teachers should look for books and other materials that deal with the realities of students' lives and the diverse communities in which they live. The next section offers examples for each content areas.

Sheltered Instruction in the Content Areas

Sheltered content teachers can make math, science, and social studies comprehensible to the ELLs in their classes. For each area, the following discussion looks at five topics: the language of the content area, making instruction comprehensible to ELLs, modifying instructional materials, using literature, and integrating students' cultures. Charts showing the sample performance indicators from the TESOL standards for math, science, and social studies are also included. These are followed by a brief discussion of the importance of art, music, and physical education for ELLs. (Music, document; Art, document; Physical Education, document)

Mathematics

Math is one of the main subjects covered on state high-stakes tests, and therefore, along with language arts, it tends to get the most attention in the classroom. Unfortunately, teachers may feel pressure to push through math instruction at a rapid pace in order to cover all concepts that may appear on the test. Math learning is cumulative and basic concepts must be mastered before students can learn more advanced concepts. It is therefore imperative that ELLs receive comprehensible math instruction to avoid falling far behind their grade-level peers. (For the sample performance indicators from the TESOL standards for math, see Figure 9.2.)

1: One strategy for avoiding this problem is to discretely use photocopies of relevant sections of the textbooks, rather than require students to hold up textbooks with the lower grade-level emblazoned on the front or side for all their peers to see. Or, teachers could put covers on the textbooks to obscure this information.

Standard 3: Language of Math
Grade level cluster: pre-K–K

Domain: Speaking Topic: Numbers and operations				
Level 1	Level 2	Level 3	Level 4	Level 5
Use number words to count (up to 10) objects (e.g., candies, crayons) with a partner.	Repeat phrases involving addition and subtraction (e.g., in choral chants such as "Five Little Monkeys.").	Use comparative phrases (e.g., "more than," "less than," "bigger") with a partner to describe the relationship between two objects.	Pose comparative questions (e.g., "What is one more than . . . ?") to classmates.	Discuss grade-level math stories using comparative language (e.g., "one more," "less than," "more than").

Grade level cluster: 1–3

Domain: Listening Topic: Time (digital and analog)				
Level 1	Level 2	Level 3	Level 4	Level 5
Draw or show on clocks responses to oral directions (e.g., "Put the big hand on the 5.").	Role-play activities associated with different times of day in response to oral statements (e.g., "I got to bed at half past 8.").	Illustrate, by drawing or using clocks, responses to oral questions or statements (e.g., "Show me a time between 6 and 9 o'clock" or "When do we eat lunch?").	Estimate elapsed amount of time from oral word problems using visual or graphic support.	Make inferences from oral grade-level story problems or classroom narratives.

Figure 9.2 TESOL ELP Standards, sample performance indicators for math. (Source: TESOL, 2006a, p. 78.)

The Language of Mathematics

A major misperception about math is that it is easy for ELLs because it's mostly numbers. Research shows, however, that math tests have high language demands that pose significant difficulties for ELLs (Abedi & Lord, 2001). My own research has documented the tremendous challenges math can pose for newcomer ELLs (Wright & Li, 2006, 2008). Clara Lee Brown (2005) argues that math has a language all its own and constitutes a third language ELLs have to learn.

Theresa C. Dale and Gilberto J. Cuevas (1992) analyzed the mathematics register and found that it has unique vocabulary, syntax, semantic properties, and text features. Words such as *divisor, denominator,* and *quotient* are rarely used outside of math, and many common words, such as *table, column,* and *face,* have specific meanings in math contexts. Imagine the confusion an ELL might feel when the teacher says, "Look at the table to find the answers." In addition, the math register has a unique set of complex phrases, such as *least common multiple* and *negative exponent.*

The syntax of math can be very confusing for ELLs. There is often no one-to-one correspondence between words and the symbols they represent. For example, "*x* is less than twenty-two" takes more words to say than symbols to write "$x < 22$." Also, word order may differ from the way numbers and symbols appear in a numeric sentence. For example, $(x + y)^2$ would be read, "The square of the sum of *x* and *y*." As Dale and Cuevas (1992) have noted, mathematical texts are dense and conceptually packed. They require left-to-right as well as up-and-down eye movement and must be read more slowly than natural language texts and often several times. Furthermore, the texts are often crowded with symbolic devices, such as charts and graphs.

Word problems can be particularly challenging because they typically contain complex syntax and difficult—and usually irrelevant—vocabulary. Solving word problems correctly requires advanced skills in English reading comprehension. Brown (2005) found that there is a high correlation between English reading ability and performance on math tests. ELL students who are highly skilled in math will have difficulty demonstrating those skills until they attain enough proficiency to handle the linguistic demands of math instruction and assessment in English.

Another challenge for newcomer ELLs is that they may have learned mathematical symbols and algorithms for problem solving in their home country that differ from those taught in the United States. For example, in several Asian countries the decimal is used to separate place value and the comma is used for number values less than 1—the exact opposite of how they are used in the United States (e.g., 5,300,200.10 would be written 5.300.200,10). And algorithms for long division differ substantially in other countries, where more emphasis is put on mental math.

Making Math Instruction Comprehensible for ELLs

To help students learn the vocabulary and language structures of math, teachers can make illustrated math word charts to go along with math units, such as geometric shapes or measurement words. Or better, they can make these word charts with the students during shared or modeled writing. Note the wide variety of charts and visuals in the photograph in Figure 9.3 of an elementary school classroom, including a number line, a 100 chart, a calendar, coins, a clock, a list of ordinal numbers, a chart of skip counting by 2s, 5s, and 10s, math facts, and clue words for word problems signaling the correct operation. Charts like these provide visual support and offer opportunities for daily practice of these concepts.

ELL students can get hands-on practice with pattern blocks, sorting manipulatives, counting manipulatives, base-10 blocks for teaching place value and regrouping, pie-slice manipulatives for learning fractions, clocks, play money, rulers, protractors, compasses, three-dimensional shapes, measuring spoons and cups, balance scales, and weights. These and other manipulatives help ELLs understand concepts that they might not fully grasp if they were only to hear them explained or see them in print. They also allow ELLs to demonstrate what they know, without having to rely only on words, spoken or written.

Teachers can also make math comprehensible for ELLs with primary language support and technology designed to enhance or support math instruction. For example, several software programs use the computer's multimedia capabilities to

Figure 9.3   Calendar wall from Mrs. Armstrong's classroom, Scobee Elementary School, Northside Independent School District, San Antonio, Texas, 2007.

(Photo by author.)

help students understand and practice math concepts, often in the context of games and other entertaining activities. Students can also use multimedia programs such as KidPix, Kidspiration/Inspiration, and PowerPoint to create their own presentations that demonstrate their understanding of math and can use programs such as Excel to create their charts and graphs.

Modifying Math Instructional Materials

Teachers can use role playing to help ELL students understand new vocabulary and unfamiliar concepts in word problems. In a unit on money and how to make change, for example, the math textbook might offer the following word problem:

> Michael's mother pays him $20 for mowing the front lawn. Michael goes the store and buys a toy train for $8, and a music CD for $10. He also wants to buy a video game for $15, but he realizes he does not have enough money. If he pays the cashier with a $20 bill, how much change should he get in return after his purchase?

To solve this problem, ELL students must know how to read English. Even if they have some reading ability, however, they may have trouble understanding the problem. Some of the contextual information may be unknown to them, such as mowing the lawn (many may not have lawns or lawn mowers). The words *cashier* and *purchase* may be unknown to them. Also, with limited proficiency in English, they might well be confused by the irrelevant information about the cost of the video game. ELLs will be unable to simply pull out the numbers and figure out the operation. To determine which numbers and what operation to use to set up the problem, students must be able to read and fully comprehend the text.

To modify this and other word problems, the teacher could have students role play similar situations, using, in this instance, a toy cash-register, play money, and several items marked with different prices. Once the teacher has helped students learn the vocabulary and language needed for this activity, they could take on the roles of customer and cashier and practice counting out their money and making change. After role playing, students could be guided in writing word problems to record the situations they acted out (e.g., Reggie has a $10 bill. He bought a magazine for $3 and a candy bar for $2. How much change should he receive?). Eventually, the students would be able to answer other word problems without the hands-on manipulatives and role playing. Note how the same math concepts are being covered, but modified and scaffolded in this way, the content becomes more accessible to ELLs.

Using Literature to Support Math Instruction

Many books are available, both fiction and nonfiction, with mathematical themes. My students loved the *M&M's Brand Counting Book*. Despite its blatant advertising of candy to impressionable young children, the book provides an entertaining way to explore number concepts and easily leads to extension activities involving the use of yummy manipulatives. *The Doorbell Rang* tells the story of a family's batch of cookies that gets further and further divided as more and more friends come over and the cookies must be evenly shared. Cindy Neuschwander has written a series of books appropriate for upper elementary and lower secondary students in which solving math problems is central to the plot; titles include *Sir Cumference and the First Round Table: A Math Adventure, Mummy Math: An Adventure in Geometry,* and *Patterns in Peru: An Adventure in Patterning*. For students in the secondary grades, *What's Your Angle, Pythagoras? A Math Adventure* provides a fictionalized account of Pythagoras discovering his theorem that can help readers understand the relevant math.

Integrating Students' Cultures into Math Instruction

Integrating students' cultures into math instruction is not simply a matter of writing word problems with ethnic names that deal with supposedly "cultural" content. While word problems should have a diversity of names, great care must be taken to avoid introducing offensive stereotypes.

A better and more effective approach is to help students connect math to their own lives in their families, their communities, and the world. For example, an elementary school in Livermore, California, undertook a project through a collaborative on-line project called Connecting Math to Our Lives.[2] The students started by learning about biographies and practiced writing some on their own. They then went to their school library, where they examined and categorized the biographies by race, class, disability, and gender, using percentages, fractions, and bar graphs. After sorting, classifying, recording, and using math to summarize and analyze their data, the students found that the vast majority of the biographies were about dead White men. The project did not end there. The findings inspired the students to ask questions that led to discussions about equity and representation. Their work extended to collaboration with another school, whose students also analyzed their library's biography collection. Later, the two groups worked together to analyze the biography collection of the main branch of the San Francisco Public Library, where they found imbalances similar to the ones at their own school libraries. Students from both schools met with the public librarians to present their findings and their concerns about the collection. Note that the students also used oral and written language for expository and persuasive purposes in this authentic task.

Math instruction can also include discussions of the multicultural history of math and in particular the contributions of Indian and Arabic mathematicians. The 10 digits of our number system (0 1 2 3 4 5 6 7 8 9), for example, are called Hindu-Arabic numbers, a reflection of their origin. Explanations and charts illustrating the history and origins of our number system can be found on the Internet by googling "Hindu-Arabic numeral system." Also, *algebra* is an Arabic word (*al-gebra;* originally *al-jebr*), first used in writing by the mathematician Muhammad ben Musa al-Khwarizmi in the 9th century CE (Daney, 2007). Students may be surprised to learn that the *al-* prefix in Arabic is a definite-article prefix roughly equivalent to *the* in English. Presenting this history to students may help counter confusing messages they receive in the post 9/11 United States about the Middle East and the Arab world.

Science

Science has always been a popular subject for sheltered instruction because its tangible concepts and processes, which facilitate hands-on learning, make it fairly easy to shelter for ELL students. Furthermore, students are naturally curious about how things in the world work and thus respond well to science instruction. The science experiments on the children's television show *ZOOM* and other children's television shows with a science theme, such as *Bill Nye, the Science Guy; Fetch! with Ruff Ruffman; The Magic School Bus;* and the zany animal show *Zoboomafoo,* are very popular. Even shows that are less educationally oriented, such as *Jimmy Neutron, Boy Genius,* owe their success to children's scientific wonder. Many science fiction television shows and movies captivate viewers of all ages.

Unfortunately, when NCLB testing requirements focused on math and reading soon after passage of the legislation, science received less attention, especially in

---

2: Their story appears on the Connecting Math Web site (www.orillas.org/math/projex.html) under the title "Counting Biographies to See Whose Stories Are Being Told." It is also described in Cummins, Brown, & Sayers, 2007.

schools in high-poverty areas with large number of ELLs. Teachers there felt pressure to teach to the test, and science was all but eliminated. But NCLB also requires students must be tested in science three times between 3rd grade and high school. When science tests were first developed and administered, many schools realized the cost of their having neglected science instruction for several years, and science is making a comeback as an important content area. Many educators remain concerned, however, that high-stakes science tests will result in narrow teach-to-the-test science instruction, focused more on memorization than on discovery and substantive learning. (For the sample performance indicators from the TESOL standards for science, see Figure 9.4.)

The Language of Science

The language of science can be confusing for ELL students because, like the language of math, it uses many words from everyday life that have different meanings. ELL students may know that they eat off a *plate*, but in studying earth science, they will encounter *plate tectonics.* They may know words such as *cell* (as in *cell phone*), *tissue* (something to use when you sneeze), and *organ* (a musical instrument at church), but in the life sciences these words have very different meanings. In addition, students will need to learn many new vocabulary words for each topic they encounter in science.

Just as important as specialized science vocabulary is the way language is used to learn and talk about science (i.e., the Discourse of science). Students learn to ask questions and form hypotheses just as scientists do. Students make predictions and come up with explanations. They design experiments, collect data, identify and manipulate variables, record results, and draw conclusions. In moving through the scientific process, students collaborate with others in a group. They also com-

Standard 4: Language of Science
Grade level cluster: 4–5

Domain: Reading				
Topic: Properties of matter; energy sources				
Level 1	Level 2	Level 3	Level 4	Level 5
Find examples of forms of energy from billboards, magazines, and newspapers.	Sequence steps of energy use and depletion from phrases and illustrations.	Follow illustrated directions to test hypotheses about energy in scientific inquiry.	Interpret results of inquiry from illustrated text (e.g., in lab reports).	Infer applications of information about energy gathered from modified grade-level text or inquiry-based projects.

Domain: Writing				
Topic: Solar system; Earth's history				
Level 1	Level 2	Level 3	Level 4	Level 5
Replicate labeled representations of models of the planets or solar system.	Make notes from observations from videos or illustrations.	Compare features from models, videos, or illustrations using graphic organizers.	Maintain illustrated records, logs, or journals of features, events, or observations.	Explain the physical world with examples of features, events, or observations.

Figure 9.4 TESOL ELP Standards, sample performance indicators for science. (Source: TESOL, 2006a, p. 75.)

municate their findings in the unique genre of science reports; even oral reports of scientific findings are expected to use specific language forms. Each of these is representative of different language functions that are often unique to science. Thus, to be successful in science, ELLs must learn how to talk the talk of science.

Mary J. Schleppegrell (2002) acknowledges that even non-ELL students must learn new concepts and related vocabulary in science instruction. However, she points out that ELLs are at a particular disadvantage because in addition to their lack of proficiency in English, they may also have less experience with the genre and register expected in their science assignments. One particular challenge in science is the writing of lab and other science reports—a specific genre which requires a unique discourse style and textual structure. Schleppegrell notes:

> This means that ESL students need to learn to adopt the register features that give their work the authoritativeness and the textual structure that realize the meaning expected in standard academic English. Academic registers have evolved the way they have because they are functional for their purposes, and if students do not draw on appropriate register features, they fail to achieve the purposes of the text. (p. 140)

Barbara J. Merino and Lorie Hammond (2002) explain how teachers must go beyond a simple focus on grammar and help students gain sociolinguistic competence as they learn to write within the culture of scientists:

> Teachers have to become aware of the complexity of learning to write the discourse of science. They must understand that grammatical competence is only one aspect of what children are learning as they write. Sociolinguistic competence, defining the audience for whom they write and knowing how that affects how they write, is critically important. Teachers need to be aware that the discourse of science adheres to the rules of a culture of scientists. These rules are complex and involve not only grammatical competence, but also sociolinguistic discourse, and strategic competence used in unique ways depending on the genre or task. (p. 241)

Making Science Instruction Comprehensible for ELLs

Research conducted by Olga A. Amaral (2002) has shown that discovery (or inquiry-based) science is an effective means for helping ELL students successfully learn science concepts and develop English language skills. James H. Rupp (1992) emphasizes that in all grades discovery science should include the processes that are at the heart of science instruction: observing, using space–time relationships, using numbers, measuring, classifying, communicating, predicting, inferring, interpreting results, formulating hypotheses, controlling variables, defining operations, and experimenting. Rupp notes that hands-on activities provide rich language opportunities for students to explore real experiences using purposeful language in a meaningful context.

Dobb (2004) describes a hands-on science classroom as a rich, highly motivating language laboratory, pointing out that discovery science offers an arena in which ELLs can try out their maturing ideas about scientific phenomena using their expanding English language skills. He adds, "It is only through expressing oneself about 'something' that another language adheres to our lives and becomes part of our identities. Science content becomes that 'something.' What is learned in science through English remains as part of one's understanding of the universe and represents a step in one's growth into a second language" (p. 14).

Teachers, however, need to ensure that their science classroom is indeed a language laboratory. Juliet Langman and Robert Bayley (2007) tracked the progress of a newcomer ELL student they called "little Manuel" in a middle school science classroom in a large urban South Texas school district. They found that little Manuel had very few opportunities to develop his English language skills in the science classroom. Part of the problem, they found, stemmed from the teacher's false assumption that simply hearing English all day would be sufficient for little Manuel to learn English. An in-depth analysis of audio and video recordings made throughout the semester revealed, however, that little Manuel had few opportunities to practice sustained English while focusing on scientific tasks. Of particular concern was that even though the science teacher had received some SIOP training and acknowledged the need to provide specialized assistance for her ELLs, she was unclear about how to provide that assistance. Some of her attempts to help little Manuel were actually counterproductive in facilitating his English language development. What may have been lacking in this teacher's classroom were clearly articulated language objectives and a system for monitoring and assessing little Manuel's progress in meeting these objectives.

Consider the following example of an inquiry-based science lesson called Mystery Powders, that enables students to learn new vocabulary and provides opportunities for students to practice sustained English.[3] Students are organized into cooperative learning groups with four members. Each group is given a bag containing a different white powder (e.g., baking soda, flour, powdered milk, cleaning powder), a magnifying glass, a cup of water, a spoon, waxed paper, and a recording sheet (see Figure 9.5). The students' task is to figure out what their powder is by using their senses of sight, smell, and touch. (They may not use their sense of taste, because some of the powders may be inappropriate to eat.) They then make a hypothesis about what their powder is and what will happen when it is mixed with water. Next they conduct their experiment and record their results. Based on the results, they decide whether they want to keep or revise their hypothesis.

In this lesson, the main content objective is that students will use the scientific process to identify their mystery powder, and the main language objective is that students will interact with each other in English, using their language skills to complete the assignment (e.g., *asking* questions, *discussing* results, *recording* observations, *reporting* findings). Each student in the group is given a specific role:

Student #1 – Pick up and set up materials
Student #2 – Lead group in observations and conducting the experiment
Student #3 – Record results on the sheet
Student #4 – Report findings to class

To meet the content and language objectives for this lesson, students will need vocabulary to describe how powders might look, smell, and feel. One way to provide it is to create a vocabulary chart with the students (through modeled or shared writing or as a separate ESL lesson) before they conduct the experiment (see Figure 9.6). To be particularly effective, the teacher could bring in items (realia) for students to see, feel, and smell that illustrate the meanings of these words. Once the chart is completed and students begin the science project, the teacher monitors each group, helping students refer back to the chart as necessary to find the words to discuss and record their observations of their mystery powder. Students can use the completed recording sheet when making an oral report of their findings to their class, and the teacher can use it to assess the students' performance.

Modifying Science Instructional Materials

Mainstream science textbooks pose considerable challenges for ELL students. As Dobb (2004) points out:

> The factual and direct style of scientific writing can be dull, impersonal, and decidedly harder to understand than narrative fiction. The English classroom, where the most

---

3: I did not invent this activity, nor do I know who did, but it is popular among science teachers. I learned about it from Dr. Marilyn Thompson, one of my statistics professors, who is a former high school science teacher. I did, however, create the forms in Figure 9.5 and Figure 9.6 that accompany this lesson.

🌱 Mystery Powders 🔭

What do you think your mystery powder is? Use your senses and the scientific process to find out!

Observe:

How does the powder look?_____

_____

How does the powder feel?_____

_____

How does the powder smell?_____

_____

Hypothesis:

What do you think your powder is? _____

Based on your hypothesis, what do you think will happen to your powder when mixed with water?_____

_____

Experiment:

Mix your powder with small amounts of water.

Results:

What happened?_____

_____

Did this result confirm or reject your hypothesis?_____

    If reject, what is your new hypothesis (i.e., what do you think your powder
    is now?) _____

What other experiments could you perform to determine what your mystery powder is?_____

_____

Figure 9.5　**Mystery Powder recording sheet**

direct teaching of language occurs, rarely exposes the EL to expository writing with complex content. In the textbook, content is often unfamiliar, and new vocabulary is introduced rapidly and constantly. Details are usually presented before general ideas and concepts. Dense passages require rereading. There is infrequent repetition or restatement of information.

When faced with fact-packed textbooks and the necessity to slow down and reread material, even the most motivated EL complains of fatigue and frustration. Students

SIGHT	SMELL	TOUCH
It looks ...	**It smells ...**	**It feels ...**
white	good	hard
brown	bad	soft
dirty	sweet	powdery
off-white	sour	fine
tan	bitter	coarse
bright		rough
hard	**Like ...**	dry
soft	(name of	wet
powdery	food or	smooth
shiny	powder)	sticky
sandy		
fine	**Or ...**	**Like ...**
coarse	it has	small rocks
rough	no odor	crystals
dry		
wet		(name of
smooth		food or
messy		powder)
dusty		
Like ...		
crystals		
small rocks		
snow		

Figure 9.6 Vocabulary helper for Mystery Powder science lesson

with strong academic preparation in their primary language may need two or three times as long to read the textbook as they would to read the same material in their stronger language. Without careful instruction, their engagement with the text and comprehension tend to be low. Frequently, they miss the major science concepts and find little positive reinforcement in their attempts to keep up. (pp. 27–28)

One of the best ways to give ELL students access to the concepts of science is to get the concepts off the pages of the textbook. Students will learn a concept if they experience and discover it rather than just read about it. No teacher, however, can realistically turn every concept in the textbook into a hands-on, inquiry-based lesson. Other options are to provide students, especially those at the intermediate and advanced levels, with instruction in the structure and supports in the textbook. Outlines and graphic organizers can help them identify the main ideas and information structure of the text. Teachers can also rewrite parts of the text in simplified English and use supplemental science textbooks, designed for ELL students, such as *Access Science* by Elva Duran, Jo Gusman, and John Shefelbine or *Gateway to Science* by Tim Collins and Mary Jane Maples.

Using Literature to Support Science Instruction

Nonfiction books can be found on a multitude of scientific themes. A thematic unit on the solar system, for example, could incorporate books by Seymour Simon, such as *Our Solar System,* and others by the same author on the sun, the moon, the individual planets, stars, and comets, meteors, and asteroids. Older students with higher levels of English proficiency would benefit from supplemental books such as Kenneth C. Davis's *Don't Know Much about Space* and *Don't Know Much about the Solar System,* written and illustrated in a much more lively manner than the typical grade-level textbook. On the fiction side, there are dozens of titles in the Magic School Bus series, from simple picture books to longer chapter books, on a wide variety of scientific topics. Students' interest in science could also be piqued by reading science fiction.

Students can also make their own science books to develop and practice their written English language skills and to demonstrate their knowledge of science. The California Science Project features on its Web site several books on science topics written by ELL students in collaboration with their teachers (csmp.ucop.edu/csp/ ScienceBook/sciencebooks.html). These books provide an excellent illustration of what ELLs can do with appropriate and effective guidance and scaffolding.

Integrating Students' Cultures into Science Instruction

The National Science Teachers Association (NSTA, 2000), in a position paper on multicultural science, declares, "Curricular content must incorporate the contributions of many cultures to our knowledge of science." Echoing this sentiment, the Saint Paul Public School District Multicultural Resource Center (n.d.) stresses the importance of recognizing diversity in the classroom, noting that educators often overlook cultural beliefs and perspectives in science education. Their statement on multicultural science education reads in part:

> It is vital that students understand not only the hows and whys of science, but also the whos. Children have a strong image of a White male, with glasses and messy hair, as the standard scientist, but it is our job to erase that image and show them that scientists look just like them. In fact, there are scientists of every race, ethnicity, gender, and socioeconomic background. Teachers need to provide this diverse curriculum that exposes students to women, people of color, and people with disabilities in history, science, mathematics, and so on. Presently, America needs more scientists and engineers and students must realize that they do not have to be a stereotypical scientist. . . . We as teachers need to be sure that in our own classrooms science instruction stresses real-life applications and acknowledges individual differences so that our students understand that every person is a scientist no matter their ethnicity, gender, religion, or sexual orientation.

The statement concludes with a list of resources to support multicultural science teaching, as well as links to lessons plans, activities, and information teachers can use in their classrooms.

Upper elementary and middle school students can also be encouraged to read about the origins of science in other cultures in books by George Beshore, including *Science in Ancient China,* which discusses rockets, water wheels, the compass, and other inventions, and *Science in Early Islamic Culture,* which discusses advances in medicine and surgery by Middle Eastern scientists in ancient times. A key part of multicultural science should be for students to engage in scientific inquiry about issues that affect them, their families, and their communities. Students in the agricultural community of Oxnard, California, for example, learned about the strawberry fields surrounding their school, where many of the ELL students' parents worked as agricultural laborers (Cummins, Brown, & Sayers, 2007). Through Project Fresa ("strawberry" in Spanish), the students realized they knew very little about strawberries and generated a list of questions about how they are planted, grown, and harvested. Students' parents became sources of expert knowledge on the topic, and children were able to learn from the funds of knowledge within their communities. The students' inquiries, however, went well beyond science. They began asking questions about the business aspects of strawberry farming, including the low pay and poor working conditions of the laborers. Thus, what started as a scientific inquiry was extended to a powerful social studies inquiry.

Social Studies

Social studies, unfortunately, has received less attention since the passage of NCLB. The National Council for Social Studies (NCSS) is conducting political advocacy and public awareness campaigns to promote social studies education in schools and prevent the further erosion of this important content area.

The NCSS advocacy campaign is carried out under the theme "Today's Social Studies . . . Creating Effective Citizens." An advocacy kit prepared by the council (NCSS, n.d.) explains that social studies is much more than looking at maps and memorizing dates: "Today's social studies provides students with the knowledge, thinking skills and experiences that will allow them to grow into effective citizens." The ultimate outcome is to "prepare people to take their place in a democracy."[4]

Social studies is a broad label covering several disciplines. NCSS defines it as "the integrated study of the social sciences and humanities to promote civic competence." In response to the question, "What is social studies education?" NCSS states:

> The accurate answer to this question is many, many topics. After all, social studies includes such disciplines as anthropology, archaeology, economics, geography, history, law, philosophy, political science, psychology, religion, and sociology. Parts of the humanities, mathematics and the natural sciences also touch on the broad topic of social studies. This is what makes social studies so important to a complete education.

(For the sample performance indicators from the TESOL standards for social studies, see Figure 9.7.)

The Language of Social Studies

The language of social studies poses unique challenges to ELLs. Unlike the language of science which, for the most part, describes tangible or readily observable processes, social studies deals largely with abstractions. Concepts such as *government, law, democracy, freedom, rights, justice, poverty, immigration,* and *elections* cannot be illustrated with simple drawings, and they frequently defy simple explanations. In social studies, terms such as the *American Revolution, slavery, westward expansion,* and *the Trail of Tears* are abstractions of very complex events, chains of events, or intricate webs of related events (Martin, 2002).[5] These abstractions enable us to talk about complex social and historical phenomena as if they were a tangible thing (e.g., "The American Revolution led to America's independence from England"). But these abstractions carry a heavy semantic load and require substantial background to understand and substantial language skills to use properly within the discourse of social studies.

For example, for an ELL student unfamiliar with the abstraction *American*

4: For more about the campaign, visit the NCSS home page at www.ncss.org

5: Note that the abstraction *slavery* is free from agency. In this form, it is simply something that exists. *Enslavement,* in contrast, suggests agency—some people were enslaving other people. Thus, this term carries a heavier moral indictment than the first term. Think about how other abstractions used in social and political discourse may also mask responsibility or misrepresent a socially complex issue.

Standard 5: Language of Social Studies
Grade level cluster: 6–8

Domain: Speaking
Topic: Rights and responsibilities; freedom and democracy; slavery

Level 1	Level 2	Level 3	Level 4	Level 5
Respond to questions with words or phrases related to illustrated historical scenes.	Make general statements about illustrated historical scenes (e.g., "Women do vote now. Women did not vote in 1900.").	Describe or enact historical scenarios based on illustrations or historical cartoons.	State a stance or position using conditional language (e.g., "If I lived in the 1850s ...") from visually supported historical scenarios.	Evaluate or imagine different historical scenarios and their impact or consequences (e.g., "Imagine if we could not vote.").

Grade level cluster: 9–12

Domain: Reading
Topic: Global economy; supply and demand; money and banking

Level 1	Level 2	Level 3	Level 4	Level 5
Make connections between areas on maps or globes and their products or monetary units using illustrated sources.	Glean information about places, products, or monetary units from newspapers, charts, and graphs.	Detect trends or fluctuations in monetary values or production from summaries and information presented in charts, tables, and graphs.	Predict future trends in monetary values or production presented in graphically supported text.	Interpret economic trends based on modified grade-level materials (e.g., business reports, magazine articles).

Figure 9.7   TESOL ELP Standards, sample performance indicators for social studies.
(Source: TESOL, 2006a, pp. 86, 97.)

Revolution, this term would have to be "unpacked," by explaining the following facts and events:

America was originally a colony of England.
Many Americans did not feel England was treating them fairly.
They wanted to be independent from England.
They fought a war against England from 1775 to 1783.
This war was called the American Revolution.
America won the war and became an independent nation.

The American Revolution was of course much more complex than these few sentences suggest, but even within this simple unpacking are more abstract terms that may need further unpacking: *colony, fairly, independent, war, nation,* and *revolution.*
    Another linguistic challenge in social studies involves how time is marked and making the distinction between sequence and setting in time. Students writing about something they experienced in the past would need to know words such as *first, then, next,* and *finally* and how to use them appropriately to mark the sequence of events in their story. Setting in time, in contrast, combines a series of events into one "chunk" that historians may conventionalize under names such as the Middle Ages, the Renaissance, or the cold war (Martin, 2002). Such chunking of time enables us to talk about periods ranging from a whole day (e.g., Black Friday) to mil-

lions of years (e.g., the Jurassic Period) as if they were singular events. Understanding and using named time chunks appropriately in spoken and written discourse can be very difficult for ELLs, particularly those who may be encountering such concepts for the first time. Thus, teaching key vocabulary to ELLs in social studies is more involved than it is in other areas.

Making Social Studies Instruction Comprehensible for ELLs

One of the first ways to make social studies instruction comprehensible to ELLs is to find out what students already know about the particular topic or concept to be taught. A three-column K-W-L chart can be very useful here. Students brainstorm and list what they *know* in the first column, then what they *want to know* in the second column. Later they will fill in what they *learned.* Filling out the columns on the K-W-L chart also gives teachers of ELLs a way to find out what vocabulary knowledge they already have on the topic. For a unit on transportation, for example, ELLs might show that they know the words *car,* boat, *airplane*, and *street* but not *ship, ferry, tanker, pickup truck, semi-truck, highway,* or *freeway.*

The language of social studies focuses on abstract concepts, but the field itself offers a wide variety of visuals that can help make instruction more comprehensible. Portraits of historical people, photographs of historical places, and drawings, photographs, or video clips of historical and contemporary events can go a long way in helping students comprehend concepts, and they can have a lasting effect. When I think about the civil rights movement, for example, my mind goes back to the disturbing images of "White Only" signs and the inspiring audio and video recordings of Martin Luther King Jr. speaking before massive cheering crowds. Appropriate images to support social studies instruction can be found though a quick search using Google images (images.google.com). Social studies also relies heavily on visuals such as charts, graphs, maps, globes, and historical political cartoons. Realia such as authentic or replicas of historic items like uniforms, period clothing, coins, stamps, documents, flags, and artifacts from different cultures can also create a great deal of interest among students and help make instruction more comprehensible.

Role playing can be a very effective form for making social studies concepts comprehensible. For example, students can get a better grasp of democracy and the electoral process if they hold an election in class. When working as a bilingual paraprofessional in a high school social studies class, I helped the ELL students make a video about their rights under the U.S. Constitution. The students acted out various scenes in which their rights were being violated. When students experience concepts, they are much more likely to comprehend and remember them.

Social studies also enables students to explore current events and the history behind them and understand the ways these events affect them, their families, and their communities. Including current events in the social studies curriculum can be as simple as clipping articles from newspaper, magazines, or the Internet to use as read-alouds, shared readings, or guided readings, and facilitating a discussion with the students about the events. *Time* magazine's *Time for Kids* and the *Weekly Reader* are excellent commercial resources designed for younger students. Other excellent and free resources for teaching older ELLs about current events are available on the Internet (Website Resources, links).

Modifying Social Studies Instructional Materials

The abstract language of social studies can make social studies textbooks especially challenging for ELL students. To make the text more accessible, teachers can simply read it aloud, using the before-during-and-after strategies described in

Chapter 7 and stopping to look at and discuss the illustrations, tables, charts, graphs, captions, boxes, and so on. Lower-level ELLs could also be paired with a reading buddy when reading the text (Reiss, 2005). Another strategy is for the teacher or a student with strong reading ability to make an audio recording of the text for ELLs to listen to as they follow along in the text. Among the advantages of this strategy for ELLs, Reiss points out, is that "they learn pronunciation of unfamiliar words." Also,

> they may make new associations of words in their oral and written forms, words they may know in spoken form but not recognize in writing because they are spelled so differently from the way they are pronounced. . . . Simultaneously seeing and hearing these words in context may help students to understand and remember the different meanings and usages. (p. 61)

Teachers also can use graphic organizers with students to break down the text to its most basic structure and content. For example, here is some text from a 5th grade social studies textbook, describing how farmers in the middle colonies made a living:

> Farmers raised livestock such as cattle and pigs. They grew vegetables, fruits, and other crops in the fertile soil. Farmers grew many different grains, such as wheat, corn, and barley. In fact, they grew so much grain used to make bread that the middle colonies became known as the "breadbasket" of the thirteen colonies.[6]

From this text, the teacher, along with the students, could create a graphic organizer like the one in Figure 9.8. Note how that organizer presents the same information but in fewer words and with visual organization and support to facilitate comprehension. Students who may have struggled with the meanings of the words *livestock, cattle,* and *grains* in the text can easily determine their meaning with the support of illustrations added to the graphic organizer.

Some teachers have found the "ten important sentences" strategy, developed by George Gonzalez (2005), to be useful in helping students focus on the main ideas and basic essence of a social studies text. The teacher and students identify the 10 most important sentences in the text, which are copied onto the board or on a chart, then read by the class and discussed. This strategy can also be used with fiction and other genres.

Some textbook companies recognize that not all students will be reading at grade level and thus may have trouble accessing the core grade-level social studies textbook. Houghton Mifflin, for example, has a series of supplemental, leveled social studies readers for grades K–6. Great Source Education Group offers two textbooks for students in grades 5–12: *ACCESS American History* and *ACCESS World History.*

Using Literature to Support Social Studies Instruction

Books can easily be found to support whatever content is covered in the main social studies textbook. But teachers should also consider using external literature to fill in gaps or deal with topics given only slight mention in a textbook. For example, the internment of Japanese Americas during World War II is a topic rarely explored in-depth in mainstream textbooks. Younger students can learn about this great injustice in U.S. history through fiction books, such as *Baseball Saved Us* by Ken Mochizuki, *So Far From the Sea* by Eve Bunting, and *Flowers from Mariko* by Rick Noguchi and Deneen Jenks, or nonfiction books, such as *The Children of Topaz: The Story of the Japanese American Internment Camp* by Michael O. Tunnell and George W. Chilcoat. Books appropriate for older students include *I Am an Ameri-*

6: *Houghton Mifflin Social Studies, 5th Grade,* 2005, p. 197.

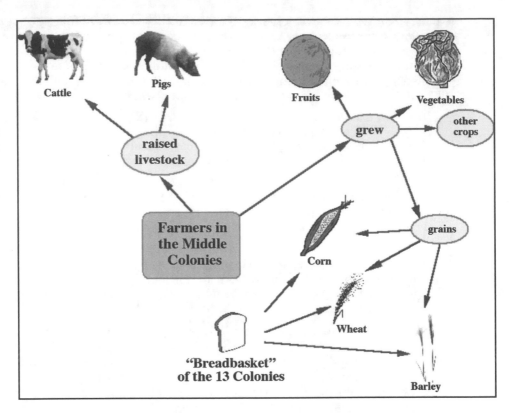

Figure 9.8 **Modification of text with a graphic organizer** (created by the author with Kidspiration software).

can: A True Story of Japanese Internment by Jerry Stanley and *Farewell to Manzanar* by Jeanne Wakatsuki Houston and James D. Houston.

Integrating Students' Cultures into Social Studies Instruction

In recent years, publishers of social studies and history textbooks have made efforts to better represent the ethnic and cultural diversity of the United States. Often, however, what makes it into textbooks that may be reflective of the cultures of ELL students is limited and relegated to sidebars and boxes.

The easiest way to incorporate students' cultures into social studies is to make them a focus of study. If the ethnic and cultural groups represented by the students in your class, school, and community are not represented in your social studies texts, you can create your own units. Be careful, however, not to make assumptions about what the students already know. For example, one of my former colleagues suggested that there was no need for me to teach my Cambodian American students about Cambodian history and culture, yet few of my students understood the tragedy of the Cambodian genocide and what had caused their families to flee as refugees and ultimately resettle in the United States. Because of the trauma of their experiences, the students' parents did not talk about them much, making it all the more important to include that history in social studies instruction.

I also created my own material for a unit on community workers to make it more relevant for my Cambodian American students. I was unsatisfied with the books, visuals, and other materials provided in our somewhat dated curricular program because all the community workers were White, and so I headed out into the local community with a digital camera. Within a 1-mile radius of the school, I took photos of several Cambodian Americans who worked in the community, including a doctor, a teacher, a police officer, a librarian, a social worker, a business person, and a shop owner, and photographs of African Americans and Latino community workers, including a firefighter, a bus driver, and a crossing guard. I used the photos to create a bulletin board display and a book. The students enjoyed learning about community workers with these materials, because they were an accurate depiction of workers in their community, some of whom they even recognized.

Students' own communities also offer an excellent resource for learning about cultures other than their own. The school where I taught was in the inner city, where in a single year nearly a hundred youths died in a major gang war between Cambodian and Mexican gangs. Every one of my students and their families was affected in one way or another by the gang violence and ethnic tensions in the community. And because our bilingual program further separated some Cambodian and Mexican students from each other, I felt it was important to teach my Cambodian students about Mexican Americans. Many students thought *Mexican* was a bad word and equated it solely with gang members, since this was the only context in which they heard the word used within their immediate families. Students would say, for example, "A Mexican shot my uncle" or "Some Mexicans chased my brother after school and beat him up." My young students, a few of whom declared outright, "I hate Mexicans," were shocked to find out that some of their favorite teachers, staff members, and even their beloved principal were Mexican Americans. We had some social studies lessons where these individuals came and talked with the students about their culture. We read multicultural literature together, including *Bread, Bread, Bread* by Ann Morris (a book about different kinds of bread eaten around the world), which was followed by a visit from the PTA president, who came in and taught us how to make tortillas like the ones in the book. Through such activities, my students gained a broader, more accurate, and much more positive view of their fellow community members.

Art, Music, and Physical Education

Art, music, and physical education (PE) have been receiving the short shrift in schools where instruction focuses narrowly on preparing ELLs and other students for state high-stakes tests. Because these content areas are not on the test, they tend to get deemphasized or even eliminated altogether. This trend is of great concern to educators because these content areas are as crucial as all the other areas to a well-rounded education.

A strong argument for including the arts in a well-rounded education comes from the Consortium of National Arts Education Associations (see MENC, n.d.), which reminds us, "The arts are inseparable from the very meaning of the term education." The consortium established the National Standards for Arts Education, covering the areas of dance, music, theater, and the visual arts, and issued a summary statement that includes a list of reasons for this assertion (see Box 9.2).

The implication of this statement is that to deny ELLs and other students arts instruction is to deny them the opportunity to become educated. Note the emphasis on the arts as a means of reflection, high-order thinking, expression, and communication, and the role of the arts in developing skills valued in the workplace. These and other points made in the statement show why it is imperative for teachers of ELL students to resist the pressure to exclude art from the classroom.

An equal emphasis should be put on PE. Regular PE instruction in the schools

Box 9.2

The Importance of Arts Education

The National Standards for Arts Education, established by the Consortium of National Arts Education Associations, includes the following statement on the importance of arts education.

Knowing and practicing the arts disciplines are fundamental to the healthy development of children's minds and spirits. That is why, in any civilization—ours included—the arts are inseparable from the very meaning of the term education. We know from long experience that no one can claim to be truly educated who lacks basic knowledge and skills in the arts. There are many reasons for this assertion:

■ The arts are worth studying simply because of what they are. Their impact cannot be denied. Throughout history, all the arts have served to connect our imaginations with the deepest questions of human existence: Who am I? What must I do? Where am I going? Studying responses to those questions through time and across cultures—as well as acquiring the tools and knowledge to create one's own responses—is essential not only to understanding life but to living it fully.

■ The arts are used to achieve a multitude of human purposes: to present issues and ideas, to teach or persuade, to entertain, to decorate or please. Becoming literate in the arts helps students understand and do these things better.

■ The arts are integral to every person's daily life. Our personal, social, economic, and cultural environments are shaped by the arts at every turn—from the design of the child's breakfast placemat, to the songs on the commuter's car radio, to the family's night-time TV drama, to the teenager's Saturday dance, to the enduring influences of the classics.

■ The arts offer unique sources of enjoyment and refreshment for the imagination. They explore relationships between ideas and objects and serve as links between thought and action. Their continuing gift is to help us see and grasp life in new ways.

■ There is ample evidence that the arts help students develop the attitudes, characteristics, and intellectual skills required to participate effectively in today's society and economy. The arts teach self-discipline, reinforce self-esteem, and foster the thinking skills and creativity so valued in the workplace. They teach the importance of teamwork and cooperation. They demonstrate the direct connection between study, hard work, and high levels of achievement.

Source: From *National Standards for Arts Education.* Copyright © 1994 by Music Educators National Conference (MENC). Used by permission. The complete National Arts Standards and additional materials relating to the Standards are available from MENC: The National Association for Music Education, 1806 Robert Fulton Drive, Reston, VA 20191; www.menc.org

can help reduce the increasing rates of obesity in the United States and, more important, PE is an essential component of a complete education for all children. According to the American Academy of Child and Adolescent Psychiatry (2008), childhood obesity in the United States has grown considerably in recent years with estimates that between 16 and 33 percent of children and adolescents are obese. The organization cites unhealthy weight gain due to poor diet and lack of exercise as the cause of over 300,000 deaths each year. Key to resolving this crisis and preventing overweight children from becoming overweight adults is to encourage students to adopt and maintain healthier patterns of eating and exercise.

Despite these well-publicized statistics, more and more schools are reducing their PE programs. Some elementary schools no longer have PE teachers or a schoolwide program, relying instead on classroom teachers to provide their own PE instruction. But because of the overemphasis on preparation for high-stakes tests, many teachers have found little time left in the day to include the "luxury" of PE. Even schools with full-time PE teachers have felt the pressure to reduce the amount of time for PE instruction, and some have the coaches regularly drilling students with test preparation materials. Many schools have even eliminated recess to make more classroom time for test preparation (Ohanian, 2002).

The place of PE in the curriculum is defined in the *National Standards for Physical Education,* established by the National Association for Sport and Physical Education (NASPE, 2007). The document declares that physical education has academic standing equal to other subject areas. The standards describe a physically educated person as one who achieves and maintains a health-enhancing level of physical fitness and who values physical activity for such reasons as health, enjoyment, challenge, self-expression, and social interaction, in addition to being able to demonstrate understanding of and competency in motor skills and movement patterns to perform physical activity. Thus, PE instruction is not just about participation; rather, like other academic content areas, it focuses on helping students gain important knowledge and skills necessary for success in life.

Because art, music, and PE typically carry less of a language demand than math, science, and social studies, ELLs can often participate in them more easily and quickly and excel in them from the beginning. Artistic, musical, and physical talent easily transcends language barriers. Thus, students who developed these talents before beginning school in the United States bring in strengths that can be built on immediately. As with the other content areas, however, there is a unique language associated with art, music, and PE, as well as content, concepts, and theories beyond the surface-level activities of these subjects that require higher levels of English proficiency to comprehend. Teachers can make instruction in these content areas more comprehensible for ELLs with the support of literature and the use of other strategies similar to those suggested for math, science, and social studies. (Website Resources, links; Examples of Strategies, video links)

Assessing the Content Areas

When assessing students' work in content areas, teachers must ensure that the assessment is a valid measure of the students' knowledge of the content and not a measure of their language proficiency. For example, giving students a math test consisting only of word problems on measurement may be more of a test of the students' English reading comprehension skills than of their math knowledge and skills. In this instance, a better approach for ELLs who lack English sufficient English reading skills would be to give them objects and measurement tools, with a simplified answer sheet to record their answers.

Performance assessments and other forms of alternative assessment should mirror the activities students do when learning in each content area. For example, in science, students' understanding of different cycles (e.g., water cycle, animal life cycles, cell division) can be assessed by asking students to arrange pictures depicting each stage in the cycle in the correct sequence. In social studies, maps students make of their neighborhood can be assessed using a rubric with items such as, "map includes: house, school, street, library, park"; "map includes a key"; "map includes a scale"; and "map includes a compass rose." In art, if students are making masks from different cultures, they could use a checklist for self-assessment or peer assessment to evaluate their final projects (e.g., "My mask is original, not a copy of the teacher's model"; "My mask is based on masks from a particular culture"; "I used a variety of materials to create my mask"). In music, the teacher could use an observational checklist to monitor and assess a student's performance (e.g.,

"Student is able to do the movements that go with the song"; "Student is able to sing all the words to the song"). In PE, students could self-assess by keeping a log of their exercise, heart rates, calories burned, and other physical activities in class and at home. These and other types of performance assessments can remove the language barriers and allow students to show what they know and can do.

The language objectives associated with each content area should also be assessed using the formal and informal assessments described in earlier chapters. Teachers should use on-going alternative and authentic assessments along with formal assessments to ensure that they have multiple measures of their students' knowledge and skills.

SUMMARY

To be successful in school, and in life, ELLs must be given access to the core curriculum that equals that of their native English-speaking peers. To ensure that ELLs receive that access, instruction in the content areas must be comprehensible, if not through native language instruction, then through sheltered instruction. The SIOP is one popular model that can help teachers plan, deliver, and evaluate effective sheltered content-area instruction. One key to effective content-area lessons for ELLs is the inclusion of both content and language objectives. The language objectives should address the challenges posed by the language (or registers) of each content area, including the unique vocabulary, language structures, discourse styles, and genres. Objectives should be appropriate to students' levels of language proficiency and content knowledge. Because of the wide range of abilities across ELL (and other) students, it is imperative that teachers differentiate their instruction. The sample performance indicators of TESOL's English Language Proficiency Standards provide examples of how academic tasks can be differentiated for students at different levels of English proficiency. Textbooks and other content-area instructional materials are designed for English-proficient students and therefore must be modified and adapted to make them accessible to ELLs. Thematic teaching ties together the different content areas by building background knowledge, making it possible for skills developed in one content area to facilitate comprehension and further learning in other areas. Teachers can find books outside the core textbook that may be more appropriate to the academic and English proficiency levels of some students and that may inspire discussions and activities that further reinforce core-content area concepts while promoting English language development. Integrating different cultures into content-area instruction, particularly those of the ELL students, can make lessons more meaningful and motivating. On-going formal and informal authentic assessments in the content areas offer multiple measures and therefore a valid depiction of ELL students' academic achievement. The results of these assessments help teachers plan further content-area instruction tailored to students' unique linguistic and academic needs.

Discussion Questions

1. Why is it important for content-area lessons for ELLs to have both content and language objectives? What would the consequences be if lessons consistently had one but not the other?

2. **On-line Discussion Board**   Why do ELL students need effective instruction in every content area? What are some of the harmful effects of providing ELL students with instruction only in the content areas that are on a state's high-

stakes test? Despite the pressure to prepare students for high-stakes tests and to raise test scores, what are some ways teachers can ensure that they are providing effective instruction for their students in all the content areas and not just the tested ones? Give examples from your personal experiences or observations.

 3. **On-line Discussion Board**   What are some of the challenges content-area instruction and textbooks pose to ELLs? If English is not your first language, describe some of your experiences with the challenges you faced in learning academic content and using grade-level textbooks. Discuss different strategies for sheltering instruction and modifying textbooks to make instruction and materials more accessible for ELLs.

4. Some teachers feel it is necessary to use textbooks from a lower grade level to meet the needs of their ELL students. What are your thoughts on this practice? If these textbooks are used, how can teachers keep ELL students from feeling the stigma of using below-grade-level materials?

Research Activities

1. Interview a classroom teacher of ELL students. Ask the teacher about the challenges of teaching different content areas to ELLs students and what strategies and techniques he or she uses to shelter content-area instruction to make it more comprehensible for ELLs.

 2. **Wiki This**   Interview a former ELL student and ask which content areas were the most challenging for him or her in school. Ask what strategies and techniques the teacher used (if any) that were helpful in making the content areas more accessible.

3. Observe a content-area lesson and evaluate it using the SIOP. Present and discuss the results in class, including what changes could be made, if any, to improve the lesson and make it more comprehensible for ELLs.

 4. **Wiki This**   Look at a fairly recent content-area textbook or curricular program that claims to have incorporated strategies and techniques for ELL students. Evaluate it using the criteria established by Dobb that appears in Box 9.1.

Recommended Readings

Carr, J., Sexton, U., & Lagunoff, R. (2007). *Making science accessible to English learners: A guidebook for teachers.* San Francisco: WestEd.
Background on inquiry-based science and how to provide it for ELLs in a manner that helps them learn science content while supporting their English language development.

Clements, R. L., & Kinzler, S. K. (2002). *A multicultural approach to physical education: Proven strategies for middle and high school.* Champaign, IL: Human Kinetics.
The authors make a strong case for multicultural PE instruction and offer many great ideas for incorporating games and physical activities from around the world.

Dobb, F. (2004). *Essential elements of effective science instruction for English learners* (2nd ed.). [Electronic version]. Los Angeles: California Science Project. http://csmp.ucop.edu/downloads/csp/essential_elements_2.pdf
Covers issues related to the language of science, affective factors, classroom talk, vocabulary development, use of science textbooks and materials, assessment, and professional development.

Laminack, L. L., & Wadsworth, R. M. (2006). *Reading aloud across the curriculum:*

How to build bridges in language arts, math, science, and social studies. Portsmouth, NH: Heinemann.

The authors make a strong case that reading is the bridge across the content areas. They provide many examples of using literature across the curriculum and provide lists of suggested book titles. Although the book does not target ELLs, teachers of ELL students will nonetheless find excellent ideas and resources.

Reiss, J. (2005). *Teaching content to English language learners: Strategies for secondary school success.* White Plains, NY: Longman.

In this important book, the author offers suggestions about how to provide effective sheltered content instruction for ELL students at the middle and high school levels.

10

Primary Language Support

When you explain it in Khmer, it's so easy!
—Nitha, a newcomer ELL student from Cambodia,
to her bilingual classroom volunteer

KEY TERMS

- primary language support (PLS)
- concurrent translation
- Preview-review
- cognates
- dual language books

GUIDING QUESTIONS

1. What is primary language support?
2. How can primary language support enhance English language development and sheltered English content-area learning?
3. What are effective strategies for providing primary language support?

Imagine attending school in a new country where you do not speak the language used for instruction. Perhaps you do not need to imagine because this was your own experience. How difficult would it be to pay attention, follow directions, complete class work, and, in short, learn? For many ELLs across the country, these challenges are a daily reality. Most ELL students are not in bilingual programs. This does not mean, however, that these students' native language skills should be ignored or that their classrooms should be strictly English-only.

When bilingual education cannot be provided, children still should have the right to attend a school that shows full respect for their home language and encourages its use. Effective programs for ELLs, regardless of program type, view the native language of ELLs as a resource and thus provide primary language support to help students learn English and academic content. Even teachers who do not speak the students' native languages can provide this support. In this chapter, we define *primary language support* and then review the theoretical background and research literature that supports its use. Finally, we review a variety of effective ways teachers can provide primary language support for the ELLs in their classroom.

What Is Primary Language Support?

Primary language support (PLS), also called native language support, refers to the use of students' first language to *support* sheltered content and ESL instruction. It is different from primary language *instruction,* which refers to the teaching of entire lessons in the native language of students, as in bilingual education programs. The purpose of PLS is to make instruction in English as comprehensible as possible for ELL students so they can learn the content and acquire more English. Thus, PLS is especially important in sheltered English immersion and other nonbilingual program models. Indeed, PLS is an essential component of nearly all program models for ELLs.

Theories and Research Supporting the Use of PLS

Several learning theories in general and language-learning theories in particular support the concept of PLS. A few research studies have been conducted on PLS, all of which found it to be an effective strategy for helping ELL students learn English and academic content through English.

PLS is consistent with Stephen Krashen's (1985) input hypothesis and its associated notion of comprehensible input ($i + 1$). When properly provided, PLS maximizes ELL students' comprehension of instruction in English, enabling them to acquire more English. PLS is also consistent with Krashen's affective filter hypothesis: when PLS is used properly, it can lower students' affective filters and thus provide students with greater access to comprehensible input.

Schemata theory also incorporates primary language support. By building students' background knowledge and activating their prior knowledge through their first language, PLS activates their schema, and thus the students are better prepared to learn more about the topic in their second language. As explained by Sharon H. Ulanoff and Sandra L. Pucci (1999):

> Second language learners can make use of what they know in their native language to better understand what they are learning in English. When used appropriately the primary language assists in promoting meaningful learning, which further builds the network of schemata available to the second language learner. The connections made between the students' first and second languages thus serve to facilitate new learning (p. 320).

PLS is also a form of scaffolding. According to Lev Vygotsky's (1978) theories of social interaction and cognitive development, students need to work within their zone of proximal development (ZPD) to acquire new knowledge. The ZPD marks the area between what students know and can do on their own and what they can potentially learn and do with expert guidance from a teacher or more knowledgeable peers. The supports that teachers or others provide within the ZPD are scaffolds. The use of the students' native language provides substantial support as new concepts are introduced. Once students understand a particular concept, the scaffold (PLS) used to present that concept is removed and students are left better prepared to learn the new concepts through English. Further scaffolding through PLS is provided each time new concepts are introduced.

PLS is featured prominently in the Sheltered Immersion Observation Protocol (SIOP). Item 19 of the SIOP calls for ample opportunities for students to clarify key concepts in L1 as needed with an aide, peer, or L1 text. As explained by the authors of the SIOP:

> Best practice indicates that English learners benefit from opportunities to clarify concepts in their native language (L1). Although sheltered instruction involves teaching subject-matter material in English, students are given the opportunity to have a concept or assignment explained in their L1, as needed. . . . We believe that clarification of key concepts in students' L1 by a bilingual instructional aide, peer, or through the use of materials written in the students' L1 provides an important support for the academic learning of these students who are not yet fully proficient in English. (Echevarria, Vogt, & Short, 2007, pp. 106–107)

Even those opposed to bilingual education recognize the need for PLS in non-bilingual programs. Keith Baker (1998), a long-time opponent of bilingual education, agrees that PLS can maximize the effectiveness of instruction and has suggested that 10–30% of instruction time in SEI classrooms should be reserved for PLS. He points out that PLS makes the students more comfortable and helps them get through difficult communication problems with teachers more quickly. It also motivates students and boosts their self-esteem.

The need for PLS is recognized even within the English for the Children laws that have restricted bilingual education in California (Proposition 227), Arizona (Proposition 203), and Massachusetts (Question 2). Although these laws mandate sheltered English immersion, they also state that teachers "may use a minimal amount of students' native languages when necessary." Since the terms "minimal amount" and "when necessary" are not defined, teachers in these states are entitled to make their own professional judgments about how much PLS is needed, and when necessary, to make their English language instruction for ELLs as comprehensible as possible.

In the following discussion we look at three studies on the use of PLS: a teacher action research study in an English immersion classroom, a case study of two newcomer ELL students, and an experimental study on the use of the preview-review method of providing PLS in bilingual classrooms.

Teacher Action Research in an English Immersion Classroom

Nina Weber (2000), a certified bilingual teacher in California who was a member of the UCLA Teacher-Research Program in 2000, conducted an action research project in her sheltered English immersion classroom on the use of PLS. As a teacher in the Los Angeles Unified School District, Weber was authorized to provide PLS for up to 25% of the instructional time. Weber speaks Spanish, and all of the ELLs in her classroom were Spanish speaking.

Weber found, among the many beneficial effects, that PLS enabled her to *affirm understanding* or *identify misunderstandings.* Her students would sometimes answer in Spanish when she asked questions in English. These students did not feel ready to answer in English but were still able to demonstrate their understanding of the content they had learned. Listening skills in a second language are often more developed than speaking skills. When her students answered correctly in Spanish, Weber would repeat their answer in English, affirming their knowledge while modeling the English they would have needed to answer the question. If the answer was wrong, Weber knew she needed to re-teach the concept.

With PLS, Weber was able to *extract details* and her students were able to *provide explanations.* Some of her students would begin an answer in English but then elaborate in Spanish because they could not yet fully express themselves in English. Again, this use of their L1 allowed students to fully demonstrate their understanding in ways they would not have been able to if they were restricted to using English. Weber also found that PLS enabled her to *engage students* who otherwise would be lost during English language instruction, and it helped her *discuss problems* her students were having at home or in the schoolyard during recess. Weber notes that when tears are flowing, students need to be able to express themselves in the language they know best. Finally, Weber describes how she used PLS to *help students write:*

> Many of our writing activities such as thank-you notes, student of the week books, and daily news involved oral discussion first. I would post a piece of chart paper on the whiteboard with the students seated on the rug or in their chairs. Students would tell me what should be written. If a student spoke in Spanish, we would discuss how that could be written in English. In this way, students of all language abilities could participate. (p. 10)

Weber allowed some students to write in their journals first in Spanish, "and then, together, we would find the words to write their ideas in English" (p. 10).

Case Study of Newcomer ELL Students

Some of my own research has looked at the benefits of PLS. In one study (Wright, 2006b), I had the privilege of working with two newly arrived 5th grade students from Cambodia, Nitha and Bora, at an intermediate school in the San Antonio, Texas area. Nitha and Bora, sisters from an impoverished village in Cambodia where they spoke Khmer, could not speak a single word of English when they arrived two months after the school year began. Their classroom teacher had little experience working with ELL students and felt overwhelmed at first by their presence. Nonetheless, she did several good things in the classroom to provide PLS. She gave the girls a bilingual Khmer-English picture dictionary, allowed them to write notes and translations in Khmer on their school papers, and let them work together and help each other in Khmer. Still, she was frustrated because she felt they needed much more help than she was able to give them. A sympathetic colleague suggested they seek out someone from the community who could speak Khmer and volunteer in the school to provide PLS. The search led to me, and I volunteered about an hour and a half a week at the school with the girls.

I found Nitha and Bora a joy to work with. They were extremely intelligent and highly motivated. One of the first things I did, at the teacher's request, was to determine their level of literacy in Khmer and how much math they knew. I found they had excellent reading and writing skills and could do basic math computations. Their math skills would have been considered at or even above grade level in Cambodia, but they were far below what was expected of 5th grade students in Texas (Wright & Li, 2006, 2008). The teacher decided to have my weekly PLS sessions with the girls focus on math because they would be required to the take the state math test—the TAKS—in English at the end of the school year.

The girls made great progress in math over the next several months, particularly as their proficiency in English improved. They were able to pick up new math concepts from their teachers' sheltered instruction, which included lots of modeling and simplified explanations. But the girls struggled with word problems because they did not yet have the vocabulary or reading skills in English to comprehend them. Also, some new math concepts proved too difficult for the teacher or paraprofessionals to explain because of the language barrier. Thus, these word problems and difficult new concepts were saved for our weekly PLS sessions.

During our sessions, I explained the word problems in Khmer and taught them strategies for solving them. Once they understood what the questions were asking, they could easily answer them. They also quickly grasped the new concepts they had struggled to learn in English, once they were explained to them in Khmer. I remember vividly one occasion where their teacher had been trying hard to help them learn the concept of fractions, but they just were not getting it. When I met with the girls, I explained and modeled the basic concepts of fractions, and both girls let out an audible, "Ohhhhhh!" They both quickly started completing their fractions worksheets, getting all the answers right. About halfway through the worksheet, Nitha smiled and said, "When you explain it in Khmer, it's so easy!"

Our PLS sessions also provided opportunities for the girls to ask questions about things taught in class that they did not fully understand. Some of these conversations went into great depth about the political organization of the United States, space exploration, Native Americans, poverty, enslavement, the civil rights movement, disabled students, religious differences, and U.S. holidays and traditions. Our PLS sessions were only about 90 minutes a week, but they were long enough to help Nitha and Bora deepen their understanding of academic concepts and issues that otherwise would not have been fully accessible to them.

I also observed Nitha and Bora in their regular classroom, in their pull-out ESL classroom, in tutoring sessions with a nonbilingual paraprofessional, and in the computer lab. In all settings they were allowed to speak to each other in Khmer. Most of their conversations were related to the learning tasks at hand as they tried to figure out what was said what was being asked of them, or as they tried to figure out the work they had been given to do.

During a social studies lesson I observed in their classroom, on the topic of how to use the U.S. map and identify the 50 states, I saw Nitha perk up and then pull out of her backpack one of the Khmer-language social studies books I had given her. She brought the book to me where I was sitting at the back table and proudly showed me a map of the United States with explanations and the names of each state written in Khmer. The Khmer-language textbook helped her develop the background knowledge needed to understand her classroom instruction in English.

Despite great progress in learning math, the girls did not pass the Math TAKS test at the end of the year. The reason was simple—passing the Math TAKS test (in English) is an unreasonable expectation for newly arrived ELL students because of the high level of English language proficiency required to read and understand the test items (Wright & Li, 2006, 2008). Fortunately, their teacher and others in the school understood this well and were nonetheless greatly impressed with the progress the girls made after just six months of schooling in the United States. By the end of the school year, the girls were able to have basic conversations with their teachers and peers in English, and they could read in English at about the 2nd grade level with some comprehension. When they first arrived, they were doing math at around the kindergarten and 1st grade level, but by the end of the school year, they were able to do some math work at the 5th grade level.

At the end of the school year, I asked their classroom and ESL teachers to evaluate the PLS sessions. They both described it as extremely beneficial. The classroom teacher said: "First of all, it was helpful for me to see them light up when they knew you were coming. They loved it. And you can imagine, I mean, it was the one day a week where they got to hear their language and they got to understand what was going on that whole afternoon period." She also reported that Nitha and Bora were able to do work independently after our PLS sessions. The girls' ESL teacher said, "I can't say enough about all that you've done for the girls, . . . taking time to visit with them, clarifying things, giving them some additional instruction. You have made the process so much better, not only for the kids, but [also] for us as their teachers" (Wright & Li, 2006, p. 130).

Experimental Study of Preview-Review

Sharon Ulanoff and Sandra Pucci (1999) conducted an experimental study in 3rd grade bilingual (Spanish-English) classrooms in a Los Angeles area school. They found empirical evidence that PLS—when provided appropriately—is effective in helping ELL students acquire new vocabulary in English. The study used a pretest/post-test design with a vocabulary test based on words from the picture book *The Napping House*. Students in all three classes were a given the pretest, and then the classrooms were randomly assigned to one of three groups. Group 1, the control group, received no PLS; Group 2 received concurrent translation; and Group 3 received PLS in the form of preview-review. (Concurrent translation and preview-review are discussed later in this chapter.) After administering the posttest, Ulanoff and Pucci found that the students in Group 3 (preview-review) acquired more new vocabulary words in English than did the students in the other two groups.

Ineffective and Effective Ways to Provide PLS

Providing PLS is easiest when the teacher or a classroom paraprofessional can speak the native language of the students. But even when neither can and even when there are multiple languages within the same classroom, there are still ways teachers can provide effective PLS. Some methods of PLS, however, are ineffective.

Ineffective PLS

PLS is ineffective when it inhibits rather than supports the students' efforts to obtain comprehensible input from oral or written English.

Translation

The worst use of students' native language or languages in the classroom is concurrent translation, also referred to as direct translation. Either the teacher speaks first in English and then repeats everything in the students' native language or a paraprofessional translates everything the teacher says. When students hear a translation, they have no need to attend to the English and thus they acquire little English. In the study by Ulanoff and Pucci, the group that received concurrent translation acquired fewer English vocabulary words than the preview-review group and also fewer than the group that received no PLS.

Substituting Written English Text with Oral L1 Translation

Another ineffective use of PLS is to substitute text written in English with oral L1 translation. During reading instruction, for example, rather than reading the actual words on the page of a book written in English, the teacher or paraprofessional translates the book aloud as if it were written in the students' L1. All students hear is the translation. They make no connection with the written English words on the page. The same problem occurs when teachers or paraprofessionals point to words on a worksheet in English and simply translate them aloud. Under these circumstances, there are no attempts to have the students engage with the text in English. The instructional construct is changed from reading in English to listening comprehension in the native language. Students are unlikely to acquire any English, since no English is presented for them to comprehend. Furthermore, it is very confusing for students to look at sentences written in English but then hear them spoken in different language.

Effective PLS

The following questions can be used as a guide to determine whether a PLS strategy or technique is effective:

1. Does the strategy allow the ELL student to quickly grasp a concept that was previously inaccessible when taught or explained only in English?
2. Does the strategy prepare the ELL to attend to instruction or print in English and receive greater amounts of comprehensible input?
3. Does the strategy lower the affective filter of ELLs and thus allow greater amounts of comprehensible input?
4. Does the strategy enable greater interaction between the ELL student and others in the classroom for social and academic purposes?

5. Does the strategy enable the teacher to determine the ELL students' understanding of content taught in English?

Each of the following strategies addresses one or more of these questions.

Preview-Review

Researchers have found preview-review to be one of the most effective forms of PLS (Freeman & Freeman, 2000, 2008; Ulanoff & Pucci, 1999). Preview-review takes just a few minutes before and after a lesson or read-aloud and maximizes students' comprehension in English. If the teacher cannot speak the students' native language or languages, preview-review may be provided by a bilingual paraprofessional or classroom volunteer.

Preview involves having a brief discussion with students in their native language to activate prior knowledge or build background knowledge related to the book to be read or lesson to be taught. For example, if a teacher is doing a unit on plants, he or she asks students in their L1 everything they know about plants and guides the discussion to cover the key ideas that will be taught in English. For a read-aloud, the teacher activates prior knowledge about the topic of the book and builds background knowledge by discussing the cover, doing a picture walk to help students understand the characters and settings and allow them to make predictions about what they think will happen. Teachers can also use the student's L1 with other prereading strategies.

After this preview, the teacher presents the lesson or reads the book in English, using appropriate sheltered strategies and techniques. Next, the teacher or paraprofessional briefly reviews with the students in their L1 the key ideas in the lesson or asks comprehension questions about the book read. This discussion and students' answers will reveal how much of the instruction or read-aloud in English the students were able to understand. If there are any minor misunderstandings, they can be resolved immediately. If it becomes clear that the students understood little, the teacher knows that re-teaching will be necessary with appropriate adjustments to facilitate greater comprehension.

In contrast to line-by-line translation, which diverts students' attention away from the English input, previewing in the L1 prepares the students to pay attention to the English and thus maximizes comprehensible input. Reviewing then provides a check to determine how much of the English input students were able to comprehend.

Give Quick Explanations during Whole-Class or Small-Group Instruction

The easiest way to provide PLS is to give quick explanations in the L1 during a lesson taught in English to the whole class or a small group. Quick explanation should be given when it becomes clear that some ELL students are not getting it, or when the concept is too difficult to explain or demonstrate in English. For example, during a social studies lesson on the American government, it may be difficult for a teacher to convey the meaning of the word *freedom*. Abstract concepts are difficult to explain by the techniques that work for concrete nouns and verbs, such as gesturing, pointing to objects, or drawing pictures. Many Spanish-speaking ELLs, however, would quickly understand if the teacher simply said that *freedom* is *libertad* in Spanish. Once students have the concept, the teacher can go on and develop it further in English.

Some teachers in classrooms with both ELLs and monolingual English-speaking students are hesitant to provide PLS in a whole class setting because it can interrupt instruction and the monolingual English speakers will not understand the explanations. Although this may be a legitimate concern, many explanations take just a few seconds, and there is no research evidence that monolingual English speakers are harmed by hearing a few words spoken in another language. On the contrary, it may beneficial for them to learn a few words in the language or languages of their classmates. Chances are they are already learning some from them informally.

For concepts that may require more extensive explanation, such as a math lesson on probability, the teacher or a bilingual paraprofessional can work with a group of ELLs who need the support while the other students work on their own.

Give Quick Explanations for Individual Students

Good teachers monitor students while they are working independently. They look for students who appear to be struggling and quietly provide assistance. If the student is an ELL and is not able to understand the assistance in English, the teacher can provide the assistance in the L1 or ask the bilingual paraprofessional to do so. Often simple explanations in the L1 are all students need to complete their work.

If students are having trouble understanding written directions, the teacher or bilingual professional should ask the student to read the directions aloud or read them aloud to the student, in English, while tracking the text and then ask the student what he or she thinks the instructions say to do. The teacher or paraprofessional should provide an explanation in the L1 based on the student's response rather than provide a word-for-word translation of the directions. This response avoids the problem associated with substituting English written text with oral L1 translation and ensures that students are at least attempting to attend to the English text. This form of PLS supports the students' efforts to read and comprehend English text. It does not replace the English reading with L1 listening comprehension. In addition, an explanation tailored to a student's partial understanding of the instructions ensures that the student will know what do in a way that merely providing a direct translation of the instructions does not.[1]

Pull Students Aside to Re-teach Concepts

If it becomes apparent during independent working time that some of the ELL students are having difficulty, the teacher or paraprofessional can pull a group of students aside and re-teach the concepts in the L1.

Read Aloud L1 Books
That Reinforce Concepts Taught in English

In thematic teaching, teachers identify books that can be used across the curriculum relevant to a selected theme. Some of these books could be in the L1 of the ELL students and could be read aloud to students during appropriate times. For example, in connection with a lesson on plant growth, the teacher could read aloud to her Spanish-speaking ELLs the book ¡Tiempo de calabazas! [It's Pumpkin Time!] by Zoe Hall and Shari Halpern, which describes how pumpkins grow. This book would help activate students' prior knowledge on the topic or help them build background knowledge so that they are more likely to receive greater comprehensible input.

1: For a standardized high-stakes state test, a teacher or paraprofessional may be allowed to provide only a direct translation of the instructions. To avoid confusion, however, the text should not be tracked as the oral translation is given, because there would be no direct correspondence between the English text and the oral translation.

Accept Students' Contributions in the L1 during Class Discussions

Teachers who speak the native language of their ELL students can allow them to contribute to class discussions in their L1. For example, if the teacher is reading a book about pets, an ELL student may wish to tell something about her pet dog. The teacher would allow her to speak in the L1 and then would repeat back in English what she said. The repeating back should not be a translation but an acknowledgment that conveys the same information the student shared. For example, "Oh, how cute! Your puppy likes to jump on you and lick your face when you come home from school." This type of response fits the flow of the discussion, acknowledges the student's contribution to the discussion, makes her comments accessible to all students in the class, and models back to her in English the information she shared. The student feels included, and also the teacher knows the student was able to follow and comprehend the discussion in English because she was able to contribute to the discussion in an appropriate way.

If the teacher does not speak the L1 of the student, and if no paraprofessional is available, it may be possible to have another student in class who is bilingual translate for the ELL. Teachers do need to be careful not to over-rely on other students as translators, though allowing one student to translate for another on occasion is a wonderful way to acknowledge and value that student's bilingual skills.

Label the Classroom in English and the Students' Native Language or Languages

An effective language and literacy strategy is to label classroom objects with word cards (e.g., *door, desk, chair, computer, clock, pencil sharpener*). Teachers can make these labels bilingual or multilingual, in keeping with the languages spoken by ELLs in the classroom. This exercise is particularly effective if the students help make the labels. These labels not only help students learn the names of classroom objects in English but also send students the message that their native language is valued as a resource for learning in the classroom (Freeman & Freeman, 1994). They can also help monolingual English-speaking students in the class learn vocabulary in the L1 of the ELL students. If the teacher and paraprofessional do not know the native language or languages of the students, the labels could be made by more advanced students with L1 literacy skills or by a parent or community volunteer. The teacher could also look up the translations in a bilingual dictionary or use an on-line translation tool and then check with the students (or parents or bilingual staff member) to make sure they are correct.

Other L1 Instructional Wall Displays

Effective teachers use the classroom walls to display and celebrate student work and to display instructional resources, such as charts and posters—commercially produced, teacher-made, or student-made—that relate to themes or content-area lessons they are working on. Teachers can easily add to or modify these displays to provide information in the native language or languages of their ELL students. Many commercially made charts, posters, and other displays are available in Spanish. For example, if the students are learning about weather, the teacher could display two identical weather posters—one in English and one in Spanish—or simply add Spanish text to the English version by creating labels on a computer and gluing them to the poster next to the corresponding English texts. For languages other than Spanish, gluing on labels may be the only option, but it is not hard to do. If the teacher does not speak the native language or languages of the ELLs in the class, the project could be given to a bilingual paraprofessional or volunteer, or to more advanced students in the class with bilingual skills. When referring to these displays during instruction, the teacher could call on ELLs to read aloud the texts in the L1 before discussing the displays in English.

Create Cognate Word Studies

One underexplored strategy that could be very beneficial especially in helping Spanish-speaking ELLs quickly acquire English vocabulary and improve their English reading comprehension, is to create lessons on cognates. Cognates are related words in the two languages that come from the same root, such as *education* (in English) and *educación* (in Spanish) (Bravo, Hiebert, & Pearson, 2007). Cognates, however, can be misleading because two words that appear to be similar may differ slightly in meaning (partial cognates) or may be unrelated altogether (false cognates). Cognate word study should also include instruction about these partial and false cognates.

Some partial cognates are specific in one language but general in another. For example, the English words *casserole* and *parents* have specific meanings, whereas the Spanish words, from the same roots, *cacerola* ("saucepan") and *parientes* ("relatives") are more general. In some cognate pairs, the meaning of the English word may have a more negative connotation than the Spanish word, as in *disgrace* and *desgracia* ("misfortune"), and vice versa, as in *to be interested* and *ser interesado* ("have an ulterior motive"). Some words may have related meanings but are nonetheless different, such as *library* and *librería* ("bookstore"). And finally, some words, false cognates, may appear to be similar but are not at all similar in meaning, such as *exit* and *éxito* ("success").[2]

There are many great stories illustrating the danger of false cognates. One true story involves an American Mormon missionary in Mexico. On her first Sunday at church in Mexico, the bishop called on her to come to the pulpit to introduce herself to the congregation. The missionary was a bit flustered because she had studied Spanish for only two months prior to her arrival. She wanted to begin by saying, "I'm embarrassed, and it's the bishop's fault," so she said in Spanish, *"Yo estoy embarazada y es la culpa del bishop."* The congregation burst into laughter, and the bishop's face turned bright red. Only later did she learn she had announced to the congregation, "I'm pregnant, and it's the bishop's fault!"

Despite the potential dangers, with proper instruction, cognates can be a very useful tool. Box 10.1 provides some excellent Internet resources for Spanish cognate word study lessons. Even if teachers do not speak Spanish, these resources can help them prepare lessons for students and discuss the words. Just as these are easy words for Spanish-speaking students to learn in English, so too are these easy words for English-speaking teachers to learn in Spanish.

Use the L1 to Support Writing in English

Writing is really hard, and one of the hardest parts for students is just figuring out what to write about and how to organize their thoughts. The prewriting activities discussed in Chapter 8 may be easier for ELLs to do first in their L1, with the help of a bilingual teacher or paraprofessional who can talk with them and help them brainstorm ideas. If the ELLs can write in their L1, they could use it to create graphic organizers, such as word webs, or create outlines. In some instances, it may even be appropriate to allow students to write their first draft in their L1. The teacher or

---

2: All examples of cognates are from Crandall, 1981.

Box 10.1

Spanish-English Cognates

The following Internet resources may be useful to teachers in preparing Spanish-English cognates word study lessons for Spanish-speaking ELLs:

Spanish Cognate Dictionary

www.latinamericalinks.com/spanish_cognates.htm

A free, comprehensive, on-line cognate dictionary provided by Latin America Links.

"Fickle Friends" and "False Friends"

spanish.about.com/cs/vocabulary/a/partcognates.htm

spanish.about.com/cs/vocabulary/a/obviouswrong.htm

Articles by Gerald Erichsen; one includes a list of partial cognates ("fickle friends"), the other a list of false cognates ("false friends").

paraprofessional can provide assistance as needed with vocabulary when they begin to write in English. Even if the teacher or paraprofessional does not speak the L1 of the ELLs, he or she can still allow them to use their L1 in prewriting activities and initial drafts.

Provide Bilingual Dictionaries

Bilingual dictionaries can be an important resource for ELL students who are literate in their L1. Schools should have a collection of dictionaries for students who do not already have their own. Simply having the dictionaries, however, is not enough. Teachers will need to show students how to use them and encourage their use when appropriate. The dictionary is also a resource for teachers who do not speak the students' L1. These teachers can look up words in English and point to the translation for the students. For example, a teacher who is reading with a small group of students notices that one of her Korean ELL students does not know the meaning of the word *uncle*, which appears in the book. The teacher could quickly look up the word *uncle* in the student's dictionary and point to the translation. The teacher does not need to know how to read Korean, or any other non-English language for that matter, to look up words in a bilingual dictionary.

Bilingual picture dictionaries are also an excellent resource. Many are organized by topic (body parts, family members, food, clothing, classroom, doctor's office, etc.) and provide illustrations with numbered objects. The numbers correspond to a list of vocabulary words below the picture in the two languages. The popular *Oxford Picture Dictionaries,* published by Oxford University Press, are available in 12 bilingual editions: Arabic, Brazilian Portuguese, Cambodian (Khmer), Chinese, Haitian, Japanese, Korean, Polish, Russian, Spanish, Thai, and Vietnamese. Teachers who are familiar with these dictionaries can coordinate them with classroom themes and lessons.

Electronic bilingual and multilingual dictionaries or translation devices offer another resource (see Figure 10.1). These handheld devices contain thousands of words. The user types a word or phrase on a small keyboard and then pushes a button to bring up the translation. Some models also have a speaker that provides a pronunciation of the word. The dictionaries are available in many languages. During oral conversations, an ELL student may hear a word he or she does not know the meaning of and would like to look up. But if the student also does not know how the word is spelled, the teacher, or another student in the conversation, with the ELL's

Figure 10.1   English-Vietnamese talking dictionary (GD-315V), ECTACO Electronic Translators (www.ectaco.com)

permission, could type in the word for the student to get the translation. Newer models of translation devices, however, may make the typing step unnecessary. These models have built-in voice recognition. Students (or teachers) can simply say a word in one language, and the device will display and speak the translation.

The role of bilingual dictionaries in the language classroom is a subject of debate, with some educators concerned that students will rely on them, rather than using other vocabulary-learning strategies, such as figuring out the meaning of words based on context, or even using an English-only dictionary. Educators seem to agree, however, that some bilingual-dictionary use, particularly for ELLs at the lower levels of English proficiency, is beneficial. As with any scaffold, to be effective, the scaffold of bilingual dictionary use should be taken away at some point. As students' proficiency in English grows, they will rely less on their dictionaries. I believe, however, that even ELLs who are more advanced should be allowed to access dictionaries when needed, particularly when they are writing, because a bilingual dictionary can help them find the right words in English to express thoughts that are still in their L1.

Accept Initial Writing in Students' L1 as They Transition to English Writing

Newly arrived ELLs with low levels of English proficiency are unlikely to be able to write much in English. If these students have literacy skills in their L1, teachers should consider allowing them initially to write in their journals in their L1. Even if the teacher cannot read what is written, at least the students are writing! As a teacher, I would much rather have L1 writing than a blank page. Teachers may be able to find a colleague or friend who can read the language and tell them what it says. But eventually teachers will notice that the students will begin to write in English when they feel ready. Most likely, by the end of the school year, the journal entries will be entirely in English.

Read Aloud Native-Language Versions of Books Used in Class

Some English-language books teachers use for read-alouds in class, or that students might read independently during sustained silent reading, are available in other languages, particularly Spanish. Teachers can use these books in other languages to benefit ELL students. For example, a teacher, as part of a unit on the five senses, plans to read the book *The Magic School Bus Explores the Senses* by Joanna Cole and Bruce Degen. She obtains the Spanish-language version of this same book, *El autobus magico explora los sentidos,* and either she or a paraprofessional reads the Spanish-version aloud to the Spanish-speaking ELLs before she reads the English-version aloud to the class. If the teacher does not speak Spanish but has a recording of the book in Spanish (one that was recorded commercially or one recorded by a paraprofessional or volunteer), she could make the book and audio recording available at the listening center. She could also make the book available for students to read on their own or take home to read with their families.

When students have had a chance to read or listen to the L1 version of the book, they will have become familiar with the characters, setting, plot, and the science concepts covered in the book. Then, when the teacher reads the same book aloud in English, these students will be able to understand much more because of their background knowledge of the book. In other words, comprehensible input will be maximized. In using this technique, teachers should take care not to read the L1 version and the English versions back-to-back, because this would be too much like the ineffective concurrent translation method discussed earlier.

Provide Native Language and Dual Language Books for At-Home Reading Programs

Teachers encourage their students to read at home and encourage parents to read with their children. Many ELLs, however, come from low-income homes with few books. Also, many parents of ELLs do not read English well, if at all, and thus have difficulty reading aloud to their children English books brought home from school. To solve this problem, teachers can obtain a collection of books in the native languages of their ELLs and create a classroom lending library of books children can check out to read at home. Reading is reading. For ELLs, reading or being read to at home in the native language promotes literacy development. Sending home native language books allows parents of ELLs to participate in their children's education. Along with the linguistic and literacy skills that can transfer from L1 to English is the enjoyment of reading, the development of life-long readers, and a model of parents as fluent readers.

In dual language books the text of the two languages may appear one above the other or side by side or on opposite pages. These books can be very useful because teachers, students, and students' family members can read either the English or the native language text or both in the same book. Recordings can be sent home along with the book in both languages, or better yet, the teacher could send home a blank tape or a digital audio recorder for a family member to record the book in the native language. Having the two languages side-by-side does not necessarily recreate the problem of concurrent translation in print, because the students do attend to the English language text and the L1 text provides support to make the English text comprehensible.

Native and dual language books are easy to find. Many school libraries and most public libraries have non-English collections. Spanish-language books, including dual language books—can be ordered through book clubs, such as Scholastic's Club Leo, or purchased from a bookstore. Children's books in languages other than Spanish and English can be ordered on-line through booksellers such as Amazon or companies that specialize in foreign language books for schools. Shen's Books (www.shens.com), for example, carries native and dual language children's books in over 25 different languages. A simple Google search for "children's books" and the name of the language you are looking for will usually return a surprising number of relevant resources.

Students can also create their own dual language books. A good example is a project by students at Thornwood Public School, an elementary school near Toronto, Canada, who created dual language books in 17 languages with assistance from family, friends, teachers, and older ESL students in the school. These dual language books are featured on their Web site (thornwood.peelschools.org/Dual/). Thornwood has a multilingual student body representing over 40 languages and cultural groups from all over the world. The project got started when six of the school's classroom and ESL teachers, in partnership with faculty at local universities, began collaborating to find effective ways to address the literacy-learning needs of their ESL students by forging stronger home-school connections.

Key to their efforts are activities drawing on the strengths of students' and their families' native languages through the creation and use of dual language books and recordings. A statement on the group's Web site explains the rationale for this project:

> We believe that reading in any language develops reading ability. We want to engage parents in reading with their children at home and to encourage discussion and the sharing of their experiences and realities. As a result, the group decided to create dual language book bags, comprising of dual language books and multilingual audio tapes, for use at school and at home. Non-English speaking parents could enjoy reading the stories to their children in their own language and elaborating on the ideas, values, skills, and concepts introduced in this "expanded" home literacy program. Student/parent/community volunteers would record the multilingual stories on audiocassette.
>
> Through the use of audiocassettes, ESL students and parents would be exposed to basic English vocabulary, grammatical structures, and conventions of text.
>
> Promoting literacy development in the ESL student's first language will facilitate the acquisition of literacy in English. Accessing prior knowledge through the use of their first language provides the framework for new learning.

The site also offers links to research and other relevant sources, including an article written by the teachers with Jim Cummins published in *Educational Leadership* (see Recommended Reading). Thornwood's efforts illustrate the possibilities for PLS even in schools that are highly multilingual and where teachers do not know all the languages spoken by their students.

Send Home Letters in the Students' Native Languages

Many effective teachers send home monthly or weekly letters to parents describing what students are learning in class, suggesting ways parents can help and reporting other classroom news. For ELL students, these letters could be sent home in their native language, preferably with English on one side and the native language on the other. Some parents may not be able to read in their L1 but can find someone who can either read the L1 version to them or translate the English for them. Many schools employ bilingual community workers or liaisons who can assist teachers with translation of letters like these, and some districts even maintain a translation office where such assistance can be provided.

Another often overlooked source is the teacher's guides for major curriculum programs, some of which include monthly letters in several different languages that can be sent home. These letters explain what students will learn in the next month, with suggestions on ways parents can help at home. Teachers can simply copy these letters and send them home.

Students Helping Students

Students who are proficient in both English and their native language are an excellent source of PLS. Teachers just need to facilitate their help in an appropriate and effective manner. When newcomer ELLs arrive with little or no English proficiency, teachers can assign them a buddy who can speak their language. This buddy can help orient the new student to the classroom and school routines. The teacher can make seating arrangements so that lower-level ELLs are seated next to or in a table group with a bilingual student to make it easier for the lower-level student to have someone to ask for quick clarifications and assistance when needed. When students work in centers, teachers can arrange for lower-level ELLs to partner with higher-level ELLs or fluent bilingual students who can guide the lower-level student through the required tasks.

Teachers must be careful, however, that newly arrived students do not rely on their bilingual buddies to the extent that the buddies are just translating for them all day. This is a form of concurrent translation and therefore would not be effective in helping the new ELL learn English. Teachers need to establish clear guidelines to ensure that the buddy's own learning is not disrupted and the lower-level ELL does not become overly dependent.

Computer Software and Internet Resources

Many educational software programs come with built-in PLS, typically in Spanish but occasionally in other languages as well. This support could range from running the program completely in another language to translations and explanations to help students interact with the program in English. For example, the Living Books series, which brings to life popular children's books, such as *Arthur's Teacher Trouble* by Marc Brown, and traditional stories, such as "The Tortoise and the Hare," give students the option of listening to and interacting with the story in English or Spanish (and even Japanese for some titles). The popular multimedia program KidPix Deluxe 4 includes a "Spanish mode" with help, menu options, tool dialogues, and foreign language character support to help Spanish-speaking ELLs successfully interact with the program. In some ESL software programs, PLS is often just the click of a mouse away.

The latest versions of Microsoft Office Suite programs (e.g., Word, PowerPoint, Excel, Outlook) have built-in translation tools that offer translations of single words, phrases, sentences and even an entire document into French, German, Italian, Japanese, Korean, Chinese (People's Republic of China or Taiwan), Spanish, Dutch, Greek, Portuguese, and Russian. In Microsoft Word, the translation tool can be accessed by selecting then right-clicking text, then choosing "translation" from the pop-up menu. The Internet offers free translation tools (see Box 10.2) and on-line bilingual dictionaries for over a hundred different languages (On-line Translation Tool, links).

Box 10.2

Online Translation Tools

The following Internet resources can translate individual words, phrases, sentences, paragraphs or even entire documents or Web pages into and between several different languages. They should be used with caution for translations of larger chunks of text.

AltaVista Babel Fish Translation
babelfish.altavista.com
Dictionary.com Translator
dictionary.reference.com/translate/text.html
Free-Translator.com
www.free-translator.com
Google Language Tools
www.google.com/language_tools?hl=en
Systran
www.systransoft.com
Translation Booth
www.translationbooth.com/tb/aojb/Tpl
World Lingo Free On-line Language Translator
www.worldlingo.com/en/products_services/worldlingo_translator.html

These translation tools are generally effective for translating single words. Students and teachers must use extreme caution, however, when using them to translate entire sentences, paragraphs, and documents. Translation is a difficult task and a fine art that requires an expert human touch. Computers can only approximate this task. The translations tools listed in Box 10.2 are notorious for producing translations riddled with errors. They are intended to give users just a rough idea of what a text is about. Under no circumstances should a teacher use these programs to translate letters or other communications with parents or to create classroom materials without having them first checked and corrected by a knowledgeable translator.

A growing number of educational Web sites include bilingual interfaces. For example, at StoryPlace: The Children's Digital Library (www.storyplace.org), students can decide whether they want to interact with the on-line stories and activities in English or Spanish. The Enchanted Learning Web site (www.enchantedlearning.com) features on-line activities and reproducible educational materials that can be printed and used in the classroom. Many resources are available in English and Spanish, and a few resources are available in other languages.

VoyCabulary (www.voycabulary.com) is a free on-line tool that can make all the words on a Web page link to any number of reference works, including bilingual dictionaries. Two steps are required: cut and paste the URL of the Web page onto the VoyCabulary page and select the reference work or bilingual dictionary you want all the words to be linked to. For example, if a student is reading from a Web site about electricity and runs into an unfamiliar word, such as *circuit,* if he has linked to Voycabulary, he simply clicks on the word and up pops a Web page with the translation! Currently VoyCabulary works with bilingual dictionaries for over 30 different languages.

Seek Bilingual Parent or Community Volunteers

A final source for PLS is to seek out bilingual volunteers who can help out on occasion in the classroom. Even assistance of just an hour or so a week can go a long way, as my experience with the two newcomer Cambodian students shows. Many schools have active parent volunteers, and some of these parents may be bilingual in English and one of the languages spoken by ELLs in the school. If no parent volunteers are available for a particular language, schools may be able to find volunteers through community-based organizations, particularly those that serve ethnic communities. Another source of bilingual volunteers is through service-learning programs in high schools, colleges, and universities.

When volunteers can be found, teachers should plan ahead to maximize the use of their time, keeping, for example, a running list of concerns or questions for them to address the next time they come in to work with the students. Also, the teacher should save any work the students had difficulty completing in class and provide instructional materials the volunteers can use to re-teach difficult concepts in the students' native language. Teachers should also set up a system that allows the volunteers to report back to the teacher the students' progress and provide feedback.

SUMMARY

Primary language support, when provided properly, can maximize ELLs' comprehension of English-language instruction and thus help the students acquire English more quickly and effectively. PLS is consistent with a variety of learning and language-learning theories, and researchers have documented evidence of its effectiveness as an instructional strategy for ELL students. Concurrent translation and replacing written English text with oral L1 translation are ineffective ways of providing PLS. More effective ways of providing PLS include strategies that (1) enable ELLs to quickly grasp concepts they were struggling to learn in English, (2) prepare students to attend to English instruction or print in order to receive greater amounts of comprehensible input, (3) lower students' affective filters, (4) enable ELLs to interact at greater levels with their teacher and peers, and (5) enable teachers to assess the level of their students' comprehension of instruction in English. PLS sends students a strong message that even in an English-medium classroom, their native language is valued and is a viable resource for learning. This message creates a very positive environment for ELL students conducive to effective language and content-area teaching and learning.

Discussion Questions

1. How can the use of students' native languages facilitate their English language development and maximize their comprehension of sheltered English content-area instruction?

 2. **On-line Discussion Board**   Describe any experiences you have had (as a student or as a teacher) with the PLS strategies discussed in this chapter. Describe other strategies for providing PLS you know about that are not mentioned here. How effective did you find these strategies to be in helping students learn English and academic content taught in English?

3. There is sometimes a fine line between primary language *instruction* and primary language *support*. What is the difference, and why is primary language support so important, particularly in nonbilingual classrooms?

 4. **On-line Discussion Board**   The press has reported cases of principals or teachers who outlaw any use of ELL students' languages in the classroom or school. Describe any instances you may have heard about or seen personally. Why is this a mistake? What do these educators misunderstand about the role native languages can play in helping ELLs learn English and academic content through English?

Research Activities

 1. **Wiki This**   *Classroom Primary Language Support Inventory.* Visit an ELL classroom or do an evaluation of your classroom if you are already teaching. How many of the following evidences of PLS can you find in the classroom? Discuss your findings with the classroom teacher or with a colleague.
   - Bilingual/multilingual classroom labels (wall, door, desk, chair, clock, etc.)
   - Bulletin boards and other wall displays that include students' L1
   - Bilingual dictionaries
   - Books and other instructional materials in the students' L1
   - Bilingual computer software or use of bilingual resources on the Internet
   - Student writing in their L1
   - Preview-review
   - Assistance in L1 provided by the teacher
   - Acceptance by the teacher of L1 comments and answers during classroom discussions
   - PLS provided by students for each other
   - Bilingual paraprofessional or classroom volunteers who provide PLS
   - Cognate word study lessons
   - Other _____

2. **Wiki This**   Interview a teacher about his or her use of PLS using the questions below as a guide.
1. What languages are spoken by your ELL students?
2. Do you speak any of the languages spoken by your ELLs?
   a. (yes) What are some ways you provide PLS for these students?
   b. (no) Have you been able to find ways to provide PLS for your ELLs, even though you cannot speak their L1? If so, what are some things you do?
3. Do you allow your students to speak to each other in their native languages in class? Why or why not?
4. Do you believe that PLS can help ELLs learn English and academic content through English? Why or why not?
5. Do you have any written materials in the native languages of your students? If so, how do you use these materials to provide PLS?
6. Do you encourage the parents of your ELLs to read books to their children in their native language? Why or why not?
7. How do your school or district administrators feel about PLS?
8. What resources do you wish you had so that you could provide more effective PLS?
9. Do your ELL students feel their native language is valued by you and the school?
10. If you have been providing PLS for your students, how effective has it been in helping them learn English and academic content?

 3. **Wiki This**   Pick two or three languages spoken by ELL students in a school with which you are familiar. Do an Internet search and make a list of resources that could be used to provide PLS for these students. Show your list to school administrators and teachers. Add any item not already listed.

Recommended Readings

Cummins, J., Bismilla, V., Chow, P., Cohen, S., Giampapa, F., Leoni, L., et al. (2005). Affirming identity in multilingual classrooms. *Educational Leadership, 63*(1), 38–43.
A report prepared by Cummins, in collaboration with teachers from Thornwood Public School; provides a rationale for the use of dual language books and describes the process the teachers used with their ELL students to create dual language books in 17 languages.

Ulanoff, S. H., & Pucci, S. L. (1999). Learning words from books: The effects of read aloud on second language vocabulary acquisition. *Bilingual Research Journal, 23*(4), 319–332.
The authors report the findings of their research investigating the use of preview-review as a primary language support strategy to increase ELL students' English-language vocabulary.

Weber, N. (2000, August). *Sink or swim? A look into an English immersion class.* ldt.stanford.edu/~ninaweb/Sink%20or%20swim.pdf
The author describes the importance of primary language support and how it benefits her ELLs in her elementary school classroom.

Wright, W. E., & Li, X. (2006). Catching up in math? The case of newly-arrived Cambodian students in a Texas intermediate school. *TABE Journal, 9*(1), 1–22. www.tabe.org/members/Catching%20_up_in_Math.pdf
Findings of a case study detailing, in part, the primary language support provided for two newcomer ELL students from Cambodia; also calls into question federal and state policies for testing newcomer ELLs.

11

Technology

> Without question, our ability to easily publish content online will force us to rethink the way we communicate with our constituents, the way we deliver our curriculum, and the expectations we have of our students.
>
> —Will Richardson (2006)

KEY TERMS

- computer-assisted language learning (CALL)
- Read/Write Web
- WebQuests
- VOIP (voice-over-Internet protocol)
- blog
- wiki
- podcast

GUIDING QUESTIONS

1. How can ELL educators use technology to support their teaching?
2. How can teachers use technology with ELLs in the classroom?
3. How can ELLs use technology to support their content learning and English language acquisition?
4. What are some promising uses of technology for ELLs?

When computers first became widely available during the 1970s and 1980s, there were many debates in the field about whether or not they should be used for language learning. This debate was long over by beginning of the 21st century. Technology is so entwined with our daily lives that the use of technology in language-learning classrooms is beyond question (Chapelle, 2001). Now the debate is squarely centered on how to use technology effectively to facilitate, enhance, or even accelerate the second language acquisition process.

Carol Chapelle (2001), an early pioneer and one of the leading authorities in the field of computer-assisted language learning, explains in her important book *Computer Applications in Second Language Acquisition: Foundations for Teaching, Testing and Research*, that the earliest experiments with computers and language learning began in the early 1950s with massive mainframe computers, though nothing was documented until the 1960s. In the 1970s two universities—Brigham Young and the University of Illinois at Urbana-Champaign—were involved in large federal grants to explore the potential of computer-assisted language instruction. In the early 1980s, personal computers became readily available and affordable, and in 1983, at the annual TESOL conference, the term computer-assisted language learning (CALL) was agreed on and an interest section by that name was added to the organization the following year. Participants from the 1983 conference also formed a new organization, the Computer-Assisted Language Instruction Consortium (CALICO), which remains a leading organization in the field today.

The widespread availability of the Internet beginning in the mid 1990s revolutionized the field for students and for CALL professionals, who now had universal access to materials and information in the field. For example, the on-line journal *Language Learning & Technology* published its first issue in summer 1997, and other on-line journals related to the field have appeared since. For language learners, Chapelle (2001) points out, "interesting opportunities for autonomous language learning and self-assessment became widely available rather than being tied to a particular institution." Furthermore,

> CALL activities were no longer limited to interaction with the computer and with other students in the class, but included communication with learners in other parts of the world—either learners from specific classes chosen by instructors or self-selected participants who choose to spend time in computer-mediated communication for language learning. (p. 23)

At the beginning of the 21st century, a revolution began in language learning and technology. The latest developments in Internet technology have changed how we interact with the Internet—we no longer just "surf" the Internet. Now we also read on it and write to it, using tools that are easy enough for anyone to use (Richardson, 2006). New technologies are emerging that also make it very easy to collaborate with people nearby and those half a world away. Jim Cummins, Kristin Brown, and Dennis Sayers (2007) document case studies that highlight the use of technology and the Internet by ELL teachers and their students in transformative ways as they collaborate to question their world and share their findings with others.

Will Richardson (2006) refers to this "new Internet" as the Read/Write Web (or Web 2.0) and points out that educators are just now coming to terms with how the new technology can revolutionize education:

> Without question, our ability to easily publish content online will force us to rethink the way we communicate with our constituents, the way we deliver our curriculum, and the expectations we have of our students. It also has the potential to radically change what we assume about teaching and learning, and it presents us with important questions to consider: What needs to change about our curriculum when our students have the ability to reach audiences far beyond our classroom walls? What changes must we make in our teaching as it becomes easier to bring primary sources to our students? How do we need to rethink our ideas of literacy when we must prepare our students to become not only readers and writers, but editors and collaborators as well? (p. 5)

These same questions apply equally to teachers of ELL students. But beyond them are even more basic questions for educators and researchers in the CALL field. Chapelle (2001) raises the important point that much of the attention in CALL has focused on learning new technologies and looking for ways to apply them to language classrooms, but we currently lack a research base and framework for evaluating the effectiveness of these technology applications. The central question is whether or not, for language learners, the use of these technologies adds value, that is, what is the technology adding that otherwise would not be there, and is this addition something of real benefit? Chapelle (2001) points out the need to define "value added" and to find a way to assess the extent to which value has been added for learners who use CALL. In her book, she lays the groundwork for such an assessment.

Although addressing Chapelle's concerns is beyond the scope of this chapter, readers should keep her point in mind, recognizing also that many technology applications have great potential for helping ELLs learn English, but we have to be careful about doing technology just because it is fun. Teachers should constantly evaluate their use of technology and ask, "What value is being added for my students through my use of this technology?" Answers to this question will help teachers implement technology with their students in the most effective and beneficial ways possible.

In this chapter, we explore CALL in its broadest sense, encompassing all potential uses of technology—including those that do not necessarily require a computer—for language learning and teaching. First we look at different types of technology resources available to teachers and students. Next we point out some poor uses of technology that, unfortunately, are quite common. Finally, we explore a few of the many promising practices for the effective use of technology to facilitate second language acquisition in the classroom and make suggestions about how teachers can find their own resources that address specific needs within their classrooms.

Technology Resources for Language Learning and Teaching

Technology resources may be thought of in three broad areas: those that teachers may find beneficial for their own use, those that teachers can use with their students, and those that students can use on their own, inside and outside of the classroom.

Resources for Teachers for Their Own Use

Technology can help teachers who work in programs with a canned (predetermined and designed) curriculum by helping to fill the need for supplemental lessons and resources for their ELLs. It can help teachers who work in schools that lack funding for resources and materials and teachers who may feel isolated in their classrooms—particularly those who are the lone ESL, bilingual, or sheltered English instruction teacher in their school.

Planning Lessons and Adding Resources

The Internet is an excellent source for lesson plans and activities for ELL classrooms. In the past teachers had to create their own lessons and activities or settle for whatever was outlined in the teacher's guide of their school's curriculum. Those days are over. Just as colleagues within a school might share lessons plans with each other, there are now vast networks of thousands of ESL teachers around the world happily sharing their lesson plans and activities with each other over the Internet.

Do you have some students who are struggling with verb tenses when asking questions? Try a lesson activity from About.com: English as 2nd Language (esl.about.com/library/lessons/blintro_lower_intermediate.htm). Do you need to teach a science lesson on the weather that is appropriate for beginning ELLs? The everythingESL.net Web site offers a lesson plan called "Be a Weather Reporter!" with reproducible materials in pdf format (www.everythingesl.net/lessons/weather_vocab.php). Are you looking for quick game ideas that are appropriate for the ESL classroom? Take a look at some of the games under the Idea Cookbook at Dave's ESL Café that have been submitted by ESL teachers from around the world (www.eslcafe.com). See Box 11.1 for a list of just a few of the Web sites out there that offer free ESL lesson plans and ideas. Specific ideas and resources for teachers to incorporate technology into their teaching can be found at 4teachers.org: Teach with Technology (4teachers.org).

The Internet is also great for finding supplemental resources for lessons.[1] Need clip art or photos to help teach and reinforce key vocabulary? A simple search of

---

1: Copyright may be an issue in using on-line text, photos, videos, or other materials in multimedia presentations you or your students create for use in class or for publishing on the Internet. Although much of what is used for education purposes falls under fair use (as long as proper citation is given to the original source), not everything found on the Internet can be used. TESOL's *Essential Teacher* magazine offers a guide for ESL teachers on these issues at www.tesol.org/s_tesol/secetdoc.asp?CID=1222&DID=5722

Box 11.1

ESL Lesson Plan Web Sites

Dave's ESL Café
www.eslcafe.com
EFL/ESL Lessons and Lesson Plans from the Internet TESL Journal
iteslj.org/Lessons
English Baby!
www.englishbaby.com
English Lesson Plans for ESL EFL Classes fromAbout.com: English as a 2nd Language
esl.about.com/od/englishlessonplans/English_Lesson_Plans_for_ESL_
EFL_Classes.htm
ESL Activities.com
www.eslactivities.com
ESL Kids Lab
www.english-4kids.com
ESL Lesson Plan
esl-lesson-plan.com
everythingESL.net
www.everythingesl.net
TEFL.net (TEFL Networks for English Teachers)
www.tefl.net

free clip art sites such as Microsoft Office Online (office.microsoft.com/en-us/clipart/default.aspx) with thousands of free images (and sounds) is a great place to start. You can find photos or images of just about anything with a simple search on Google Images (images.google.com). Flickr (www.flickr.com)—a site where people all over the world freely share their photos, and photos are tagged with useful searchable keywords—is another rich resource for ESL teachers looking for photos to include in lessons. Video clips on practically any topic can be found on YouTube (www.youtube.com) and video-sharing sites specifically for educational purposes, such as TeacherTube (www.teachertube.com) and SchoolTube (www.schooltube.com).[2]

Audio and video clips from the Internet can add immeasurably to a lesson. For example, I once taught a lesson about Martin Luther King Jr. and wanted my students to hear his voice. A quick search of the Internet provided several sources from which I could download sound bites from his famous speeches. Those brief recordings brought the lesson to life and the students were enthralled by King's powerful voice and speaking style, so much so that I overheard them at recess repeating lines from his speeches. On another occasion, we read the book *Ayu and the Perfect Moon* by David Cox, about an Indonesian girl learning the traditional dance of her culture. I wanted my students to hear the traditional gamelan music described and beautifully illustrated in the book. A simple Google search led me to free downloads of gamelan music. We listened to the recordings while we read the book and also while we did postreading activities in connection with the book. The gamelan music really brought the book to life, and students were able to relate it to traditional music in their culture. One other example: I once had my students make flags of other countries as part of a social studies unit. When the students presented

---

2: Teachers should be careful about allowing students to search YouTube, Flickr, and Google Images, because they may return inappropriate material. These services offer filtering to prevent the most offensive material from being displayed, but it may never be possible to block all inappropriate content. The contents of School Tube and TeacherTube are closely monitored to ensure that all content is appropriate for educational use.

their flags to the class, we used a CD-ROM-based encyclopedia to listen to each country's national anthem and to listen to and view traditional music and dance from each country.

Creating Your Own Materials

Over the years teachers have spent a small fortune at their local teacher supply store buying bright, colorful posters and wall displays and workbooks containing reproducible activities to supplement the curriculum provided by their school districts. But with advances in technology, teachers can now easily create professional-looking materials on their own. I frequently visited my local teacher supply stores and took note of anything that looked useful, then went home to my computer and made the overpriced materials myself. Word processing, desktop publishing software, and cheap color ink-jet printers make it easy to combine text and images to create professional-looking classroom resources. A growing number of Web sites help teachers create their own worksheets, language games such as word searches and crossword puzzles, and assessment tools such as rubrics and quizzes (ESL Lesson Plan Websites, links).

Interacting and Networking with Other ELL Professionals

The Internet offers a virtual teachers' lounge where ESL teachers from all over the world can gather to share ideas and resources, discuss the latest research, boast about recent accomplishments or student achievements, or simply vent their frustrations. This form of social and professional networking is a very effective antidote to the isolation ESL teachers, who may be the only one in their school, often feel. The same is true for bilingual or sheltered classroom teachers, who often make up a small minority of teachers within their schools.

Newsgroups and on-line discussion boards were some of the first mediums available for teacher networking and continue to be popular through services such as Google Groups. They are organized by topic, and anyone can post messages or respond to others' messages. Users can post new topics for discussion and others will respond. As a new teacher of bilingual Cambodian students, I actively participated in on-line discussion boards related to teaching and also those related to Cambodian Americans. These sites gave me many great ideas to try out in my classrooms, and through them I became aware of many issues in the Cambodian American community that affected my students and their families. Listservs also were an early medium that remain popular. A listserv is a discussion group handled through e-mail. In California I was on a listserv affiliated with the California Association of Teachers of English that dealt with literacy issues, both pedagogical and political. As a teacher, I found it thrilling to receive e-mail messages and engage in discussion with well-known scholars who actively participated on the list. I read with great interest major debates between listserv members. What I learned from these on-line discussions went well beyond what I had read and learned in college. In Arizona, I actively participated (and continue to do so) on a listserv that focuses on bilingual education and policy for ELLs in that state. Like the California listserv, this one brings together leading scholars, administrators and teachers, and other advocates for ELL students. I also started my own listserv for educators and community leaders focused on the education of Asian and Pacific American students (APAlist).

For these who want more immediate interaction, there are now live chat rooms where ESL teachers can gather and type messages back and forth to each other in real time. Instant messaging offers another avenue for the live interactions between ELL professionals. An emerging technology is voice chat rooms, where groups of people can meet and talk about specific topics rather than typing. These technologies can be great resources for students. Twitter (www.twitter.com), a microblogging service, is also rapidly becoming a way for teachers to share ideas and resources, and even for teachers and schools to communicate with parents. Users post "tweets," messages limited to 140 characters, which can then be read by followers on their computers, cell phones, or other handheld communication devices.

Virtual conferences and professional development workshops are also now a reality. TESOL began organizing these in the mid 2000s. In one such workshop, Margo Gottlieb, an assessment expert, discussed issues related to testing ELL students. Participants from all over the country were able to hear Gottlieb's voice clearly and to see her PowerPoint slides while she discussed them. With the simple push of the control key, they could ask questions through their computer microphones. A later TESOL virtual workshop featured two ELL experts, Kate Menken and Debora Short, who discussed strategies for meeting the needs of adolescent ELL students, featured live video, and viewers were able to e-mail in questions that were answered during the Web cast. The on-line virtual reality world Second Life (www.secondlife.com) has also been used for on-line conferences, where users' avatars (computerized representations of themselves) enter a virtual conference hall, sit in virtual chairs, listen to presentations, and ask questions. Behind the avatars and virtual setting are real people sharing knowledge for use in the real world. As this technology develops and catches on, it will become easier than ever to organize gatherings of ELL professionals without the time and financial constraints of attending face-to-face meetings.

New forms of educator collaboration began to emerge in the mid 2000s with the emergence of blogs, wikis, and podcasts. These tools of the Read/Write Web have made it much easier for teachers to share ideas and resources and are discussed in a later section.

Resources for Teachers to Use with Students during Lessons

With a single computer connected to a projector or classroom television, teachers can use a multimedia presentation program such as PowerPoint, Keynote or Google Docs Presentation for their lessons, bringing in text, graphics, and video that can provide excellent scaffolding support for ELLs. I frequently used a word-processing program for modeled and shared writing with my students. This technology made it very easy to revise when we composed texts together. I also created simple slideshows using PowerPoint, KidPix, or Hyperstudio for students to learn and practice new vocabulary.

Teachers can incorporate interactive activities from ESL and educational software programs into their lessons. For example, during a lesson about regrouping in addition and subtraction, I used a simple software program with animated interactive visuals that allowed students to drag and drop base-10 block manipulatives to the 1s, 10s, and 100s places to regroup numbers. I would model how to do this and then allow individual students to come up and use the program to solve problems. I could have done the same thing with paper-based manipulatives on the board, but the software program's sound effects and vivid graphics and the speed and ease of manipulating the virtual manipulatives made it all the more engaging and interesting for my ELL students (i.e., value added) and prepared them to work in small groups and on their own with real base-10 manipulatives to solve problems similar to those we worked on as a class.

If Internet access is available through the classroom computer, teachers have the vast resources of the World Wide Web to incorporate into their lessons. They can easily include relevant photos, graphics, animations, sounds, and videos into their lessons and have the whole class participate in on-line interactive activities. Teachers can even take their students on virtual field trips. I once observed a bilingual teacher at a newcomer school for Hmong students using a zoo's Web site to teach his students about animals. These newcomer students did not yet have sufficient language proficiency in English or technology skills to navigate and read the sites on their own, but the teacher used the photos and graphics on each page to describe, explain, and discuss each animal with the students in Hmong. I did not have the benefit of having a live Internet connection in my own classroom when I was a teacher, so I saved interesting and relevant Web pages on a disk from home and then copied them to my classroom computer to share with students.

Resources for Students to Use on Their Own

One important software application is word-processing programs for students to type and publish their final drafts of their writing produced through Writer's Workshop, or to use with other writing projects. Students can also be taught how to use PowerPoint, Keynote, Google Docs Presentation, KidPix, or Hyperstudio to create multimedia presentations to demonstrate what they know and can do in language and in the content areas. They can use programs such as Inspiration or Kidspiration to create graphic organizers to assist them with the prewriting stage (see Figure 11.1), or with postreading comprehension activities.

Many software programs are available to help students learn English as a second language by engaging them in structured listening, speaking, reading, and writing activities in English. The better and more sophisticated programs assess students and start them out at the appropriate level, monitor their progress, and increase the difficulty as their English language proficiency improves. These programs can also produce detailed progress reports for students and their teachers.

Other computer software programs in reading, writing, math, science, and social studies that are not necessarily designed for ELLs are nonetheless appropriate (or can be made appropriate) for ELL students. They often use vivid animation and other graphics and audio instructions and other sounds that help make the input comprehensible for ELL students. Some of the activities are in the form of games that, because they are fun and are played in a low-risk environment, can lower students' affective filters. These programs may also support differentiated instruction, with students starting at the appropriate level and moving through the program at their own pace.

In addition to commercial software, more and more educational resources are

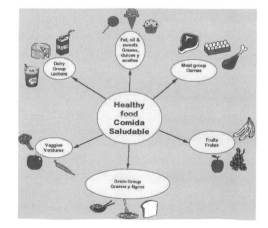

Figure 11.1   Graphic organizer created using Kidspiration by Marysol Trevino, Adrienne Padilla, and Rosa Jonasz, graduate students at the University of Texas at San Antonio in 2007
(www.inspiration.com/productinfo/kidspiration/index.cfm)

appearing on the Internet that are designed for ESL students, ranging from on-line ESL curricular programs to Web-based resources that help ELLs learn vocabulary and grammar, improve their pronunciation, and develop their listening, speaking, reading, and writing skills. Although some commercially developed ESL curricular programs are delivered on-line and require a fee, many other on-line programs and resources are free.

Also, teachers are finding it easy to use commercial, government, entertainment, and other Web sites to enhance student interaction and learning. The most effective uses of technology involve student collaboration to use such Internet sites to find information and create multimedia presentations to share with the rest of the class (Macy, 2002). As just a few examples, students can prepare a budget for a vacation by visiting travel Web sites to research the prices of airline tickets and hotel reservations; they can plan a menu by visiting restaurant Web sites; they can compare and contrast the prices of consumer goods by visiting different online retailers; or students can watch and summarize on-line news reports on a particular topic of interest.

The computer is now also a major tool for communication that is opening up all kinds of possibilities for ELL students to engage in computer mediated communications (CMC) with proficient English speakers (or with other students learning English) though the use of on-line discussion boards, e-mail, chat, and even live talk through the use of voice-over-Internet protocol (VOIP) programs such as Skype (www.skype.com). Blogs, wikis, and podcasts are also providing new and exciting ways for ELL students to practice using their English in authentic contexts. These and other technologies are discussed later in this chapter. With these programs, students engage in social activities that can enhance their English language development.

Poor Uses of Technology

Simply using technology is not enough. Educators need to consider *how* technology is used. Just as with any other tool, strategy, or technique a teacher can use, teachers should define a specific learning goal that technology helps to facilitate. And as Chapelle (2001) stresses, there needs to be value added beyond what could be done without the computer. In what follows we discuss four examples of poor uses of technology that are all too common in classrooms today.

- Using Technology to Keep ELLs Busy
  In mainstream classrooms where an untrained teacher has only a handful of ELLs and thus chooses to focus instructional attention on the fluent English speakers, he or she may find a few computer programs or on-line activities that amount to little more than busy work, with no real language or content-area goals. Worse yet, sometimes students are just told to "go use the computer" and are left on their own to find things to do.
- Using Technology to Recreate Poor Teaching Approaches and Methods
  Just because something is on a computer, it is not necessarily representative of effective teaching methods. Many computer programs for ELLs and other students are nothing more than old-fashioned drill-and-kill worksheets with a few bells and whistles. With any software program, teachers should look beyond fancy graphics and sound effects and analyze the actual task students are being asked to complete. What methods or approaches does the task represent? What does the computer add that goes beyond a traditional worksheet

or beyond what a teacher or student can do without the computer? Many software programs provide little more than tasks common in outdated methods, such as the grammar-translation method or the audiolingual approach.

■ Using Technology to Supplant Rather Than Support Teacher Instruction
Computers and other technology resources should be used to support teacher instruction; they should never supplant a teacher's instruction. Even in schools that purchase comprehensive ESL curricular software, the computer should never replace the teacher. One of the worst abuses I have ever seen was in an elementary school where a new sheltered English immersion teacher had only a couple of hours in the afternoon to teach her newcomer ELL students, because the school required the students to spend almost the entire morning in the computer lab using a program ill-suited to their language and literacy needs. Clearly, the amount of time spent on computers should be limited, and teachers should integrate the software programs into their instruction by first teaching new concepts and then inviting students to practice them on the computer. And skills and concepts practiced on the computer should be reinforced through classroom activities off the computer.

Adhering to the following guidelines will ensure that computers support rather than supplant teacher instruction.

1. Students should never spend more time on the computer than they spend with their teacher.
2. Students should never spend more time interacting alone with a computer than with their teacher and fellow students in the classroom.
3. Software programs used with ELLs must be reviewed to ensure that they are appropriate for addressing the students' specific language and academic needs.
4. Teachers should never place faith in a piece of computer software to teach their students English. The computer is no replacement for a teacher. (See Box 11.2 for an example of how students can get away with things on a computer in manner that would never work with a good teacher.)

■ Using Computers for a Single Software Application
Sometimes administrators and teachers get so excited about a particular software program, they buy computers exclusively for its use. I recall walking into one ELL classroom that had five brand new Macintosh computers. I was anxious to see how the teacher integrated technology into her classroom but was disappointed to learn that the computers were used only for Accelerated Reader, a reading comprehension program, the merits of which are debatable, as discussed in Box 7.5. It was disheartening to see that those powerful and expensive computers were not being used to their full potential in ways that would have been much more beneficial for the ELL students.

Promising Practices
for Technology Use with ELLs

Now let's look at some of the more promising ways that educators are using technology to facilitate the language and content-area learning of their ELL students. What follows is a brief overview of the possibilities. Readers interested in more are encouraged to look into the books listed at the end of this chapter and to explore the links in this chapter and on the companion Web site. Any mention of specific

Box 11.2

What's Wrong with This Picture?

Monica Uses the Computer

The following vignette is based on an actual observation in a middle school computer lab.

Monica, a newly arrived 8th grade ELL student with beginning English proficiency, is working with a math computer program in her school's lab. The lesson she is working on covers the concept of place value for up to ten-digit numbers. The computer first presents text explanations and graphics to model the mathematical concepts and steps for solving problems.

With a click of the mouse the text can be read aloud to help students understand if they are poor readers. But Monica does not wear the headphones. She says they hurt her ears. Furthermore, her lack of English vocabulary means she probably would not understand the read-aloud anyway.

Monica is expected to advance slowly through several screens of instruction to read the content and learn the concept. At the end of the lesson, there is a five-question quiz. If students miss any of the questions, they have to repeat the lesson and try the quiz again.

Monica flies through the lesson, advancing each instructional screen by rapidly clicking on the mouse without even attempting to read the text. She gets to the quiz and tries her best to answer the questions. She gets three of the five questions wrong and has to repeat the lesson. She quickly advances through the lesson screens again with no attempt to read them, in order to get back to the quiz as quickly as possible. She remembers she missed questions 1, 4, and 5. When she gets to these questions, she does not try to read them again. Instead she just randomly picks a different answer than last time. Now she has only two incorrect answers. She repeats this process two more times (within a matter of minutes) and gets a perfect score. She is congratulated for mastering the lesson and is allowed to proceed to the next lesson.

How effective is this computer program in helping Monica learn new math concepts? What does this example demonstrate about the dangers of computers replacing teacher instruction? How could the use of this software program be made more effective for Monica?

software titles or Internet resources are for illustrative purposes only. There is a vast and growing number of fantastic programs and resources available and it is simply not possible to list and describe all of them.

ESL Software

A walk around the exhibition hall at the annual TESOL conference will present one with a dizzying array of computer programs designed to help ELLs learn English. These software programs range from those that focus on a specific skill, such as pronunciation, to comprehensive curricular programs addressing listening, speaking, reading and writing. Much of the software is geared to high school students and adults, but there are a growing number of programs for younger ELL students.

Appropriate ESL computer software in the hands of effective teachers offers another avenue for ELL students to learn English in nonthreatening and potentially highly motivating ways. Many ESL software programs can provide comprehensible input while lowering the affective filter. For example, programs typically include multiple levels so students can start at their level of proficiency and move through the program at an appropriate pace. In other words, computer software can allow for differentiated instruction—a big need for classrooms with students at different levels of English proficiency. Most programs incorporate music, sound effects, and spoken English that can be part of the activities or that students can activate to have instructions read aloud or repeated as many times as needed. Some offer written or oral translations in several languages. These programs are also typically visually stimulating, and many include animations or video and present learning tasks in the form of games. Most programs also provide immediate feedback on errors and students are given multiple chances to relearn and redo tasks until they are mastered. Some programs also keep track of students' progress and generate detailed reports to the teacher.

Despite the promises of ESL software, remember that ESL software is only as effective as the teacher who makes use of it, and it should always be used supplementally. The computer should not replace the teacher or regular ESL instruction during which the student interacts with the teacher and other students. After all, the main purpose of learning a new language is to be able to communicate with fellow human beings, not computer software.

Internet-Based Resources

There is virtually no limit to Internet-based resources that can be used with or by ELLs. Teachers are challenged to find authentic and interesting material for students to listen to and read. Written materials are available on just about any topic at any reading level and often formatted in highly appealing ways with graphics and images and links to related information. Finding these materials starts with a search on Google or other search engine. There are thousands of Web sites designed by educators for students that can easily be adapted and made more accessible for ELL students. As starters, try BrainPop (www.brainpop.com) for games and entertaining educational videos and also try Scholastic (www.scholastic.com/kids), PBS Kids (pbskids.org), and Disney (www.disney.com), which offer educational games and activities with popular characters from books and TV that may appeal to students. The *Internet TESL Journal* offers Activities for ESL Students (a4esl.org), a collection of activities and quizzes for ESL students to improve their vocabulary and grammar skills, and ESL: Kids (iteslj.org/links/ESL/Kids), with links to sites and resources that are especially appropriate for younger ELLs. Or check out Interesting Things for ESL Students (www.manythings.org) for hundreds of activities in listening, speaking, reading, and writing. Among the resources at Dave's ESL Café are idiom, phrasal verb, and slang dictionaries and message boards for student interaction. Another popular site is English, Baby! (www.englishbaby.com), which includes a daily lesson with an audio dialogue between native speakers, along with full transcripts and hyperlinked text to define and explain any difficult vocabulary or cultural concepts. These and many other ESL Web sites tend to target secondary and adult students, but teachers of younger ELLs will find plenty of content that is appropriate and a growing number of resources for younger ELLs, such as the EFL Playhouse (www.esl4kids.net), the ESL Young Learners section of English Club (www.englishclub.com/young-learners/index.htm), and ESL Kids.com (www.esl-kids.com), which provides song lyrics and links to on-line games and many other resources.

Word Processing and Multimedia Applications

The most obvious application of word processing is for student writing associated with Writer's Workshop, but it can also be used for any other student writing projects, with the advantage that final drafts can be shared electronically by e-mail or posted on a classroom or school Web site.

The ease of making corrections and revising the text with a word processor makes it more likely that students will revise. Teachers need to advise all students, especially ELLs, that they may use the spell-check and grammar-check features but they should not just accept the first correction the computer offers. I once had a student type a caption for a photo of his two friends that read "Bora Sam and Sath Kimseng under a tree." After the computer's grammar and spelling suggestions were accepted, the caption read, "Bora and Sam sat kissing under a tree."

Microsoft Word offers additional writing tools, including an on-line dictionary, thesaurus, and encyclopedia that can be accessed without leaving the program. A simple right-click on the target word brings up a menu from which students can look up the word in a dictionary or even instantly select a synonym. Another little-used support, as mentioned in Chapter 10, is the option to translate a word, phrase, sentence, paragraph, or even an entire document from a pop-up menu. Students can also type English words directly into the translation tool to check the meaning in their native language, for example, to make sure they are using the word correctly, or they can type in a word in their native language and get the English translation so they can use that word in their writing. As with the spell-check, students need to be taught how to use these tools effectively and to be aware that the results they get may not necessarily be what they were looking for.

Another little-known feature of Microsoft Word makes it an ideal tool for listening and speaking practice with many potential uses. Teachers can easily embed audio clips, including recordings of their own voice. A small speaker icon appears where audio clips are available, and the student double-clicks on it to listen. With this tool, for example, students could complete a worksheet on the computer and the teacher could record instructions to help those who still have difficulty reading or imbed an audio-clip with instructions in the students' native language. Audio clips could be placed throughout the worksheet to provide helpful hints or suggestions in areas where students might have difficulty. Or the teacher could create a worksheet that focuses on listening comprehension, where students listen to an audio clip and then complete tasks related to it. Students could listen to the clip many times if necessary. The students could also be taught how to use the audio recording feature and thus complete tasks that require them to respond orally. The document could be saved and the teacher could open it later and listen to and assess the students' oral responses. Video can also be embedded within a Word document, adding visual support to listening comprehension tasks.

Teachers can use the comment feature in Microsoft Word (available by clicking on the "Insert Comment" icon on the toolbar or by clicking on the "Insert" menu and choosing "Comment") to add support within an electronic worksheet. For example, a reading passage could be glossed with definitions, explanations, synonyms, translations, or even pictures to help the student read and comprehend the passage. Thus, for example, the student might come across an unknown word, such as *supper*. By accessing the comments for the word, the student could read a definition or see that *dinner* is a synonym, or see a picture of a dinner plate filled with food, or perhaps all three.

Microsoft's office suite programs are quite expensive. Fortunately, there are free alternatives. OpenOffice (www.openoffice.org), by Sun Microsystems, is a suite of programs very similar to those in the Microsoft Office suite and can be downloaded free from the Internet. A similar suite of free productivity programs is Google Docs (docs.google.com), which is used directly on the Internet and thus does not require downloading or installation (see Figure 11.2).

Figure 11.2   **Screenshot of Google Docs**

Besides being free, Google Docs has many advantages over traditional word processing and productivity programs. The program, and the documents created with it, can be accessed from any computer anywhere in the world that is connected to the Internet. If a student begins working on a paper at school, for example, and he has the Internet at home, he can open the file and continue working on it when he returns from school. If he does not have Internet access at home, he could access the file from a computer at the public library, an Internet café, or a friend's house. Even if the student has to return temporarily to his home country, he can still access and work on his files, if he can find a place to access the Internet. There is no need to carry around or worry about losing a disk or flashdrive and no worries about transferring viruses between computers and no worries over whether their computers have the required software program or correct version. But this is just the beginning.

These documents are accessible by anyone the student allows. Thus, for example, a teacher could have instant access to a student's work in progress, inserting suggestions and comments to help him or her revise and further develop the work. A teacher or a peer could also help out with proofreading. Students could work on the same document in collaborative groups outside of class. Parents could be given access to their children's work, so they could monitor their progress and provide assistance where needed. Google Docs makes it easy for students to publish their completed documents on-line, available for anyone to read. This feature brings the notion of "publishing" to a whole new level that goes beyond sticking a story on a classroom wall or including it in the classroom library. Imagine students' sense of audience if they know their published stories are available literally all over the world.

Students use multimedia software typically to create presentations. This software is great for ELL students because it allows them to incorporate photos, clip-art, or other images and sound or video clips to illustrate what they know and what they learned about a particular topic. These presentations can be a good alternative to traditionally written reports in English, which ELLs naturally struggle with. A completed presentation also provides an excellent support (scaffolding) for students' oral presentations to the class.

WebQuests

With the evergrowing number of fantastic resources on the Internet, the challenge for teachers, particularly teachers of ELLs, is guiding students to appropriate Web sites. One effective way to address this challenge is through WebQuests, activities designed by teachers to structure students' time on the Internet by directing them to specific Web sites and giving them tasks to complete as they visit each site.

For ELLs, these tasks are a form of scaffolding. Simply telling an ELL to go use the Internet to research butterflies, for example, could be overwhelming for the student. The number of hits returned from an Internet search will be in the millions. Even if students end up on an appropriate Web site, the reading level may be too difficult. But through a WebQuest, the teacher scaffolds the experience by first selecting appropriate Web sites and then designing a task appropriate to the student's level of language proficiency. A beginning student, looking for information on butterflies, for example, could be sent to a site with photos of different butterflies and asked to select one, then draw it and write its name. More advanced beginning-level students could be sent to a site that illustrates the life-cycle of a butterfly and use this information to complete their own butterfly life-cycle charts. Intermediate and advanced students could start with these activities as warm-ups and then be sent to sites with extended written information and questions to answer. An assignment like this scaffolds their reading by helping them read for a specific purpose. Figure 11.3 provides a sample of the beginning of a WebQuest on butterflies for ELLs.

The easiest way to prepare a WebQuest is to use a word processing program, such as Microsoft Word or Google Docs, that allows teachers to embed links students can click on. Below each link, the teacher inserts a description of the task and the space needed for students to complete the task (draw a picture, complete a graphic organizer, write or select answers, report results of an on-line experiment, etc.). PowerPoint works just as well. Some teachers prefer to use a Web-page design program to create their WebQuests in html format so that they can be used directly within the Internet browser. Students can also be given paper worksheets to record their answers. Note that WebQuests created in Word or PowerPoint can easily be saved in html format, so there is no need to learn to use Web-page design software.

WebQuests are becoming a very popular tool in education and can be found ready made on many different topics and grade levels on several Web sites. Most of these sites enable teachers to create and share their own WebQuests. A great place to start is WebQuest.Org (www.webquest.org), which includes a blog on WebQuests and links to a database created by San Diego State University containing over 2,500 WebQuests. The database can be searched by content area and grade level. Keep in mind when using a predesigned WebQuest, however, that most were not designed to accommodate ELL students and may require modification to make them appropriate for students at different levels of language proficiency. Also, be aware that the Internet is constantly changing. Links that worked last year, last week, or even this morning may no longer be working when students begin their quest. Always check to make sure all the links are working properly just before students begin working, and have alternative links as a backup.

E-mail, Message Boards, Instant Messaging, and VOIP

One challenge facing ELL educators is they are sometimes the lone model of proficient English for their students. Students in the class may all be ELLs and come from homes or neighborhoods where little English is used. Effective teachers create

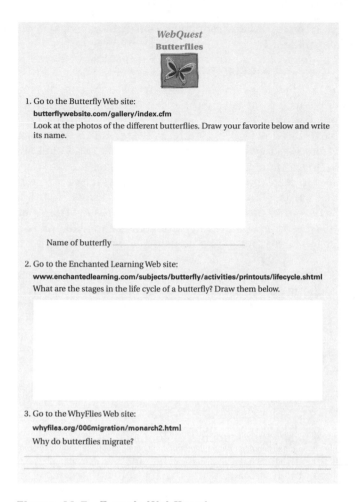

Figure 11.3   Sample WebQuest

opportunities for their ELL students to interact as much as possible with native or fluent English speakers. In the past, creating these opportunities meant arranging buddies from other classrooms or finding community volunteers to be conversation partners or finding pen pals with whom students can exchange letters. Although these are still great strategies, technology is making it easier for teachers to create opportunities for students to interact with proficient English speakers.

E-mail is the easiest and most common means for connecting students. Yesterday's pen pal is today's *key* pal. The regular exchange of e-mail messages allows ELL students to use their new language in an authentic way. In the best of circumstances, ELLs are paired with native-English speakers who have been trained to be patient and to use their responses to model back the correct spelling and grammar usage their ELL partners have trouble with, rather than to overtly correct their errors (Sauro, 2007, 2009).

Sometimes ELLs are paired with other ELLs as key pals. Although such pairings raise the concern that the students may not be modeling correct English for each other, what is important is that the students are practicing their new language for authentic communication purposes. Teachers can guide the students' participation by suggesting topics and pre-teaching appropriate vocabulary and structures. They can also monitor the interactions and provide assistance where needed.

The text of the interaction, which can easily be saved, also provides teachers a rich resource for identifying the needs of the students and planning instruction accordingly. The texts of these interactions (with students' names removed) can also be used for effective mini-lessons.

On-line message boards usually focus on a specific topic, and anyone with knowledge or interest in that topic can participate by posting information or asking or answering questions. Currently, most, if not all, of the available on-line message boards designed for ESL students are for adults, though a number of "kid sites" incorporate message boards that ELLs can read and contribute to. If students are matched to a topic of high interest—for example, video games—they may be highly motivated to read and write. Teachers should take care to monitor students' use of message boards. Many message boards on kid sites are moderated by responsible adults who either prevent inappropriate messages from being posted or remove students who post such messages. Teachers can also create and control their own message board for their students using Google Groups, or through the free course management system Moodle (www.moodle.com).

Instant messaging, a phenomenon that took off in the early 2000s, refers to the quick exchange of written text with one or more people who are simultaneously connected to the Internet. It is like e-mail, except that messages are shorter and responses are received in real time. It is essentially having a live conversation through your fingertips, which, for an ELL student can be a huge advantage. The conversation has features of spoken discourse but because it takes place in written language, there is enough of a delay that the recipient can reread the message a few times to fully comprehend it and still have time to think through the answer carefully, reviewing and revising it as necessary before sending it (Sauro, 2007, 2009). In other words, it provides built-in wait time, something quite rare in oral conversations. At the end of the session, there is a written record or a "chat script" that the student can save to go back and review, and even look up words—more things you cannot do with oral conversation! Teachers can also review the chat script, glean important data to inform future instruction, and use it the script for mini-lessons.

Teachers should be involved in pairing up students up with an appropriate partner, just as in the key pal program. For obvious safety reasons, teachers should never allow students to interact with unknown people over the Internet. Teachers therefore should avoid the use of chat rooms (unless it is a room they have created and control), which work much like instant messaging but typically include a large number of people in an unmoderated environment.

All the technologies described so far require the use of text and typing to interact with others through the Internet. This feature is great for developing students' vocabulary and writing ability but does little to directly address their listening and speaking needs. VOIP (Voice-over-Internet protocol), however, a technology that began taking off in popularity in the mid-2000s, has great potential for providing authentic oral communication opportunities for ELLs. Many of the instant messaging services include the option to communicate by speaking rather than typing. All that is needed is for both computers to have a microphone connected. Another option is to add a video camera (or "webcam"), so that the people talking can see each other. Most new computers, including laptops, now come with built-in video cameras for this purpose. This option is great for ELLs, because they now can have visual cues while interacting with their partner, which can facilitate greater comprehensible input. Another nice feature that goes beyond the telephone is the ability to send files back and forth, such as photos or written documents, which give the speakers something additional to talk about and adds further visual support for the ELL student.

VOIP has taken off because it essentially allows people with computers to make

Box 11.3

Blocking Access to Internet Resources

Most schools use filters to block content that is not appropriate for students. But filtering software is never 100% effective, and it also blocks access to many legitimate educational Web sites. Some districts go even further by only allowing access to a limited number of approved websites. Teachers can request additional sites to be added, but these are submitted and approved one at a time. This policy gives students (and teachers using the Internet at school) access to only the tiniest fraction of on-line resources.

Many schools, in their concern for student safety, also block access to e-mail, instant messaging programs, on-line discussion boards, VOIP programs, such as Skype, and even blogs, wikis, and podcasts.

If you were (or are) a teacher in a school or district that blocks these sites, what are some ways you could argue for their educational value, particularly for ELLs? What are some measures you, your school, or your district could take to find ways to balance the need to keep children safe with the need to prepare students for the reality of communications, knowledge construction, and knowledge sharing in the 21st century?

free long-distance phone calls with families and friends over the computer. Skype emerged in the mid-2000s as a leading company in this area. The program is free to download and use. The only time a charge is incurred is when it is used to call another person's landline telephone or cell phone. Skype also offers the ability to video conference. There are a few other key features of Skype, however, that make it a particularly powerful language-learning tool. First, Skype makes it easy to record the conversation (including the video if videoconferencing is used). The captured audio and video can be reviewed by the students after the conversation to go over any areas of difficulty. They can also incorporate the recordings into multimedia presentations. Thus, if students were studying idioms, for example, they could put real examples from their conversations into a PowerPoint presentation they create for the class.

With any of the technologies described here, teachers must be vigilant and monitor their use to ensure that they are used appropriately. Although these technologies pose great language learning possibilities, there is also a great potential for abuse. Students must be taught how to interact appropriately with others on-line and what to do if someone attempts to interact with them in an inappropriate way. Most schools have developed policy statements related to the appropriate use of technology. ELL teachers should make themselves familiar with their school's policy and make sure their students and their families fully understand it. Some schools block these types of Web sites on school computers. See Box 11.3 for a discussion on this controversial issue.

Another issue to consider is the style used by many native speakers in their on-line interactions. As mentioned in Chapter 8, a new variety of English is emerging with truncated words, alternative spellings, and new acronyms to accommodate this new communication mode that has prescriptivists worrying about the decline of English (Kolesnikova, 2008) and descriptive linguists arguing that languages are always changing. David Crystal (2004) refers to the variety of language emerging from computer-mediated communications as "Netspeak." To teachers of ELLs who wonder how to help ELLs learn both the standard English needed for academic success and these new forms of communication, I suggest that when students use these technologies, they (and their partners) be required to use standard English. The native English speakers should be reminded that they are models for the ELL students and thus should write the same way on-line as they would in their regular student work. As ELLs continue to acquire standard English, they will also figure out the more contemporary ways their peers are using English (or Netspeak) on-line on their own.

Blogs

A blog (short for Web log) is an easy-to-create and easy-to-update Web page that requires no advanced technology skills and no specialized software. No programs need to be downloaded or installed. And most blogging services are free. A blog can be updated from any computer with an Internet connection. Bloggers (those who blog) can even update their blogs by e-mail, cell phones, or other handheld communication devices.

Unlike regular Web sites, where information is posted by the owner and retains its same look and organization, a blog is more like a journal where new entries are added regularly. The most recent entry appears on the top, and the others move down. As a page gets full, older entries are removed and archived (typically by week or month) on other pages. Entries are given titles and sometimes also tagged with keywords, which facilitate searching for past postings and information. Besides text, bloggers can include hyperlinks to interesting things they saw or read on the Internet. For example, bloggers frequently comment on news articles they read on-line and provide the link directly to it so others can read it too. They can also add photos or even videos to their postings. Such postings are easy to do through on-line photo and video sharing sites, such as Flickr, YouTube, TeacherTube, and SchoolTube. This feature allows ELLs, for example, to post a photo from their home country to their blog and write about it, or they can post humorous video clips and describe why they find them funny. The photos and videos provide visual support for language learning, and they can be highly motivating for students to write about.

Blogs also allow users to post items to the left or right column of the blog, which do not move each time new postings are added. These postings can be links, lists, photos, videos, or other information. For example, a student could write a brief autobiography that is accompanied by links to some favorite Web sites, a list of favorite television shows, movies, or musicians and bands, or a list of books they are currently reading. The entries along the side of the blog allow a student to present his or her interests and personality to the world.

The best feature of blogs, however, as Richardson (2006) explains, is that they are not built on static chunks of content but instead are made up of reflections and conversations that are regularly updated, often daily and even several times a day. "Blogs," he adds, "engage readers with ideas and questions and links. They ask readers to think and to respond. They demand interaction" (p. 18). That final point is what makes this technology particularly beneficial for ELLs. Many teachers require students keep dialogue journals or literature response journals. Typically the entries are read only by the teacher. Why not have the students keep these journals as a blog? Suddenly students' thoughts and ideas are no longer just a school assignment to satisfy the teacher but are open to a much bigger audience. Blog entries—called postings—can be read by the blogger's fellow classmates, other teachers or administrators in the school, family members, or anyone else who is interested. And these readers can post their own comments on the student's entries, thus enabling meaningful interaction surrounding the student's work. Because blog postings are permanent (unless a user deletes his or her blog) and are indexed by keyword and therefore searchable, for an ELL student, a blog becomes in essence an on-line portfolio of his or her progress in learning and using English.

David Lindsay, an elementary school teacher in Southern California who has used a variety of Read/Write Web technologies with his students, has found blogs to be particularly beneficial for ELL students. He explains, "For ELL students, the blog

Box 11.4

Important Rules About Blogging

Break the Rules and You Will Not Blog!

1. Do not include your name—use your student number/class code.
2. Do not include the name or address of our school.
3. Check your post for spelling errors, grammar errors, etc. Paste your post into WORD and run spell check.
4. Do not write about anyone else in your blog without his or her permission—No Names!
5. Use appropriate language.
6. Do not write anything that could hurt someone's feelings.
7. Never touch anyone else's blog entry.
8. NOTE: You cannot leave comments for someone else unless you are logged in. Comments should be kind.

Source: Grandview Library's blog, Grandview Elementary School, Monsey, NY (www.grand viewlibrary.org/StudentBlogs.aspx).

allows them to respond asynchronously—taking part in a conversation that does not bear the threat of requiring the rapid response that classroom discussion does. It also provides a media-rich environment that engages different modalities."[3] The blog he and his students contribute to is a districtwide blog for the Saugus Union School District, which has helped to create a sense of community among the students and teachers and the students' families (students.saugususd.org/_weblog/everyone.php).

A major challenge in motivating students to read is finding interesting things for them to read. Blogs can help solve this problem because students are often genuinely interested in reading what their friends write. This fact is made evident by the explosion in popularity of social networking sites, such as MySpace and Facebook, where networks of friends check out and comment on each other's postings.

As with all the other technologies discussed so far, students should be taught never to reveal any personal information on their blogs that could identify them. Also, users can set up their blogs so that only people they allow (e.g., teachers, friends, family members) can post comments. This measure prevents creepy strangers from posting inappropriate comments on their blogs and also keeps out the spammers. Schools and teachers need to teach students how to blog responsibility and establish a set of ground rules. An example of one school's rules appears in Box 11.4.

As mentioned earlier, Twitter provides a "microblogging" service that took off in the late 2000s and by 2009 quickly became one of the most widely used social networking services. The appeal of Twitter to ESL teachers is that postings on the service—tweets—are limited to 140 characters, which is about the number of characters in this sentence. Thus these short, highly communicative texts may be of great interest to students because they do not take long to read or write. At the time of this writing, ESL teachers and other educators are just beginning to explore the potential educational applications of Twitter (see, e.g., Twitter for Teachers twitter forteachers.wetpaint.com/).

Wikis

A wiki is a Web site that is easy to create and update. Unlike a blog, a wiki can be developed and updated by many people in collaboration. Richardson (2006) notes

---

3: Personal communication, August 29, 2009.

the important value this has for students: "As we continue to move towards a world where everyone has access to ideas and where collaboration is the expectation rather than exception, wikis can go a long way to teaching our students some very useful skills for their future" (p. 63). A wiki Web site can potentially be changed by anyone, anywhere who wants to add to or edit the Web site, though it is possible for the creator to control who can access and change it. No special software is needed, and wikis can be updated through any computer with an Internet connection.

The most well-known wiki is Wikipedia (www.wikipedia.org)—the largest encyclopedia in the world. It includes millions of articles in over a hundred different languages. Wikipedia is being created by millions of users, just like you. Anyone can add an article, and anyone can edit an existing article. In other words, anyone can be an author or editor of this major work. The founder of Wikipedia explains that the goal of this project is for "every single person on the planet" to be "given free access to the sum of all human knowledge" (quoted in Richardson, 2006, p. 59).

Although the accuracy of articles in Wikipedia and even the appropriateness of its use in schools has been the subject of much debate (see discussion in Richardson, 2006), the fact remains that when there are errors in Wikipedia, unlike those in traditional print-based encyclopedias, they can be corrected right away, and new articles are added daily. Important events sure to be of historical significance are added almost immediately after they happen and are continually updated as new details become known.

Wikipedia can be a great source of information for ELLs because they will find entries there for things they would never find in the encyclopedia in their classroom or school library, and they can find articles that explain cultural references that puzzle them or on topics that interest them. And with a couple of clicks and keystrokes, ELL students can add their own knowledge on their topic of interest and thus contribute to the sum of all human knowledge.

Wikis go well beyond just Wikipedia, which is just one example of a wiki. At Wikibooks (en.wikibooks.org/wiki/Main_Page), for example, books are being written collaboratively by many people in the same manner as Wikipedia encyclopedia articles and, like those articles, the books are free. At the time of this writing there were hundreds of books (more than 40 on education), with a combined total of over 37,000 pages, in various stages of development.

Wikijunior (en.wikibooks.org/wiki/Wikijunior), a subsection of Wikibooks, is a collaborative effort to create high quality books for young students in about a dozen different languages. Current titles in development or near completion include *Solar System, Big Cats, How Things Work, Bugs, Dinosaurs, Human Body, South America,* and *Ancient Civilizations.* These books contain easy-to-read text and are full of pictures and illustrations that make them ideal for ELLs, who can read them but also help write them. Within each book are incomplete or less developed sections (called stubs) just waiting for students to add their knowledge.

One book in development that may be of interest to teachers of ELLs is called *Languages* (en.wikibooks.org/wiki/Wikijunior_Languages). It is designed to help 8- to 12-year-old children learn about different languages around the world. Students can add information to the sections waiting to be developed, and if their language is not listed, they can add an entry about it. Once a Wikibook is considered complete, it can be downloaded as an eBook in Adobe Acrobat file format (pdf) or even purchased as a traditional bound book (see *Big Cats,* for example).

Besides reading or editing existing wikis, students can collaborate with their teacher and their classmates to create their own. Among several free wikis that schools can use is PBwiki (pbwiki.com), which is popular with K–12 schools. The site describes wikis as something like a shared white board on-line and is so named, as the site's subtitle declares, because "you can make a free wiki as easily as a peanut butter sandwich." Wikispaces (www.wikispaces.com) is another free site commonly used by schools. Using the free version requires putting up with advertisements on the site. A payment of a monthly fee of around $5 will turn off the advertising. (Wikispaces offers ad-free "K–12 Plus" at www.wikispaces.com/site/for/teachers100K.) Schools can also purchase wiki software to run off their own servers and thus maintain full control of the content and access.

Most wiki sites allow users to apply password protection to their sites and thus control who has the right to make contributions and changes. With the history tool, teachers can keep track of which students made which contributions or edits to the page. No more guessing or worrying about whether one student is doing all the work in a group project. Also, if an individual student is assigned to a particular section of the wiki to develop during the semester or the school year, the history tool can track the updates and changes made by the student and in essence function as a portfolio that tracks the student's progress. In addition, if a student accidentally messes up a page, a few clicks of the mouse within the history tool can restore the site to the point just before the damage was done.

Students could use the space on a wiki site to create their own versions of Wikipedia or Wikibooks based on things they are learning in class. They could use the wiki to post drafts of their stories. The teacher and their peers (or even their parents) could go in and assist with edits and revisions, or leave messages for authors with suggestions for improving their writing. Wikis could also be used for shared writing. In a graduate course on language learning and technology, my students and I created a wiki project for which each student—all of whom were bilingual or multilingual—described embarrassing moments they experienced while learning their second languages (see esl6973.wikispaces.com). For another course I taught, students created a wiki to document various heritage language programs we visited in the community and to report the findings of demographic research on different heritage language communities (saheritagelanguages.wiki spaces.com).

A project by an elementary school that uses wikis provides an example of their flexibility. The students in a third grade class that was working on a research project added their thesis statements to their class wiki (grandviewlibrary.pbwiki. com). One student, identified only by his first name, Argedis, posted the following thesis statement:

> I selected this topic because it is about my country, the Dominican Republic. I like my country because it's never cold and it's never winter so it never snows but it does rain. I will teach others about why I like my country and why it's special to me. My opinion is that the Dominican is a wonderful place and I could stay there forever. I could chill out there for my whole life. I am trying to prove that if you visit, it will be really fun and it's the best place.

When students completed their research projects, they edited their thesis entries to link to a new page where they shared their research findings.

Links and multimedia (images, sound, and video) can easily be incorporated into wikis. For a well-developed elementary school classroom wiki, check out this example David Lindsay developed for his class (community.saugususd.org/dlindsay/page/). It includes many links, images, and even blogs and podcasts produced by the students.

On a class wiki, an ELL teacher could, for example, post a photograph or video for students to view, and then students could each edit the page to add their thoughts about it. If they make spelling or other errors in their postings, they can always go back and fix it. Perhaps they will want to once they acquire more English and become aware of the mistakes they made in previous work.

Student-created wikis naturally will contain student errors related to their development as writers. To address this issue, Mr. Lindsay once had the following note posted on his class wiki:

Note to public—

This is a website that evolves under the care and efforts of an entire classroom of grade school students. As such, misspellings and grammatical errors will most likely be present, but one of the goals of the site is to encourage students to take responsibility for authorship and to push themselves to constantly revise and edit these pages that are available for the public eye. I do view the site daily and will correct any incorrect information that I find, as well as make suggestions for editing, style, organization, and content. For the most part, I will rely on students to make those changes because this is effectively their website.

Parents—

If you do happen to spot problems of a more serious nature (before I do) please let me know immediately so I can right them.

—Mr. Lindsay[4]

A note like this would be appropriate for a wiki developed by ELLs who are simultaneously developing their English language proficiency and their writing ability in English.

Podcasts

A podcast is an audio or video program available free on the Internet. Podcasts are like radio or television programs to which new episodes are added regularly. Most are created by amateurs and thus may lack the polished quality of professional radio and television programs. Anyone with a computer, a microphone, and an Internet connection can create a podcast using free, easy-to-use audio editing software, such as Audacity (audacity.sourceforge.net) or Garage Band, and make it available on-line for anyone in the world to listen to. With the addition of a digital video camera anyone can create a video podcast. You can find podcasts on just about any topic imaginable, including ESL, and there are a growing number of podcasts produced by ESL teachers and other professionals to help ESL students around the world learn vocabulary, grammar, idioms, and improve their listening comprehension (see Box 11.5). And ESL students can create their own podcasts. For example, ESL students at Central Middle School in Oregon created podcasts of themselves reading their favorite poems (available on Mr. Horne's ESL class blog at esltechnology.com/blog/?cat=10).

Podcasts can be listened to directly on the computer or downloaded and listened to on an iPod or other MP3 player. ESL educators are starting to realize the potential power of students' having their own MP3 players to use outside the classroom to practice listening and speaking. Teachers and students can make podcasts on the topics and themes they are studying in class and make them available through their classroom blog or just locally through the classroom computer. Some schools have set up syncing stations where new lessons can be downloaded to several MP3 players at once. With a system like that, students can download their daily or weekly lessons along with activities to help them practice listening and speaking at home. Many university professors podcast their weekly lectures through their course Web sites (or through iTunes University), where students can download them to their MP3 players and review them. Teachers of ELLs could easily do the

---

4: This note appeared on a former version of Mr. Lindsay's class wiki, which is archived at mrlindsay.pbworks .com

Box 11.5

ESL-Related Podcasts

English as a Second Language Podcast
> Center for Educational Development
> www.ESLPOD.com

A podcast for ESL students who want to improve their English listening and speaking. Produced and hosted by Lucy Tse and Jeff McQuillan, former professors of applied linguistics and education. New podcasts are added every few days. Each podcast is 15 to 20 minutes long.

Just Vocabulary
> www.justvocabulary.com

This daily (Monday through Friday) podcast provides short, 4 minute lessons introducing vocabulary words with example sentences, full explanations, and synonyms. Hosted by Jan Folmer.

English Grammar HELP and Podcasts for the Inquisitive ESL Student
> eslhelpdesk.com

Lessons to help ESL students learn a few "dos and don'ts" of English grammar. Each podcast is 4 to 7 minutes long.

ESL News Podcast
> eslpodcast.blogspot.com

A podcast that uses the news to help students learn English. Produced and hosted by an ESL teacher from New York City. Podcast averages 2 to 3 episodes a month, and each episode is 5 to 10 minutes.

a4esl.org—English as a Second Language Podcasts
> a4esl.org/podcasts

A Web site that lists the 30 most recent ESL podcasts from several different podcasts.

The CALLspot
> callspot.libsyn.com

A podcast for ESL teachers hosted by Shannon Sauro, a CALL expert from the University of Texas at San Antonio. Each episode features conversations with CALL practitioners and experts.

Edgycation TESOL
> edgycation.org

Scott Shinall and Scott Duarte, professors at Kansai Gaidai University in Osaka, Japan, talk about real-life topics that ESL teachers constantly face in secondary and post-secondary classrooms.

same. Key to language learning is repetition, and ELLs frequently do not understand everything their teachers say the first time they hear it.

With MP3 players that can also be used as digital audio recorders, individual students can make a recording that can be uploaded to a classroom computer for teacher review or turned into a podcast. Or they can create a podcast by using a program such as Audacity or Garage Band to record their voices, edit out or add in voice recordings, create intros, and add a musical background.

Stand-Alone Technology

Not all technology-assisted language learning requires a desktop or laptop computer. Personal digital assistants (PDAs), the iPod Touch, the iPad, and sophisticated mobile phones, such as the Palm Pre, Blackberry, and the iPhone, put the power of computers in the palm of the hand. Teachers and students more and more are using these handheld computers for language learning. These devices can run many kinds of software applications, including dictionaries and translation programs, as well as applications designed specifically for language learning. For example, the iTunes Application Store has over 100 applications related to ESL for the iPhone, the iPod Touch, and the iPad. As the technology in this area continues to develop, handheld computers and smart phones will likely become the technology of choice for language learning. Imagine the power of an ESL student learning and practicing new vocabulary and forms on his or her own device, and then with a few clicks being connected to a live English native speaker who engages the learner in conversation to help him or her practice what was just learned.

LeapFrog (www.leapfrog.com) produces resources that are becoming popular for use in ELL classrooms. Their main line of products includes interactive books in which students can point to sentences or words with a specialized stylus to hear them read aloud or to illustrations to hear their names in English. Many of the books also incorporate interactive tasks and games designed to help students improve their listening, speaking, and reading ability. LeapFrog has developed a series of interactive books for ELL students called Language First and also a series of interactive books in Spanish.

SUMMARY

The use of technology in language-learning classrooms is a relatively new phenomenon, beginning with the advent of readily available personal computers in the 1980s, the Internet in the 1990s, and tools of the Read/Write Web that began emerging in the 2000s. Although new educational technologies emerge faster than researchers can determine their effectiveness for language learning, many ELL professionals see great potential in new technology and are finding creative ways to use it to benefit themselves and their students.

Teachers in language-learning classrooms use tools available on the Internet to plan lessons, find resources, and create their own materials, as well as to network with other ELL professionals. The availability of computers—particularly those with Internet access—opens up many possibilities for teachers to incorporate technology for use with students while teaching lessons and conducting activities. Computers have also become an important tool for students to use on their own—both in and out of school.

Despite the potential, there are many poor uses of technology. Computers should never be used for just a single software application, to supplant teacher instruction, to just keep ELLs busy, or to implement outdated teaching methods such as drill-and-kill exercises. Technology can be an excellent tool in the hands of a skillful teacher who uses it to supplement ESL and sheltered instruction and sees it as a means for providing differentiated instruction and opportunities for authentic collaboration and communication.

To ELL students, technology is cool and fun and thus can be highly motivating. But when integrating technology into the classroom, teachers must constantly monitor and evaluate its use to ensure that the technology goes beyond the coolness factor, that value is added, and that it is really helping to facilitate and accelerate ELLs' English language development.

Discussion Questions

1. How was technology used, if it was used at all, when you were in school? How effective was this use of technology in helping you learn? What technologies described in this chapter do you use regularly and how do they benefit you?

2. **On-line Discussion Board** Describe any of your own experiences in using computer software or other types of technology to learn another language. How effective was this technology in helping you reach your goals?

 3. **On-line Discussion Board** Describe any uses of technology you have observed or experienced in schools. Explain why you feel these uses were poor or effective. Describe other uses of technology that are not discussed in this chapter but that hold great promise in helping ELLs learn English and academic content.

4. The "digital divide" refers to the problem of unequal access to computers and other technology. Indeed, one usually finds the best computers and computer labs in schools in upper- and middle-class neighborhoods rather than in poor neighborhoods. What are the implications for ELL students, and how can this inequity be resolved?

5. Some scholars and educators have questioned whether schools should be using their limited school funds to buy computers and other expensive computer hardware and software, particularly when they are typically underutilized. Some note the number of books that could be bought for the price of a single computer. Do you agree or disagree with these scholars and educators? If you disagree, what arguments would you make to defend the use of school funds to buy computers for classroom use?

Research Activities

 1. **Wiki This** Select a software program designed for ESL students and evaluate it. Go through the entire program as if you were an ESL student, trying out all aspects of the program. Document what you feel are the strengths and weaknesses of the program in helping students learn English. Explain whether or not you would use this program in you classroom, and justify your decision.

2. Do an extensive Internet search and create an annotated bibliography of Web sites and other Internet-based tools and programs you found that you believe would be beneficial for ELL students. Use the following headings to format your annotated bibliography

   URL:
   Title:
   Producer/creator:
   Description:
   Benefits for ELLs:
   Limitations:

3. Listen to (or watch) several episodes of a podcast designed for ESL students. Write a review of the podcast in which you discuss what you believe are the best features and what could be done to improve the podcast. Share your review with the creator of the podcast.

 4. **Wiki This** Visit an ELL classroom, or do a self-evaluation of your classroom if you are currently teaching. Make an inventory list of all the computer hardware and software available in the classroom. Observe the classroom for at least a day or up to a week. How much time did students spend using the technology? What software programs did they use? How effective was the use of this technology in addressing the language and learning needs of the ELL students?

Recommended Reading

Butler-Pascoe, M. E., & Wiburg, K. M. (2003). *Technology and teaching English language learners*. Boston: Pearson/Allyn & Bacon.
  This introductory textbook, grounded in second language acquisition research,

shows teachers of K–12 ELLs simple but powerful applications of technology that can help students develop communicative competence in English.

Cummins, J., Brown, K., & Sayers, D. (2007). *Literacy, technology, and diversity: Teaching for success in changing times.* Boston: Pearson-Allyn & Bacon.
Offers real life examples of students using technology as a tool for collaborative projects, which supports their language and literacy development while also helping them understand and critically view our multicultural society and world.

Egbert, J. (2005). *CALL essentials: Principles and practices in CALL classrooms.* Alexandria, VA: Teachers of English to Speakers of Other Languages.
A very readable overview of the principles of computer-assisted language learning for classroom ESL teachers, with examples of how these principles can be put into effective practice.

Levy, M., & Stockwell, G. (2006). *CALL dimensions: Options and issues in computer-assisted language learning.* Mahwah, NJ: Erlbaum.
A synthesis of the CALL field outlining the progress made and current issues; offers an in-depth look at the dimensions of design, evaluation, computer-mediated communication, theory, research, practice, and technology.

Macy, M. D. (Ed.). (2002). *Teaching ESL/EFL with the Internet: Catching the wave.* Upper Saddle River, NJ: Merrill Prentice Hall.
Offers dozens of sample lessons using the Internet that can easily be put into practice in ESL classrooms. Rather than listing Web sites designed for individual ESL student use, the contributors show how groups of students can collaborate using Internet resources to complete projects in a manner that builds their communicative competence.

Richardson, W. (2010). *Blogs, wikis, podcasts, and other powerful Web tools for classrooms* (3rd ed.). Thousand Oaks, CA: Corwin Press.
The author argues with passion and provides convincing evidence that the tools of the Read/Write Web will transform education and force us to rethink what it means to be literate and how to teach our students. He gives many of examples of educators making use of powerful new technologies.

Glossary

academic language proficiency. Refers to the level of language proficiency students need to successfully comprehend and perform grade-level academic tasks. The level of proficiency needed varies widely depending on the language demands and nature of the tasks.

accommodations. In testing ELLs, refers to modifications in the testing environment or testing procedures, or modifications to the test instrument itself, that are intended to make up for a student's lack of proficiency in the language of the test (e.g., providing extra time, oral interpretation of test directions or items, native-language versions of the test).

additive bilingualism. A situation in which a second language is eventually added to a student's native language without replacing it.

adequate yearly progress (AYP). The amount of progress a school or school district must make each year toward reaching target objectives (see AMAOs) under the federal No Child Left Behind Act of 2001. Determined mainly by student scores on state-wide tests. To make AYP under Title I of NCLB, increasingly higher percentages of students in each subgroup in each tested grade-level must pass the state tests each year. To make AYP under Title III, increasingly higher percentages of ELL students must make progress in learning English, attain English proficiency, and also make AYP under Title I.

affective filter. Refers to affective factors, such as fear, anxiety, shyness, and lack of motivation, that can block comprehensible input and thus prevent second language acquisition. Lowering the affective filter allows learners to receive more comprehensible input and thus enables them to acquire more of the second language.

analytic scoring. A form of assessment that focuses on several aspects of a student's performance, normally guided by a rubric that includes separate analytic scales. For example, a rubric to assess student writing may contain separate analytic scales for composing, style, sentence formation, usage, and mechanics.

annual measurable achievement objectives (AMAOs). Targets set by each state, as required by the federal No Child Left Behind Act of 2001, that indicate the percentage of students at each grade level expected to pass each state test. The AMAOs increase toward the goal of 100% of students passing each test by 2014.

assessment. The process of collecting and analyzing a wide variety of data from students that provides evidence of their learning and growth over an extended period.

before, during, after (BDA). In literacy instruction, refers to strategies used before, during, and after reading a text, to maximize student's comprehension. Also referred to as intro-through-and beyond.

bias. In testing, refers to the unfair advantages or disadvantages that may be given to certain students that can impact their performance. For example, a test given in English will be biased in favor of proficient English speakers and biased against students who lack proficiency in English.

Bilingual Education Act. Added in 1968 as Title VII of the Elementary and Secondary Education Act. Before passage of No Child Left Behind, it provided federal support for bilingual and other programs for ELL students and their families on a competitive grant basis.

bilingual immersion programs. For language minority students who are English dominant and native English speakers who desire to become bilingual. Students are initially instructed 90–100% in the non-English target language for the first 2 years of the program. Instruction evens out gradually to 50% instruction in English and 50% in the non-English language as students move up in grade level.

blog. Short for "Web log," refers to easy to create and update interactive Web sites where the most recent postings appear at the top and older content appears below (or is archived) in reverse chronological order. Blogs enable readers to interact with the blog creator and other readers by posting comments and questions related to the content.

cognates. Words that are similar in two languages because they come from the same root (e.g., *education* in English and *educación* in Spanish).

communicative competence. The ability to use a language to communicate effectively and appropriately with other speakers of the language. Includes grammatical, discourse, sociolinguistic, and strategic competence.

communicative language teaching (CLT). Language teaching approaches, methods, strategies, and techniques that focus on helping students develop communicative competence.

comprehensible input. Oral or written language that is slightly above a second language learner's current level of proficiency in the second language and thus provides linguistic input that leads to second language acquisition. Represented by the formula $i + 1$, where i is the current level of proficiency, and +1 is input slightly above this level.

comprehensible output. Oral or written language produced by a second language speaker that is comprehensible to the individual or individuals with whom he or she is communicating. Second language learners' need to produce comprehensible output pushes them to pay attention to gaps in their proficiency and thus may prompt them to notice more in the input and motivate them to learn the language they need to express their intended meanings.

computer assisted language learning (CALL). Refers to the use of technology in second language teaching and learning.

concepts of print. Refers to such reading-related issues as understanding the differences between letters and words and words and spaces, knowing where to start reading and how to do a return sweep to continue reading the next line, and understanding the basic features of a book, such as title, front and back cover, and even how to hold it properly.

concurrent translation. Providing line-by-line translation of teacher instruction or texts into the students' native language. Considered a poor use of the native language because it removes the need for students to attend to the second language and thus interferes with second language acquisition.

content-based instruction (CBI). An approach to second language instruction in which content-area subjects and topics are used as the basis of instruction.

cooperative learning. A process in which small groups of students collaborate and interact to accomplish a specific learning task or activity.

criterion-referenced test. Test designed to measure the degree to which students have mastered tested content.

developmental bilingual education (DBE). A form of bilingual education for ELL students, who initially receive about 90% of content-area instruction in their native language (L1) and 10% of content-area instruction through sheltered instruction. L1 instruction decreases slowly as sheltered English instruction increases as students move up in grade level. Instruction continues in both languages until the end of the program, even after students attain proficiency in English, to ensure that students attain strong bilingual and biliteracy skills. Also referred to as maintenance late-exit bilingual education.

differentiated instruction. Instruction that is tailored to the unique language and academic needs of each student.

dual language books. Books printed in two languages in which one language appears above the other or the two languages are written side by side on one page or on opposite pages.

dual language programs. A variety of bilingual program models for ELL and English-proficient students designed to help them become bilingual and biliterate. In a 50/50 model, half of the students are fluent English speakers and half are ELLs,

and 50% of instruction is English and 50% in the native language of the ELLs. In the 90/10 model, for the first few years, 90% of instruction is in the non-English language and 10% is in English. Instruction gradually reaches 50% in each language. Other variations exist. Also called two-way immersion.

Elementary and Secondary Education Act (ESEA). The main body of federal education policy and law and source for education funding to state and local education agencies. Passed in 1965 and binding on all states and entities that accept federal education funding.

emergent bilingual. An alternative label for ELLs that draws attention to the other language or languages in the learners' linguistic repertoires, situates these learners in a continuum of bilingual development, and emphasizes that a fundamental goal of programs for these learners should be to help them attain high levels of proficiency in both their first language and English.

emergent, early, early fluency, and fluency levels of literacy development. The stages or levels beginning readers go through during their literacy development.

English as a second language (ESL). Instruction that focuses on helping ELLs attain proficiency in English.

English for the Children initiatives. Referendums put to voters in four states with large ELL student populations that would place severe restrictions on bilingual education programs. In 1998 California voters approved Proposition 227, in 2000 Arizona voters approved Proposition 203, and in 2002 Massachusetts voters approved Question 2. An attempt to pass a similar initiative in Colorado (Amendment 31) failed.

English language development (ELD). An alternative label for English as a second language (ESL) programs and instruction, commonly used at the elementary school level.

English language learner (ELL). A label for students who are non-native speakers of English and are in the process of attaining proficiency in English. Sometimes shortened to English learner (EL).

Equal Educational Opportunities Act of 1974 (EEOA). A federal law that declares, "No state shall deny educational opportunities to an individual on account of his or her race, color, sex, or national origin." Includes the mandate that educational agencies take appropriate actions to help (ELL) students overcome language barriers that impede equal participation of students in education programs.

evaluation. The use of assessment data to make judgments about the progress of students' learning, the effectiveness of teacher instruction, or the quality of educational programs.

fluent English proficient (FEP). The official designation for former ELL students who have attained sufficient English proficiency to meet their state's criteria for redesignation.

formative assessment. The use of on-going assessments that help to identify a student's strengths and needs and thus informs subsequent instruction, building on these strengths while addressing these needs.

14th Amendment. An amendment to the U.S. Constitution ratified in 1868: "No State shall make or enforce any law which shall abridge the privileges or immunities of citizens of the United States; nor shall any State deprive any person of life, liberty, or property, without due process of law; nor deny to any person within its jurisdiction the equal protection of the laws." Several lawsuits regarding the education of ELLs have been argued under the 14th Amendment.

guided reading. A form of literacy instruction in which small, homogenous groups of students are matched to texts at their appropriate instructional level, and the teacher provides support as students attempt to read the texts on their own.

guided writing. A form of literacy instruction designed to address an area of need within students' writing development. Typically, guided writing lessons start with a mini-lesson on some aspect of writing; students practice the writing principle or strategy they were just taught, under the teacher's supervision, and then share their final written projects.

heritage language. In the United States, refers to a non-English language to which one has a family tie. Both ELLs and students who are proficient in English and may have little to no proficiency in their heritage language, as is common for 2nd- and 3rd-generation immigrant students, may be designated heritage language students.

heritage language programs. Programs for language minority students to develop or maintain their heritage language; includes bilingual programs for ELLs, foreign language classes targeting native speakers in K–12 and post-secondary education, and community-based after-school or weekend programs.

holistic scoring. A form of assessment in which a student's performance (e.g., a writing sample) is given a single score that represents an overall judgment of the performance as a whole.

independent reading. Reading students are able to do on their own with little or no support.

independent writing. Writing students are able to do on their own with little or no support.

interactive writing. Writing instruction for ELL students who are at the beginning stage of writing, in which the teacher and the students compose a short sentence or paragraph. The teacher helps the students construct the sentence or sentences in enlarged text (e.g., on chart paper) by guiding individual students as they come up to add individual letters or words, and helping them to make relevant sound-symbol correspondences.

invented spelling. Also called developmental spelling, transitional spelling, or temporary spelling; refers to a temporary stage emergent writers may go through as they rely on their knowledge of sound-symbol correspondences to write words as they sound to them.

journals. Notebooks in which students write regularly to practice and develop their writing skills.

language-as-resource orientation. A point of view in which the native language of ELL students is viewed as a strength to be developed and built on to help the students learn English and academic content.

language experience approach. A literacy instruction approach in which students dictate stories based on their own experiences and teachers transcribe the students' dictations into texts and then use these texts for reading instruction.

language majority students. Describes students who are native speakers of the standard language variety spoken by the dominant group of a given society. In the United States, the term covers students who speak standard English.

language minority students. Describes students who are not native speakers of the language spoken by the dominant group of a given society. In the United States the term covers all students who speak languages other than standard English

Lau Remedies. Regulations issued by the U.S. Department of Education Office of Civil Rights following the U.S. Supreme Court Decision *Lau v. Nichols* (1974), outlining requirements for school districts and schools to address the needs of ELL students.

lexicon. The vocabulary of a language.

limited English proficient (LEP). A label for students who have not yet attained proficiency in English. Although the English language learner (ELL) label is preferred, LEP remains an official legal designation in federal and in many states' legislation.

minimal pairs. Words that differ by single phoneme (e.g., *sand/hand, bit/bet, rag/rat*), typically used to help students distinguish specific sounds that change the meanings of words and help students improve their pronunciation.

modeled writing. Writing instruction in which the teacher constructs a text in enlarged print (e.g., on chart paper), demonstrating a variety of writing strategies and techniques students are expected to learn and use in their own writing.

morphology. The study of the structure of words. The central unit of study is the morpheme, the smallest unit of meaning or grammatical function.

multiple measures. Different forms of formal and informal formative and summative assessments used together to provide accurate measures of what a student knows and can do.

multi-trait scoring. Refers to scoring a piece of student writing by considering several traits, for example, clear opinion (main idea), adequate details to support the opinion, and a strong conclusion.

narrow reading. A form of independent recreational reading that entails reading several books on the same subject, by the same author, or in the same genre.

native language (L1) instruction. Instruction in one or more content areas in the native language of ELL students. A distinguishing feature of bilingual education models.

newcomer programs. For beginning level ELL students who have been in the United States for only 1 or 2 years. Programs typically provide intensive English instruction and may include some native language instruction and ample primary language support.

No Child Left Behind Act of 2001 (NCLB). A reauthorization of the Elementary and Secondary Education Act. Places heavy emphasis on accountability through standards and high-stakes testing.

norm-referenced test. A test designed to compare a student's score to those of other students. Test results are usually reported as percentile rankings (e.g., a student at the 71st percentile rank scored higher than 71% of the students in the test's norming population, that is, a group of students who have already taken the test).

peer assessment. Students' assessment of each other's work or performances.

performance assessment. A form of assessment in which students are evaluated on their ability to perform a specific academic task or set of related tasks (e.g., use oral language to role play interactions at the market, write an essay, conduct a science experiment, measure and compare a set of objects using a scale).

personal word book. A book provided for each student that contains a list of high frequency words and other words students commonly ask for when they write, and space under each letter section for students to record their own words as they progress through the school year.

phonics. A component of reading instruction in which students learn the phonetic value (i.e., sounds) of individual letters and combinations of letters.

phonology. The study of the sound systems of languages.

podcast. Free audio or video programs that can be streamed over or downloaded from the Internet. Includes professional and amateur productions.

portfolio assessment. Assessment of student work collected throughout the school year and organized in a portfolio. Enables the assessment of students' progress and growth based on authentic samples of student work.

pragmatics. The study of language in use, that is, how individuals produce and interpret language in social interaction in specific contexts.

preview-review. A form of primary language support in which a lesson or read-aloud to be conducted in English is previewed, and then reviewed, in the native language of the ELL students.

primary language support (PLS). Using student's native language during ESL or sheltered English content-area instruction to make the English instruction more comprehensible.

primary trait scoring. Refers to scoring a piece of student writing by focusing on a specific trait, for example, the ability to craft a thesis statement in a persuasive essay.

process writing. A form of writing instruction in which students are guided through five stages: prewriting, drafting, revising, editing, and publishing. Often taught through a collaborative approach called Writer's Workshop.

Proposition 203. An English for the Children voter initiative passed in Arizona in 2000, placing restrictions on bilingual education.

Proposition 227. An English for the Children voter initiative passed in California in 1998, placing restrictions on bilingual education.

pull-out ESL. A program model for ELLs in which students are placed in mainstream or sheltered English immersion classrooms but are regularly pulled out of class for ESL lessons taught by an ESL teacher.

Question 2. An English for the Children voter initiative passed in Massachusetts in 2002, placing restrictions on bilingual education.

read-alouds. Refers to any time a teacher, parent, or other proficient reader reads books or other texts to one or more students.

Reader's Workshop. A structure for reading instruction often used in secondary schools that enables teachers to tailor instruction to students' strengths, interests, and needs.

reading self-assessments. Tools or procedures used by students to assess their own reading performance.

reading wars. Refers to a political battle over approaches to reading instruction between those who favor a bottom-up direct skills instruction approach to reading (e.g., direct systematic phonemic awareness and phonics instruction) and those who favor a top-down approach, which takes a more holistic view of reading (e.g., whole language).

Read/Write Web. The interactive feature of the Internet that allows users to both read and write Internet content.

redesignation. The reclassification of a student from English language learner (ELL), or limited English proficient (LEP), to fluent English proficient (FEP), based on criteria established by a school district or state.

register. Variation in the use of language based on the context in which the language is used.

reliability. The consistency with which a test or assessment measures what it is measuring.

running record. A reading assessment tool that

provides a visual record of a student's reading performance word by word on a specific text.

sample performance indicators. A feature of the TESOL English Language Proficiency Standards that provides examples of how to implement the standards. Grade-level academic tasks are broken down into descriptions of the level of performance that can be reasonably expected from ELL students at each of the five levels of English proficiency.

scaffolding. Support or assistance provided to a student within his or her zone of proximal development by a more knowledgeable other (e.g., teacher, peer) to help the student learn a new concept or develop new skills.

self-assessment. Students' assessment of their own performance, typically guided by a checklist or rubric.

semantics. The study of the meaning of words, phrases, and sentences.

shared reading. Reading instruction in which the teacher reads a big book or other source of enlarged text with the students, modeling a variety of reading strategies and using the text (once it is familiar to the students) to teach reading skills.

shared writing. Writing instruction in which the teacher, in collaboration with the students, constructs an enlarged text (e.g., on chart paper). Students suggest sentences and revisions and the teacher models the use of a variety of writing strategies students are expected to use in their own writing.

sheltered English immersion (SEI). A program model for ELLs that combines ESL, sheltered content-area instruction, and primary language support. Sometimes called structured English immersion

sheltered instruction. Grade-level content-area instruction provided in English in a manner that makes it comprehensible to ELLs while supporting their English language development.

Sheltered Instruction Observation Protocol (SIOP). A tool for planning, implementing, and evaluating sheltered English content-area instruction.

silent period. A period many new learners of a second language go through before they feel comfortable speaking in the new language.

SOLOM (Student Oral Language Observation Matrix). An assessment of student's oral language proficiency using an analytic scoring rubric that focuses on the aspects of comprehension, fluency, vocabulary, pronunciation, and grammar.

specially designed academic instruction in English (SDAIE). Another term for sheltered instruction, preferred in California and other states because it places emphasis on the fact that such instruction is academically rigorous but specially designed to match the linguistic needs of the student.

standard error of measurement (SEM). A statistical measure that indicates a range of trustworthiness of an individual student's standardized test

score. For example, the actual score of student who earned a score of 50 on a test with an SEM of 3 would be between 47 and 53 (e.g., 50 +/− 3).

submersion. The process of placing ELL students in a mainstream classroom where they do not receive any ESL, sheltered content instruction, or primary language support. Also called "sink-or-swim."

subtractive bilingualism. A situation in which a second language eventually replaces a student's native language.

summative assessment. Assessments that provide a summary of what students know and can do. Typically given at the end of a unit or at the end of a school year.

syntax. The study of the rules governing the relationships between words and the ways they are combined to form phrases and sentences.

testing. The administration of tests, singular instruments designed to systematically measure a sample of a student's ability at one particular time.

thematic teaching. Teaching a series of content-area lessons across different content areas focusing on a unifying topic or theme.

thematic word chart. A list of key vocabulary related to a theme currently under study.

total physical response (TPR). A language teaching approach in which students physically respond to language input (e.g., commands) to internalize the meaning and to demonstrate their comprehension of the language.

transitional bilingual education (TBE). A program model for ELL students in which native language content-area instruction is provided for the first few years of the program, in addition to sheltered English content-area instruction and English as a second language. The amount of native-language instruction decreases as sheltered English immersion increases. Students are transitioned to mainstream classrooms after just a few years in the program.

validity. The accuracy of a test or assessment in measuring what it purports to measure.

voice-over-Internet protocol (VOIP). Technology that allows the use of live voice over the Internet in real time. Used for Internet telephone service and audio chatting.

wait time. The period after a question has been posed during which students can think and formulate answers in their head before being required to answer out loud. Particularly important for ELLs who may need extra time to process input and formulate output in their second language.

WebQuests. A theme-based activity in which a teacher selects a series of Web sites for students to visit, and designs learning tasks for students to complete while visiting each site.

whole language. A philosophy of reading instruction that takes a top-down approach to literacy development, that is, instruction begins with a focus on comprehension of the whole text and then helping students develop reading and comprehension strategies and skills within the context of these meaningful texts.

wiki. A Web site that can easily be created and maintained collaboratively by multiple users.

word study. Short (mini-) lessons focusing on the morphological or semantic properties of words and related sets of words.

word wall. An enlarged list of words organized alphabetically and displayed on a classroom wall to support students' vocabulary and literacy development.

Writer's Workshop. An instructional approach to writing in which students work independently and at their own pace as they move through the five stages of process writing with teacher and peer guidance and support.

zone of proximal development (ZPD). Refers to a metaphorical space between what an individual can do on his or her own, and what he or she can do with support from a teacher or other more knowledgeable person.

Bibliography
of Children's and Youth
Literature Cited in the Text

Beshore, George W. *Science in Ancient China*. New York: Franklin Watts, 1998.

———. *Science in Early Islamic Culture*. New York: Franklin Watts, 1998.

The Big Hot Pot. Boston: Houghton Mifflin Harcourt, Rigby, 2004.

Brown, Marc. *Arthur and the Lost Diary*. Boston: Little, Brown, 1998.

———. *Arthur's Teacher Trouble*. Boston: Little, Brown, 1986.

Bunting, Eve. *So Far from the Sea*. Boston: Clarion, 1998.

Bunting, Eve, and Beth Peck. *How Many Days to America? A Thanksgiving Story*. New York: Houghton Mifflin, 1990.

Cole, Joanna, and Bruce Degen. *The Magic School Bus Explores the Senses*. New York: Scholastic, 2001.

Coleman, Evelyn. *White Socks Only*. Morton Grove, IL: Albert Whitman, 1999.

Coles, Robert. *The Story of Ruby Bridges*. New York: Scholastic, 2004.

Collins, Tim, and Mary Jane Maples. *Gateway to Science: Vocabulary and Concepts*. Boston: Thomson/Heinle, 2008.

Cox, David. *Ayu and the Perfect Moon*. Des Moines, IA: National Geographic School Publishing, Hampton-Brown Books, 1984.

Davis, Kenneth C. *Don't Know Much about Space*. New York: HarperCollins, 2001.

———. *Don't Know Much about the Solar System*. New York: HarperCollins, 2001.

Duran, Elva, Jo Gusman, and John Shefelbine. *Access Science. Building Literacy through Language*. Wilmington, MA: Great Source/Houghton Mifflin, 2007.

Ellis, Julie, and Phyllis Hornung. *What's Your Angle, Pythagoras? A Math Adventure*. Watertown, MA: Charlesbridge, 2004.

Hall, Zoe, and Shari Halpern. *¡Tiempo de calabazas!* [It's pumpkin time!]. New York: Scholastic, 2002.

Houston, Jeanne Wakatsuki, and James D. Houston. *Farewell to Manzanar*. New York: Houghton Mifflin, 2002.

Hunter, Miranda. *The Story of Latino Civil Rights: Fighting for Justice*. Broomhall, PA: Mason Crest, 2005.

Hutchins, P. *The Doorbell Rang*. New York: HarperTrophy, 1989.

Lobel, Arnold. *Frog and Toad Are Friends*. New York: Harper Collins, 1970.

McGrath, B. B. *The M&M's Brand Counting Book*. Watertown, MA: Charlesbridge, 1994.

Mochizuki, Ken. *Baseball Saved Us*. New York: Lee & Low, 1993.

Morris, Ann. *Bread, Bread, Bread*. New York: Harper Trophy, 1993.

Noble, Trinka Hakes. *The Day Jimmy's Boa Ate the Wash*. New York: Puffin Books, 1992.

Neuschwander, Cindy, and Wayne Geehan. *Sir Cumference and the First Round Table: A Math Adventure*. Watertown, MA: Charlesbridge, 1999.

Neuschwander, Cindy, and Brian Langdo. *Mummy Math: An Adventure in Geometry*. New York: Henry Holt, 2005.

———. *Patterns in Peru: An Adventure in Patterning*. New York: Henry Holt, 2007.

Noguchi, Rick, and Deneen Jenks. *Flowers from Mariko*. New York: Lee & Low, 2001

Shaw, Charles. *It Looked Like Spilt Milk*. New York: Harper Trophy, 1992.

Simon, Seymour. *Our Solar System*. Updated ed. New York: Collins, 2007.

Stanley, Jerry. *I Am an American: A True Story of Japanese Internment*. New York: Crown, 1994.

Tunnell, Michael O., and George W. Chilcoat. *The Children of Topaz: The Story of the Japanese American Internment Camp*. New York: Holiday House, 1996.

Waters, Kate. *Sarah Morton's Day: A Day in the Life of a Pilgrim Girl*. New York: Scholastic, 1989.

Williams, Vera. B. *A Chair for My Mother*. 25th Anniversary ed. New York: HarperTrophy, 2007

Wood, Audrey, and Don Wood. *The Napping House*. San Diego, CA: Harcourt Brace, 1989.

References

Abedi, J. (2004). The No Child Left Behind Act and English language learners: Assessment and accountability issues. *Educational Researcher, 33*(1), 4–14.

Abedi, J., & Lord, C. (2001). The language factor in mathematics tests. *Applied Measurement in Education, 14*(3), 219–234.

Adams, M. J. (1995). *Beginning to read: Thinking and learning about print.* Cambridge, MA: MIT Press.

Alamillo, L., & Viramontes, C. (2000). Reflections from the classroom: Teacher perspectives on the implementation of Proposition 227. *Bilingual Research Journal, 24*(1 & 2), 155–168.

Alexander v. Sandoval, 534 U.S. 275 (2001).

Alvarez v. Lemon Grove, Superior Court, San Diego County, No. 66625 (1931).

Amaral, O. M. (2002). Helping English learners increase achievement through inquiry-based science instruction. *Bilingual Research Journal, 26*(2), 213–239.

American Academy of Child and Adolescent Psychiatry. (2008, May). Obesity in children and teens. [Electronic version]. *Facts for Families,* no. 79.

American Education Research Association (AERA). (2004). Closing the gap: High achievement for students of color. *Research Points: Essential Information for Education Policy, 2*(3), 1–4.

American Education Research Association (AERA), American Psychological Association (APA), & National Council on Measurement in Education (NCME). (1999). *Standards for educational and psychological testing.* Washington, DC: American Education Research Association.

American Institutes for Research & WestEd. (2006, January 24). *Effects of the implementation of Proposition 227 on the education of English learners, K–12: Findings from a five-year evaluation.* Washington, DC, and San Francisco, CA: Authors.

Amrein, A. L., & Berliner, D. C. (2002a). *An analysis of some unintended consequences of high-stakes testing.* Tempe, AZ: Education Policy Research Unit, Education Policy Studies Laboratory, Arizona State University.

Amrein, A. L., & Berliner, D. C. (2002b). High-stakes testing, uncertainty, and student learning. *Education Policy Analysis Archives, 10*(18). epaa.asu.edu/epaa/v2010n2018

Arizona Department of Education. (2004). *Arizona's school accountability system technical manual: Vol. 2. Adequate yearly progress.* Phoenix: Author.

Asher, J. J. (1977). *Learning another language through actions: The complete teacher's guidebook.* Los Gatos, CA: Sky Oaks Productions.

Asher, J. J. (1995). A conversation with Dr. James J. Asher . . . TPR and education. [Electronic version.] *Ideas for Excellence: The Newsletter for ESL/Bilingual Education, 3*(4), 1–4.

Asher, J. J. (2000). *Learning another language through actions* (6th ed.). Los Gatos, CA: Sky Oaks Productions.

Aspira v. Board of Education of the City of New York, 394 F. Supp. 1161 (1975).

Atwell, N. (1987). *In the middle: Writing, reading, and learning with adolescents.* Portsmouth, NH: Boyton/Cook.

August, D. (2006). How does first language literacy development relate to second language literacy development? In E. Hamayan & R. Freeman (Eds.), *English language learners at school: A guide for administrators* (pp. 71–72). Philadelphia: Caslon.

August, D., & Hakuta, K. (1997). *Improving schooling for language-minority children: A research agenda.* Washington, DC: National Academy Press.

August, D., & Shanahan, T. (Eds.). (2006a). *Developing literacy in second-language learners: Report of the National Literacy Panel on language-minority children and youth.* Mahwah, NJ: Lawrence Erlbaum.

August, D., & Shanahan, T. (Eds.). (2006b). *Executive summary. Developing literacy in second-language learners: Report of the National Literacy Panel on language-minority children and youth.* www.cal.org/projects/archive/nlpreports/Executive_Summary.pdf

August, D., & Shanahan, T. (Eds.). (2008). *Developing reading and writing in second-language learners: Lessons from the report of the National Literacy Panel on language-minority children and youth.* New York: Routledge, Center for Applied Linguistics, and International Reading Association.

Bailey, F., Burkett, B., & Freeman, D. (2008). The mediating role of language in teaching and learning: A classroom perspective. In B. Spolsky & F. M. Hult (Eds.), *The handbook of educational linguistics* (pp. 606–625). Malden, MA: Blackwell.

Baker, C. (2006). *Foundations of bilingual education and bilingualism* (4th ed.). Clevedon, U.K.: Multilingual Matters.

Baker, C., & Jones, S. P. (1999). *Encyclopedia of bilingualism and bilingual education.* Clevedon, U.K.: Multilingual Matters.

Baker, K. (1998, November 11). *Structured English immersion breakthrough in teaching limited-English-proficient students.* www.pdkintl.org/kappan/kbak9811.htm

Banks, J. (1994). *An introduction to multicultural education.* Boston: Allyn & Bacon.

Bear, D. R., Helman, L., Invernizzi, M., Templeton, S. R., & Johnston, F. (2006). *Words their way with English learners: Word study for spelling, phonics, and vocabulary instruction.* Upper Saddle River, NJ: Prentice Hall.

Berliner, D. C. (2006). Our impoverished view of educational reform. [Electronic version.] *Teachers College Record, 108*(6), 949–995.

Bhabha, H. K. (1994). *The location of culture.* London: Routledge.

Birdsong, D., & Park, J. (2008). Second language acquisition and ultimate attainment. In B. Spolsky & F. Hult (Eds.), *The handbook of educational linguistics* (pp. 424–436). Malden, MA: Blackwell.

Blanton, C. K. (2004). *The strange career of bilingual education in Texas, 1836–1981.* College Station, TX: Texas A&M University Press.

Bravo, M. A., Hiebert, E. H., & Pearson, P. D. (2007). Tapping the linguistic resources of Spanish-English bilinguals: The role of cognates in science. In R. K. Wagner, A. Muse, & K. Tannenbaum (Eds.), *Vocabulary acquisition: Implications for reading comprehension* (pp. 140–156). New York: Guilford.

Brown v. Board of Education of Topeka, 347 U.S. 483 (1954).

Brown, C. L. (2005). Equity of literacy-based math performance assessments for English language learners. *Bilingual Research Journal, 29*(2), 337–364.

Bushwick Parents Organization v. Mills, 5185–95 (Sup. C. Albany County 1995).

Butler, Y. G., Orr, J. E., Guiterrez, M. B., & Hakuta, K. (2000). Inadequate conclusions from an inadequate assessment: What can SAT-9 scores tell us about the impact of Proposition 227 in California? *Bilingual Research Journal, 24*(1 & 2), 141–154.

Butler-Pascoe, M. E., & Wiburg, K. M. (2003). *Technology and teaching English language learners.* Boston: Pearson/Allyn & Bacon.

California Reading Task Force. (1995). *Every child a reader.* Sacramento: California Department of Education.

California Teachers Association v. Davis, 64 FSupp 2d 945 (CD Calif. 1999).

Calkins, L. (2000). *The art of teaching reading.* Boston: Allyn & Bacon.

Canale, M., & Swain, M. (1980). Theoretical bases of communicative approaches to second language teaching and testing. *Applied Linguistics, 1*(1), 1–47.

Capps, R., Fix, M., Murray, J., Ost, J., Passel, J. S., & Herwantoro, S. (2006). *The new demography of America's schools: Immigration and the No Child Left Behind Act.* [Electronic version].Washington, DC: Urban Institute.

Cardenas, J. A., & Cardenas, B. (1977). *The theory of incompatibilities: A conceptual framework for responding to the educational needs of Mexican American children.* San Antonio, TX: Intercultural Development Research Association.

Carr, J., Sexton, U., & Lagunoff, R. (2007). *Making science accessible to English learners: A guidebook for teachers.* San Francisco: WestEd.

Carrell, P. L., Devine, J., & Eskey, D. E. (Eds.). (1998). *Interactive approaches to second language reading.* New York: Cambridge University Press.

Carson, J. G., & Leki, I. (1993). *Reading in the composition classroom: Second language perspectives.* Boston: Heinle and Heinle.

Castañeda v. Pickard, 648 F2d 989 (5th Cir 1981).

Chamot, A. U. (2009). *CALLA handbook: Implementing the Cognitive Academic Language Learning Approach* (2nd ed). Boston: Pearson.

Chandler, J. (2003). The efficacy of various kinds of error feedback for improvement of accuracy and fluency of L2 student writing. *Journal of Second Language Writing, 12*(3), 267–296.

Chapelle, C. A. (2001). *Computer applications in second language acquisition. Foundations for teaching, testing, and research.* New York: Cambridge University Press.

Chun, K.-T. (1995). The myth of Asian American success and its educational ramifications. In D. T. Nakanishi & T. Y. Nishida (Eds.), *The Asian American educational experience* (pp. 95–112). New York: Routledge.

Clements, R. L., & Kinzler, S., K. (2002). *A multicultural approach to physical education: Proven strategies for middle and high school.* Champaign, IL: Human Kinetic.

Cohen, A. C. (1994). *Assessing language ability in the classroom.* Boston: Heinle & Heinle.

Coles, G. (2000). *Misreading reading: The bad science that hurts children.* Portsmouth, NH: Heinemann.

Collier, V. P. (1995). A synthesis of studies examining long-term language-minority student data on academic achievement. In G. González & L. Maez (Eds.), *Compendium of research on bilingual education* (pp. 231–243). Washington, DC: National Clearinghouse for Bilingual Education.

Collins, J. (n.d.) *Collins Writing Program.* The Writing Site. www.thewritingsite.org/resources/approaches/collins/default.asp.

Combs, M. C., Evans, C., Fletcher, T., Parra, E., & Jiménez, A. (2005). Bilingualism for the children: Implementing a dual-language program in an English-only state. *Educational Policy, 19*(5), 701–728.

Corson, D. (1999). *Language policy in schools: A resource for teachers and administrators.* Mahwah, NJ: Lawrence Erlbaum.

Crandall, J. A. (1981). *Teaching the Spanish-speaking child: A practical guide.* Washington, DC: Center for Applied Linguistics.

Crawford, J. (Ed.) (1992). *Language loyalties: A source book on the official English controversy.* Chicago: University of Chicago Press.

Crawford, J. (2000). The political paradox of bilingual education. In J. Crawford (Ed.), *At war with diversity: U.S. language policy in an age of anxiety* (pp. 84–103). Clevedon, U.K.: Multilingual Matters.

Crawford, J. (2003). *Hard sell: Why is bilingual education so unpopular with the American public?* Tempe: Language Policy Research Unit, Education Policy Studies Laboratory, Arizona State University.

Crawford, J. (2004). *Educating English learners: Language diversity in the classroom* (5th ed.). Los Angeles: Bilingual Education Services.

Crawford, J., & Krashen, S. (2007). *English learners in American classrooms: 101 Questions, 101 Answers.* New York: Scholastic.

Crystal, D. (2001). *A dictionary of language* (2nd ed.). Chicago: University of Chicago Press.

Crystal, D. (2004). *A glossary of netspeak and textspeak.* Edinburgh: Edinburgh University Press.

Cuban, L. (2001). *Oversold and underused: Computers in the schools.* Cambridge, MA: Harvard University Press.

Cummins, J. (1979). Linguistic interdependence and the education development of bilingual children. *Review of Educational Research, 49,* 222–251.

Cummins, J. (1981). The role of primary language development in promoting educational success for language minority students. In California State Department of Education Office of Bilingual Education (Ed.), *Schooling and language minority students: A theoretical framework* (pp. 3–49). Los Angeles: Evaluation, Dissemination, and Assessment Center, California State University, Los Angeles.

Cummins, J. (1984). Wanted: A theoretical framework for relating language proficiency to academic achievement among bilingual students. In C. Rivera (Ed.), *Language proficiency and academic achievement* (pp. 2–19). Clevedon, U.K.: Multilingual Matters.

Cummins, J. (1992). Language proficiency, bilingualism, and academic achievement. In P. A. Richard-Amato & M. A. Snow (Eds.), *The multicultural classroom: Readings for content-area teachers* (pp. 16–26). New York: Longman.

Cummins, J. (2000). *Language, power, and pedagogy: Bilingual children in the crossfire.* Clevedon, U.K.: Multilingual Matters.

Cummins, J. (2006). How long does it take for an English language learner to become proficient in a second language? In E. Hamayan & R. Freeman (Eds.), *English language learners at school: A guide for administrators* (pp. 59–61). Philadelphia: Caslon.

Cummins, J. (2008a). BICS and CALP: Empirical and theoretical status of the distinction. In B. Street & N. Hornberger (Eds.), *Encyclopedia of language and education* (2nd ed.). Vol. 2: *Literacy,* pp. 71–83. New York: Springer.

Cummins, J. (2008b). Teaching for transfer: Challenging the two solitudes assumption in bilingual education. In J. Cummins & N. H. Hornberger (Eds.), *Encyclopedia of language and education* (2nd ed.). Vol. 5: *Bilingual education,* pp. 65–75. New York: Springer.

Cummins, J., Bismilla, V., Chow, P., Cohen, S., Giampapa, F., Leoni, L., et al. (2005). Affirming identity in multilingual classrooms. *Educational Leadership, 63*(1), 38–43.

Cummins, J., Brown, K., & Sayers, D. (2007). *Literacy, technology, and diversity: Teaching for success in changing times.* Boston: Pearson/Allyn & Bacon.

Dale, T. C., & Cuevas, G. J. (1992). Integrating mathematics and language learning. In P. A. Richard-Amato & M. A. Snow (Eds.), *The multicultural classroom: Readings for content-area teachers* (pp. 330–348). New York: Longman.

Daney, C. (2007, February 7). A brief history of algebra. *Science and Reason*. Message posted to scienceandreason.blogspot.com/2007/02/brief-history-of-algebra.html

Davies, A. (2001). Native speaker. In R. Mesthrie (Ed.), *Concise encyclopedia of sociolinguistics* (pp. 512–519). New York: Elsevier.

Davis, J. L. (2008). Danevang, Texas. In *The Handbook of Texas*. www.tshaonline.org/handbook/online/articles/DD/hnd4.html

de Cohen, C. C., Deterding, N., & Clewell, B. C. (2005). *Who's left behind? Immigrant children in high and low LEP schools*. Washington, DC: Urban Institute.

de Jong, E., Gort, M., & Cobb, C. D. (2005). Bilingual education within the context of English-only policies: Three districts' response to Question 2 in Massachusetts. *Educational Policy, 19*(4), 595–620.

de Jong, E., & Howard, E. (2009). Integration in two-way immersion education: Equalising linguistic benefits for all students. *International Journal of Bilingual Education and Bilingualism, 12*(1), 81–99.

Del Valle, S. (2003). *Language rights and the law in the United States: Finding our voices*. Clevedon, U.K.: Multilingual Matters.

Deschenes, S., Cuban, L., & Tyack, D. B. (2001). Mismatch: Historical perspectives on schools and students who don't fit them. *Teachers College Record, 103*(4), 525–547.

Diaz-Rico, L. T., & Weed, K. Z. (2006). *The crosscultural, language, and academic development handbook: A complete K–12 reference guide* (3rd ed.). Boston: Pearson/Allyn & Bacon.

Dixon, C., Green, J., Yeager, B., Baker, D., & Franquiz, M. (2000). "I used to know that": What happens when reform gets through the classroom door. *Bilingual Research Journal, 24*(1 & 2), 113–126.

Dobb, F. (2004). *Essential elements of effective science instruction for English learners* (2nd ed.). [Electronic version]. Los Angeles: California Science Project.

Doe v. Los Angeles Unified School District, 48 Fsupp 2d 1233 (CD Calif. 1999).

Dworin, J. E. (2006). The family stories project: Using funds of knowledge for writing. *Reading Teacher, 59*(6), 510–520.

Echevarria, J. (2007). *Sheltered content instruction: Teaching English language learners with diverse abilities* (3rd ed.). Boston: Allyn & Bacon.

Echevarria, J., & Graves, A. (2007). *Sheltered content instruction: Teaching English language learners with diverse abilities*. Boston: Pearson/Allyn and Bacon.

Echevarria, J., Vogt, M., & Short, D. (2007). *Making content comprehensible for English learners: The SIOP model* (3rd ed.). Boston: Pearson/Allyn & Bacon.

Echevarria, J., Vogt, M., & Short, D. J. (2010a). *Making content comprehensible for elementary English learners: The SIOP model*. Boston: Pearson/Allyn & Bacon.

Echevarria, J., Vogt, M., & Short, D. J. (2010b). *Making content comprehensible for secondary English learners: The SIOP model*. Boston: Pearson/Allyn & Bacon.

Edelsky, C. (2006). *With literacy and justice for all: Rethinking the social in language and education* (3rd ed.). Mahwah, NJ: Lawrence Erlbaum.

Edelsky, C., Hudelson, S., Flores, B., Barkin, F., Altwerger, B., & Jilbert, K. (1983). Semilingualism and language deficit. *Applied Linguistics, 4*(1), 1–22.

Egbert, J. (2005). CALL *Essentials: Principles and practices in CALL classrooms*. Alexandria, VA: Teachers of English to Speakers of Other Languages.

Escamilla, K., Shannon, S., Carlos, S., & Garcia, J. (2003). Breaking the code: Colorado's defeat of the anti-bilingual education initiative (Amendment 31). *Bilingual Research Journal, 27*(3), 357–382.

Eskey, D. E. (1998). Holding the bottom: An interactive approach to the language problems of second language readers. In P. L. Carrell, J. Devine, & D. E. Eskey (Eds.), *Integrative approaches to second language reading* (pp. 93–100). New York: Cambridge University Press.

Fagan, J. F., & Holland, C. R. (2002). Equal opportunity and racial differences in IQ. *Intelligence, 30*(4), 361–387.

Farrington v. Tokushige, 273 U.S. 284 (1927).

Feinberg, R. C. (2002). *Bilingual education: A reference handbook*. Santa Barbara, CA: ABC-CLIO.

Ferris, D. R., & Hedgcock, J. (2004). *Teaching ESL composition: Purpose, process, practice*. Oxford: Routledge.

Fillmore, L. W. (1991). When learning a second language means losing the first. *Early Childhood Research Quarterly, 6*(3), 323–346.

Fillmore, L. W., & Snow, C. E. (2000). *What teachers need to know about language*. Washington, DC: Clearinghouse on Languages and Linguistics.

Finegan, E. (2004). *Language: Its structure and use* (4th ed.). Boston: Thomson/Wadsworth.

Fish, J. M. (Ed.). (2002). *Race and intelligence: Separating science from myth*. Mahwah, NJ: Lawrence Erlbaum.

Flores v. Arizona, 172 F. Supp. 2d 1225 (D. Ariz., 2000).

Flowerdew, J., & Miller, L. (2005). *Second language listening: Theory and practice*. New York: Cambridge University Press.

Folse, K. S. (2006). *The art of teaching speaking: Research and pedagogy for the ESL/EFL classroom*. Ann Arbor: University of Michigan Press.

Foorman, B. (1998). The role of instruction in learning to read: Preventing reading failure in at-risk children. *Journal of Educational Psychology, 90*(1), 37–55.

Fountas, I. C., & Pinnell, G. S. (2006a). *Leveled books, K–8: Matching texts to readers for effective teaching*. Portsmouth, NH: Heinemann.

Fountas, I. C., & Pinnell, G. S. (2006b). *Teaching for comprehension and fluency: Thinking, talking, and writing about reading, K-8*. Portsmouth, NH: Heinemann.

Freedom Writers. (1999). *The Freedom Writers diary: How a teacher and 150 teens used writing to change themselves and the world around them*. With E. Gruwell. New York: Doubleday.

Freedom Writers Foundation. (n.d.) *About Freedom Writers*. Available from www .freedomwritersfoundation .org

Freeman, D. E., & Freeman, Y. S. (1994). *Between worlds: Access to second language acquisition*. Portsmouth, NH: Heinemann.

Freeman, D. E., & Freeman, Y. S. (2004). *Essential linguistics: What you need to know to teach reading, ESL, spelling, phonics, and grammar*. Portsmouth, NH: Heinemann.

Freeman, R. D. (1996). Dual-language planning at Oyster bilingual school: "It's much more than language." *TESOL Quarterly, 30*(3), 557–582.

Freeman, R. D. (1998). *Bilingual education and social change*. Clevedon, U.K.: Multilingual Matters.

Freeman, R. D.(2004). *Building on community bilingualism: Promoting multiculturalism through schooling*. Philadelphia: Caslon.

Freeman Field, R. (2008). Identity, community and power in bilingual education. In J. Cummins & N. H. Hornberger (Eds.), *Encyclopedia of language and education* (2nd. ed.). Vol. 5: *Bilingual education*, pp. 77–89. New York: Springer.

Freeman, Y. S., & Freeman, D. E. (1992). *Whole language for second language learners*. Portsmouth, NH: Heinemann.

Freeman, Y. S., & Freeman, D. E. (2000). Preview, view

review: An important strategy in multilingual classrooms. *NABE News, 24*(2), 20–21.

Freeman, Y. S., & Freeman, D. E. (2008). English language learners: Who are they? How can teachers support them? In Y. S. Freeman, D. E. Freeman & R. Ramirez (Eds.), *Diverse learners in the mainstream classroom: Strategies for supporting all students across content areas* (pp. 31–58). Portsmouth, NH: Heinemann.

Freire, P. (1993). *Pedagogy of the oppressed* (20th Anniversary ed.). New York: Continuum.

Gandara, P. (2000). In the aftermath of the storm: English learners in the Post-227 era. *Bilingual Research Journal, 24*(1 & 2), 1–14.

García, E. E., & Curry-Rodriguez, J. E. (2000). The education of limited English proficient students in California schools: An assessment of the influence of Proposition 227 in selected districts and schools. *Bilingual Research Journal, 24*(1 & 2), 15–36.

Garcia, O. (2009). Emergent bilinguals and TESOL: What's in a name? *TESOL Quarterly, 43*(2), 322–326.

García, O., Kleifgen, J. A., & Falchi, L. (2008). *From English language learners to emergent bilinguals.* New York: Campaign for Educational Equity, Teachers College, Columbia University.

Gardner, H. (1999). *Intelligence reframed: Multiple intelligences for the 21st century.* New York: Basic Books.

Gass, S., Mackey, A., & Pica, T. (1998). The role of input and interaction in second language acquisition. *Modern Language Journal, 82*(3): 299–307.

Gee, J. P. (1996). *Social linguistics and literacies: Ideology in discourses* (2nd ed.). Oxford: Routledge.

Genesee, F. (1995). The Canadian second language immersion program. In O. García & C. Baker (Eds.), *Policy and practice in bilingual education* (pp. 118–133). Clevedon, U.K.: Multilingual Matters.

Genesee, F., & Gandara, P. (1999). Bilingual education programs: A cross-national perspective. *Journal of Social Issues, 55*(4), 665–685.

Genesee, F., Lindholm-Leary, K., Saunders, W. M., & Christian, D. (2005). English language learners in U.S. schools: An overview of research findings. *Journal of Education for Students Placed at Risk, 10*(4), 363–385.

Genesee, F., Lindholm-Leary, K., Saunders, W. M., & Christian, D. (2006). *Educating English language learners: A synthesis of research evidence.* New York: Cambridge University Press.

Gersten, R., Baker, S. K., Shanahan, T., Linan-Thompson, S., Collins, P., & Scarcella, R. (2007). *Effective literacy and English language instruction for English learners in the elementary grades.* Washington, DC: Institute of Education Sciences, U.S. Department of Education.

Geva, E. (2006). Second-language oral proficiency and second-language literacy. In D. August & T. Shanahan (Eds.), *Developing literacy in second-language learners: Report of the National Literacy Panel on Language-Minority Children and Youth* (pp. 123–152). Mahwah, NJ: Lawrence Erlbaum.

Glovin, D. (2000). Welcome to Measurement, Inc. In B. Miner & K. Swope (Eds.), *Failing our kids: Why the testing craze won't fix our schools* (pp. 20–22). Milwaukee, WI: Rethinking Schools.

Glovin, D., & Evans, D. (2006, December). How test companies fail your kids. *Bloomberg Markets,* 126–142.

Gollnick, D. M., & Chin, P. C. (2002). *Multicultural education in a pluralistic society* (6th ed.). Upper Saddle River, NJ: Merrill Prentice Hall.

Gomez v. Illinois State Board of Education, 811 F.2dm1030 (7th Cir. 1987).

Gómez, L., Freeman, D. E., & Freeman, Y. S. (2005). Dual language education: A promising 50–50 model. *Bilingual Research Journal, 29*(1), 145–164.

Gonzalez, G. (2005). *Ten important sentences.* Boston: Addison Wesley.

González, J. (2002). *Bilingual education and the federal role, if any. . . .* Tempe, AZ: Language Policy Research Unit, Education Policy Studies Laboratory, Arizona State University. www.language-policy.org/content/features/article1.htm

González, N., Moll, L. C., & Amanti, C. (Eds.). (2005). *Funds of knowledge: Theorizing practices in households, communities, and classrooms.* Mahwah, NJ: Lawrence Erlbaum.

Gonzalez, V., Yawkey, T., & Minaya-Rowe, L. (2006). *English-as-a-second-language (ESL) teaching and learning: Pre-K–12 classroom applications for student academic achievement and development.* Boston: Peason/Allyn & Bacon.

Goodman, K. S. (1986). *What's whole in whole language?* Portsmouth, NH: Heinemann.

Goodman, K. S. (2005). DIBELS: The perfect literacy test. *Language Magazine, 5*(1), 24–27.

Goodman, K. S. (Ed.). (2006). *The truth about DIBELS: What it is, what it does.* Portsmouth, NH: Heinemann.

Gordon, R. G. (2005). *Ethnologue: Languages of the world* (15th ed.). Dallas, TX: SIL International. Available at www.ethnologue.com

Gottlieb, M. H. (2006). *Assessing English language learners: Bridges from language proficiency to academic achievement.* Thousand Oaks, CA: Corwin Press.

Gottlieb, M. H., & Nguyen, D. (2007). *Assessment and accountability in language education programs.* Philadelphia: Caslon.

Gould, S. J. (1981). *The mismeasure of man.* New York: Norton.

Guarino, A. J., Echevarria, J., Short, D., Schick, J. E., Forbes, S., & Rueda, R. (2001). The sheltered instruction observation protocol. *Journal of Research in Education, 11*(1), 138–140.

Guey Heung Lee v. Johnson, 404 US 1215 (1971).

Grabe, W. (2003). Reading and writing relations: Second language perspectives on research and practice. In B. Kroll (Ed.), *Exploring the dynamics of second language writing* (pp. 242–262). New York: Cambridge University Press.

Greene, J. P. (2002). *High school graduation rates in the United States.* [Electronic version]. New York: Manhattan Institute for Policy Research.

Hadaway, N. L., Vardell, S. M., & Young, T. A. (2002). *Literature-based instruction with English language learners, K–12.* Boston: Allyn and Bacon.

Hakuta, K. (1986). *The mirror of language: The debate on bilingualism.* New York: Basic Books.

Hakuta, K., Butler, Y. G., & Witt, D. (1999). How long does it take English learners to attain proficiency? *University of California Linguistic Minority Institute Newsletter, 9*(1), 1.

Hakuta, K., Butler, Y. G., & Witt, D. (2000). *How long does it take English learners to attain proficiency?* Santa Barbara, CA: University of California Linguistic Minority Research Institute.

Haladyna, T. (2002). *Essentials of standardized testing.* Boston: Allyn and Bacon.

Haley, M. H., & Austin, T. Y. (2003). *Content-based second language teaching and learning: An interactive approach.* Boston: Allyn & Bacon.

Halliday, M. A. K. (1994). *An introduction to functional grammar* (2nd ed.). London: Edward Arnold.

Hamayan, E. (2006). What is the role of culture in language learning? In E. Hamayan & R. Freeman (Eds.), *English language learners at school: A guide for administrators* (pp. 62–64). Philadelphia: Caslon.

Hamayan, E., Marler, B., Sanchez-Lopez, C., & Damico, J.

(2006). *Special education considerations for English language learners: Delivering a continuum of services*. Philadelphia: Caslon.

Haney, W. (2000). The myth of the Texas miracle in education. *Education Policy Analysis Archives, 8*(41). epaa.asu .edu/epaa/v2008n2041

Haney, W. (2002). Revealing illusions of educational progress: Texas high-stakes tests and minority student performance. In Z. F. Beykont (Ed.), *The power of culture: Teaching across language difference*. Boston: Harvard Education Publishing Group.

Haycock, K. (2006). No more invisible kids. *Educational Leadership, 64*(1), 38–42.

Heath, S. B. (1982). What no bedtime story means: Narrative skills at home and school. *Language in Society, 11*(1), 49–76.

Heath, S. B. (1983). *Ways with words: Language, life, and work in communities and classrooms*. New York: Cambridge University Press.

Herrera, S. G., Murry, K. G., & Cabral, R. M. (2007). *Assessment accommodations for classroom teachers of culturally and linguistically diverse students*. Boston: Pearson/Allyn & Bacon.

Herrnstein, R. J., & Murray, C. A. (1994). *The bell curve: Intelligence and class structure in American life*. New York: Free Press.

High, J. (1993). *Second language learning through cooperative learning*. San Clemente, CA: Kagan Cooperative Learning.

Hill, E. G. (2004). *A look at the progress of English learner students*. Sacramento, CA: Legislative Analyst's Office.

Hill, E. G. (2006). *Update 2002–2004: The progress of English learner students*. Sacramento, CA: Legislative Analyst's Office.

Hornberger, N. H. (1996). Mother-tongue literacy in the Cambodian community of Philadelphia. *International Journal of the Sociology of Language, 119*, 69–86.

Horwitz, E. K. (2008). *Becoming a language teacher: A practical guide to second language learning and teaching*. Boston: Pearson/Allyn & Bacon.

Hout, M. (2002). Test scores, education, and poverty. In J. M. Fish (Ed.), *Race and intelligence: Separating science from myth* (pp. 329–354). Mahwah, NJ: Lawrence Erlbaum.

Hudelson, S. (1989). *Write on: Children writing in ESL*. Washington, DC: Center for Applied Linguistics and Prentice Hall Regents.

Hymes, D. (1972). On communicative competence. In J. B. Pride & J. Holmes (Eds.), *Sociolinguistics*. Harmondsworth: Penguin Books.

Independent School District v. Salvatierra, 33 S.W.2d 790, 791 (Tex. Civ. App. 1930).

Institute of Education Sciences (2008). *Reading First: Interim report*. Washington, DC: U.S. Department of Education.

Jameson, J., H. (2003). *Enriching content classes for secondary ESOL students: Trainer's manual*. Washington, DC: Center for Applied Linguistics.

Jencks, C., & Phillips, M. (Eds.). (1998). *The Black-White test score gap*. Washington, DC: Brookings Institution Press.

Jensen, A. R. (1995). The differences are real. In R. Jacoby & N. Glauberman (Eds.), *The Bell Curve debate: History, documents, opinions* (pp. 617–629). New York: Times Books.

Jensen, A. R. (1998). *The g factor: The science of mental ability*. Westport, CT: Praeger.

Jesness, J. (2004). *Teaching English language learners K–12: A quick-start for the new teacher*. Thousand Oaks, CA: Corwin Press.

Johnson v. San Francisco Unified School District, 500 F.2nd 349, 353. (9th Cir. 1974).

Kagan, S. (1997). *Cooperative learning*. San Clemente, CA: Kagan Cooperative Learning.

Kendall, J., & Khuon, O. (2005). *Making sense: Small-group comprehension lessons for English language learners*. Portland, ME: Stenhouse.

Kendall, J., & Khuon, O. (2006). *Writing sense: Integrated reading and writing lessons for English language learners*. Portland, ME: Stenhouse.

Kern, R. (2000). *Literacy and language teaching*. New York: Oxford University Press.

Keyes v. School District No. 1, 413 U.S. 189 (1983).

Kloss, H. (1998). *The American bilingual tradition*. Washington, DC: Center for Applied Linguistics and Delta Systems. (Original work published 1977)

Kohn, A. (2000). *The case against standardized testing: Raising the scores, ruining the schools*. Portsmouth, NH: Heinemann.

Kolesnikova, M. (2008, May 15). Lolspeak isn't so clever when it infiltrates essays. *San Antonio Express News*.

Kozol, J. (2005). *The shame of the nation: The restoration of apartheid schooling in America*. New York: Crown.

Krashen, S. D. (1982). *Principles and practice in second language acquisition*. Oxford: Pergamon.

Krashen, S. D. (1985). *The input hypothesis: Issues and implications*. London: Longman.

Krashen, S. D. (1992). *Fundamentals of language education*. Torrance, CA: Loredo.

Krashen, S. D. (1993). *The power of reading*. Englewood, CO: Libraries Unlimited.

Krashen, S. D. (1995). School libraries, public libraries, and the NAEP reading scores. *School Library Media Quarterly, 23*(4), 235–237.

Krashen, S. D. (1996). *Every person a reader: An alternative to the California Task Force Report on Reading*. Culver City, CA: Language Education Associates.

Krashen, S. D. (1998). Comprehensible output. *System, 26*, 175–182.

Krashen, S. D. (2003). *Explorations in language acquisition and use*. Portsmouth, NH: Heinemann.

Krashen, S. D. (2004a, November). *Applying the comprehension hypothesis: Some suggestions*. Paper presented at the 13th International Symposium and Book Fair on Language Teaching (English Teachers Association of the Republic of China), Taipei, Taiwan. www.sdkrashen. com/articles/eta_paper/all.html

Krashen, S. D. (2004b, April). *Free voluntary reading: New research, applications, and controversies*. Paper presented at the RELC conference, Singapore. www. sdkrashen.com/articles/singapore/singapore.pdf

Krashen, S. D. (2004c). *The power of reading: Insights from the research* (2nd ed.). Portsmouth, NH: Heinemann.

Krashen, S. D. (2005/2006). Read-alouds are good for literacy development: A comment on Freakonomics. *Reading Today, 23*(2), 19.

Krashen, S. D. (n.d.). *88 generalizations about free voluntary reading*. www.sdkrashen.com/ handouts/88Generalizations/88Generalizations .pdf

Krashen, S. D., & Brown, C. L. (2007). What is academic language proficiency? *STETS Language and Communication Review, 6*(1), 1–4.

Krashen, S. D., & Terrell, T. (1983). *The natural approach: Language acquisition in the classroom*. San Francisco, CA: Alemany Press.

Kroll, B. (Ed.). (1990). *Second language writing: Research insights for the classroom*. New York: Cambridge University Press.

Kroll, B. (1993). Teaching writing is teaching reading: Training the new teacher of ESL composition. In J. G. Carson & I. Leki (Eds.), *Reading in the composition classroom: Second language perspectives* (pp. 61–84). Boston: Heinle and Heinle.

LaCelle-Peterson, M., & Rivera, C. (1994). Is it real for all kids? A framework for equitable assessment policies for English language learners. *Harvard Educational Review, 64*(1), 55–75.

Laminack, L. L., & Wadsworth, R. M. (2006). *Reading aloud across the curriculum: How to build bridges in language arts, math, science, and social studies.* Portsmouth, NH: Heinemann.

Langman, J. (2008a). The effects of ESL-endorsed instructors: Reducing middle school students to incidental language learners. In D. E. Murray (Ed.), *Planning change, changing plans: Innovations in second language teaching* (pp. 108–121). Ann Arbor: University of Michigan Press.

Langman, J. (2008b). Language socialization. In J. M. González (Ed.), *Encyclopedia of bilingual education* (pp. 489–493). Thousand Oaks, CA: Sage.

Langman, J., & Bayley, R. (2007). Untutored acquisition in content classrooms. In Z. Hua, P. Seedhouse, L. Wei, & V. Cook (Eds.), *Language learning and teaching as social inter-action* (pp. 218–234). New York: Palgrave Macmillan.

Lantolf, J. P. (Ed.). (2000). *Sociocultural theory and second language learning.* Oxford: Oxford University Press.

Lantolf, J. P., & Appel, G. (Eds.). (1994). *Vygotskian approaches to second language research.* Norwood, NJ: Ablex.

Lau v. Nichols, 414 U.S. 563 (1974).

Lee, S. J. (2005). *Up against whiteness: Race, school, and immigrant youth.* New York: Teachers College Press.

Lee, J. F., & VanPatten, B. (2003). *Making communicative language teaching happen* (2nd ed.). New York: Longman.

Leibowitz, A. H. (1971). *Educational policy and political acceptance: The imposition of English as the language of instruction in American schools.* Washington, DC: Center for Applied Linguistics. (Eric Document No. 047 321)

Leibowitz, A. H. (1974, August). *Language as a means of social control: The United States experience.* Paper presented at the VIII World Congress of Sociology, University of Toronto, Toronto, Canada.

Leibowitz, A. H. (1976). Language and the law: The exercise of political power through official designation of language. In W. M. O'Barr & J. F. O'Barr (Eds.), *Language and politics* (pp. 449–466). The Hague: Mouton & Co.

Leibowitz, A. H. (1980). *The Bilingual Education Act: A legislative analysis.* Washington, DC: National Clearinghouse for Bilingual Education.

Lesaux, N., & Geva, E. (2006). Synthesis: Development of literacy in language-minority students. In D. August & T. Shanahan (Eds.), *Developing literacy in second-language learners: Report of the National Literacy Panel on Language-Minority Children and Youth* (pp. 53–74). Mahwah, NJ: Lawrence Erlbaum.

Levy, M. & Stockwell, G. (2006). *CALL dimensions: Options and issues in computer assisted language learning.* Mahwah, NJ: Erlbaum.

Lightbrown, P. M., & Spada, N. (2006). *How languages are learned* (3rd ed.). New York: Oxford University Press.

Lindholm-Leary, K. J. (1994). Promoting positive cross-cultural attitudes and perceived competence in culturally and linguistically diverse classrooms. In R. A. DeVillar, C. J. Faltis, & J. P. Cummins (Eds.), *Cultural diversity in schools: From rhetoric to practice* (pp. 189–206). Albany: State University of New York Press.

Lindholm-Leary, K. J. (2001). *Dual language education.* Clevedon, U.K.: Multilingual Matters.

Lindholm-Leary, K. J., & Fairchild, H. H. (1990). Evaluation of an elementary school bilingual immersion program. In A. M. Padilla, H. H. Fairchild, & C. M. Valadez (Eds.), *Bilingual education: Issues and strategies* (pp. 126–136). Newbury Park, CA: Sage.

Lipka, J., Sharp, N., Adams, B., & Sharp, F. (2007). Creating a third space for authentic biculturalism: Examples from math in a cultural context. *Journal of American Indian Education, 46*(3), 94–115.

Long, M. H. (1983). Native speaker/non-native speaker conversation and the negotiation of comprehensible input. *Applied Linguistics 4*(2), 126–141.

Long, M. H. (1996). The role of the linguistic environment in second language acquisition. In W. Ritchie & T. Bhatia (Eds.), *Handbook of second language acquisition* (pp. 413–468). New York: Academic Press.

Lynch, J. (2005). *Making word walls work.* New York: Scholastic.

Lyons, J. (1995). The past and future directions of federal bilingual education policy. In O. García & C. Baker (Eds.), *Policy and practice in bilingual education: Extending the foundations* (pp. 1–15). Clevedon, U.K.: Multilingual Matters.

MacSwan, J. (2000). The threshold hypothesis, semilingualism, and other contributions to a deficit view of linguistic minorities. *Hispanic Journal of Behavioral Science, 22*(1), 3–45.

MacSwan, J., & Rolstad, K. (2003). Linguistic diversity, schooling, and social class: Rethinking our conception of language proficiency in language minority education. In C. B. Paulston & R. Tucker (Eds.), *Sociolinguistics: Essential Reading* (pp. 329–341). Oxford, England: Blackwell.

MacSwan, J., Rolstad, K., & Glass, G. V. (2002). Do some school-age children have no language? Some problems of construct validity in the Pre-Las Español. *Bilingual Research Journal, 26*(2), 213–238.

Macy, M. D. (Ed.). (2002). *Teaching ESL/EFL with the Internet: Catching the wave.* Upper Saddle River, NJ: Merrill Prentice Hall.

Madsen, S. A. (1991). The effect of music paired with and without gestures on the learning and transfer of new vocabulary: Experimenter-derived nonsense words. *Journal of Music Therapy, 28*, 222–230.

Mahoney, K., Thompson, M., & MacSwan, J. (2004). *The condition of English language learners in Arizona: 2004.* Tempe, AZ: Education Policy Studies Laboratory, Arizona State University. epsl.asu.edu/aepi/EPSL-0405-106-AEPI.pdf

Mahoney, K., Thompson, M., & MacSwan, J. (2005). *The condition of English language learners in Arizona: 2005.* Tempe, AZ: Education Policy Studies Laboratory, Arizona State University. epsl.asu.edu/aepi/Report/EPSL-0509-110-AEPI.pdf

Manning, M. S. (2001). Writing checklist. *Write away! A student guide to the writing process* [On-line module]. cuip.uchicago.edu/ %7Emmanning/2001/chklist.htm

Martin, J. R. (2002). Writing history: Construing time and value in discourses of the past. In M. J. Schleppegrell & M. C. Colombi (Eds.), *Developing advanced literacy in first and second languages: Meaning with power* (pp. 87–118). Mahwah, NJ: Lawrence Erlbaum.

Matsuda, P. L. (2003). Second-language writing in the 20th century: A situated historical perspective. In B. Kroll (Ed.), *Exploring the dynamics of second language writing* (pp. 15–34). New York: Cambridge University Press.

McCafferty, S. G., Jacobs, G. M., & Iddings, A. C. D. (Eds.). (2006). *Cooperative learning and second language teaching.* New York: Cambridge University Press.

McKinney, C., & Norton, B. (2008). Identity in language and literacy education. In B. Spolsky & F. M. Hult (Eds.), *The handbook of educational linguistics* (pp. 192–205). Malden, MA: Blackwell.

McLaughlin v. State Board of Education, 75 Cal. App. 4th 196, 89 Cal. Rptr 2d 295 (First Dist. 1999).

McNeil, L. M. (2000). *Contradictions of school reform: Educational costs of standardized testing.* New York: Routledge.

McQuillan, J. (1998). *The literacy crisis: False claims, real solutions*. Portsmouth, NH: Heinemann.

Meier, D. (Ed.). (2000). *Will standards save public education?* Boston: Beacon Press.

Meir, D., & Wood, G. (2004). *Many children left behind: How the No Child Left Behind Act is damaging our children and our schools*. Boston: Beacon Press.

MENC (National Association for Music Education). (n.d.) *Summary statement: What students should know and be able to do in the arts*. menc.org/resources/view/summary-statement-what-students-should-know-and-be-able-to-do-in-the-arts

Méndez v. Westminster School District, 64 Supp. 544 (S.D. Cal. 1946), *aff'd*, 161 F.2d 774 (9th Cir. 1947).

Menken, K. (2008). *English learners left behind: Standardized testing as language policy*. Clevedon, U.K.: Multilingual Matters.

Mensh, E., & Mensh, H. (1991). *The IQ mythology: Class, race, gender, and inequality*. Carbondale: Southern Illinois University Press.

Merino, B. J., & Hammond, L. (2002). Writing to learn: Science in the upper-elementary bilingual classroom. In M. J. Schleppegrell & M. C. Colombi (Eds.), *Developing advanced literacy in first and second languages: Meaning with power* (pp. 227–243). Mahwah, NJ: Lawrence Erlbaum.

Messick, S. (1995). Standards of validity and the validity of standards in performance assessment. *Educational Measurement: Issues and Practices, 14*(4), 5–8.

Meyer v. Nebraska, 262 U.S. 390 (1923).

Mitchell, R., & Myles, F. (2004). *Second language learning theories* (2nd ed.). New York: Oxford University Press.

Moll, L. C. (Ed.). (1992). *Vygotsky and education: Instructional implications and applications of sociohistorical psychology*. Cambridge, UK: Cambridge University Press.

Morales v. Tucson Unified School District (D Ariz. 2001).

Multilingual/Multicultural Office. (2001). Project KEEP [videotape]. Fresno, CA: Fresno Unified School District.

National Association for Sport and Physical Education (NASPE). (2007). *Moving into the future: National Standards for physical education* (2nd ed.). [Electronic version]. Reston, VA: NASPE.

National Clearinghouse for English Language Acquisition (NCELA). (2009). *The growing numbers of limited English proficient students, 1995/96–2005/06*. www.ncela.gwu.edu/files/uploads/4/GrowingLEP_0506.pdf

National Council for the Social Studies (NCSS). (n.d.) *Toolkit: Today's social studies . . . creating effective citizens*. www.socialstudies.org/toolkit

National Education Association. (1966). *The invisible minority . . . pero no vencibles: Report of the NEA-Tucson Survey on the Teaching of Spanish to the Spanish-Speaking*. Washington, DC: Department of Rural Education, National Education Association.

National Education Association. (2008). Joint organizational statement on "No Child Left Behind" Act. Washington, DC: Author. www.nea.org/home/19426.htm

National Reading Panel. (2000). *Teaching children to read: An evidenced-based assessment of the scientific research literature on reading and its implications for reading instruction. Summary report*. Washington, DC: Author.

National Science Teachers Association (NSTA). (2000, July). *Multicultural science education*. NSTA Position Statement. www.nsta.org/about/positions/multicultural.aspx

Nichols, S., & Berliner, D. C. (2007). *Collateral damage: How high-stakes testing corrupts America's schools*. Cambridge, MA: Harvard University Press.

Nisbett, R. E. (1998). Race, genetics, and IQ. In C. Jencks & M. Phillips (Eds.), *The black-white test score gap* (pp. 86–102). Washington, DC: Brookings Institution Press.

Ochs, E., & Schieffelin, B. (1984). Language acquisition and socialization: Three developmental stories and their implications. In R. Schweder & R. LeVine (Eds.), *Culture theory: Essays in mind, self and emotion* (pp. 276–320). New York: Cambridge University Press.

Ohanian, S. (1999). *One size fits few: The folly of educational standards*. Portsmouth, NH: Heinemann.

Ohanian, S. (2002). *What happened to recess and why are our children struggling in kindergarten?* New York: McGraw Hill.

Oller, D. K., & Eilers, R. E. (Eds.). (2002). *Language and literacy in bilingual children*. Clevedon, U.K.: Multilingual Matters.

Olsen, L. (2001). Khmer Emerging Education Program. In L. Olsen et al. (Eds.), *And still we speak: Stories of communities sustaining and reclaiming language and culture*. Oakland, CA: California Tomorrow.

Olson, L., & Manzo, K. K. (2005, October 20).Despite NCLB law's emphasis on reading and math, national test scores show little change. *Education Week*.

O'Malley, J. M., & Pierce, L. V. (1996). *Authentic assessment for English language learners: Practical approaches for teachers*. Reading, MA: Addison Wesley.

Otero v. Mesa County Valley School District No. 51, 628 F.2d 1271 (1980).

Ovando, C., Combs, M. C., & Collier, V. P. (2006). *Bilingual and ESL classrooms: Teaching in multicultural contexts* (4th ed.). Boston: McGraw Hill.

Palmer, D. K., & García, E. E. (2000). Voices from the field: Bilingual educators speak candidly about Proposition 227. *Bilingual Research Journal, 24* (1 & 2), 169–178.

Palmer, D. K., & Lynch, A. W. (2008). A bilingual education for a monolingual test? The pressure to prepare for TAKS and its influence on choices for language of instruction in Texas elementary bilingual classrooms. *Language Policy, 7*(3), 217–235.

Pang, V. O., & Cheng, L.-R. L. (1998). *Struggling to be heard: The unmet needs of Asian Pacific American children*. Albany: State University of New York Press.

Park, C. C., & Chi, M. M.-Y. (1999). *Asian-American education: Prospects and challenges*. Westport, CT: Bergin & Garvey.

Pearson, P. D. (2006). Forword to K. S. Goodman (Ed.), *The truth about DIBELS: What it is, what it does* (pp. v–xx). Portsmouth, NH: Heinemann.

Peregoy, S. F., & Boyle, O. F. (2008). *Reading, writing and learning in ESL: A resource book for K–12 teachers* (5th ed.). Boston: Allyn & Bacon.

Perez, B. (2004). *Becoming biliterate: A study of two-way bilingual immersion education*. Mahwah, NJ: Lawrence Erlbaum.

Peske, H. G., & Haycock, K. (2006). *Teaching inequality: How poor and minority students are shortchanged on teacher quality*. Washington, DC: Education Trust.

Philips, S. U. (1983). *The invisible culture: Communication in classroom and community on the Warm Springs Indian reservation*. Prospect Heights, IL: Waveland Press.

Pica, T. (1994). Research on negotiation: What does it reveal about second language acquisition? Conditions, processes, and outcomes. *Language Learning, 44*(3), 493–527.

Plessy v. Ferguson, 163 U.S. 537 (1896).

Poliakoff, A. R. (2006, January). Closing the gap: An overview. *INFObrief* (Association for Supervision and Curriculum Development), no. 44. Available at www.ascd.org

Popham, W. J. (2004). *Classroom assessment: What teachers need to know* (4th ed.). Boston: Allyn and Bacon.

Portes, A., & Rumbaut, R. G. (2006). *Immigrant America: A portrait* (3rd ed.). Berkeley: University of California Press.

Pray, L. (2003). An analysis of language assessments used

in the referral and placement of language minority students into special education. *Dissertation Abstracts International, 64*(3), 766.

Pu, C. (2008). Chinese American children's bilingual and biliteracy development in heritage language and public schools. *Dissertation Abstracts International, 69*(7), 766.

Quiroz v. State Board of Education, Sacramento Superior Court, Case No. 97CS01793 (1997).

Raimes, A. (1991). Out of the woods: Emerging traditions in the teaching of writing. *TESOL Quarterly, 25*(3), 407–430.

Ramirez, J. D. (1992). Executive summary. *Bilingual Research Journal, 16,* 1–62.

Ramirez, J. D., Yuen, D. D., Ramey, D. R., & Pasta, D. (1991). *Final report: Longitudinal study of structured English immersion strategy, early exit and late-exit bilingual education programs for language minority children.* Vol. 1 (Publication no. 300–87–0156). Washington, DC: U.S. Department of Education.

Randolph-McCree, I., & Pristoop, E. (2005). *The funding gap 2005: Low-income and minority students shortchanged by most states.* Washington, DC: Education Trust.

Regents of the University of California v. Bakke, 438 US 265 (1978).

Reiss, J. (2005). *Teaching content to English language learners: Strategies for secondary school success.* White Plains, NY: Longman.

Renaissance Learning. (n.d.). *143 research studies support the effectiveness of Accelerated Reader.* www.renlearn.com/ar/research.aspx

Richards, J. C., & Rodgers, T. S. (2001). *Approaches and methods in language teaching* (2nd ed.). Cambridge: Cambridge University Press.

Richardson, W. (2008). *Blogs, wikis, podcasts and other powerful web tools for classrooms* (2nd ed.). Thousand Oaks, CA: Corwin Press.

Rickford, J. R. (2005). Using the vernacular to teach the standard. In J. D. Ramirez, T. G. Wiley, G. de Klerk, E. Lee & W. E. Wright (Eds.), *Ebonics: The urban education debate* (2nd ed., pp. 18–40). Clevedon, U.K.: Multilingual Matters.

Rigby. (n.d.). *Rigby on our way to English overview brochure for grades K-3.* Orlando, FL: Harcourt Supplemental.

Rios v. Reed, 480 FSupp 14 (EDN 1978).

Rivera, C., & Collum, E. (Eds.). (2006). *State assessment policy and practice for English language learners.* Mahwah, NJ: Lawrence Erlbaum.

Rolstad, K. (2004). Rethinking academic language in second language instruction. In J. A. Cohen, K. T. McAlister, K. Rolstad & J. MacSwan (Eds.), *ISB4: Proceedings of the 4th International Symposium on Bilingualism* (pp. 1993–1999). Somerville, MA: Cascadilla Press.

Romaine, S. (1995). *Bilingualism* (2nd ed.). Oxford, UK: Blackwell.

Routman, R. (1996). *Literacy at the crossroads: Crucial talk about reading, writing, and other teaching dilemmas.* Portsmouth, NH: Heinemann.

Ruiz, R. (1984). Orientations in language planning. *NABE Journal: Journal of the National Association for Bilingual Education, 8*(2), 15–34.

Rumbaut, R. G., & Portes, A. (2001). *Ethnicities: Children of immigrants in America.* Berkeley: University of California Press.

Rumberger, R. W., Gándara, P., & Merino, B. (2006). Where California's English learners attend school and why it matters. *UC Linguistic Minority Research Institute Newsletter, 15*(2), 1–2.

Rupp, J. H. (1992). Discovery science and language development. In P. A. Richard-Amato & M. A. Snow (Eds.), *The multicultural classroom: Readings for content-area teachers* (pp. 316–329). White Plains, NY: Longman.

Sacks, P. (1999). *Standardized minds: The high price of America's testing culture and what we can do to change it.* Cambridge, MA: Perseus Books.

Saint Paul Public Schools. Multicultural Resource Center. (n.d.). *Multicultural science education.* mrc.spps.org/Multicultural_Science_Education .html

Samway, K. D. (2006). *When English language learners write: Connecting research to practice, K–8.* Portsmouth, NH: Heinemann.

San Antonio Independent School District v. Rodriguez, 411 U.S. 1 (1973).

Saunders, W. M., & O'Brien, G. (2006). Oral Language. In F. Genesee, K. Lindholm-Leary, W. M. Saunders, & D. Christian (Eds.), *Educating English language learners: A synthesis of research evidence* (pp. 14–63). New York: Cambridge University Press.

Sauro, S. (2007). A comparative study of recasts and metalinguistic feedback through computer mediated communication on the development of L2 knowledge and production accuracy. Retrieved from ProQuest Digital Dissertations. (AAT 3271810)

Sauro, S. (2009). Strategic use of modality during synchronous CMC. *CALICO Journal, 27*(1), 101–117.

Savignon, S. J. (2001). Communicative language teaching for the twenty-first century. In M. Celce-Murcia (Ed.), *Teaching English as a second or foreign language* (3rd ed., pp. 13–28). Boston: Heinle & Heinle.

Sayer, P. (2008). Demystifying language mixing: Spanglish in school. *Journal of Latinos and Education, 7*(2), 94–112.

Schleppegrell, M. J. (2002). Challenges of the science register for ESL students: Errors and meaning-making. In M. J. Schleppegrell & M. C. Colombi (Eds.), *Developing advanced literacy in first and second languages: Meaning with power* (pp. 119–142). Mahwah, NJ: Lawrence Erlbaum.

Schmidt, R. (1990). The role of consciousness in second language learning. *Applied Linguistics, 11*(1), 17–46.

Schmidt, R. (2001). Attention. In P. Robinson (Ed.), *Cognition and second language instruction* (pp. 3–32). Cambridge, UK: Cambridge University Press.

Schunk, H. A. (1999). The effect of singing paired with signing on receptive vocabulary skills of elementary ESL students. *Journal of Music Therapy, 36*(2), 110–124.

Serna v. Portales 351 FSupp 1279 (D New Mexico, 1972), aff'd, 499 F2d 1147 (10th Cir 1974).

Shohamy, E. G. (2001). *The power of tests: A critical perspective on the uses of language tests.* New York: Longman.

Short, D., & Boyson, B. (2004). *Creating access: Language and academic programs for secondary school newcomers.* McHenry, IL: Delta Systems.

Smith, F. (1994). *Understanding reading* (5th ed.). Mahwah, NJ: Lawrence Erlbaum.

Smith, F. (1999). Why systematic phonics and phonemic awareness instruction constitute an educational hazard. *Language Arts, 77*(2), 150–155.

Smith, F. (2004). *Understanding reading* (6th ed.). Mahwah, NJ: Lawrence Erlbaum.

Smith, F. (2006). *Reading without nonsense* (4th ed.). New York: Teachers College Press.

Smith, M. L. (2004). *Political spectacle and the fate of American schools.* New York: Routledge.

Smith, M. L., Heinecke, W., & Noble, A. J. (1999). Assessment policy and political spectacle. *Teachers College Record, 101*(2), 157–191.

Sotomayor and Gabaldon v. Burns, Arizona Supreme Court NO CV-00–0305-SA, 2000.

Spellings, M. (2008). Notice of Final Interpretations: DEPARTMENT OF EDUCATION: Title III of the Elementary and Secondary Education Act of 1965 (ESEA), as Amended by the No Child Left Behind Act of 2001 (NCLB). *Federal Register, 73*(202), 61828–61844.

Spolsky, B. (1984). A note on the dangers of terminological

innovation. In C. Rivera (Ed.), *Language proficiency and academic achievement*. Clevedon, UK: Multilingual Matters.

Stainback v. Mo Hock Ke Lok Po, 336 U.S. 368 (1949).

Steinberg, J. (2000, August 20). Increase in test scores counter dire forecasts for bilingual ban. *New York Times*.

Stewner-Manzanares, G. (1988). *The Bilingual Education Act twenty years later (Occasional Papers in Bilingual Education, No. 6)*. Washington, DC: National Clearinghouse for Bilingual Education.

Student Oral Language Observation Matrix (SOLOM). (n.d.). www.cal.org/twi/EvalToolkit/appendix/solom .pdf

Suzuki, B. H. (1995). Education and the socialization of Asian Americans: A revisionist analysis of the "model minority" thesis. In D. T. Nakanishi & T. Y. Nishida (Eds.), *The Asian American educational experience* (pp. 113–132). New York: Routledge.

Swain, M. (1985). Communicative competence: Some roles of comprehensible input and comprehensible output in its development. In S. Gass & C. Madden (Eds.), *Input in second language acquisition* (pp. 235–253). Rowley, MA: Newbury.

Swain, M. (2000). The output hypothesis and beyond: Mediating acquisition through collaborative dialogue. In J. P. Lantolf (Ed.), *Sociocultural theory and second language learning*. Oxford, UK: Oxford University Press.

Swain, M., & Suzuki, W. (2008). Interaction, output, and communicative language learning. In B. Spolsky & F. M. Hult (Eds.), *The handbook of educational linguistics* (pp. 557–570). Malden, MA: Blackwell.

Tamura, E. H. (1993). The English-only effort, the anti-Japanese campaign, and language acquisition in the education of Japanese Americans in Hawaii, 1914–1940. *History of Education Quarterly, 33*(1), 37–58.

Taylor, D. (1998). *Beginning to read and the spin doctors of science: The political campaign to change America's mind about how children learn to read*. Urbana, IL: National Council of Teachers of English.

Terman, L. M. (1916). *The measurement of intelligence*. Boston: Houghton Mifflin.

Terrell, T. (1977). A natural approach to second language acquisition and learning. *Modern Language Journal, 61*, 325–336.

TESOL (Teachers of English to Speakers of Other Languages). (2006a). *PreK–12 English language proficiency standards*. Alexandria, VA: Author.

TESOL. (2006b, March). TESOL revises preK–12 English Language Proficiency Standards. www.tesol.org/s_tesol/ sec_document.asp?CID=1186&DID=5349

Texas Education Agency. (2004). *Texas Assessment of Knowledge and Skills: Grade 5* (Released Spring 2004 test). www.tea.state.tx.us/student.assessment/ resources/release/taks/2004/gr5taks.pdf

Texas Education Agency. Student Assessment Division. (2005). *Texas Observation Protocols: Training on the Proficiency Level Descriptors [PowerPoint presentation]*. Austin: Texas Education Agency.

Texas Education Agency. (2008, Spring). TELPAS [Texas English Language Proficiency System Assessment System] proficiency level descriptors. www.tea.state.tx.us/ student.assessment/admin/rpte/telpasrater/ spring2008pld.pdf

Thomas, W. P., & Collier, V. P. (2002). *A national study of school effectiveness for language minority students' long term academic achievement*. Santa Cruz, CA: Center for Research on Education, Diversity, and Excellence.

Thompson, M. S., DiCerbo, K. E., Mahoney, K., & Mac-Swan, J. (2002). ¿Exito en California? [Success in California?]: A validity critique of language program evaluations and analysis of English learner test scores. *Educa-*

tion Policy Analysis Archives, 10(7). epaa.asu.edu/epaa/ v10n7

Trujillo, A. (2008). Latino civil rights movement. In J. M. González (Ed.), *Encyclopedia of bilingual education* (pp. 505–510). Thousand Oaks, CA: Sage.

Tyack, D. B., & Cuban, L. (1995). *Tinkering toward utopia: A century of public school reform*. Cambridge, MA: Harvard University Press.

Ulanoff, S. H., & Pucci, S. L. (1999). Learning words from books: The effects of read aloud on second language vocabulary acquisition. *Bilingual Research Journal, 23*(4), 319–332.

United States v. Texas, 342, F. Supp 24 (E.D. Texas 1971).

United States v. Texas, 506 F. Supp 405 (E.D. Texas 1981).

U.S. Department of Education. (2001). *Language backgrounds of limited English proficient (LEP) students in the U.S. and outlying areas, 2000–2001*. www.ncela.gwu .edu/stats/4_toplanguages/langsrank.pdf

U.S. Department of Education. (2003a). *Non-regulatory guidance on the Title III State Formula Grant Program. Part II: Standards, assessments, and accountability*. Washington, DC: Office of English Language Acquisition, Language Enhancement, and Academic Achievement for Limited English Proficient Students.

U.S. Department of Education. (2003b). *Standards and assessment: Non-regulatory guidance (Draft)*. Washington, DC: Author.

U.S. Department of Education. (2004, February 19). Remarks of U.S. Secretary of Education Rod Paige at the press conference announcing new policies for English language learners [Press release]. Washington, DC: Author.

U.S. Department of Education. (2006a). *New No Child Left Behind regulations: Flexibility and accountability for limited English proficient students*. www.ed.gov/admins/ lead/account/lepfactsheet.html

U.S. Department of Education. Office of Inspector General. (2006b). *The Reading First Program's Grant Application Process: Final Inspection Report*. www.ed.gov/ about/offices/list/oig/ aireports/i13f0017.pdf

U.S. Department of Education. (2008). *Biennial Report to Congress on the Implementation of the Title III State Formula Grant Program, School Years 2004–06*. Washington, DC: Office of English Language Acquisition, Language Enhancement, and Academic Achievement for Limited English Proficient Students.

U.S. Department of Education. Institute of Education Sciences. (2008). *Reading First impact study: Interim report*. ies.ed.gov/ncee/pdf/20084016.pdf

U.S. Department of Education. (2009a, March 7). Education Department to distribute $44 billion in stimulus funds [Press release]. www.ed.gov/print/news/press releases/2009/03/03072009.html

U.S. Department of Education. (2009b, July 24). President Obama, U.S. Secretary of Education Duncan announce national competition to advance school reform [Press release]. www.ed .gov/news/pressreleases/2009/07/ 07242009.html

Valdés, G. (1997). Dual-language immersion programs: A cautionary note concerning the education of language-minority students. *Harvard Educational Review, 67*(3), 391–429.

Valdés, G. (2001). Heritage language students: Profiles and possibilities. In J. K. Peyton, D. A. Ranard, & S. McGinnis (Eds.), *Heritage languages in America: Preserving a national resource* (pp. 37–77). Washington, DC: Center for Applied Linguistics.

Valdés, G., & Figueroa, R. A. (1994). *Bilingualism and testing: A special case of bias*. Norwood, NJ: Ablex.

Valdés, C., MacSwan, J., & Martínez, C. (2002). Toward a new view of low achieving bilinguals: A study of linguistic competence in designated "semilinguals." *Bilingual Review, 25*(3), 238–248.

Valenzuela, A. (2004). *Leaving children behind: How "Texas-style" accountability fails Latino youth.* New York: State University of New York Press.

Valeria G. v. Wilson, No. C-98-2252-CAL (N.D. Ca. 1998).

Vandrick, S. (2003). Literature in the teaching of second language composition. In B. Kroll (Ed.), *Exploring the dynamics of second language writing* (pp. 263–284). New York: Cambridge University Press.

VanPatten, B. (2003). *From input to output: A teacher's guide to second language acquisition.* Boston: McGraw Hill.

VanPatten, B. (Ed.). (2004). *Processing instruction: Theory, research, and commentary.* Mahwah, NJ: Lawrence Erlbaum.

von Raumer, K. (1858). Wolfgang Ratich. *American Journal of Education, 5*(13), 229–256.

Vygotsky, L. S. (1978). *Mind in society: The development of higher mental processes.* Cambridge, MA: Harvard University Press.

Wagstaff, J. (1999). *Teaching reading and writing with word walls (grades K-3).* New York: Scholastic.

Weber, N. (2000, August). *Sink or swim? A look into an English immersion class.* ldt.stanford.edu/~ninaweb/Sink%20or%20swim.pdf

Weinberg, M. (1977). *A chance to learn: The history of race and education in the United States.* New York: Cambridge University Press.

Weinberg, M. (1997). *Asian-American education: Historical background and current realities.* Mahwah, NJ: Lawrence Erlbaum.

Wiley, T. G. (1998). The imposition of World War I era English-only policies and the fate of German in North America. In T. Ricento & B. Burnaby (Eds.), *Language and politics in the United States and Canada: Myths and realities* (pp. 211–241). Mahwah, NJ: Lawrence Erlbaum.

Wiley, T. G. (2001). On defining heritage languages and their speakers. In J. K. Peyton, D. A. Ranard, & S. McGinnis (Eds.), *Heritage languages in America: Blueprint for the future* (pp. 29–36). Washington, DC, & McHenry, IL: Center for Applied Linguistics and Delta Systems.

Wiley, T. G. (2002). Accessing language rights in education: A brief history of the U.S. context. In J. W. Tollefson (Ed.), *Language policies in education* (pp. 39–64). Mahwah, NJ: Lawrence Erlbaum.

Wiley, T. G. (2005). *Literacy and language diversity in the United States* (2nd ed.). Washington, DC: Center for Applied Linguistics.

Wiley, T. G., & Hartung-Cole, E. (1998). Model standards for English language development: National trends and a local response. *Education, 119*(2), 205–221.

Wiley, T. G., & Wright, W. E. (2004). Against the undertow: The politics of language instruction in the United States. *Educational Policy, 18*(1), 142–168.

Williams v. California, Superior Court, San Francisco County, No. 312236 (2004).

Wisconsin Literacy Education and Reading Network Source. n.d. Assessing print understanding. Retrieved March 25, 2007 from wilearns.state.wi.us/apps/PDF/print_prompts.pdf

Worthy, J. (2005). *Readers theater for building fluency.* New York: Scholastic.

Wright, W. E. (1998). The education of Cambodian American students in the Long Beach Unified School District: A language and educational policy analysis. *Dissertation Abstracts International, 37*(2), 409.

Wright, W. E. (2002). The effects of high stakes testing on an inner-city elementary school: The curriculum, the teachers, and the English language learners. *Current Issues in Education, 5*(5). cie.asu.edu/volume5/number5

Wright, W. E. (2003a). Language policy issues in the U.S. Press. In J. Cohen, K. T. McCallister, K. Rolstad & J. MacSwan (Eds.), *Proceedings of the 4th International Symposium on Bilingualism.* Somerville, MA: Cascadilla Press.

Wright, W. E. (2003b). The success and demise of a Khmer (Cambodian) bilingual education program: A case study. In C. C. Park, A. L. Goodwin & S. J. Lee (Eds.), *Asian American identities, families, and schooling* (pp. 225–252). Greenwich, CT: Information Age.

Wright, W. E. (2004a). What English-only really means: A study of the implementation of California language policy with Cambodian American students. *International Journal of Bilingual Education and Bilingualism, 7*(1), 1–23.

Wright, W. E. (2004b). Intersection of language and assessment policies for English language learners in Arizona. *Dissertation Abstracts International, 65*(2), 389.

Wright, W. E. (2005a). *Evolution of federal policy and implications of No Child Left Behind for language minority students* (No. EPSL-0501-101-LPRU). Tempe, AZ: Language Policy Research Unit, Education Policy Studies Laboratory, Arizona State University. www.asu.edu/educ/epsl/EPRU/documents/EPSL-0501-101-LPRU.pdf

Wright, W. E. (2005b). The political spectacle of Arizona's Proposition 203. *Educational Policy, 19*(5), 662–700. DOI: 610.1177/0895904805278066.

Wright, W. E. (2006a). A catch-22 for language learners. *Educational Leadership, 64*(3), 22–27.

Wright, W. E. (2006b). Meeting the needs of newcomer non-Spanish-speaking ELLs: A case study of two Cambodian students in a suburban intermediate school. In M. Cowart & P. Dam (Eds.), *Cultural and linguistic issues for English language learners* (pp. 108–141). Arlington, VA: CANH NAM; San Marcos: Texas Woman's University.

Wright, W. E. (2007). Heritage language programs in the era of English-only and No Child Left Behind. *Heritage Language Journal, 5*(1), 1–26.

Wright, W. E. (2008). No Child Left Behind Act of 2001, Title I. In J. M. González (Ed.), *Encyclopedia of bilingual education* (pp. 607–612). Thousand Oaks, CA: Sage.

Wright, W. E., & Choi, D. (2005). *Voices from the classroom: A statewide survey of experienced third-grade English language learner teachers on the impact of language and high-stakes testing policies in Arizona.* Tempe: Educational Policy Studies Laboratory, Arizona State University. epsl.asu.edu/epru/documents/EPSL-0512-104-LPRU.pdf

Wright, W. E., & Li, X. (2006). Catching up in math? The case of newly arrived Cambodian students in a Texas intermediate school. *TABE Journal, 9*(1). www.tabe.org/members/Catching%20_up_in_Math.pdf

Wright, W. E., & Li, X. (2008). High-stakes math tests: How No Child Left Behind leaves newcomer English language learners behind. *Language Policy, 7*(3), 237–266.

Wright, W. E., & Pu, C. (2005). *Academic achievement of English language learners in post Proposition 203 Arizona.* Tempe: Language Policy Research Unit, Educational Policy Studies Laboratory, Arizona State University. www.language-policy.org/content/features/EPSL-0509-103-LPRU.pdf

Index

Note: Page numbers followed by f refer to figures; page numbers followed by t refer to tables; page numbers followed by b refer to boxes.